CELTIC COINAGE OF BRITAIN

# CELTIC COINAGE
## of BRITAIN

R. D. Van Arsdell

SPINK

LONDON
1989

© SPINK AND SON LTD., 1989
PUBLISHED BY SPINK AND SON LIMITED
LONDON
1989


British Library Cataloguing in Publication Data

Van Arsdell, R. D. (Robert D.)
   Celtic coinage of Britain.
   1. Great Britain. Celtic coins, to B.C. 54
   I. Title
   737.49361

   ISBN 0 907605 24 9

Printed in Great Britain by BAS Printers Limited,
Over Wallop, Hampshire

TO JOANNE

# CONTENTS

CONTENTS

# FOREWORD

The Celtic coinage of Britain has been served well by writers in the past. Sir John Evans' seminal work *Coins of the Ancient Britons* published in 1864 provided the standard textbook for nearly ninety years until Commander Mack brought out the first edition of *The Coinage of Ancient Britain* in 1953. Mack's book was made necessary by the greatly increased number of coins that had come to light in the intervening period and, more particularly by Derek Allen's detailed study of the British dynastic rulers of the late Iron Age published in Archaeologia in 1944. That Mack's book was a work of sound connoisseurship was amply demonstrated by the appearance of a second edition in 1964 and a third edition in 1975. The 1964 edition took account of Allen's far-reaching reassessment *The Origins of Coinage in Britain: a Reappraisal* which appeared in 1958 as well as the results of Allen's detailed studies of the coinage of the Dobunni and Coritani, while the third edition incorporated Allen's views on the Durotrigan series and the potin issues.

Since 1975 a great deal has been written on Celtic coinage. But recent studies have tended to concentrate on social and economic matters rather than on the intricacies of coins series. This has been a healthy development and has led to many new insights but inevitably there has been a tendency to neglect the actual raw data—the coins—and to rely on identification conforming with classifications that were fast becoming out-of-date. Meanwhile the rate at which new coins were being recovered, largely as metal-detector finds, has meant there have been considerable difficulties in keeping a record of the new finds on the Index of Celtic Coins maintained at the Institute of Archaeology, Oxford. In other words, scholars using the coin record for their syntheses have been increasingly relying on out-of-date classifications, little knowledge of the actual coins and access to only a partial record.

The appearance of Bob Van Arsdell's *Celtic Coinage of Britain* is an event of considerable importance in Celtic coin studies, for in a single book he has provided us with a thoroughly revised classificatory system founded, not only on his incomparable knowledge of the coins themselves but also on a range of entirely new metallographic data and a precise, statistically valid, assessment of coin weights. In bringing together an impressive battery of analytical techniques, he has placed the study on a new, and scientifically sound, footing.

What emerges from his study is a reassignment of many obscure types, previously lumped together in rag-bag categories, to their appropriate series, allowing the three denominational sets of most issuing authorities to be reconstructed. Moreover the weight assessments and metallurgical compositions have led to a more soundly based method of dating. What is presented here is a well-ordered, well-dated series from which the clutter of old preconceptions has been totally stripped.

*Celtic Coinage of Britain* is not only invaluable to the collector, it is an essential research tool of incomparable value for everyone working in the field of Iron Age Studies.

Barry Cunliffe
Institute of Archaeology
Oxford
1988

# INTRODUCTION

## A High-Technology Society

Scientists are uncovering a Celtic Britain no one has ever seen before. A sophisticated, technology-driven one—the roots of today's industrialized society.

The long-held view of the British Celts as colourful, barbaric people, ripe for conquest by the more advanced Mediterranean civilization of Rome is crumbling. The Roman invasion of Britain, as Barry Cunliffe recently stated, was not the conquest of a primitive society by a more advanced one, it was the blending of two advanced civilizations.

Roman greatness is easy to see and appreciate—the Romans were masters of organization and their architecture survives for us to marvel at. But Celtic greatness lies hidden. The Celts cared little for monumental architecture—they directed their brilliance instead to the PROCESS TECHNOLOGIES.

Everyone can appreciate today's spacecraft and high-speed computers. But surprisingly, the highest technological sophistication is applied to simple items like razor blades and cheese wrapper. Today's metallurgists, polymer chemists, electronic engineers, statisticians and physicists work to improve the manufacture of everyday items—to optimize the manufacturing processes.

Similarly, the Celts devoted their energies to the control of their environment and the manufacture of everyday goods. At Danebury, twenty years' excavations are revealing the sophistication of Celtic agriculture, animal husbandry and land-use. Studies at Butser Iron Age Farm are showing an unsuspected level of efficiency in Celtic agriculture, and an early knowledge of aseptic food-preservation techniques.

Meanwhile, scientists at the Department of Metallurgy and Science of Materials at Oxford are unravelling the complexities of Celtic metal-working—and are discovering an astounding knowledge of alloys and the methods of mass-production. A high degree of social organization must have existed to create and nurture this technology.

Celtic technology shows its brilliance most clearly in the coinage, however, and this book focusses attention on that story. The coins of the Celtic tribes are masterpieces of abstract beauty. But behind those abstract images lies the story of one of the world's most complex and sophisticated coinages.

British staters were made of three-part alloys of gold, silver and copper. The tribes were forced to debase them because of economic pressures, but they did this in a clever way. Over time, they gradually decreased the weight of the coins and reduced the gold content. But as they did this, they manipulated the ratio of gold, silver and copper to keep the colour almost constant. The moneyers placed secret marks on the coins so they could tell the gold content and weight by sight. However, the average person would have had difficulty detecting the debasement over the span of a lifetime.

In Kent, an early series of cast bronze coins show marks caused by mould-making experiments. The moneyers were trying out different ways of producing the moulds to speed up production and produce better-quality coins. The experimenting, testing and innovating are akin to the procedures of modern industrial engineering.

These are only two examples of the things discovered during the last few years that are revolutionizing our thinking about Celtic coinage. In preparing this book, I have integrated the results of metallurgical studies, statistical analyses of coin weights, die-cutting studies, findspot and hoard analyses, typological studies and the testimony of the ancient authors. I have had to restructure much of the catalogue as a result of this synthesis, and the views presented in this book are often different from those of earlier writers.

Robert D. Van Arsdell
New York
July 1988

# ACKNOWLEDGEMENTS

Of the dozens of people who have added to our understanding of Celtic coins, two should be singled out for their special contribution.

My friend, Henry Mossop has quietly worked on the coinage for over thirty years. His insight into the privy-marks and keen eye for typology gave me the tools to reorganize the coins. Much of the section on the Corieltauvian coinage reflects his ideas, and the overall theme of 'sophistication' owes its existence to his studies. I will always remember the many hours spent at Henry's home discussing the coinage and studying his collection. The kind hospitality of his wife, Marjorie, always made the trip to the Mossop's home more pleasant.

Peter Northover, of the Department of Metallurgy and Science of Materials at Oxford, has revolutionized our knowledge of Bronze and Iron Age metal-working. His Electron Microprobe studies of the coins have revealed, for the first time, the sophistication of Iron Age alloys. He successfully identified the progression of alloy-types, which provided much of the support for the dating used in this book. Additionally, Peter performed all the metallurgical studies used to expose the Haslemere forgeries.

Originally, this book was to have been co-authored by Lyn Sellwood. She contributed greatly to the original concept of the book. To a great extent, the choice of material, and the order of its presentation reflect her thinking. She helped with the early stages of the writing and cataloguing, and offered much valuable criticism and insight. Her work on die-identities was instrumental to the exposure of the Haslemere forgeries, and she made important contributions to the work on the cast coinage of Kent. The usefulness of the Index of Celtic Coins at the Institute of Archaeology, Oxford, owes much to her years of upgrading the records, and the outgoing spirit she brought to the task of tracking down new finds. The demands of a career-change prevented her from continuing as co-author—the book would have benefited had she been able to do so.

The support and advice of the archaeological community throughout Britain was greatly appreciated. Clare Conybeare of the Salisbury and Wiltshire Museum helped with material from the Pitt-Rivers collection, Jeffrey May of the University of Nottingham provided information on the Corieltauvi, Paul Sealey of the Colchester and Essex Museum informed me of new Trinovantian/Catuvellaunian coins, while Andrew Fitzpatrick of the West Essex Archaeological Group offered his insights on the coinage of Tasciovanus and Cunobeline. David Allen of the Museum of the Iron Age, Andover, provided information about hoards of Atrebatic coins found in Hampshire. Niall Sharples provided information about the recent excavations at Maiden Castle.

George Boon, Curator of the National Museum of Wales, spent considerable time discussing the collection of Celtic coins held at Cardiff—an important resource for Celtic studies. He offered many useful suggestions about· the manuscript, and his encouragement was always helpful.

Tony Gregory of the Norfolk Archaeological Unit provided information about recent finds of Icenian coins. He has worked with the local metal detector community, often providing archaeological training. As a result of this cooperation, the prehistory of Norfolk is being carefully recorded.

Randy Bingley and Terry Carney of the Thurrock Local History Museum, Grays, working with Allen Bennett, a numismatist, provided information about the recent find of cast coins known as the Thurrock Types. Mr. Bennett's appreciation of the importance of the find, and his work to record it deserves special mention. The quick thinking and insight of the three men has preserved a major find for future workers.

Chris Going helped with discussions of amphorae, archaeological contexts and chronology. He also kept me informed of finds of cast bronze coins in Essex. Lisa Brown helped with pottery chronologies. Paula Thomas and Thom Richardson suggested hoard-analysis methods.

Ian Brooks offered help by analyzing ancient tool-marks on damaged coins. His incomparable knowledge of ancient tools and their uses was helpful in distinguishing the work of the Haslemere forger from that of ancient die-cutters.

Finally, the encouragement of the Danebury excavation team was a great help. The archaeologists, finds specialists, supervisors and excavators all took time to look at the coins and offer their comments. Appreciation is extended to Cynthia Poole, Assistant Director, Graham Barton, Andy Brown, Rosemary Goodyer, Kathy Laws, Beth McFarlane, Vivian Mead, Simon Pressey, Julian Rouse, Paolo Scremin, John Taylor and Sandra Turton.

Several Museums were particularly helpful in supplying photographs for illustration. The help of the British Museum stands out because of the special effort of Dr. J. P. C. Kent, Dr. Andrew Burnett and the Photographic Department. Most of the coins illustrated are in the BM collections, and the cooperation extended made the publication of this book possible. Other museums furnished important photographs: The Colchester and Essex Museum, the Norwich Castle Museum, the Museum of the Iron Age, Andover, and the National Museum of Wales. Richard Bartlett of the Harlow Museum provided photographs from the recent excavations at Harlow Temple. Other illustrations were supplied by the Institute of Archaeology, Oxford; Robert Wilkins of the Photographic Department was particularly helpful.

The help of the numismatic community deserves special recognition.

David Sellwood offered his expert advice on ancient coining methods many times over a period of years. The sections on coin manufacture, metallurgy, the cast coinage of Kent, and the Haslemere forgeries could not have been written without his help.

Dr. J.P.C. Kent, Keeper of Coins and Medals at the British Museum, kindly read the manuscript and offered many useful suggestions; his help with literature references was most appreciated.

Melinda Mays helped with the typology of the Durotrigan coinage. Daphne Nash offered encouragement in the study of modern forgeries. John Casey offered insights into monetary matters. Edward Besly and Andrew Burnett offered encouragement and assistance.

The outstanding work of the numismatic and archaeological communities of Belgium, France, the Federal Republic of Germany and Spain also deserves special mention. Much of the pioneering work in Celtic coinage is being done on the Continent, and the help offered by these workers was crucial to my studies. Simone Scheers offered much insight into chronologies, M.J. DeBord helped with the continental potin coinages and ancient forgeries of Gallo-Belgic coins. Brigette Fischer offered advice on potin coins. W. Binsfeld of the Rheinisches Landesmuseum, Trier provided access to the collection of Celtic coins and helped with literature references. Mr. Pare and Dr. Pferdehist of the Roemisch-Germanisches Zentralmuseum, Mainz helped with chronologies and literature references. Michael Egger of the Praehistorisches Staatssammlung, Muenchen helped with discussions of typology and modern forgeries.

Katherine Gruel was especially helpful. Her outstanding work in blending typology, metallurgy and metrology, and her application of statistics to coin studies is well-known. She offered valuable assistance in the chronology of late Armorican coinages.

The work of the Asociación Numismatica Española on the pre-Roman Celtiberian coinage deserves mention. Leandre Villaronga and Jose Pellicer Bru helped with the continental background of Iron Age coinage.

Some of the most consistent and enthusiastic help came from coin collectors and dealers.

Of the collectors, Robert Clarke's help in obtaining photographs of new types was especially crucial to the completeness of the catalogue. Others who deserve mention for their advice and support are Ian Finney, J.C. Sadler, G. Dunger, Frank Payton, A.W Harrison, P. Thompson, Dan Dolata, Irwin Schneider, Albert Levy, Frank Greco, Dieter Kaltz, Hans Denk and David Johnson.

Many dealers helped with information. Peter Mitchell and Michael Sharp of A.H. Baldwin and Sons were especially helpful—they brought many new types to my attention and put their exceptional cabinet of coins at my disposal. The work of C. J. Martin, Paul Withers and Joseph Linzalone in this area was also crucial. David Miller worked diligently to bring new types and modern forgeries to my attention so the catalogue would be as complete as possible. The extent to which the catalogue is illustrated would have been impossible without the photographs supplied by these dedicated numismatists.

Other dealers who helped were Lloyd Bennett, Leo Dardarian, Jean Elsen, Victor England, Richard Gladdle, Robert Ilsley, Paul-Francis Jacquier, Dr. Lanz in Munich, the staff of Muenz Zentrum in Cologne, Mr. Ritter in

Duesseldorf, Dr. Arnold Saslow, Peter Sheen, Frank Sternberg, Carl Subak, Jon Subak, Italo Vecchi, Paul Vecchi, and the staffs of Vinchon in Paris, Coin Galleries in New York and X. and F. Calico in Barcelona.

Three book dealers provided the background materials that made my studies possible. Douglas Saville and George Kolbe tracked down all of the obscure numismatic works I required. Simon Westall of Island Books, London, did an absolutely phenomenal job of finding hundreds of rare archaeological books, historical works and excavation reports. It is seldom mentioned how important the work of antiquarian book dealers is to numismatic studies.

Several people read early manuscripts of the book and offered valuable criticism—the help of Dr. J.P.C. Kent of the British Museum, Dr. John Collis of the University of Durham, Douglas Saville and Patrick Finn of Spink and Son, and Joseph Linzalone was much appreciated.

The staff of Spink and Son deserve special appreciation as publishers of the book. May Sinclair and Susan Barker kept everything glued together despite the difficulties of writing a book on one continent and publishing it on another. Douglas Liddell encouraged my studies on the coinage and helped me locate many rare types for publication. Douglas Saville worked with the typesetters and printers to produce the book, and did just about everything connected with its production from the selection of the format, to overseeing the binding operation.

I have reserved the end of this section to single out the contribution of two people for special comment.

First, the help and guidance of Patrick Finn of Spink and Son paved the way at every step. He was the first person to recognize the need for a new publication on Celtic coins, and was the champion of the book from the very start. He introduced me to many of the people mentioned above, solicited help on my behalf, and put the exceptional cabinet of Celtic coins at Spinks at my disposal. He encouraged my work on the exposure of the Haslemere forgeries, and did not hesitate to publish my early articles on Celtic coins in the Numismatic Circular. I have always accepted his sound advice in numismatic matters.

Finally, the encouragement and guidance of Barry Cunliffe provided the balance required to complete the work. It was Barry's suggestion that prompted me to work out a new classification system for the British-made coins. My appreciation of Celtic sophistication owes much to his writings on Danebury, Hengistbury, and the Cross-Channel trade.

                                                        Robert D. Van Arsdell
                                                        New York
                                                        July, 1988

# CELTIC COINAGE OF BRITAIN: THE HISTORY

## THE EARLIEST USE OF MONEY

Julius Caesar gives us the only contemporary account of coinage in Iron Age Britain (1). In his 54 B.C. report on military campaigns there, he observes: 'For money they use either bronze or gold coins or iron ingots of fixed weights'. This mention, tantalizingly brief, does not confirm whether he actually saw the currency he describes. However, finds of both coins and ingots today substantiate Caesar's report.

## IRON CURRENCY BARS

Iron ingots, commonly called CURRENCY BARS (2) exist in large numbers today—there are over a thousand known examples. They occur in four varieties: sword-shaped, spit-shaped, ploughshares and bay-leaf shaped. Most are retained in museums, however, some are held in private collections. Iron objects require chemical treatment to remove corrosive agents and stabilize the metal; ideally they should be conserved in a humidity-controlled environment.

Currency bars were introduced in Britain during the Second Century B.C. and continued in use until the middle of the First. It is not certain whether all served as money, nor is there evidence they circulated side by side with normal coins.

The most common variety, the sword-shaped bars, certainly did function as a form of currency. They show two common attributes of money: they conform to a weight standard and have a standard, easily recognized appearance. Furthermore, iron was a valuable commodity at the time and the bars were often hoarded. In this manner, they functioned as a means of wealth-storage. On a number of hillforts bars have been found cut up, perhaps to be used as smaller denominations. It is also possible they were in the process of being converted to scrap metal for fashioning iron tools. The suggestion that sword-shaped bars served as weapons has been disproved by recent metallurgical analysis showing the metal quality was not good enough for this purpose.

Sword-shaped bars had a flat, narrow blade between 780 and 890 mm long and weighed between 400 and 500 gms. The hilt was pinched and formed around a wooden dowel. Traces of mineralized wood have been found inside some of them. This variety of bar was used in what would later become the territories of the Coritani, Dobunni, Durotriges and Atrebates.

The three remaining varities of bar, all rare, are found individually, not hoarded. The ploughshare-bars, with a thick, heavy blade are found along the Thames Valley, and some may have been votive offerings, deposited in the river. A few findspots also occur in the West Midlands. The spit-shaped bars have a thinner blade and shorter hilt, and are found in the area later associated with the Dobunni. The Bay-leaf type bars, known from only a few Cambridgeshire examples, have a long hilt with semi-circular section. It is uncertain whether any of these three varieties functioned as currency.

## RING MONEY

Alternate forms of currency include personal ornaments such as the tradition-ally-styled RING MONEY. Rings similiar to those identified as money were in use in Britain on Bronze Age sites prior to 1000 B.C. The Iron Age examples may have had multiple functions: as items of personal adornment (many were hair-ornaments), as a means of displaying wealth and as a medium of exchange. The weights and diameters vary, making it difficult to establish whether denominations existed.

The gold rings surviving today occur in three varieties, all of them open-ended. The commonest variety is made from a thin, single-strand of twisted gold with plain, tapering ends. The second type, also reasonably common, is thicker and appears to be of twisted silver, with a gold-plating or wash. They have a smooth surface with the ends square-cut. This type occasionally appears with some of the gold worn off, revealing the silver core. The third type, which is extremely rare, is made of two strands of twisted gold soldered together at one point to form a double ring. The strands have has plain, tapering ends, much like the first type of ring.

Large bronze rings are known from the Iron Age, and these are sometimes described as ring money. These are probably nothing more than bracelets, and are not likely to have been a form of currency.

## THE PERIOD OF IMPORTED COINAGE
### 125 – 100 B.C.

Ancient Britain was far from isolated from the rest of Europe. The British tribes had active contact with the Celtic peoples on the Continent and a lively commodities trade was carried on cross-Channel. As early as the late Bronze Age, about 1000 B.C., finished metal objects and also scrap metal for local manufacturing were imported into Britain (3). This trade continued into the Iron Age, mirroring the use of metals on the Continent. As iron first began to replace bronze for high-prestige goods in Gaul, the same replacement occurred in Britain. As the use of iron became common in Gaul, it became widely used in Britain as well. The British tribes, rather than being isolated, appear to have been well-connected with those on the Continent.

By the Second Century B.C., the growing trade in commodities between Britain and the Continent became more intense (4). Wine, prestige metal goods and exotic plants and animals were all imported in exchange for British raw metals and other commodities. The British tribes also supplied manpower to the Gallic tribes in the form of mercenary warriors or slaves for the Roman slave trade. The cross-Channel trade eventually expanded until coinage was needed to facilitate negotiations. At this point, coins already in use on the Continent, began to flow from Gaul to the British tribes. They were brought to Britain in several ways: some were used in actual trading transactions, others were brought back as pay by returning mercenaries, and yet others may have been carried over by raiding-parties or settlers from the Continent. Gifts between tribal leaders could account for the appearance of others. There is some debate as to the date of the first importations, but 125 B.C. is a reasonable estimate.

There were two trade routes, the most important of which supplied the Roman economy. The Roman world was in perennial need of raw materials, particularly tin and iron, and was especially dependent on slave labour. Both commodities had to be obtained outside the empire because domestic sources were inadequate to satisfy Roman needs. Britain, significantly, had both manpower and metals in abundance (5).

The Romans occupied Southern Gaul in 125 B.C., and used this as a base for trade. They encouraged the taste for wine amongst the Celtic tribes, an addiction that created a market for an abundant Roman product. The Romans then traded cheap wine for expensive tin, iron and slaves at a four hundred percent profit. Although this trade was conducted by private Roman merchants, it is known the Roman government encouraged it. Initially, the Romans traded with local Celtic tribes around Massilia who, in turn, traded with other tribes up the Rhone. These intermediates then sent the wine down the Garonne, where it was placed on Venetic ships, which travelled by ocean to the Armorican peninsula (Brittany, today), whence it was re-exported to Southern Britain. St. Malo, on the north coast of Brittany, and the British ports of Mount Battan, Hengistbury, and a possibly submerged one at Selsey were active trading partners. Shards of thirty Roman wine amphorae have been found at Hengistbury, dating to the early First Century, and Armorican coins have been found throughout the south coast of Britain. Finds of similiar amphorae in Armorica attest to the trade route and the commodity traded.

In the beginning, it is likely the Romans had no idea of the origin of the goods they received, and the Celtic intermediaries tried to retain the secret. The information could not be concealed indefinitely, however, and the Romans soon learned about the British trade. Ultimately, they tired of the long chain of distribution, and sought direct contact. Strabo gives an account of a Roman war galley sent to follow Phoenician trading ships to discover the British trade route. Rome's desire for direct trade was one of the motives for the Claudian invasion many years later.

A second trade route is also known, cross-Channel from the Belgic part of Gaul (northern France and Belgium, today) to Kent and the mouth of the Thames. Whether the Romans instigated this trade is unknown, but it occurred at the same time as the Armorican wine trade. Gaulish coins of the Ambiani tribe, dated to 125-100 B.C., are found in great numbers throughout southeast Britain today (6).

In the past, the existence of Gaulish coins in Britain was taken as sign of a series of invasions from the Continent. Certain tribes, such as the Atrebates, Parisii, and possibly the Iceni had groups on both sides of the Channel. The movement of coins from the Continent to Britain, in the case of these tribes, could have indicated the movement of people as well as goods—but these groups were not the ones involved. Furthermore, there is no archaeological evidence of the wide-scale disruption such invasions would have caused. Coin imports are believed today to give testimony to trade, not military activity (7).

The situation existing about 100 B.C., a quarter of a century after the first coin imports, is one in which the tribes of the Armorican peninsula were trading with the British southern coast, and the Belgic tribes were trading with Kent and tribes around the mouth of the Thames. A lively cross-trade along the British coast from the southwest to the Thames area is a probability. Coastal trading would explain why small numbers of Armorican coins are found in Kent, around the Thames and in Essex; and why Ambiani coins are found similarly along the coast of Dorset, Devon and Cornwall.

## THE FIRST IMPORTED COINS

Sometime around 125 B.C., two types of imported gold coins appeared in southeast Britain: the LARGE FLAN TYPE of the Ambiani and the DE-FACED DIE TYPE of the Caletes. The attribution of the Defaced Die Type to the Caletes is not entirely certain because the original dies may have been Ambianic in origin. In any event, these tribes occupied the coastal districts opposite Kent and were ideally situated for controlling trade and social interaction cross-Channel. Consequently, the presence of their coins in Britain probably reflected trade and other ties. Modern findspots of the coins indicate the tribes had links with the Atrebates/Regni, Trinovantes/Catuvellauni and the Cantii (8). There is some difference in the use of the coins, however, since the Ambianic link used more staters than quarter staters, whereas the Caletic one used mostly quarters. Indeed, Defaced Die Type staters are extremely rare and almost all have British findspots. The difference in use suggests the nature of the trade was different, but there is no proven explanation for the phenomenon.

The Large Flan Type, the largest and heaviest coin used in Ancient Britain, circulated in considerable numbers. The types—a head of Apollo on the obverse and a horse and chariot on the reverse—were ultimately derived from the staters of Phillip II of Macedon. However, the Ambiani were not content to copy the designs slavishly. The Celtic spirit demanded a flowing transformation of the image to produce a masterpiece of abstract beauty. The design, several copying-stages from the Macedonian original, became fully Celticized. The

Apollo head, though still naturalistic, expanded to fill the entire surface of the die and overspilled the edges of most flans. The obverse was dominated not by the face, but by the lively pattern of the god's curling hair and laural wreath. The horse on the reverse, even more abstract in form, was shown with disjointed legs, whilst the charioteer now floated freely above the animal. The surrounding field, ornamented by a series of pellets and lines, had a crude flower-motif springing from the ground—all these details utterly foreign to the Macedonian original.

The two varieties, in which the head and horse faced either right or left in unison, appear to have been used simultaneously because they have the same standard weight. Two mules, one head-right/horse-left, the other head-left/horse-right were once thought to prove the contemporaneity of the types, but both have proven to be modern forgeries (9). Genuine staters are almost always found worn to a great degree—they evidently saw heavy use over an extended period, perhaps 30 or 40 years.

The staters and quarter staters of the Defaced Die Type are slightly smaller in diameter than the Large Flan Type, but are thicker and thus have the same standard weight (10). On the reverse, the horse is still recognizable as an animal, but is stylized to a greater degree than on the Ambianic coins. The head of Apollo on the obverse is obliterated by a series of crude, deliberate chisel cuts to the die. Two varieties circulated: with the first, a normal Large Flan Type die was defaced, because remnants of the Apollo head can be detected between the chisel cuts (11). With the second, an unusual thing happened—the chisel cuts were made on a blank die. Evidently, the defaced image had become a standard design feature; when new dies were needed, the motif was retained.

The retention of the chisel-cut motif could indicate several things. First, the Celts may have used these particular coins as money. Often, coins of high intrinsic value are struck with minimal design changes over time. The reason for conservatism is that continuity facilitates acceptance; people are reassured by familiarity with the design. If acceptance had not been an issue, there would have been little reason to continue the chisel-cutting practice. Second, the decision to obliterate the head of Apollo in the first place suggests some important event necessitated the change—a schism between the Caletes and some other group, for example. It is possible the Defaced Die Type's appearance in Britain chronicles not only trade or social contact, but a movement of people from the Continent in the late Second Century B.C.

## LATER IMPORTED COINS 100—50 B.C.

In about 100 B.C., a new series comprising only gold staters was imported from Belgic Gaul. The ABSTRACT DESIGN TYPE appears to have replaced the Large Flan Type in the territory of the Trinovantes/Catuvellauni and Cantii (12). In general, they were smaller and lighter than the earlier type. The Abstract Design Type has been suggested as the coinage of Diviciacus of the Suessiones, whom Caesar described as ruling on both sides of the Channel (13).

The coins were issued in five distinct varieties (14); the increasing stylization of the design matched by a corresponding decrease in weight. The head of Apollo on the two earliest varieties was still representational, in fact very close to that of the Large Flan Type. The design on the third variety was more abstract and the head less unrecognizable. On the last two varieties, the Apollo head was stylized to the extent that it is barely recognizable as a portrait.

The commonest of the five types, on both sides of the Channel, tend to be the later ones (15). The earlier, heavier types were either melted down and reminted or they were initially struck in smaller quantities. The commonest variety, the third, appeared about 80 B.C., and the last was imported about 65 B.C.

A new series of staters, the GALLIC WAR TYPE, appeared about 65 B.C. (16) actually in advance of the war, but the commonest varieties date to the war years—hence the name. These uniface coins, with the design confined to the reverse, display a spirited, highly stylized horse. The first Gallic War Type staters are only slightly lighter than the latest issue of the Abstract Design Type. However, the series suffered a rapid decline in weight after the beginning of the war. The coins circulated in vast numbers on both sides of the Channel and it seems likely the issue was struck by the Gallic tribes to finance the resistance against Caesar (17). Presumably, this included payment to the British tribes for mercenaries and supplies. Caesar pointed to British assistance as one of the reasons for his sorties across the Channel in 55 and 54 B.C. Quarter staters which carry the Gallic War Type design have proved to be modern forgeries (18).

A final type of stater, the TRIPLE-TAILED HORSE TYPE, used extensively on the Continent in the territory of the Suessiones, appeared in Britain about 60 B.C. The issue is represented in Britain by only a couple of coins, but the type is important to British numismatics because it became the prototype for the coinage of several of the southern tribes during the Gallic War (19).

The final imported Belgic issue was the GEOMETRIC TYPE, comprising quarter staters only. These appeared in Britain about 65 B.C.; either at the very end of the Abstract Design Type or at the inception of the Gallic War Type. It circulated along the Sussex coast and to a lesser extent throughout the southeast, and must have been the corresponding fractional denomination to one of the stater issues. On balance, it was probably the quarter stater of the Gallic War Type, but this has not been proven. The obverses possibly represent a highly-stylized wolf-and-twins motif, or if the coins are inverted, a boat with oars having three occupants or sails. The most speculative suggestion is the Geometric Type represented an abstraction of the obverse and reverse of the Monnaies à la Croix series of southern Gaul.

Some coins also flowed into Britain along the trade route between the Armorican peninsula and the trading ports of Hampshire, Dorset and Devon. Coins of the Osismii, Coriosolites, Baiocasses, Venetii and Redones appeared, principally in the ports with only a thin scattering inland (20). Few coins were involved and these tended not to travel far, so it is possible they were considered curiosities. Armorican coin finds do not provide much evidence for a money economy in southwest Britain in the early first century. These Armorican coins, initially imported around 100 B.C. and continuing at least to the time of the Gallic War, had no stylistic influence on British coinage. Instead, it appears the coinage of Belgic Gaul was used as a prototype, even in the territory of the Durotriges (21).

The trade axes between the southeast and Belgic Gaul, and the southwest coast and Armorica were not mutually exclusive. Armorican coins appear in small quantities along the southeast coast and around the mouth of the Thames. Similarly, Belgic coins appear along the southwest coast. It is likely there were coastal traders plying between the major ports, moving coins along with goods. Armorican tribes possibly had direct trading contact with the southeast coast, and the Belgic ones had similiar contact with the southwest coast.

## THE EARLIEST BRITISH COINAGE
### 100 — 75 B.C.

During the Second Century, the British tribes imported coins from Gaul to meet their currency needs. By 100 B.C., however, a market economy had developed in Kent and it required large quantities of low-value coins (22). This need for small change was to foster the first British-made coins. Early in the opening decade of the First Century, a Kentish tribe, probably the Cantii, began to cast coins in a high-tin bronze alloy. Using the bronze coinage of Masillia as a prototype, they placed a head of Apollo on the obverse and a charging bull on the reverse. A similar type appeared shortly thereafter north of the Thames, probably the first coins of the Trinovantes/Catuvellauni (23).

Previously, these early British pieces had been considered copies of the coins of the Leuci, a tribe in eastern Gaul. The coins of the Leuci are adapted from the same Masilliote bronzes. However, the earliest extant British examples are closer in style to the Masilliote prototype, indicating a direct derivation (24). Furthermore, Masillia bronzes have been found at Richborough and Canterbury, and they may have arrived in Britain as a result of the wine trade with southern Gaul. The Kentish tribes were likely to have been familiar with them, when the time came to produce their own cast bronze coinage.

The KENTISH CAST BRONZES are amongst the most fascinating of all British coins, because they demonstrate Celtic ingenuity at its best (25). The Cantii were required to produce large quantities, and because each coin had a low intrinsic value, they had to produce them economically. Initially, the moneyers experimented with manufacturing techniques—the earliest examples appear to be made from moulds produced by impressing a mother coin into the clay. Soon, textile, wood and perhaps other materials were used to produce the runner system, and a stylus was used to scribe the design. Once the most efficient method was discovered, the coins became standardized and were subsequently issued in enormous quantities throughout the first half of the first century, to be replaced ultimately by struck bronzes (26).

Although the cast bronzes were used primarily in Kent, other findspots indicate they travelled beyond the territory of the Cantii (27). Large numbers have been found near London, in the vicinity of the Thames, possibly votive deposits, and the Durotriges imported them as scrap metal during the Gallic War.

## EARLY STRUCK COINAGES IN BRITAIN
### 75 — 60 B.C.

Shortly after the inception of the cast coinage in Kent, several tribes made their first fitful attempts to strike gold staters (28). About 75 B.C., or shortly thereafter, the Atrebates/Regni produced a copy of the Abstract Design Type, struck to the standard weight of the Gallic stater. This coin, named the WESTERHAM TYPE, was somewhat more stylized than its Gallic prototype. The Atrebatic/Regnan coinage induced the Durotriges, the neighbouring tribe to the west, to issue the CHUTE TYPE around 65 B.C. Five other types appeared by 60 B.C.: the YARMOUTH TYPE, possibly Durotrigan, the NORFOLK WOLF TYPE of the Iceni, the CLACTON TYPE of the Trinovantes/Catuvellauni, the WALDINGFIELD TYPE, probably Trinovantian/Catuvellaunian, as well and the NORTH EAST COAST TYPE of the Corieltauvi.

In all, six British tribes issued coins before the Gallic War, giving us the first glimpse of tribal structure in Britain. Caesar substantiated the testimony of the coins by confirming a tribal structure in his writings. The Durotriges, Atrebates/Regni, Cantii, Trinovantes/Catuvellauni, Iceni and Corieltauvi had all, by this time, progressed sufficiently to require coinage and all struck coins to the pre-war standard weight of the Celtic stater. The Trinovantes and Catuvellauni, seemingly distinct in the historical record, cannot be distinguished in the numismatic one (29). Although Cassio Dio mentions the Catuvellauni in his account of the Claudian invasion, they are not mentioned by Caesar. The historical importance of the Catuvellauni has been exaggerated by earlier interpretations of the numismatic evidence.

The Dobunni, later to issue coins, were not a part of the early activity and cannot be identified in the numismatic record until after the Gallic War (30). The Cantii, perhaps because they had access to large quantities of Gallic War type staters, did not strike their own gold coins until after the war and contented themselves with issuing the cast bronze pieces (31).

Some of these early staters, notably the Atrebatic/Regnan and Trinovantian/Catuvellaunian, were short-lived and struck in small quantities. They probably represent local productions which met some local need, rather than a part of a grand tribal scheme. It is likely they were struck only sporadically and their long term influence on British coinage was minimal. The issues were soon suspended, likely a result of events during the Gallic War (32). Most of these early gold issues are today quite rare and have a small number of recorded findspots. It is sometimes difficult to establish their tribal origin with certainty. Even the commoner of the rare types, such as the Westerham, are commoner because of one or two hoards.

However, for the tribes farthest from the cross-channel trade with Gaul, the early issues were the beginning of continuous and long-lasting coinages. The North East Coast type was issued in considerable quantities and ultimately lead to the rich and varied SOUTH FERRIBY TYPES and the long run of inscribed Corieltauvian coinage. The Icenian Norfolk Wolf Type became gradually debased with first silver and then copper. Finally it became merely billon, to be replaced entirely with a restored coinage (33).

The Durotriges tried to maintain a gold coinage for external trade during the early stages of the Gallic War. However, for internal use they switched to white-gold coins, these having a very low gold content. Surprisingly, the white-gold pieces were copied from the Westerham Type, rather than the Durotriges' own Chute Type. The crab below the horse was replaced by a simple pellet, similar to that on the Westerham staters.

Although the coins were primarily used inside Durotrigan territory, some have been found to the east, in Atrebatic/Regnan territory. Perhaps, trading contacts between the two tribes were the motivation for the stylistic change (34). Soon the Durotriges removed almost all the gold from the alloy and issued the same type in the form of silver staters. These silver staters were coined in vast quantities and the coinage continued into the 30's B.C.

The first British quarter staters appeared before the Gallic War, as well, in the territory of the Atrebates/Regni. The KENTISH GEOMETRIC TYPES were copied from the continental GEOMETRIC TYPE. The Durotriges, in turn copied these and produced their own DUROTRIGAN GEOMETRIC TYPE. The first were struck in gold, but the alloy rapidly debased to white-gold and finally to silver, about the middle of the Gallic War.

## COINAGE AND TRADE AT THE OUTSET OF THE GALLIC WAR
### 60 — 55 B.C.

The Roman occupation of Gaul brought about changes in the trading patterns of the British tribes. The numismatic evidence indicates a fluid situation existed at the outset of the war—considerable trading contacts existed amongst the tribes (35). By the close of Caesar's campaigns, however, some of the inter-tribal trading networks had been severed (36). In the years that followed, tribal fortunes hinged upon the allegiances forged during the War.

By 57 B.C., the lively cross-Channel trade had created an embryronic exchange network within Britain (37). It supplied luxury items to British markets and located and procured goods required for export to Gaul. The findspots of early imported coins such as the Large Flan and Defaced Die types generally shun the extreme interior of Britain. Evidently, the inland trading network was not sufficiently developed around 100 B.C. to require money transactions. However, findspots of later issues, such as the Abstract Design, Westerham, Chute and North East Coast Types hint at a wider dispersal throughout the interior. Some of the British issues even travelled beyond tribal boundaries in small numbers. While the coins may indicate movement of people within Britain, it is much more likely they delineate inter-tribal trade.

In the early years of the Gallic War, the coins became dispersed farther and farther inland—the Gallic War Type circulated in enormous quantities, and well into the Midlands (38). Inter-tribal trade became more articulated and intense, with the Durotrigan territory and the southeast coast acting as two hubs of the networks. This trading situation reached its climax in the early years of the war as Britain became a supply depot for the fight on the Continent.

The appearance of so many Gallic War Type staters in Britain suggests Roman manipulation. By financing one tribal group to compete against another in the trading networks, they may have tried to influence the flow of war materiel to the Continent for Roman benefit. Thus, the Romans may have been the ultimate source of the Atrebatic/Regnan gold, but this has not been proven (39).

In any event, the Atrebates/Regni appear to have received immense quantities of gold staters and flooded the trading networks with them. Simultaneously, the Durotriges seem to have run out of gold bullion. Their Chute Type stater was replaced first with the CHUTE/CHERITON TRANSITIONAL TYPE in the early war years and by 57 or 56 B.C., the CHERITON TYPE. All these Durotrigan coins are linked by privy marks: the direction of the laurel leaves and an object near the horse's neck. The Transitional piece has full weight, but reduced noble-metal content, the Cheriton a drastically reduced weight and a further reduction in fineness. Cheritons, unlike other staters, can contain a surprisingly high proportion of tin—the Durotriges were obtaining Cast Bronzes from Kent and adding them to melted-down Chute staters to debase the alloy. It appears the Durotriges were trying to maintain a gold coinage for trading purposes, but as events turned out, unsuccessfully.

While the Atrebates/Regni were engaging in British trade with good-quality staters, the Durotriges found themselves having to deceive their partners with increasingly inferior ones. The networks, eventually detecting the difference, shunned the Durotrigan hub, preferring the Atrebatic/Regnan one. Since the Romans were preparing to invade Armorica, they had a strong reason for eliminating the Durotrigan trade with the Continent prior to 56 B.C. By financing Atrebatic/Regnan trade, making it more competitive in the trading networks, they would have accomplished just this.

Caesar, by smashing the Venetic fleet in 56 B.C. and invading Armorica in 57, largely cut the Durotriges off from their Continental sources of luxury goods. This effectively hobbled the Durotriges in the British trading networks, because they now lacked the luxury goods to make barter-type arrangements. Prior to the war, Italian wine, coloured glass, figs and Armorican pottery were being imported into the Durotrigan port, Hengistbury, for redistribution (40). After the war, the profitable Italian wine trade shifted to the Trinovantes/Catuvellauni as findspots of later amphorae show, and the Durotriges were forced to import wine from Spain. They may have lost trading rights for other commodities, as well. Perhaps to compensate for their loss of prestige imports, the Durotriges developed their pottery industry around Poole harbour and Hengistbury served as a distribution centre for trading this commodity.

After the war, Durotrigan coins were limited to the tribal territory and to a small extent that of the Dobunni (41). However, findspots of Atrebatic/Regnan coins in Dubunnic territory show the Durotriges had competition for the Dobunnic trade. The Durotriges probably suffered economically from the loss of their trading contacts and the competition from other tribes. Post-war Durotrigan coins became increasingly coarse and debased, suggesting increasing poverty. Although some goods continued to be imported from the Continent, trade was at a reduced level. Economic difficulties, of which we have only a hint, may have been one of the reasons why the tribe was so resolutely opposed to Vespasian during the Claudian invasion a hundred years later—they would have blamed the Romans for their losses.

When Caesar invaded Britain in 55 B.C. and again in the following year the situation in the southeast was altered as well. Henceforth, the Romans controlled the cross-channel trade and it appears they manipulated it to favour their allies during the war at the expense of the anti-Roman tribes. Roman manipulation helps explain the wealth of the post-war Atrebatic/Regnan and Trinovantian/Catuvellaunian coinages, compared to the surprisingly small output of the Cantii. The small postwar output of the Cantian mint and the earlier appearance of Kentish Cast Bronzes in Durotrigan territory may not be mere coincidence—the Cantii may have suffered repression in the cross-Channel trade after the war.

## COINAGE DURING THE CAESAREAN INVASIONS
### 55—54 B.C.

Although the Gallic War Type stater had a relatively stable value compared to the Durotrigan coinage, it too suffered a decline. Its weight was lowered during the fifteen years following 65 B.C. in several stages from 6.35 to 5.80 grammes (42). Increasingly lower-value staters flooded Britain and the reduction eventually influenced local coinages. The heavier-weight Westerham, Clacton and Waldingfield issues of the Atrebates/Regni and Trinovantes/Catuvellauni were driven out of circulation and the tribes stopped striking them. By the midpoint of the war, they struck no coins at all, the requirement for coinage being fully met by imports.

Although imports of Gallic War staters increased to an unprecedented level (43), the trading networks in Britain demanded even greater quantities. Those of the Atrebates/Regni and Trinovantes/Catuvellauni became longer as goods and manpower were sought well into the interior. By 55 B.C., the Atrebates/Regni began to strike the lighter-weight ATREBATIC ABSTRACT TYPE in great quantity to feed a trading network extending as far away as the territories of the Dobunni and Corieltauvi. Shortly thereafter, the Trinovantes/Catuvellauni began to produce their own light-weight version, the WHADDON CHASE TYPE.

At first, the Gallic War Type did not influence the outlying tribes because few of these coins reached them. Eventually, however, the weight reduction and quantity of light-weight coins became too great to ignore and the Iceni and Corieltauvi were forced to react (44). The Iceni debased the metallic content of their staters, gradually increasing the proportion of silver to gold until the coins were little more than white gold. The Corieltauvi, however, held out and refused to debase their staters. Eventually, the pressure became so great they decided to reduce the weight of the North East Coast Type in one step to make it conform. They struck a new light-weight stater, called the REDUCED WEIGHT TYPE, and identified it by reversing the direction of the horse from right to left.

The period 57—56 B.C. proved to be a turning point in British history. Caesar invaded the Armorican peninsula, eliminated Gallic resistance there and destroyed the Venetic fleet. The disruptions are chronicled in the vast hoards of Armorican coins found in the Channel Islands. Though the deposition date of the hoards is somewhat controversial and may extend into the 30's B.C., it is clear the events of 56 initiated the turmoil (45). Debased silver staters, intended to finance the Armorican resistance, found their way to Guernsey and Jersey to be deposited, unused by refugees after the Armorican resistance collapsed.

As traumatic as events may have been in Armorica, the repercussions in Britain were equally severe. The Durotriges were now largely cut off from the Continent, and although there is some evidence for continuing trade, it is evident they lost many of their contacts in Gaul. They became increasingly isolated from the mainstream of British tribal development, to become a conservative and less-prosperous enclave, amid an increasingly prosperous Britain later in the century.

The following year, 55 B.C., Caesar made a brief reconnaissance foray into Kent. Nearly meeting with disaster, he returned to Gaul to plan a more elaborate invasion the following year. In 54 B.C., he mounted a second expedition, one that would change the tribal relationships in Britain. Crossing the channel with a large force, he quickly overran Kent and pressed on to the Thames near the future site of London. Several British tribes sent envoys to offer submission, while others decided to continue the resistance. One of the defending tribes, led by a man named Cassivellaunus, had been harassing the Trinovantes/Catuvellauni earlier and Caesar set out to attack its oppidum. Cassivellaunus arranged a counterattack on Caesar's camp in Kent but this failed, thus breaking the main British resistance. After the failure in Kent, Cassivellaunus and the rest of the British tribes capitulated, ending the hostilities.

Traditionally, it has been stated that Cassivellaunus was ruler of the Catuvellauni, but no historic documentation supports this idea and Caesar never mentioned the name of the tribe. The 'Cas' of Cassivellaunus and 'Cat' of Catuvellauni were merely coincidental and did not indicate a connection. An elaborate North Thames history has been written around the conflict between the Catuvellauni and Trinovantes (46). This included a give-and-take power struggle between the two tribes that ultimately ensnared Rome in British tribal politics.

This history, written entirely from the numismatic evidence, is now considered obsolete because numismatically the Catuvellauni and Trinovantes are indistinguishable (47). For the most part, the two tribes used a single coinage and appear as a single socio-economic unit. It is difficult to see them as adversaries and consequently the tribe-of-origin of Cassivellaunus is somewhat of a mystery. It may be he was merely a strong and charismatic figure from a relatively minor tribe or sub-group who rose to lead the opposition to the Caesarian invasion only to sink back into obscurity after the threat passed.

The socio-economic results of the invasion, however, are quite plain: the Trinovantes/Catuvellauni directly benefitted from Caesar's invasion. They had not resisted him and consequently were rewarded after the campaign, becoming the recipients of the cross-Channel wine trading rights, now controlled indirectly by the Romans on the Gallic side. The Cantii may have played an active part in the resistance by supplying the troops who, at Cassivellaunus's behest, attacked Caesar's camp. If so, they were probably barred from the cross-channel trade after the war.

The Gallic War had two important effects on British coinage. The first was the weight reduction in the British staters, marked by the introduction of new types (48). The effects of the weight reduction in the earlier period of the Gallic War has already been discussed, but towards the end of the war these effects became pronounced, reflected most dramatically in the coinage of the Trinovantes/Catuvellauni. The new Whaddon Chase Type stater appeared, based partially on the Continental Triple-Tailed Horse Type, but with design elements copied directly from Republican denarii (49).

The second effect was the introduction of silver coins, the designs of which were often inspired by Republican denarii (50). The Gallic tribes had been striking silver coins during the war and some may have continued to do so afterwards. The British tribes may have been prompted to strike silver because of the Gallic practice. Also the presence of Roman troops in Britain, and the face-to-face contact with Caesar during his visits possibly hastened the introduction of silver coin throughout the southeast. By the end of the Gallic War, the Atrebates/Regni, Trinovantes/Catuvellauni, Iceni and Corieltauvi had all started striking silver coins to complement their gold issues.

At the very end of the Gallic War, one final event influenced the future of British coinage. After the defeat of the united Gallic tribes at Alesia in 51 B.C., the leader of the Continental Atrebates, Commius, fled to Britain to join his tribal cousins. Previously an ally of Caesar, he became disillusioned and joined Vercingetorix's heroic but doomed attempt to repulse the Romans. Commius, declaring he never wanted to see the face of another Roman, climbed into his ship to leave for Britain and found himself beached by a low tide. Seeing the Romans in the distance, Commius raised his sails as if he were sailing away and tricked them into giving up the pursuit. Later, when the tide came in, he sailed to Britain where he spent the rest of his days. There, he modified the Atrebatic Abstract Type staters by adding his name to the reverse of the coin, thus launching the first of the British dynastic issues.

## THE LAST UNINSCRIBED COINS AND THE EARLIEST DYNASTIC ISSUES
### 54—30 B.C.

Towards the end of the war, coin imports largely ceased and locally-made coins now circulated in specific areas, with little overlap (51). As a result, findspot maps delineated tribal territories with increasing clarity as time goes on. The story of the postwar coinage is one of three major regions: the NORTH THAMES, the SOUTH THAMES, and that of the PERIPHERAL TRIBES.

North of the Thames, the Trinovantes/Catuvellauni emerged as a powerful economic force and maintained their trading networks, evidently with success. They established an economic, if not a political hegemony over their neighbours, the Iceni, and seem to have had some influence over the Icenian coinage.

South of the Thames, the Atrebates/Regni continued as the most powerful tribe. Cantian territory, at first independent with its own coinage, came under increasing Trinovantian/Catuvellaunian influence. Eventually, it became a disputed area with the Atrebates/Regni and Trinovantes/Catuvellauni vying for control.

The Peripheral Areas included the territories of the Corieltauvi, Dobunni and Durotriges. These three tribes maintained their independence and each had its own coinage.

## COINAGE IN THE NORTH THAMES REGION
### 54—30 B.C.

In the southern part of the North Thames Region the Trinovantes/Catuvellauni continued to strike the Whaddon Chase Type after the war, gradually making the design more abstract and reducing the weight slightly. An extremely rare complementary issue of quarter staters was struck for some varieties. Towards the end of the issue, about 45 B.C., two new types appeared.

The WONERSH TYPE and its more stylized descendant, the SAVERNAKE FOREST TYPE, were both light-weight variants of the Whaddon Chase stater. Today, they are seldom found in Trinovantian/Catuvellaunian territory, but rather in those of the neighbouring tribes on all sides. It is possible they represented light-weight trade coins. These types, all relatively rare, were significant because they were the prototypes for the Trinovantian/Catuvellaunian dynastic issues that immediately followed. The first of these inscribed coins, first struck about 40 B.C., was that of Addedomaros, a ruler who struck coins for about ten years. These were replaced by the short-lived coinage of Dubnovellaunus-in-Essex.

The first silver coins appeared in Trinovantian/Catuvellaunian territory about 55 B.C., the first bronzes during the coinage of Addedomaros (52).

The Iceni, in the northern part of the North Thames Region, had severe coinage problems by the end of the war. The Norfolk Wolf Type had become so debased and widely counterfeited, it probably became a discredited currency. About 45 B.C., a new coinage was introduced, with restored gold content. A new issue of staters, the FRECKENHAM TYPE appeared, known today primarily from a single hoard. A miniscule number of quarter staters was struck to complement the staters. At this time, Trinovantian/Catuvellaunian gold coins did not circulate in Icenian teritory, however uninscribed silver coins were just beginning to appear.

Within five years, the Freckenham Type disappeared, replaced first by the coinage of Addedomaros and later by that of Dubnovellaunus-in-Essex. Either imports of Trinovantian/Catuvellaunian coins enabled the Iceni to suspend their own coinage or, more likely, Addedomaros supressed the Icenian coinage. Except for an extremely rare issue of inscribed coins around the turn of the millennium, the Iceni never struck coins in gold again (53).

The opposite was true, however, for the Icenian silver coinage. By 35 B.C., evidently prompted by the lead of the Corieltauvi, the tribe struck the first of a long series of silver coins. The earliest were similiar to Corieltauvian issues and it is difficult to assign some varieties to one tribe or the other. Significantly, the Iceni chose not to adopt Trinovantian/Catuvellaunian designs for their first silver coinage, suggesting an early attempt to free themselves from the 'North Thames socio-economic unit'.

The first inscribed Icenian coins were not struck until the very close of the First Century B.C., making the Iceni the last tribe to strike coins with legends. It was not perhaps until this late date that the tribal nobility felt sufficiently free of Trinovantian/Catuvellaunian interference to strike coins carrying their own names (54).

## COINAGE IN THE SOUTH THAMES REGION
### 54 — 30 B.C.

The two tribes occupying the South Thames Region, the Cantii in the east and the Atrebates/Regni to the west, both had sophisticated money economies before the Gallic War.

Though the Cantii had manufactured their own bronzes for fifty years, they traditionally satisfied their need for gold coins by importing them from Gaul. By the war's end, they found themselves cut off from their Continental sources and were forced to strike their own. About 50 B.C., they introduced the ORNAMENTED TYPE stater and its quarter, the KENTISH GEOMETRIC TYPE. Within five years, these were superceded by the lower-weight WEALD TYPE and its quarter, the TROPHY TYPE. The dynastic coinage began around 35 B.C., and the first inscription, not fully visible on existing coins, contained the letters IVII (55). By 30 B.C this coinage was replaced by coins in the name of Dubnovellaunus-in-Kent (56).

During this period, the tribe changed the module of the cast bronze coins as well, to make them smaller in diameter, but thicker. The change was evidently necessitated by some production difficulties with the thinner, but large-diameter Optimization Period Type. The resulting ADJUSTMENT PERIOD TYPE was produced in fairly small quantities. Soon, a manufacturing change was again instituted—casting was suspended, and struck bronzes were introduced. The cast bronzes were superceded, around 35 B.C., by the dynastic issues, first uninscribed coins under the ruler whose full name is not known, followed by inscribed issues of Dubnovellaunus-in-Kent (57).

The Atrebates continued to issue the Atrebatic Abstract Type after the war, the quarters of which were struck in a very wide variety of designs. However, the appearance of Commius in Britain forever changed the complexion of British coinage.

By 45 B.C., the Atrebates were striking a variant of the earlier staters, but now carrying a legend on the reverse, below the horse. The name COMMIOS appears on what was to be not only the first inscribed British coin but the first to carry the name of a ruler. A silver coinage was added to the Atrebatic issues, coins too small to accommodate Commius's name, but identified by a privy mark which has been attributed to him (58).

## COINAGE IN THE REGION OF THE
## PERIPHERAL TRIBES
### 54 — 30 B.C.

The peripheral tribes, the Durotriges, Dobunni, and Corieltauvi all seemed to follow their own paths during the second half of the First Century B.C.

The Durotriges, by the end of the war, had run out of gold and struck only silver coins. Although modest trade continued with the Armorican peninsula, the Armorican tribes were not in a position to add to the wealth of the Durotriges. Furthermore, fewer findspots of postwar Durotrigan coins appear in Dobunnic or Atrebatic/Regnan territory, indicating the tribe had less economic interaction with the rest of southern Britain. This isolation caused the tribe to suffer economically (59).

The Durotrigan coinage underwent a decline in silver standard over the next twenty years. As the coins became successively debased, minor changes were made to the designs (60). Sometime, probably late in this sequence, a new type silver coin was introduced, the STARFISH TYPE. There is some evidence this was struck in two denominations, but the issue was short-lived. By 30 B.C., the Durotriges were forced to debase their coinage further, until it became merely an issue of bronze staters. These were struck into the next the century.

The Dobunni were the last tribe in Britain to strike their own coins and numismatically represented a backwater. They formed part of the Atrebatic/Regnan trading network during the war, and were introduced to coinage primarily by imports of Atrebatic Abstract Type staters. After the war, this trading network became less important and the Dobunni gradually received fewer coins from the Atrebates/Regni. They then introduced their own staters, around 35 B.C., adapted from the Atrebatic issues. These carried a branched emblem on the obverse, instead of the abstract head of Apollo. The EMBLEM TYPE stater, and its quarter, the DOBUNNIC ABSTRACT TYPE were issued only in small quantities and it is possible the tribe stopped striking gold coins for a few years.

A silver Dobunnic coinage was begun about the same time. These coins were commoner and were struck in a fairly complex progression of types. Conceivably, the Dobunni used silver coins exclusively for a time, following Durotrigan practice. Durotrigan coins appeared in Dobunnic territory less at this date, however, so trading patterns do not fully explain a change in standard. Perhaps the Dobunni simply lacked the gold bullion with which to strike coins.

Later, around 30 B.C., a series of inscribed issues was struck in gold, the first with the name CORIO (61).

The Corieltauvi were still striking the Reduced Weight Type staters after the war. They had held out too long and again found themselves striking coins which were heavier than those of their neighbours. The next reduction in weight was signalled by a radical departure in the coins' artistic style. An amazingly complex and sophisticated coinage was issued starting about 45 B.C. These coins, known collectively in the past as the South Ferriby Type, comprised perhaps the most elaborate of all Ancient British coinages. A bewildering sequence of privy marks appeared as the coins were struck over the next thirty-five years.

The silver Corieltauvian coinage had begun about 55 B.C., and the boar on the reverse of the first issue, the HOSTIDIUS TYPE, was adapted from a

Roman denarius (62). The Hostidius Type gave way to a silver SOUTH FERRIBY TYPE at the time the gold coinage was changed.

The first dynastic issues of the Corieltauvi began fairly late, around 10 B.C., and replaced the last of the South Ferriby varieties.

## THE EARLY DYNASTIC COINAGES
### 30 — 10 B.C.

By 30 B.C., all seven coin-producing tribes had mints in operation, and five were producing coins with inscriptions. Commius had started the practice by placing his name on the Atrebatic/Regnan staters about 45 B.C. Addedomarus promptly responded to this display of vanity by emblazoning his entire name across the Trinovantian/Catuvellaunian ones. This one-upmanship game spread quickly to the other tribes and by the end of the milennium, all but the Durotriges and Iceni were striking inscribed types. From 30 B.C. to the end of the millennium, two additional developments shaped the coinage.

The first was a continued trend to localized coin use (63). The trade situation became increasingly rigid, with coins circulating largely within tribal boundaries. There was less and less intertribal coin flow as the century wore on and tribal areas became increasingly better-defined by the modern findspots.

The second development was the replacement of Celtic motifs by Romanized ones, especially noticable on the Trinovantian/Catuvellaunian coinage. The designs of the gold coins became less abstract as time went on and Roman images appeared on the silver and bronze—often little more than copies of the Roman originals (64).

## COINAGE IN THE NORTH THAMES REGION
### 30 — 10 B.C.

The Trinovantes/Catuvellauni benefitted from Roman favour throughout the second half of the First Century B.C., as their richly-furnished graves and elaborate and prolific coinage attest (65). Late types of wine amphora appeared in their territory indicating the Romans granted the tribe the profitable wine-trade rights. They probably received other trading rights with Roman-controlled Gaul as well. The wealth derived from cross-Channel trade enabled them to control the region north of the Thames to the degree they established an economic hegemony over the Iceni (66).

The reign of Addedomaros came to a close around 30 B.C., roughly ten years after he added his name to the staters. He struck three separate coinages, distinguished from one another by privy-marks. A short-lived ruler, Dubnovellaunus-in-Essex followed, with only a single coin issue. A Cantian ruler, Dubnovellaunus-in-Kent also appeared at this time, but the agreement of names is likely a coincidence.

The next ruler, Tasciovanus, led the tribe from about 25 to 10 B.C. and struck one of the most elaborate coinages in Celtic Britain. He struck three distinct issues, identified by the images on the gold staters. These started with two stylized wreaths of Apollo crossed on the obverse and a Celtic horse on the reverse, but these images were soon replaced by more representational ones. First the Celticized horse was replaced by a mounted warrior brandishing a carnyx, and later the stylized wreath of Apollo was replaced with the inscription TASCIOV RIGON in a box. The title RIGON, meaning 'great king', thus appeared for the first time on the British coinage. These innovations were fairly modest, as would be expected with a conservative coinage of high intrinsic value.

The silver and bronze coinages, however, were not subject to the conservatism expected of the gold staters. Thus freed of restrictions, Tasciovanus' moneyers introduced a great diversity of types: Celticized heads, mythological beasts, abstract designs and some of the earliest Roman scenes to appear on British coins. Several types had designs adapted from Roman denarii and at times the Roman images were simply copied. The head of Augustus appeared, for example, with Tasciovanus' name substituted for that of the Roman emperor. The appearance of Roman motifs at such an early date suggests close ties existed between the Trinovantes/Catuvellauni and the Romans. At a minimum, the tribe was assimilating Roman culture at a rapid pace.

The idea, suggested in the past, that Roman moneyers were sent to Britain to strike coins for the Celts need not be taken too seriously. The Celtic moneyers were perfectly capable of producing coins of the necessary artistic quality and had been demonstrating their die-cutting expertise for fifty years (67).

An important innovation which appeared on Tasciovanus' coins was the inclusion of mint names. The first mint to be so honoured was Verulamium, the modern St. Albans, indicated by VER on the coins. The inscription CAM also soon appeared, denoting Camulodunum, the modern-day Colchester.

The Iceni continued to be economically, if not politically, dominated by the Trinovantes/Catuvellauni. The post-Gallic War Icenian gold issue, the short-lived FRECKENHAM TYPE, disappeared by 40 B.C., never to be replaced. Tasciovanus' coins circulated within Icenian territory, as had those of his predecessors Addedomaros and Dubnovellaunus-in-Essex.

The Iceni continued to strike their series of uninscribed silver coins, beginning with the Boar Type, reminiscent of the Corieltauvian Hostidius and South Ferriby Types. Towards the end of this coinage, a few rare coins appeared with the inscription CAN DURO, the meaning of which is not known.

The CAN DURO type was replaced during the middle of Tasciovanus' reign by the CELTIC HEAD TYPE. The new image was decidedly not based on Corieltuavian motifs, suggesting increased Trinovantian/Catuvellaunian influence and diminished Corieltauvian. The Celtic Head Type was soon replaced by a prolific issue of silver coins, the CRESCENT TYPE.

Surprisingly, the Iceni did not strike coins with the names of their rulers during this period. They were evidently reluctant to do so, and became the last tribe in Britain to produce an inscribed coinage. The Trinovantes/Catuvellauni may have exercised sufficient influence over the Icenian nobility to suppress a dynastic coinage.

## COINAGE IN THE SOUTH THAMES REGION
### 30 — 10 B.C.

The Atrebates/Regni appear not to have benefitted from Roman favour as the Trinovantes/Catuvellauni had. Although the Continental Atrebates had been Roman allies during the early stages of the Gallic War, they must have suffered the Romans' wrath when Commius deserted Caesar and joined Vercingetorix towards the end. Commius' flight to Britain to join the British Atrebates after the battle of Alesia would have thrown them into disfavour with the Romans as well. The tribe's coinage is not very prolific in the period after the War, suggesting they did not share in the wealth from the cross-Channel trade.

The meagre coinage of Commius ended about 35 B.C., replaced by that of Tincommius, who styled himself 'son of Commius'. Tincommius' coinage had three separate issues, distinguished by the images on the staters. It appears to have been a smaller coinage than that of his contemporary, Tasciovanus, and it exhibited a narrower range of types. Tasciovanus struck more than twice the number of varieties and prior to the Wanborough hoard, his coins were much commoner. The Wanborough hoard has distorted our estimate of Tincommius' output by making his coins common today (68).

Tincommius' coinage was made up entirely of gold and silver, with no bronze coins whatsoever. The coins are found almost entirely within Atrebatic/Regnan territory. Evidently, the tribe did not enjoy the economic hegemony over their neighbours, the Cantii, that the Trinovantes/Catuvellauni had over the Iceni.

The Cantii continued to issue coins of their own, introducing inscribed types about 30 B.C. in the name Dubnovellaunus. They thus showed no particular concern for interference from the Atrebates/Regni, their neighbours to the west. Though it cannot be proven, Dubnovellaunus-in-Kent was probably a different ruler from the contemporary Trinovantian/Catuvellaunian one of the same name (69). The coins of the two were completely different in style and those of the Cantii were issued for a longer period.

Dubnovellaunus-in-Kent struck three coinages in gold, silver and bronze, all privy-marked (70). He, or his predecessor, was probably responsible for the replacement of the Kentish Cast Bronze coinage with a series of struck bronzes. His coins circulated largely within Kent, judging from modern finds, underscoring the lack of interaction between the Cantii and the Atrebates/Regni.

However, Cantian coins occasionally circulated in southern Essex because a small number have been found there (71). Similarly, the coins of the Trinovantes/Catuvellauni circulated in Kent to a degree. The economic influence the Trinovantes/Catuvellauni enjoyed over the Iceni was being carefully extended to Kent during the reign of Tasciovanus.

## COINAGE IN THE REGION OF THE
## PERIPHERAL TRIBES
### 30—10 B.C.

The Durotriges practically disappeared from the numismatic scene by 30 B.C. They had suspended all gold and silver coinage by this date and continued with only a series of struck bronze coins. These bronzes mimicked the earlier silver staters, but were poorly-made and became increasingly crude as time went on.

The Dobunni continued to issue silver coins throughout the rest of the century, but there is some question whether they struck gold continuously. The uninscribed gold coins are known today in only a handful of specimens, whereas the silver issues are relatively plentiful, with a long succession of types. By 30 B.C. staters inscribed with the name CORIO appeared, replaced around 15 B.C. by those inscribed BODVOC.

The Corieltauvi continued to issue the South Ferriby Types up to 10 B.C., changing the privy marks on the reverses in a sophisticated manner. The progression of these marks has not yet been fully determined. About 10 B.C., the tribe added the inscription VEP to the South Ferriby Type staters.

Thus by 10 B.C., seven tribal authorities were striking coins. All except the Durotrigan and Icenian issues carried inscriptions. These coinages were largely local ones and did not circulate beyond the tribal areas for the most part (72). The one significant exception to this was the coinage of the Trinovantes/Catuvellauni, the tribe which benefited from Roman sponsorship.

As the millennium drew to a close, Tasciovanus either died or lost his throne, causing turmoil throughout southeastern Britain. The ensuing events are chronicled in a shadowy manner by the coins of the Interregnum.

## THE TRINOVANTIAN/CATUVELLAUNIAN
## INTERREGNUM
### 10 B.C.—10 A.D.

The departure of Tasciovanus from the scene sometime between 10 B.C. and the end of the millennium caused several changes in the coinage almost simultaneously. These chronicled a rapidly changing picture in southeastern Britain as the Trinovantian/Catuvellaunian succession was disputed (73).

The interpretation of this period is, of necessity, speculative, but the upheaval is reasonably certain. The period starts with the appearance of the new names on the Trinovantian/Catuvellaunian coinage and a reduction in the stater's standard weight from 5.60 to 5.40 grammes. The chronological order of the names is suggested by the observation that gold and then silver goes out of circulation.

A struggle for the succession was probable, with various nobles issuing coins to finance their bid and proclaim leadership. On some types, the name Tasciovanus was coupled with other names: SEGO, RUIIS and DIAS. While these could have been mint designations, it is more likely they were the names of rulers. The coupling of the new name with that of Tasciovanus may have been an attempt to establish the legitimacy of the claimant. In any event, the appearance of several rulers or new mints was unprecedented.

The coins closest in style to those of Tasciovanus are those of SEGO, who struck in gold, silver and copper. Next, probably appeared the coins with the name ANDOCO. Andoco's staters were copied from the earliest type staters of Tasciovanus, but were struck to the lighter weight-standard of the Interregnum. The die cutter who engraved the dies was either copying from a poorly-preserved coin or was unfamiliar with the details of the design because he blundered the bucranium above the horse. The coins of DIAS, in silver and bronze, and finally RUIIS, only in bronze, followed.

In Cantian territory, the coinage of Dubnovellaunus-in-Kent ceased, replaced by that of a short-lived ruler Vosenos. Soon Vosenos disappeared, and coins of an Atrebatic/Regnan ruler, Eppillus, circulated in fairly large quantities. The Eppillus pieces carried new designs, one with a winged victory; interestingly none of these carried the Calleva mint signature.

The turmoil in Trinovantian/Catuvellaunian territory may have given the Cantii an opportunity to replace their ruler. The Atrebates/Regni may have then seized the opportunity to exert their influence in Kent, while the Trinovantes/Catuvellauni were preoccupied with internal problems.

The Iceni began to strike silver coins with the inscription ANTED, and even issued a small number of gold staters with this inscription. Although the gold staters were short-lived, the inscribed silver issues endured. Evidently the Iceni gained increased independence from Trinovantian/Catuvellaunian influence, or at least received some concession during the time of trouble.

In Atrebatic/Regnan territory, Tincommius disappeared, replaced by a new ruler named Eppillus, who styled himself 'REX'—king. Both Tincommius and Dubnovellaunus (probably the Kentish one) appeared in Rome about this time appealing to Augustus for aid.

By 10 A.D., the troubled period had passed and Cunobeline held the Trinovantian/Catuvellaunian throne. The coinages with the inscriptions AN-DOCO, SEGO, DIAS and RUIIS ended abruptly and the Atrebatic/Regnan coins disappeared from Kent. The Cantian coinage had come to an end with Vosenos, never to be reinstated and the coins of Cunobeline became the normal coinage of Kent from this time on. Cunobeline evidently drove the Atrebates/Regni from Cantian territory after consolidating his rule. The

Atrebates/Regni, as the historical record shows, were subsequently placed on the defensive by the Trinovantes/Catuvellauni until the situation became serious enough to provide an excuse for Roman intervention in 43 A.D.

## THE LATER CELTIC COINAGES IN BRITAIN
### 10 to 61 A.D.

At first, Cunobeline's accession sometime before 7 A.D. not only stabilized the situation north of the Thames, but also that of the entire south. Tincommius and Dubnovellaunus-in-Kent had fled to the Continent, removing two potentially destabilizing elements from the picture. By 10 A.D., Eppillus disappeared and a new ruler came to the Atrebatic/Regnan throne, one whose posture must have been defensive, and not a source of aggression. With no dangerous opponents to worry him, Cunobeline was able to consolidate his position.

Cunobeline evidently wanted more than stability because he soon extended his influence to Kent (74). The Cantian dynastic coinage was not reinstated after Eppillus disappeared—Cunobeline's coins circulated in Cantian territory, instead. Later, the Atrebates/Regni were subjected to Trinovantian/ Catuvellaunian schemes. Epaticcus, who claimed to be the son of Tasciovanus, gradually removed Verica from power. The encroaching opponent's coins first appeared in the northern part of Atrebatic/Regnan territory about 35 A.D. Eventually, Verica was deposed and fled to the Continent. His downfall became the Roman excuse for intervention in Britain in 43 A.D.

With the Claudian invasion, coinage came to an abrupt end in the southeast. In the beginning, the territories of the Cantii, Trinovantes/Catuvellauni and Atrebates/Regni were overrun by the Roman legions and tribal coinage was supressed. As the Romans moved westwards and northwards, the coinages of the peripheral tribes were halted one by one. The last tribe to strike coins was the Iceni, who had remained Roman allies until the revolt of Boudicca.

## COINAGE IN THE NORTH THAMES REGION
### 10 — 61 A.D.

The coinage of Cunobeline dominated the territory of the Trinovantes/ Catuvellauni from 10 to 43 A.D. During the Interregnum, the standard weight of the stater was reduced to 5.40 grammes, down from the 5.60 grammes of Tasciovanus' reign. Apparently, Cunobeline tried to restore the weight to the heavier standard of 5.60 upon his accession to the throne, but was not successful (75). By 20 A.D., the weight of his staters was reduced to 5.40 grammes. The other tribes had maintained the lower standard throughout the period and had not supported Cunobeline's attempt at restoration.

Cunobeline's coins were as varied in type as those of Tasciovanus, and carried many designs inspired by Roman images. He styled himself the son of

Tasciovanus on some of these, perhaps to legitimatize his claim to the throne. Whether he and Epaticcus were actually brothers is not confirmed in the historical record. The Trinovantian/Catuvellaunian coinage came to an end with the Roman invasion in 43 A.D.

The Iceni struck silver coins throughout the first half of the First Century A.D. and continued production until the Boudiccan Revolt of 61 A.D. The designs on the Icenian coinage showed a double-crescent emblem on the obverse and a horse with inscription on the reverse. This basic type continued with minor changes to the horse and a series of inscriptions: ANTED, ECEN, SAENU and AESU.

After the Claudian invasion, the Iceni became independent allies of Rome, eventually under the leadership of Pratsutagus. He struck silver coins with a Romanized bust and the inscription SUBRI PRASTO on the obverse and a horse with the legend ESICO FECIT on the reverse (76). Queen Boudicca assumed leadership of the tribe after Pratsutagus' death, introducing an uninscribed silver unit with a Celticized head on the obverse. These were struck in great quantities to finance the revolt against Rome (77).

## COINAGE IN THE SOUTH THAMES REGION
### 10—61 A.D.

The Cantii disappear from numismatic history after the accession of Cunobeline, with the exception of a rare Cantian series struck just before the Claudian invasion. For most of the period, Cunobeline's coins circulated in Kent, emphasizing the loss of Atrebatic/Regnan influence in the region after A.D. 7.

About 35 A.D., silver and bronze coins with the inscription AMM appeared in Kent and shortly after this, Adminius, a son of Cunobeline fled to the Continent after having a quarrel with his father. The arrival of Adminius in Gaul prompted the Roman Emperor Caligula to prepare an invasion of Britain. This was doomed never to take place. The subsequent events were hopelessly distorted in the historical record by Caligula's enemies. Apparently, the Romans were sufficiently concerned about Trinovantian/Catuvellaunian expansion by 39 A.D. to prepare for an invasion. The 'AMM' of the coins and the son of Cunobeline were likely the same man.

The numismatic record of the Atrebates/Regni is more complex. After 10 A.D., Eppillus disappeared and a new ruler, Verica, styling himself 'REX' replaced him. The Atrebates/Regni had lost their influence in Kent by this time and Verica's coins did not circulate there (78). Possibly Cunobeline orchestrated Verica's accession or alternatively Eppillus disappeared as a direct result of Cunobeline's reassertion in Kent, with Verica merely filling the vacancy in the Atrebatic/Regnan leadership.

Verica's coins displayed the same Roman influences that had characterized those of Tasciovanus prior to the Interregnum. It is possible the Romans, fearing Trinovantian/Catuvellaunian expansion, increased their contact with the Atrebates/Regni to balance the power of the two tribes. Verica eventually fell prey to Trinovantian/Catuvellaunian expansion—the coins of an encroacher appeared in the northern part of his territory about 35 A.D.

The encroacher, Epaticcus, styled himself a son of Tasciovanus as did Cunobeline. The obverses of Epaticcus' staters were copied from Cunobeline's, but the reverses were inspired by those of Verica. It seems a Trinovantian/Catuvellaunian nobleman was appealing to the Atrebatic/Regnan populace by continuing their reverse types, at the same time proclaiming affiliation with Cunobeline. The Atrebates/Regni later supported the Romans during the Claudian invasion, perhaps as a result of the encroachment of Epaticcus.

Verica was deposed and fled to the Continent by 42 A.D., prompting the Claudian invasion the following year. Epaticcus disappeared about the time of the invasion and his silver coins were replaced by identical types, now carrying the inscription 'CARA'. This man was undoubtedly the historical Caratacus, who lead the British resistance during the Roman invasion. Caratacus' coinage would have been curtailed by his capture in 51 A.D. and probably ended much earlier because he was a fugitive for the latter part of the forties.


## COINAGE IN THE REGION OF THE
## PERIPHERAL TRIBES
### 10—61 A.D.

Sometime probably after the turn of the millennium, the Durotriges stopped striking bronze staters and introduced a cast bronze coinage. The date is difficult to determine and there may have been a time gap between the two coinages. The first of the crude cast pieces displayed line-and-pellet motifs mimicking the struck bronzes. The image now only faintly echoed the Apollo head and horse derived from the staters of Phillip of Macedon. The designs on the last of the cast bronzes were extremely simple—just lines and pellets. The Durotrigan coinage probably came to an end sometime in the mid to late forties A.D., after Vespasian's invasion of their territory. Durotrigan cast bronzes do, however, occur in quite late Roman contexts.

The Dobunni continued to strike gold and silver with the names of their leaders (79). The gold staters carried an immobilized type—all had the branched emblem on the obverse and a celticized horse on the reverse. The names ANTEDRIG, COMUX, EISV, CATTI and INAM appeared in sucession above the horse, and silver units were struck with the names ANTED and EISV. The tribe's coinage would have come to an end in the late forties, as the Roman army marched westward towards Wales.

The Corieltauvi also continued to strike gold and silver with inscriptions, although it is uncertain whether all are the names of rulers. On many coins two or even three words appeared and though it has long been assumed these indicate joint rulers, this has never been established with certainty. The tribe's coinage would have come to an end in the mid to late forties as the Romans moved into their territory on the way to Brigantia.

There has always been some question whether the coins continued to circulate in Britain after the sixties A.D. Celtic coins have the annoying habit of turning up during archaeological excavations in Roman contexts well into the Second Century A.D. These stragglers, probably considered curiosities in later Roman times, need not have represented circulating money.

The experience of the Gaulish coinage after the Gallic War may help explain the end of Celtic coinage in Britain. Celtic silver coins were struck and circulated in Gaul as small change for a while after Caesar's invasion but gold coinage was largely, if not totally, suppressed. The Romans confiscated gold, leaving the Gallic tribes only lesser-value metals. Probably, the same confiscation occurred in Britain and certainly no gold coins were struck. Silver and bronze coinage would probably have been suppressed after the Boudiccan revolt, and thus Celtic coinage would have come to an end after 61 A.D.

## DENOMINATIONS

With the exception of the Durotriges, the Celtic tribes used five basic denominations throughout the late Iron Age: the gold stater and quarter stater, the silver unit and half unit, and the bronze unit.

## GOLD STATERS

Gold staters, initially imported from northern Gaul about 125 B.C., were the premier coins. The first import, the Large Flan Type, had a 27 mm diameter and weighed 7.8 gms—an impressive coin. The weight of the Celtic stater gradually dropped, however, and by 75 B.C it stood at 6.45 gms. The British tribes produced their own versions about this time and these conformed to the prevailing weight standard. As the standard continued to drop, the British tribes successively reduced the weight of their coins—the last weighed only 5.40 gms.

As the weight fell, the moneyers also reduced the gold content, at first replacing gold with silver. After the Gallic War, they replaced both gold and silver with copper. The staters are at first yellow-coloured, but when the copper content increased, they became reddish. The change was very gradual, however, and it is unlikely the average person would have detected the debasement over a ten-year period.

Measuring the gold content is not a simple matter. Specific gravity is a questionable indicator because the staters are made of three-way alloys. Normally, X-ray fluorescence or electron microprobe studies must be performed to determine the metallic content of a given coin.

All Celtic staters are struck on dish-shaped flans, with the obverse on the convex side and the reverse on the concave. For this reason, the reverses are often better preserved—the concavity protects the reverse from wear. It is not unusual for staters to carry a different preservation grade for the two sides. Staters also suffer flan splits at the edges as a result of striking between curved dies. Splits are not a grading concern in this series, but coins with minimal splitting are difficult to find. Sometimes, a flattened coin is encountered and these lack the concave form. In such cases, the flan splits are usually more severe.

## GOLD QUARTER STATERS

Gold quarter staters, as a class, are generally quite rare, although there are exceptions. Often they were issued as smaller versions of the staters at a quarter the weight, but sometimes the relationship between the fractional denomination and the stater is not so clear. Diameters run from 14 to 8 mm, and typical weights from 2.0 to 0.7 gms. Though struck on dish-shaped flans, striking splits are not as pronounced as on the staters because of the smaller diameters. Some very late quarter staters have such small diameters, they do not appear dish-shaped at all. At all times, a high level of die-cutting craftsmanship was maintained and consequently these little coins are often impressive masterpieces of pre-Roman Celtic art.

## SILVER STATERS

The largest silver coin used in Britain was the Durotrigan silver stater. The Durotriges had traditional ties to the Armorican peninsula, an area of Gaul populated by silver-using tribes. Trading contact with this area resulted in the adoption of silver coins and the Durotrigan coinage consequently remained outside the mainstream of British types for much of its history. The Durotrigan silver stater is roughly the same size as a gold stater and the stylistic devices were initially copied from the Atrebatic/Regnan Westerham Type staters. Initially, the Durotriges struck these coins in white gold, but during the Gallic War they debased them to silver, then billon, and finally to bronze. Struck on silver-plated bronze cores, forgeries of staters are fairly common and some of the so-called bronze staters may actually have been silver plated when new.

Large hoards of Durotrigan silver staters have been found and they are amongst the commonest of Ancient British coins. Unfortunately, most examples are struck in very base silver and are often corroded. Staters struck in fine silver are less common and are quite attractive when well-preserved—such specimens normally command a premium. All are struck on dish-shaped flans, as are the gold staters. Diameters run about 19 mm and weights about 4.9 to 5.8 gms. Several varieties of obverse and reverse types exist, and some are excessively rare.

## SILVER UNITS

The normal type of silver coin used in Britain has been traditionally referred to as a silver unit, for want of a better name. These were struck by all the tribes, including the Durotriges. They are small, having diameters 11 to 15 mm, and weigh 0.9 to 1.4 gms. Dish-shaped flans are the norm, though flan splits are not normally seen. The silver is generally debased, and consequently the coins are often corroded, pitted or otherwise poorly preserved. The stylistic devices have a much wider range than the gold coins, with images often copied from Roman Denarii. As a result, the series is one of fascinating diversity.

At one time, most silver units were considered rare, but the efforts of metal-detector enthusiasts have vastly increased the numbers of known examples. In the early and mid 1980's, some very large hoards of Durotrigan and Atrebatic types were discovered. Today, there are fewer rare types. Better preserved specimens tend to be scarcer, due to the poor quality of the metal, and these command a premium. Unfortunately, some people, in an attempt to improve the appearance of dark-toned or corroded specimens, subject the coins to chemical cleaning. This produces a shiny surface, but a magnifying glass will reveal a loss of sharpness caused by the etching action of the chemicals. Some will eventually tone and may one day appear acceptable again, but they will always be less attractive due to the loss of sharpness. Others have been chemically attacked to the point they are unstable and will ultimately disintegrate.

## SILVER HALF UNITS

Silver half units are generally very rare and are known primarily from the Iceni and Corieltauvi tribes. Some of the smaller Atrebatic/Regnan silver units actually represent half denominations. Flans are again dish-shaped and the silver content appears about as debased as the silver units. Usually the images are similiar to those on the silver units in the same series.

## BRONZE UNITS

Bronze units are generally common and were struck by several of the tribes after the Gallic War. Diameters and weights vary considerably and it is virtually impossible to identify distinct denominations. Possibly, they were produced so a certain number of coins were struck from a given weight of metal, none of which had to be within a given weight tolerance. Silver and gold coins, on the other hand, were each struck to a specific weight. Most bronze units are today corroded and many have a heavy green patina. As with Roman coins, true patination is highly prized by collectors, and should never be disturbed. The patina is stable and attempts to alter it may cause the coin to become chemically active and subject to corrosion. Although some bronze units are struck on dish-shaped flans, flat flans are common also and striking splits are seldom seen. Of all the coins, the bronzes show the greatest diversity of types, with designs often inspired by classical Roman art, either derived from Roman coins or engraved gemstones.

## MISCELLANEOUS DENOMINATIONS

Several coin types do not fit in with the denominations outlined above. The Cantii and Trinovantes/Catuvellauni produced cast coins in an alloy of copper and tin, most of which are common today.

The Durotriges struck bronze staters which appear to be a continuation of the silver stater series. These may reflect debased silver types, rather than a distinct bronze coinage. They also produced cast bronzes, the earliest of which appear to be a stylistic continuation of the struck bronzes. Although the cast bronzes were discovered in great quantities in two hoards, most have gone into museum collections and seldom appear for sale. Finds of individual cast bronzes are extremely rare.

The Atrebates struck a very small silver coin, called a minim. These are about 8 mm in diameter, weigh 0.3 gms and were struck on dish-shaped flans. The designs are often quite elaborate, considering the small size provided little room for the engraver's work. One of seldom-seen representations of an ornamental neck-torc occurs on one of these pieces, catalogue number 551-1.

# THE FUNCTION OF THE COINS

## CELTIC COINS WERE MONEY

People spent them, saved them and gave them as gifts. Some were donated to temples, others used to finance wars. They were even counterfeited (80).

In the past, it was argued Britain had no money economy, and thus did not need a circulating coinage. It was thought the coins must have served a ritual purpose in the primitive Celtic society. Celtic coinage, crude and barbarous, was considered to be unlike any other coinage.

Metallurgy, metrology, statistics and typology all tell a different story today (81). The coins were struck to precise weights and the proportions of gold, silver and bronze were controlled by expert metalworkers. Privy marks were routinely added to denote issues, identify weights and specify noble-metal content. Dies were cut with precision—the images may be abstract, but they are intentionally abstract (82).

The abstract images are misleading. Although Celtic die-cutters drew their inspiration from Greek and Roman coins, their work is too easily dismissed as incompetent copying. The die-cutters created exactly the images they wanted—and knew exactly what they were trying to accomplish. There is no lack of die-cutting skill to explain the distortion in a Celticized image.

The coinage as a whole suggests centralized control of production. Weights were standardized and coins were produced using quality control procedures. The silver units of the Iceni were struck to a standard of 1.25 grammes for nearly a hundred years and thousands were produced within two or three percent of the standard (83). The Icenian moneyers were measuring weight to better than five hundredths of a gramme.

The Corieltauvi had similar measurement expertise—they signalled a five percent weight reduction in their gold stater with a privy mark about 55 B.C. The manufacturing operations required to produce such skilfully-made coins argues for centralized control. People wanted confidence in the value of their money—the authorities used technology and organization to provide it.

Counterfeiting was a problem throughout most of the coin-using period. The commonest kind of forgery is a stater struck from false dies on a gold-plated bronze core. It has been suggested these were intended to pass as low-denominations (84), but have the more pleasing appearance of gold. Such a suggestion is unlikely since the plating process would have been costly in materials and time. The most probable explanation of these base coins is they are simple forgeries, intended to deceive.

The typical forgery is often unworn and has a test cut at the edge, exposing the bronze core. Often the cuts are harsher than necessary to reveal the base interior, suggesting frustration and anger on the part of the discoverer. People must have been aware of the forgery problem and were testing light-weight coins. The forgeries were immediately discarded on discovery, and today are found relatively unworn. The existence of these forgeries in such large numbers suggests a circulating coinage (85).

A disproportionate number of forgeries was discovered at the site of the Dobunnic mint at Bagendon (86). The excavators suggested the counterfeits were being produced at the mint; but a more likely suggestion is they were being brought to the experts at the mint for authentication. Counterfeiting and counterfeit-detection schemes are all common aspects of commercial transactions in money economies.

There are two arguments for a non-monetary function: one, the gold staters must have been extremely valuable and could not have been useful for money transactions; and two, there were not enough coins in circulation to facilitate a money economy.

The two arguments certainly do not hold for the period after 50 B.C. (87). Small denomination coins existed in large quantities and would have facilitated a money economy. Furthermore, the total number of gold staters and quarters in circulation was very large, especially in the first century A.D.

Allen estimated the size of Cunobeline's gold coinage based on the number of known dies and the likely number of coins struck from each (88). An output of 30,000 pieces a year was calculated, with the total output estimated at one million staters. This sum appears reasonable because it compares well with known payments in Gaul. The annual tribute paid by the Gallic tribes to Rome after the Gallic Wars was the equivalent of three million of Cunobeline's staters. An excessively high value cannot be supported for such common coins.

The more difficult question lies in the use of the coins in the earliest period. Before 100 B.C., trade between Britain and the Continent was largely controlled by the Armorican and Belgic tribes. The Romans did not have direct trading contacts of any magnitude in this period. Coinage likely served as a storehouse of wealth and may have been a circulating medium in the trading ports. It would have facilitated trading at a wholesale level. This does not preclude the use of coins as gifts amongst the noblility.

Growing trade with the continent would have required money transactions well before the Gallic War. Extensive trade is well attested, with Roman luxury goods exchanged for raw materials and slaves. By 90 B.C., low value coins circulated in large quantities in Kent—the Cast Bronzes of the Cantii. Certainly these would not have been considered 'prestige gifts'.

By 55 B.C., trading networks existed in the interior of Britain to procure war materiel for the struggle on the continent. Coins circulated in them and today great numbers are found throughout southern Britain. A money economy was probable in this period—it would have facilitated trading.

After the Caesarian invasion, the trading patterns changed. The Armorican trade was reduced and the Romans controlled that with the tribes in the southeast. Trade with the Romans would have created an impetus for the growth of a money economy in Britain. The appearance of small denomination coins in large quantities, particularly bronzes, argues this was exactly what happened (89).

## CELTIC COINS AND CELTIC ART

Celtic coins look the way they do because that's exactly the way the Celts wanted them to look. The imagery, no matter how incredible it may appear at first, is not due to lack of ability. Expert die cutters rose to practice their craft in Britain just as they did in Greece or Rome. Look at an Atrebatic Abstract Type stater under magnification and you see expert die-cutting—craftsmen working with steady hands and keen eyes. The Celts were creating exactly the images they wanted.

Although many Celtic images are derived from classical Greek and Roman prototypes, they seldom look as the originals do. In the past, they have been described as barbarous copies; lack of die-cutting skill accounting for the imperfect reproduction. But this view is clearly an uninformed one because the differences are predictable—the result of conscious preference. Celtic coins are consistently more abstract, more expressionistic than the Classical prototypes. Instead of copies, they represent adaptations of the Classical images—ideas borrowed from the Greeks or Romans, but adapted to the artistic tastes and preferences of Celtic society.

## ABSTRACTION AND EXPRESSION

Celtic society preferred non-representational art. Producing an exact likeness of an object was unimportant, exact likenesses were undesirable most of the time. Instead, the artist tried to express some feeling about the object, for example the power and speed of a horse, or the fierce attack of a boar. Usually he did not depict the object as it appeared in real life, because a mirror-like representation could obscure the desired feeling. The Celts, understanding this, rejected the Classical art of Greece and Rome.

The Celts' abstract, expressionistic art best reveals itself in images of animals. Celtic society, with a large pastoral element, had an appreciation for the qualities of animals. On the early coins, for example, horses are reduced to stick-figures—but what stick-figures they are! The images are ones of power and grace, the animals bounding across the coins with legs straining for speed and tails flying in the wind. This desire to enhance the appreciation of things by reducing them to their simplest essentials is one of the powerful elements of pre-Roman Celtic art.

The creation of striking graphic designs was another. Much of Celtic art was decorative—images were used to decorate everyday objects such as pottery, swords and harness fittings. The goal was to create images that caught the eye and delighted the viewer. The images could be of an animal or human, but could, just as well, be an abstract design.

Pre-Roman Celtic art was seldom symmetrical, that is, one half of an image was not the mirror of the other. However, there was always asymmetric balance to the design in which the elements counterbalanced one another. The easiest way to appreciate this is to rotate an early coin and note how the design seems

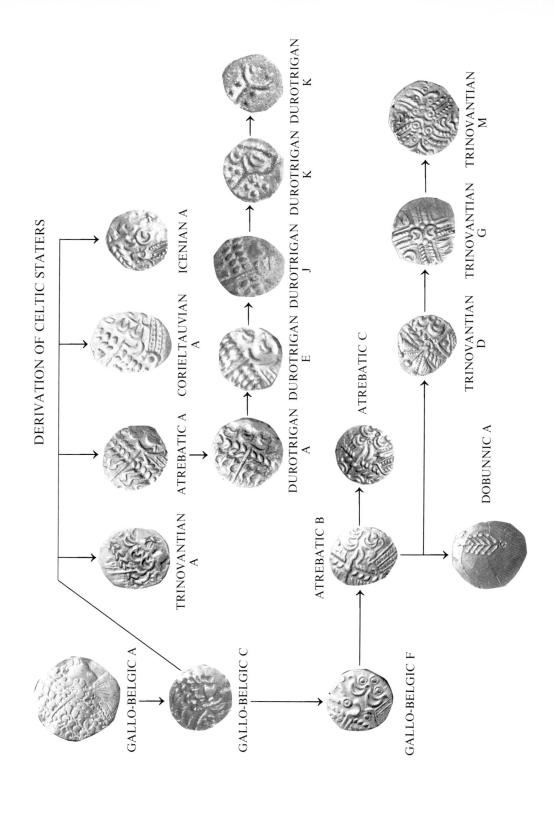

DERIVATION OF CELTIC STATERS

GALLO-BELGIC A

GALLO-BELGIC C

GALLO-BELGIC F

TRINOVANTIAN A

ATREBATIC A

CORIELTAUVIAN A

ICENIAN A

DUROTRIGAN A

DUROTRIGAN E

DUROTRIGAN J

DUROTRIGAN K

DUROTRIGAN K

ATREBATIC B

ATREBATIC C

DOBUNNIC A

TRINOVANTIAN D

TRINOVANTIAN G

TRINOVANTIAN M

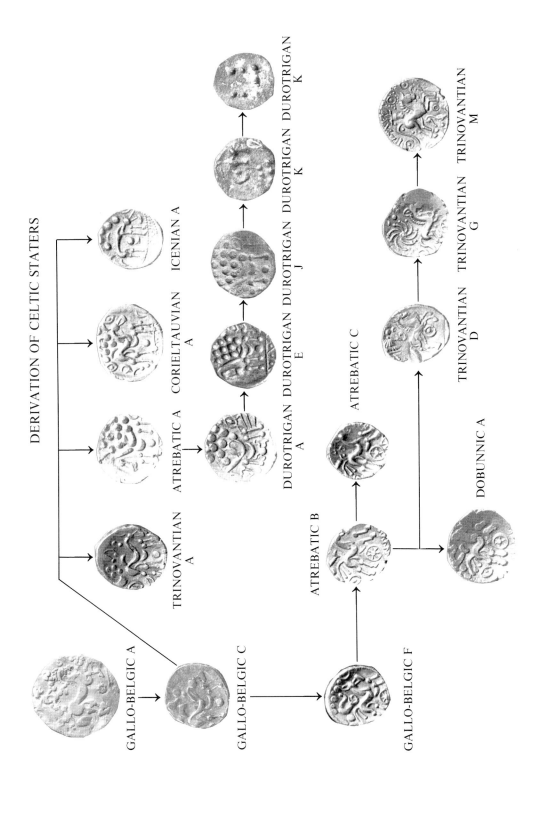

DERIVATION OF CELTIC STATERS

GALLO-BELGIC A

GALLO-BELGIC C

GALLO-BELGIC F

TRINOVANTIAN A

ATREBATIC A

CORIELTAUVIAN A

ICENIAN A

DUROTRIGAN A

DUROTRIGAN E

DUROTRIGAN J

DUROTRIGAN K

DUROTRIGAN K

ATREBATIC B

ATREBATIC C

TRINOVANTIAN D

TRINOVANTIAN G

TRINOVANTIAN M

DOBUNNIC A

balanced and pleasing regardless of the orientation. The coin does not have to be viewed right-side-up to appreciate the excellent graphic design. Indeed, by mastering asymmetric balance, the Celts created some of the most striking graphic designs ever to appear on coins.

## CONSERVATISM, COPYING AND ADAPTATION

There were, however, countervailing influences preventing the Celts from attaining a high level of artistic expression on every coin. Coins of high intrinsic value had to be accepted freely, or the coins became useless. Coin designs tended to be conservative as a result, and once an image became accepted on the coinage, it was recreated with minimal change on successive issues. It became an immobilized type. In such instances artistic expression was subjugated to economic necessity.

Furthermore, after the Gallic War, certain tribes in Britain were favoured by the Romans and were showered with Roman luxury goods. The Romans often used cultural conquest as a prelude to military invasion, softening-up the enemy prior to invasion. Thus, after the war, the Trinovantes/Catuvellauni and later the Atrebates/Regni were subjected to Romanizing influences. These were to alter Celtic thought and attitudes, and the manifestations are seen on the coins. Although purely Celtic images never quite disappear, the percentage of tribal coins with Romanized images increases over time. In some isolated instances, simple copying of Roman images occurs, but on the majority of coins, adaptation occurs, that is, the Roman image receives a Celtic transformation. Significantly, the other tribes, having less direct contact with the Romans, tended to resist the intrusion of Roman stylistic elements on their coins.

## ORNAMENTATION

The images on Celtic coins almost never float freely in an uncluttered field. Instead, the field is normally filled with a myriad of small objects and abstract designs. Occasionally these are sub-designs, like a tiny boar beneath the horse, or an ox head above it. But more often the objects are rings, pellets, crosses or floral patterns. Some of these images are added merely to decorate the available space, and present the viewer with more things to discover as he looks at the coins.

## PRIVY MARKS

However, the Celts were a technologically astute people, especially in the area of metallurgy. Their coins were remarkably well-made and the moneyers gave particular attention to controlling weight and metallurgical content. As time went on, the tribes experienced inflation, especially during the Gallic War. As a countermeasure, they reduced the standard weights of the gold coins while simultaneously replacing the gold content with first silver and later, copper. These changes were made gradually and in a remarkably complex way—it must have been the intention to render them in an imperceptible manner. Some of the ornaments in the fields have been shown to be privy marks, placed there by the moneyers so they could identify the weight and metallurgical content of the coins by sight.

## PROPAGANDA

One Romanizing influence changed the coinage after the Gallic War—the introduction of propaganda devices. Prior to the war, the designs on the coins were primarily artistic expressions. If there was any political meaning intended, it has been largely lost in time. Some differences in ornamentation, and the choice of motifs, may have denoted tribal affiliation, but this is conjecture. After the war, however, the coinage becomes an important medium of propaganda. First, the names of rulers appear: Commius and Addedomaros, then later, the names of cities: Verulamium, Camulodunum and Calleva. Tribal names may have been used, the ECE and ECEN on some Icenian silver pieces probably denotes the name of the tribe. It appears tribal rivalries manifest themselves on the coins. The coins were being used for boasting, especially as expressions of economic prowess on the part of the powerful tribes.

Direct expressions of tribal accomplishments are more difficult to detect, but some were produced. The appearance of a victory on the coins of Eppillus in Kent probably commemorated the incursion of the Atrebates/Regni into Kent. This occurred after Tasciovanus left the Trinovantian/Catuvellaunian throne, creating a power vacuum in the southeast of Britain. The later appearance of victories on later Trinovantian/Catuvellaunian coins may have commemorated the reversal of the situation. Finally, the subsequent appearance of Trinovantian/Catuvellaunian designs on the coinage of the Atrebates/Regni during the reign of Epaticcus chronicle the gradual encroachment of influence, and the subjection of the weaker tribe.

## SOME SOURCES OF ARTISTIC INSPIRATION
## ADAPTATIONS FROM GREEK COINS

The most well-known example of adaptation of a Greek design occurred on the Large Flan Type staters and their derivatives. The Greek prototype, the Phillippus, a gold stater of Phillip II of Macedon, minted 559—536 B.C., was used widely as a trade coin throughout the Classical world. Two theories account for the adoption of this type by the Celts. The first suggests Celtic mercenaries, returning from wars during the early Third Century in Greece brought back these coins as military payment or booty. Strabo's account in which the Tectosages returned to Gaul with enormous amounts of plunder from the sack of Delphi in 279—278 B.C. supported this idea.

The second explanation is Massilia, the Greek colony founded near the mouth of the Rhone in the Sixth Century B.C., used these coins to trade with the neighbouring Celtic tribes. The Romans, who occupied Southern Gaul in the Second Century B.C., continued to use the Phillipus because it was readily accepted. The Celts were trading iron and tin in exchange for luxury goods with the traders at Massilia. Thus, by this account, the Phillipus reached the Celts via the Massilia-Rhone trade route. Probably, each of these accounts was to some extent true, and the Phillipus reached Gaul by both methods. In any event, there is no question the Macedonian staters reached northern Gaul by the Second Century B.C.

The Phillipus became the preferred coin of the Celtic tribes because of its familiarity, and when they began to strike their own, they naturally chose the Phillipus as the model. The earliest Celtic staters struck in Gaul, the predecessors to the Large Flan Type, are closer in style to the Greek originals in appearance. As time went on, the designs on both sides of the coin became increasingly abstract and expressionistic. By the time the Large Flan Type was produced, the original designs were barely recognizable, having been totally transformed into Celtic motifs.

The Greek coinage of Massilia, itself, became the inspiration for yet another series of British coins. The colony had issued a series of cast bronze coins for much of the Second Century, B.C., carrying a head of Apollo on the obverse and a charging bull on the reverse. These coins travelled into the Celtic lands and eventually found their way to Britain. The Massiliote originals have been found at Richborough and Canterbury, and evidently served as prototypes for the Kentish Cast Bronze coins. In the past, it has been suggested the Gallic tribes adopted the Massiliote designs and the British tribes then adopted the Gallic coins as models. However, recent finds of very early Kentish bronzes show them to be closer to the Greek originals than the Gallic pieces. Furthermore, the early Kentish pieces have been dated as early as 100 B.C. by archaeological finds and thus predate the Gallic issues. Consequently, it is now believed the Kentish tribes were inspired directly by the Greek prototypes.

Although the earliest Celtic designs were adopted from the Greek trading coins of the day, this was not to be the only source of inspiration. As the First Century B.C. progressed, Roman coins became much more common in the Celtic lands. Thus by mid century, the Celts began to adopt Roman types for their coins and this trend accelerated in Britain after the Gallic War.

## ADAPTATIONS FROM ROMAN COINS

The first British coins with Roman themes appeared about the time of the Gallic War. An early instance was the appearance of design elements from 'Helmeted Roma' denarii on the Whaddon Chase Type staters (90). The wing from the helmeted head and the 'X' mark of value from these Republican pieces appear on the reverse of the Celtic staters. The wing was now a free-floating object above the horse and the 'X' appeared behind the amimal. Surprisingly, the two objects were engraved in the proper sizes and relationship, as if they were copied directly, but with no regard to the other design elements of the denarius. The horse on this type was also Romanized to a great extent and was no longer so abstract.

About the same time, the Corieltauvi began striking silver coins, and chose the speared boar design on the denarii of C. Hostidius C. f. Geta for the reverse (91). The boar received a completely Celtic treatment, but the adaptation of the design in detail is obvious when the two types are seen side-by-side.

About the end of the war, or shortly thereafter, gold quarters staters were struck in the south of Britain, with the design adapted from the Trophy denarii of Caesar. The designs from two different Trophy denarii were adapted for two distinct varieties of quarter stater, the differences being in the details of the trophy.

These are only three examples of Roman influence on the British uninscribed coinage. Other examples undoubtedly exist, as yet undetected, offering a potentially fruitful area for discovery. The circulation of Roman coins in Britain during the Gallic War may be better understood if additional examples can be identified.

## ROMAN INFLUENCES AFTER THE GALLIC WAR

The Celts adapted Roman types with increasing frequency after the war, especially on the silver and bronze issues (92). By the time of Tasciovanus, Roman culture had made an impression on the nobility of several southern tribes and consequently they modified their traditional artistic style. At times, the die-cutters simply copied Roman motifs, with no attempt to Celticize them. The abstraction which previously had made Celtic coins so striking was now, in isolated instances, forsaken. Gradually, more and more designs were rendered in a Classical style. At first, this might be interpreted as reduced cultural vitality amongst the effected tribes—whether it actually indicates a decline is worth exploring.

While the reluctance of the more conservative tribes, such as the Dobunni and Corieltauvi, to accept Romanizing influences could be seen as a sign of strength, it may mean nothing more than stagnation. Stagnation was not the case for the Trinovantes/Catuvellauni and Atrebates/Regni who were experiencing rapid change in their economies and social structures. The growth of large civil settlements in the southern tribal territories and the expanding trade with the continent are two indicators of the dynamic changes. By assimilating Roman artistic motifs, the southern tribes demonstrated a cultural transformation was taking place as well.

Although the instances of copying are dramatic ones, the majority of the die-cutters did not slavishly copy the Roman designs, but transformed them into Celtic motifs, instead. Thus, while acknowledging the 'modern', they retained the best from their own traditions. On balance, the acceptance of Romanizing influences suggests a dynamic and vigorous culture amongst the southern tribes.

## INSCRIPTIONS

Legends first appear on the staters of Commius, the Atrebatic leader closely allied with the Romans during most of the Gallic War. When he came to Britain, he placed his name on the coinage, a practice he undoubtedly learned from Caesar. Other Celtic rulers, not to be outdone, soon copied the idea.

The appearance of inscriptions in one sense makes the coins more interesting and informative. They give the names of rulers who would otherwise be lost to history, and names of mints are identified as well, confirming their exact locations. But the adoption of inscriptions represents a loss as well. An intrusion in the Celtic designs, they look out of place and ruin the artistic effect. Ultimately, the inscriptions become so important to the Celts, the design becomes subservient. They take over an increasing share of the available space, cramping the graphics into a diminished area. The artistic treatment degenerates to the extent the legend is emblazoned across the entire field on some coins, the beautiful Celtic design completely eliminated.

## TITLES

Titles seldom occur, but a few appear very late. The first is the RIGON or RICON of Tasciovanus, the Celtic form of REX, meaning king. RIG also appears on the Dobunnic staters of ANTED. Eppillus becomes the first to use the title REX in its latin form, about the turn of the millennium and Cunobeline and Verica continue the practice.

## ROMANIZED HORSES

The abstract rendition of the horse, a standard feature of the earliest British staters, disappeared gradually from the coinages of the southern tribes after the war. The Whaddon Chase stater had one of the earliest attempts at a more representational portrayal (93) and eventually the other southern tribes struck coins with Romanized horses. However, the peripheral tribes—the Dobunni, Iceni and Corieltauvi—continued highly stylized horses up to the end of their coinages. These three had less direct contact with the Romans and were evidently less willing to modify their artistic heritage.

## DIRECT COPYING OF ROMAN COINS

Some coins of Tasciovanus and Cunobeline, both in silver and bronze, were copied directly from the denarii of Augustus. On these, the portrait bust of the emperor is copied exactly, but the name of Tasciovanus or Cunobeline is inserted in place of that of Augustus. On others, the entire reverse design has been lifted and used on the tribal issue. It is important to note this level of artistic decline does not occur on the gold issues, which continue to bear Celticized images. Again, the need for coins of high intrinsic value to pass in commerce without problems dictated a conservative approach.

## DESIGNS ADAPTED FROM ENGRAVED GEMSTONES

The classical themes on certain late coins never appear on Roman or Greek coins. Exact parallels exist, however, on engraved gemstones (94). Evidently, the Celts received intaglios from Roman traders in the century before the Roman invasion and used these as models for some of their coins. Several coin designs of Tasciovanus and Cunobeline are duplicates of known gemstones. A bronze of Tasciovanus with a Centaur playing the double-pipes is one example and another is the seated sphinx on a silver coin of Cunobeline. The running boar on the silver of Epaticcus and the swimming Hippocamp on a silver piece of Adminius are very late examples. These coins demonstrate how surprisingly innovative the Celtic die-cutters were in seeking out images for the coins. It is possible other sorts of objects may have been reviewed, Roman votive statuary, for example. The sources of inspiration from the Classical world are not yet fully explored and present many opportunities for original work for collectors and students of the series.

It is wrong, however, to think the Celts were incapable of finding artistic inspiration within their own culture. They created images using Celtic models also, although the examples are more difficult to point out. Perhaps the fascination of the interaction between Celtic and Roman society has caused an over-emphasis on the adaptation of Roman motifs. A balanced view acknowledges the inspiration the Celts found in scenes from daily life. These images are clearly neither Roman nor Greek, but purely Celtic in origin.

## SCENES FROM CELTIC LIFE

The die-cutters definitely portray scenes from Celtic life (95), but these are usually difficult to detect because they are rendered in the abstract style. The earliest identified examples, post Gallic War, occur during the reign of Tasciovanus. One stater depicts a mounted warrior brandishing a carnyx (war-trumpet). Details on the coin are significant; perhaps the most important is the fact the rider wears chain-mail armour. Although Tacitus, writing a hundred years later, indicated the Celts were unfamiliar with chain-mail, Strabo states otherwise. The stater shows Strabo was correct—and the testimony of the coin is confirmed by modern finds of such armour in Celtic graves.

Other coins show helmets, spears, swords, shields, horse fittings and even warriors riding naked, all providing additional information about Celtic warriors, their tactics, appearance and equipment.

Abstract portraits of men give some evidence about the way Celtic men looked. Beards, moustaches and long wavy hair are all in evidence. The figures are all muscular and athletic. Surprisingly, despite the relative equality of the sexes in Celtic society compared to the Classical world, women are difficult to detect on British coins, unless adapted from Classical sources. It is possible some of the beardless portraits portray women, but it would be stretching the imagination to single out an example.

## SCENES FROM CELTIC MYTHOLOGY

Although the Celts could have created images embodying religious themes, or portrayed creatures from their imaginative mythological storehouse, such examples are actually elusive. Part of the problem is our modern understanding of Celtic mythology and religion is drawn from evidence post-dating the period of the coins. Most of what is known about the mythology is drawn from the writings of Irish churchmen starting about the Sixth Century A.D. However, the majority of the Irish sources date much later, at least a thousand years after the period of interest.

Celtic religious practices may be deduced from votive statues known from the pre-Roman period, but these are commonly analyzed in unison with a much larger assortment of objects dating from the Romano-British period. The Roman objects used for comparison date as much as four hundred years after the coins.

The result is our understanding of pre-Roman Celtic religion and mythology is irretrievably coloured—the interpretation of the votive statuary by influences emanating from the Roman objects, and the analysis of the Irish manuscripts by a thousand years' evolution in the oral tradition.

Some simple themes are known, however, which must be apropos to the coin-issuing period. The veneration of the human head as the seat of the human spirit is so widespread it cannot be ignored. That the Celts treasured the heads of ancestors and slain adversaries is well-established, and carefully buried groups of skulls are known from Celtic sites in Britain, Danebury for one. However, it is wrong to think every head appearing on a Celtic coin is a severed one. The heads floating in the fields of Armorican coins may be examples, but conclusive British ones are hard to come by. The famous Cunobeline bronze depicting a male figure holding a severed human head is more likely to be an adaptation of a Classical theme—Perseus carrying the head of Medusa—than a Druid carrying out a human sacrifice.

Various animals were venerated, some as gods. Epona, the horse goddess is probably the best-known, and most Celtic coins have horses. Whether these had religious meaning to the viewer, is a matter of pure speculation. The boar, wolf, stag and birds all appear in Celtic mythology, and most appear on the coins as well. Again, whether these images had religious significance is difficult to prove, though they may have, and the coins could have had a purpose ancillary to that of commerce.

Enormous numbers of coins normally turn up at pre-Roman temple sites, such as Harlow, Wanborough, and Sheepen. Indeed, Sheepen appears to be the site of Cunobeline's mint (96). However, temple sites also served other functions, such as market-places, and coin-loss at trading sites would be rife. Alternatively, the finds of coins at these sites may represent religious offerings. Thus, although the occurrence of coins at religious sites may indicate the coins carried religious images, there is no real proof.

## APPRECIATING CELTIC COINS

Appreciating Celtic art requires some effort because of its abstract nature. The images embody extreme distortions of reality, often with a dreamlike quality. To complicate matters, the Celts enjoyed concealing images-within-images, so the total idea can be grasped only with scrutiny and attention to detail. It is often possible to view a coin many times, only to discover something new on a closer look. You almost have to take the approach you use when analysing puzzles of the 'find twenty-eight things wrong with this picture' variety. Appreciating Celtic coins requires more concentration on the part of the viewer today, because we are not accustomed to looking at images so closely. You will be repaid many times over, however, for making the effort.

The following is an analysis of a Celtic coin-image, selected because it is not only a good example of Celtic art, but is also typical of what the coins offer. The coin is unusual in one respect: the dies and the flan were nearly matched in diameter, and as a result, almost the entire image is present. Most Celtic coins carry only about two-thirds of the die-image, because the dies were normally much larger than the flans. Often, to see an entire image, several coins must be viewed—a process leading to discovery after discovery as new coins turn up.

The coin is an Atrebatic Abstract Type stater, struck late in the Gallic War or perhaps slightly afterwards. The design is several adaptation/copying steps from the Macedonian Philippus and the horse-and-chariot design has become completely abstract.

But in what sense are they 'abstract'? While the artist who cut the dies for the Philippus was trying to portray a horse and chariot at full speed, the Celtic engraver was obviously after something else. The engraving does not suffer from a lack of skill—the die cutting is carefully executed—the engraver has created exactly what he wanted.

Our first impression of the image is of an animal trotting across the coin in a spirited and graceful manner. The area around the horse is filled with unrelated objects appearing out of place and giving the image a dreamlike quality.

Atrebatic Abstract
Stater
210–1
5X

A detailed inventory of the objects in the image is necessary at this point. The animal, a horse, has its legs spread apart as if it was leaping. The horse's knees are made up of pellets and the hooves are small wedges. The image is a stick-figure, but the body is thickened and formed into a swayed-back shape. The tail is represented, surprisingly, by three lines, each ending in a pellet. The nose is a triangle, the head a large pellet and the ear an ellipse. Below the horse is a spoked wheel floating in space and behind the animal, part of an ellipse. Above the horse appears a series of curved lines, the remnants of the chariot driver's arms on the Philippus.

How does the form of this image create the impression of a graceful animal trotting across the field? The artist has succeeded by creating a repetition of details, while carefully avoiding monotony. The image is one of near-balance, made of non-symmetrical elements. The lack of exact balance and the inexact repetition causes the viewer to feel tension, and this in turn creates the feeling of motion. First, note none of the lines is a radius of the coin—none would pass through the centre, if extended. Any line, if made a radius, would have ruined the design, made it monotonous.

The horse's back and rear legs lean forward giving the entire image a motion to the right. The motion is balanced, but not stopped, by the left-leaning front legs. The tail has been made triple to increase its mass and thus balance the head, nose and ears. The pellet above the tail skilfully balances the pellet of the head, but being slightly above, increases the motion to the right.

We enter the design at the tail, because the repetition of the strands immediately commands attention. The tail picks up the observer's view and casts it up to the arms of the rider, which in turn sends it to the nose. The end of the nose brings the eye down to the curves of the wheel and the belly of the horse. These, in turn, send the eye back to the tail, where the entire process is repeated. Thus, the viewer's eye is carried round and round in a clockwise direction, enhancing the impression of vivid motion. The major elements of the design balance nicely, but there is a preponderance of motion to the right, created by the lean of the body, the pointing head and the arms of the rider.

The artist has created the impression of an animal in motion, and has done it with great skill. While the viewer may not like the image, he is forced to admit it works admirably—and this is the essence of art, the ability to create an impression in the mind of the beholder. The artist has hidden the physical appearance of a horse, and has instead portrayed only its graceful motion. This is the process of abstraction and the Celts were masters of it.

## COIN MANUFACTURING METHODS

Ancient British coins were manufactured using the normal methods (97)—striking and casting—however, our understanding of the techniques is changing rapidly. Studies of metallurgy, mould-making and die-cutting demonstrate the Celts employed an exceptional level of technology. The knowledge of the moneyers, more advanced than previously thought, is forcing a reassessment of the 'barbarian' label imposed by the Romans. The British tribes, once thought to have imported Roman technicians to teach them how to produce better coins, are now seen controlling complex alloys with great precision, alloys the Romans never used for coins.

The Romans have long been known to debase their coins during times of economic stress and doing so with an eye to public sensibilities. They changed weights and finenesses gradually and sometimes resorted to striking plated pieces. These ploys are simplistic, however, compared to the sophisticated schemes used by the Celts. The Celtic moneyers made almost imperceptible, yet simultaneous modifications to weights and tri-metallic alloys, demonstrating an incredible application of technology to the solution of their economic problems.

There is little question the following information will have to be modified as die studies and metallurgical analyses expand our knowledge of the workings of a Celtic mint. The results will give us a better understanding of the monetary policies of the tribal leaders, as well. Today, these are only beginning to be understood, but the changes will only reinforce the sophistication of the coinage and the people responsible for it.

## THE DIE-STRUCK COINAGES

At one time, it was sufficient to describe a Celtic mint as little more than a blacksmith hammering flans between dies crudely engraved with lines and dots. All Celtic coinage was 'imitative', so the manufacturing techniques were expected to be little better. Today, there is little agreement about the methods used to cast the flans, much less the alloying techniques. The technologies are more complex than once thought and the moneyers must have been specialized craftsmen to a degree. This is especially true in the later periods when coins were produced in astounding numbers and a mint would have provided full-time employment.

## FLAN PRODUCTION

Two methods of flan-production have been suggested, both plausible. The arguments for choosing between them are irrelevant because both were probably used.

The first technique, the 'Flat Rock Method' (98), involved ladling blobs of molten metal directly onto a surface such as a flat rock. With practice, the pourer could attain considerable accuracy, and weight adjustments would be minimal. The molten metal's surface tension would cause the flans to be dome-shaped—ideal for centering on a concave obverse die. The shape would also help in striking up the image on the characteristically dish-shaped coins. The flans would have smooth edges and would not require pre-forming or edge shaping before striking. The efficiency of the technique was primarily a matter of the percentage of flans that could be poured to standard weight. Since Celtic coins appear to have been struck to a tolerance approaching plus or minus 0.05 grammes, the skill demanded of the flan-pourer was considerable.

The second technique, the 'Muffin-Mould Method' (99), involved casting the flans in clay moulds and then hammering them to shape prior to striking. The moulds supposedly used in this manufacturing process have been found in large numbers on every known mint-site. However, it should be pointed out the presence of the moulds has been used to prove the existence of a mint. Thus, a circular argument exists in which mint sites yield moulds and sites that yield moulds are mint sites. Fortunately, mints sites are also identified by the mint-names on coins, and all these sites have yielded moulds. Metallurgical studies of metal traces in the moulds have identified gold and silver alloys, strengthening the assertion the moulds were used to produce coin flans.

Reconstructions of the moulds have shown them to be of flat clay, almost square, but actually pentagonal. Seven rows of seven circular cavities, with an added cavity in the point of the pentagon produced fifty flans at a time. Two sizes of cavities are known, one about the size of the larger gold staters and the other about that of the smaller silver pieces. The smaller-cavity moulds are the commoner type, this would be expected because gold staters would be produced in smaller numbers.

The method of filling the mould cavities is a controversial topic in itself. Molten metal could be poured into the moulds directly, though this is not felt to be the method used. It would have the same skill demands on pouring as the Flat Rock Method. Instead, it has been suggested granules of metals were weighed out and placed in the cavities. These were then fused by two methods: either the entire mould was fired in a kiln or the individual cavities were fired by means of a blow torch (100). In the second method, by blowing air through a hollow tube, over a hot charcoal, and directly onto the granules, sufficient heat was produced to fuse the metal.

Thermo-Remanent Magnetic studies have proven the moulds were last subjected to heat in a horizontal position, with the cavities uppermost (101). Whenever clay is fired, its magnetic properties are modified. The analysis technique measures these properties and compares them to the magentic field of the earth to determine the orientation of the clay during its last firing. The orientation of the moulds during their last use supports the hypothesis they were used to cast molten metals.

Signs of vitrification (102) from intense heat on the bottoms of some moulds support the method by which the entire mould was fired in a kiln to fuse the granules. However, other moulds from Villenueve-Saint-Germain, France, were found with little holed covers made of clay, used to allow a blow torch access while at the same time containing its heat. Thus, it is likely both techniques were used.

Some moulds from Verulamium have been found with traces of calcium carbonate (103), probably from powdered chalk, adhering to the sides of the cavities. These suggest the Celts understood and used mould-release agents to facilitate the removal of the flans from the moulds. Chalk was pressed onto the sides of the cavities to prevent the metal from sticking to the walls.

Flans produced by the Muffin-Mould Method would have irregular edges, whereas the actual coins have smooth edges, sometimes with cracks. Thus, the mould-cast flans cannot have been used directly for striking. They would have been first hammered to the optimum thickness and then hammered around the edges to produce smooth surfaces. The additional pre-forming steps involved in the Muffin-Mould Method is not necessarily a reason to condemn the technique. Efficiencies would be obtained by the accuracy of the flan weights produced by weighing the granules prior to firing.

## METALLURGY

The alloys used to produce flans for gold coins are remarkable (104). All are three-way alloys, the predominent metals being gold, silver and copper. However, the ratio of the three was intentionally varied over time to gradually and imperceptibly debase the metal.

Around 125 B.C., the Large Flan and Defaced Die types had a ratio of about 75 percent gold, 22 percent silver and 3 percent copper. The tribes then gradually replaced gold with silver, and by the time of the Abstract Design type, around 100 B.C., the ratio had dropped to less than 70 percent gold and over 25 percent silver, with copper constant. Forty years later, the Gallic War type was struck with less than 60 percent gold and something over 30 percent silver, copper now averaging around 10 percent. The sophistication of this debasement lies in the fact the gradual change in alloy would have been imperceptible—the colour of the metal would appear constant during the lifetime of a single generation.

After the Gallic War, the British tribes evidently had insufficient bullion and were forced to replace gold not only with silver, but also with copper. The Atrebatic Abstract and Whaddon Chase types were struck fairly close to the nominal alloy of the Gallic War type, but the succeeding inscribed types are quite different. The inscribed coins generally run 45 to 50 percent gold, 10 to 20 percent silver and 30 to 40 percent copper (105). At this point, the British staters take on their characteristic reddish tinge. The colour of the metal is not, however, a guide to its origin—red gold is not necessarily native to Britain, nor is yellower gold necessarily Continental. The tribes were carefully and

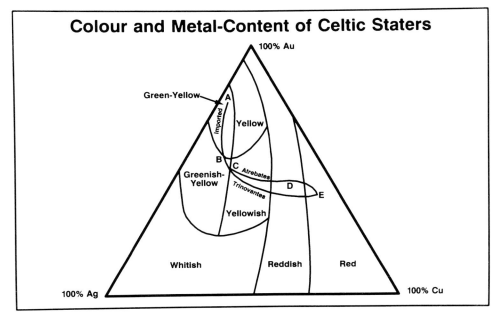

## Colour and Metal-Content of Celtic Staters

The Celts removed half the gold from their staters, bit-by-bit, over a hundred year period. They concealed the fact, however, by cleverly adjusting the other metals in the alloy, to keep the colour constant.

The earliest coins, made of naturally-occurring gold, are plotted at 'A', these have a colour described as Green-Yellow. The moneyers replaced the gold mostly with silver for the first fifty years, because this kept the colour in the Green-Yellow region. If they had added copper, instead, the coins would have gone into the Yellow or Reddish sectors—and the difference might have been noticed.

By the early years of the Gallic War (point 'B'), the moneyers were forced to reduce the gold content drastically. Unfortunately, further additions of silver at this point drive the colour into the Greenish-Yellow sector. The Celts were faced with a decision. They could produce coins that would soon look too pale (by adding more silver), or they could allow them to become yellowish, by adding copper, instead. Evidently, yellowish was more acceptable, so copper-additions were chosen. Thus, the colour-trend skirts the Greenish-Yellow sector during the Gallic War, and enters the Yellowish, about 50 B.C., at point 'C'.

About this time, two things occurred: gold staters stopped flowing to Britain and many tribes began to strike silver units. The moneyers now had to economize on both gold and silver, so they switched from simply adding copper to the alloy, to extracting silver, as well.

For a few years, the coins stayed in the Yellowish sector. But by 30 B.C., at point 'D', they had entered the Reddish one. The transition from yellowish to reddish happened reasonably quickly, and this would have been one of the few times the colour change would have been detected by the people. The transition from the Reddish sector into the Red would have been less objectionable—and coins were already red-tinged. By 20 A.D., at point 'E', the coins had developed the well-known red colour.

intentionally controlling their alloys to attain economic goals. The switch from yellow to red gold marks an intentional debasement of the coinage.


## WEIGHT

While the tribes were debasing their alloys, they simultaneously reduced the standard weights. The Large Flan and Defaced Die type staters of 125 B.C. were struck to a standard of about 7.80 grammes. The staters were then dropped in stages of an almost imperceptible five percent over the next seventy-five years. Around 100 B.C., the Abstract Design type weighed 7.25 grammes, by 75 B.C. it had dropped to 6.45. The Gallic War types, starting around 6.35 grammes, weighed only 5.80 at the end of the Gallic coinage. The British staters continued to drop, ultimately stablilizing at 5.40 grammes, around 10 B.C.

The concerted decline in weight and gold content was orchestrated carefully and deliberately (106). The changes in the types, the minor die varieties within types and the field-objects are probably indicators the moneyers used to identify intrinsic value. Knowing these privy marks, a moneyer could identify the weight and gold content of a coin by sight. Celtic staters are seldom found with the chop marks often seen on Roman denarii. The reason is clear—the moneyers and other knowledgeable individuals must have been able to evaluate the coins by eye.

The exact sequence of this gradual debasement is only now being elucidated by means of Electron Microprobe Spectroscopy, and the corresponding die studies remain to be correlated to it. However, the trends are sufficiently identified to predict the outcome—the coins were debased in a systematic way and the coins probably were marked for identification.


## DIE PRODUCTION

Celtic dies exist in both iron and bronze. Few exist today, but the iron type is rarer than the bronze. This may be due, however, to the difference in survival of the two metals. Little is known of the manufacturing techniques, but the dies were certainly hand-cut using gravers, punches and perhaps the bow-drill. Whether specialized punches, containing a finished image were used, or whether hubbing was practised cannot, however, be proven. Almost without exception, the obverse dies were concave and the reverse ones convex. The curvature facilitated positioning the flan on the lower die and holding it in place for striking.

The alloys employed in the dies varied with the knowledge of the moneyers. Those used for the Whaddon Chase staters, for example, must have been punched in a soft metal. The field around punch marks is violently heaved from the force of the blow—an effect not seen, for example on South Ferriby staters. The softness of the Whaddon Chase dies caused them to break up rapidly and signs of die damage are common in this series. The South Ferriby reverses, on the other hand, seldom show the same extent of damage and evidently wore better. Celtic dies were often used well beyond their useful life, to the extent the image is often completely obliterated. The use of irretrievably damaged dies occurs more often on silver coins than on bronze or gold.

The earliest coins are struck from dies considerably larger than the flans, and no one coin contains the entire image. However, after the Gallic War, the sizes of the dies and flans were more closely matched, and most of the image was now captured. Possibly this was a direct result of the switch to inscribed coins—the ruler's name, at the edge of the die was often struck off the flan on the early inscribed types. Naturally, the ruler would be expected to protest, and the moneyers would have responded by reducing the size of the dies.

## STRIKING

The flans, probably heated, were hand struck between the dies. Tongs have been found on at least one mint site, evidently used to handle hot flans (107). Despite heating, the gold coins normally have striking cracks at the edge. The bronze and silver coins tend not to have cracks to the same degree.

Double-struck coins are not as common for the Celtic series as they are, for example, the mediaeval. For the most part, a single blow of the hammer was sufficient to strike up the design, despite the fact Celtic dies were normally cut in high relief. Brockages, extremely rare, are known (108), usually for the commoner issues where the moneyers would have been rushed and would not have noticed the error. The hammer-men seldom paid much attention to centring the flans on the dies and off-centre strikes are more common than perfectly centred ones. Centring was improved after the change to smaller dies, probably because an off-centre strike would then result in a blank area being recorded on a portion of the flan or again because a ruler's name would be omitted.

## THE CAST COINAGES

Two distinct series of coins were cast, both in bronze. The first type, the Cast Bronze Coinage of Kent, demonstrates the Celts' innovative ability at its best (109). The moneyers attained a remarkable level of casting technology as they experimented with and improved their methods of manufacturing moulds.

The second type, the Durotrigan Cast Bronze Coinage follows the tribe's struck coinage and dates considerable later than the Kentish series. The Durotrigan coins do not seem to be the technological inheritors of the Kentish ones and the level of casting expertise is not as developed.

## THE CAST COINAGE OF KENT

The Kentish series has previously been referred to as a 'potin' coinage, using the French word for a high-tin alloy of bronze. This designation is unfortunate because the word has no exact English counterpart. Furthermore, it fails to communicate the nature of the alloy correctly because it implies a higher percentage of tin than occurs in the Kentish coins. The Kentish pieces are made of a copper-tin alloy with generally less than twenty-five percent tin. Archaeologists routinely refer to such alloys as bronze, or tin-bronze if the tin percentage surpasses twenty-five percent. Additionally, the British coins appear to be earlier than the Gallic Potin coins and are not a derivative type. Consequently, the misleading term 'potin' is no longer used for the Kentish series and instead the more accurate and descriptive 'bronze' is used.

The Kentish Cast Bronzes progressed through five stages, beginning around 100 B.C. and ending sometime after the Gallic War. The coins were all cast in clay moulds, several coins at a time, in a line, and connected by runners. The method of producing the moulds exhibited a complex series of changes, denoted by five distinct periods, as the Celtic moneyers improved the casting techniques to speed up production.

## PROTOTYPE PERIOD

The first coins, inspired by the cast bronzes of Massillia are all extremely rare and were only produced for a short period. On the very first pieces, the images appear to have been impressed on the moulds using a 'mother coin', but this technique was soon replaced by scribing the image into the mould cavities with a stylus. Both types of moulds produced rather thick and dumpy coins compared to the later issues.

## EXPERIMENTAL PERIOD

It was soon decided to reduce the metal content of the pieces, but to maintain the diameter. As a result, the coins became much thinner in the next period. The mould cavities were now made by pressing a cylindrical object into the clay, perhaps a polished wooden dowel. The edge of the coin, the sprues connecting one coin to another on the runner system, and the image were all inscribed with a blunt stylus. Production problems cropped up in this period, the moulds did not mate very well and the metal squeezed out to produce 'flash'. The moulds were often misaligned, producing an offset between the obverse and reverse. The Experimental Period coins are all extremely rare, evidently the mould production methods were quickly abandoned.

Analyses of hoard contents, the introduction of various types in different parts of Britain and typological studies have all been used to refine the dating sequence. Many of the later types carry images adapted from Roman denarii, these in turn providing dates. With the appearance of inscriptions, some of the coins can be related to historical people and events, and the rest of the coinage fitted in between these benchmarks.

## COMPLETENESS

No catalogue of Celtic coins is likely to be complete, and no claims of completeness are made for this one. The 1975 edition of Mack's Coinage of Ancient Britain listed fewer than 550 types (subtracting modern forgeries), this catalogue lists about 800 types. Three problems work against completeness.

The first is the problem of modern forgeries. About 1961, a series of forged staters appeared, and these were not condemned until the middle 1980's. The 1964 edition of Mack's *Coinage of Ancient Britain* listed several of the forgeries as genuine 'new types' and the 1975 edition added more. The forgeries attained a degree of acceptability as a result of inclusion in the catalogue, to the detriment of collectors, archaeologists and the numismatic trade.

Unfortunately, the work of the 'Haslemere Forger' has not been entirely suppressed at the time of writing and a small number of fantasy-types show up from time to time. Consequently, the inclusion of 'new types' in the following catalogue has been done conservatively and questionable ones have been rejected.

Two exceptions should be noted. The first is the listing of an important variety of stater of Eppillus of the Atrebates/Regni—the piece has been inspected by the author and it appears genuine. The second is the listing of several new types of Atrebatic/Regnan silver coins from the Wanborough hoard. These are plausible types and the circumstances of their appearance argues for authenticity. All the coins catalogued under these two exceptions are identified in the lists.

The second problem is that of coin origins. Evans' landmark work, *Ancient British Coins*, appeared in 1864 listing many Gaulish coins as British. Over the next hundred years, cataloguers struggled to delete these from the British lists. Inadvertently, several more Gaulish types were added to the later catalogues.

This catalogue continues the process of deletion of Gaulish types. Where Gaulish coins listed in the 1975 edition of Mack's work have been deleted, a note is included in the appropriate part of the catalogue. Furthermore, many 'new types' have appeared and again the process of cataloguing has been done conservatively. Unless the new coin has direct typological affinities to known tribal issues, the coin has been rejected. The bulk of these rejections have occurred in the Atrebatic/Regnan and Trinovantian/Catuvellaunian portion of the catalogue—a number of coins have been found in the tribal territories carrying animals with long, spindly legs or with two animals back-to-back.

Such images are normal for Gaulish (and some Corieltauvian) coins, but not for southern British ones. Where scholars have argued for inclusion, the type is noted in the catalogue, but not assigned a catalogue-number.

The third problem is the rapid pace with which metal-detectorists are discovering new types, compared to the long lag between discovery and reporting to the central clearinghouse for Celtic coins in Oxford. New coins, which ought to be catalogued, have been discovered but not reported for inclusion. The major problem in this area appears to be the Wanborough Hoard, many new types are now appearing in coin lists and auction catalogues. This portion of the catalogue was purposely written last to include as many new varieties as possible. Furthermore, museums, collectors, coin dealers and archaeologists have been contacted to obtain reports of new types.

Readers are urged to report finds and acquisitions of Celtic coins to the central clearinghouse in Oxford, so future cataloguers may produce better handbooks:

> Index of Celtic Coins
> Institute of Archaeology
> 36 Beaumont Street
> Oxford OX1 2PG
> United Kingdom

The inclusion of a black and white photograph, at 2x magnification if possible, is very helpful.

## DESCRIPTION OF CATALOGUE ENTRIES

CATALOGUE NUMBERS—The entries in this catalogue, unlike most coin catalogues are not consecutively-numbered. There are numbering gaps between the successive types to accommodate future discoveries. The Celtic series is unusual because new types are being continually discovered and the numbering scheme needs flexibility. The 1953 edition of Mack's *Coinage of Ancient Britain* contained 468 consecutively-numbered coins. By the third edition of 1975, a hundred new types had been inserted adding letter suffixes to the catalogue numbers. Because the suffixes already used letters up to 'G' and also because several coins had been shifted to new out-of-sequence locations, the numbering scheme was beginning to break down. It has been necessary in this catalogue to replace the numbering system used in Mack's work. The switch to a new numbering scheme is never a welcomed event in numismatics—hopefully the current one has enough flexibility for future needs.

The largest gaps in the numbering sequence have been built into the Atrebatic/Regnan and Trinovantian/Catuvellaunian portions of the catalogue, especially for the uninscribed silver. Many of the new types reported recently are in this area, and it is expected many more will be discovered as the result of the use of metal detectors.

The catalogue number has two parts—a MAIN NUMBER of up to four digits, followed by a dash, followed by a MINOR NUMBER of up to two digits (in the form XXXX-XX). The catalogue thus accommodates a million entries, 0000-00 to 9999-99, the format being fixed to facilitate computerization.

The intention is that the MAIN NUMBER represents a major type, and the MINOR NUMBER distinguishes between die varieties. Naturally, there will be disagreement over the definition of a 'die variety' and subjectivity is unavoidable. For most purposes, reporting the MAIN NUMBER is sufficient, but for very detailed studies, the MINOR NUMBER may be necessary as well.

Ancient forgeries are listed along with genuine coins in the catalogue. They have the same MAIN NUMBER as the genuine type but are distinguished by different MINOR NUMBERS.

Modern forgeries are listed in an Appendix, given the same number as the genuine coin, but suffixed with an 'F', in the form XXXX-XXF. The existence of modern forgeries is noted in the catalogue entries where appropriate. Fantasy coins—those modern forgeries for which no ancient coin exists—are listed in the same Appendix as FANTASY 1, FANTASY 2, etc.

TYPE-NAMES—Generally, the existing name of the coin, the one used in the numismatic trade, is given. Most of these names are derived from famous hoards, eg: the CHUTE TYPE. Others refer to some typological detail, eg: the TRIPLE-TAILED HORSE TYPE, and yet others refer to metrological or metallurgical properties, eg: the REDUCED WEIGHT TYPE. A chronological chart of these trade names appears in the Appendix.

DATES—Date ranges for types refer to the estimated date of manufacture, not the dates over which the coins were in use. The period of use often extends beyond the latest date given. Although firm dates are given, chronology is a controversial topic and uncertainties of plus or minus five years are usually intended.

RARITY—Rarity estimates have been assigned based on a computer study of known examples of the coins. The study included the contents of museum collections, published gazetteers, hoards, major private collections and sales via fixed price lists, auctions and bourse activity. Careful attention was paid to eliminate modern counterfeits and double-counting of individual pieces.

During the last few years, several large hoards were discovered, and it was difficult to determine the rarity of certain types. Statistical studies were conducted (113) to predict the numbers of coins found but obviously this approach lacked precision.

A survey was conducted amongst members of the numismatic trade to determine whether the statistically calculated rarities were accurate. In a few cases, the survey indicated the coins were commoner than the calculated rarity values—in these cases, a lower rarity was used for the catalogue listing, and a comment was added to the notes.

The Atrebatic/Regnan coinage was affected by this problem the most, the Durotrigan and Trinovantian/Catuvellaunian series suffered to less of an extent.

Although uncounted coins exist and new coins are found daily, the relative rarities are likely to be correct. The uniform rarity scale has been constructed as follows:

| RARITY | DESIGNATION | RECORDED EXAMPLES |
|--------|-------------|-------------------|
| C | COMMON | OVER 100 |
| S | SCARCE | 51 TO 100 |
| R | RARE | 31 TO 50 |
| VR | VERY RARE | 16 TO 30 |
| ER | EXTREMELY RARE | 1 TO 15 |

METAL/DENOMINATION—The traditional $N$, $R$ and $\mathcal{E}$ have been used to denote gold, silver and bronze coins. All Celtic gold coins have three-component alloys of gold, silver and copper. Some coins are described as White Gold, these have a high proportion of silver (the use of the misleading term 'electrum' has been avoided). Many so-called silver coins similarly have three-component alloys, with silver the major constituent. Billon coins are silver-copper alloys, with a high proportion of copper. The denominations listed are the gold stater and its quarter, the silver unit, the silver stater, the silver fraction, the silver minim and the bronze unit.

WEIGHTS—Weights are given in grammes, using two conventions. Most coins are listed with the 'typical weight'—this is the weight most existing examples exhibit. Some coins are listed with the 'standard weight'—this is the weight the coin was supposed to have when it left the mint. Standard weights have been determined statistically and represent the heaviest weight for the type, when enough heavy examples exist to determine this. If the catalogue listing does not specify which weight is reported, the typical weight is intended.

DIAMETERS—Diameters are reported in millimetres, and these are typical values. Celtic coins vary greatly in diameter from coin to coin and the flans are often irregular in shape. The largest possible diameter is intended. There has been no attempt to determine standard values, if any existed.

DESCRIPTIONS—The descriptions of the coins include conventions for naming the objects in the fields. A list of these objects, with illustrations appears in the Appendix.

CLASSIFICATION—The designations intended for use by archaeologists and other workers are given before the notes. Those devised by Derek Allen (114) for the imported coins: eg: Gallo-Belgic A, have been retained, however those for the British-made coins are out-of-date and have been replaced. A chronological chart of these classifications appears in the Appendix.

MUSEUM HOLDINGS—In the notes, an estimate is given of the proportion of coins held in museums. This entry relates to the Rarity estimate. SOME means about one-third of the existing quantity is held by museums, MANY about half, and MOST about two-thirds or more. No entry means the number held in museums is negligible compared to the total known.

# THE EARLIEST FORMS OF MONEY

The two earliest forms of money used in Britain were small rings of gold and iron bars shaped like swords. The dating of these objects is problematic, although Caesar mentions the iron bars in his writings, placing them as late as 55 B.C. There is no contemporary account of the gold rings and these objects could have been in use at any time before the Gallic War. Rings are known from Bronze age contexts, about 1000 B.C. or perhaps earlier, but at this early date they probably functioned only as hair ornaments. Their use as money probably dates to the second century B.C.

## RING MONEY

1-1 **TWISTED WIRE TYPE** ca. 1200–100 B.C.      VR
Ν Ring Money ca. 4–15 gms ca. 23 mm

OBV: Twisted loop of metal
Identifying points:
    1) plain, pointed ends
    2) ends do not touch
    3) ends tapered

REV: Same as obverse
Identifying points:
    1) same as obverse

CLASSIFICATION: None

NOTES: Weights and diameters vary considerably. Primarily used as ornaments, may have functioned as money.

1-3 **PLAIN TYPE** ca. 1200–100 B.C.      VR
Ν Ring Money ca. 3–12 gms. ca. 13–16 mm

OBV: Plain band of metal
Identifying points:
    1) ends usually blunt, do not touch
    2) often two colours of metal form banded pattern

REV: Same as obverse
Identifying points:
    1) same as obverse

CLASSIFICATION: None

NOTES: Weights and diameters vary considerably.
Primarily used as ornaments, may have
functioned as money.
Often occur plated.

1–5          DOUBLE–RING TYPE ca. 1200–100 B.C.          ER
Æ Ring Money 4.4 gms. 17 mm

OBV: Two rings of twisted metal
Identifying points:
    1) plain, pointed ends
    2) ends do not touch
    3) ends tapered
    4) two rings connected at one end

REV: Same as obverse
Identifying points:
    1) same as obverse

CLASSIFICATION: None

NOTES: Primarily used as ornaments, may have
functioned as money.

## CURRENCY BARS

5–1          SWORD TYPE ca. 200–50 B.C.          C
Iron Currency Bar 400–500 gms.
780–890 mm

OBV: Iron bar, sword shaped
Identifying points:
    1) flat, narrow blade
    2) tapered end
    3) hilt formed around wooden dowel.

REV: Same as obverse
Identifying points:
    1) same as obverse

CLASSIFICATION: None

NOTES: Traces of mineralized wood sometimes
found in hilt.
Sometimes found cut up as scrap metal
awaiting re–use.
Often found in hoards.
Iron requires special conservation treat-
ment.
Most are in museums.

5–3       **SPIT TYPE ca. 200–50 B.C.**       ER
Iron Currency Bar

OBV: Similar to Sword Type
Identifying points:
    1) thinner blade
    2) shorter hilt

REV: Same as obverse
Identifying points:
    1) same as obverse

CLASSIFICATION: None

NOTES: Not usually found hoarded.
       Iron requires special conservation treat-
       ment.
       Most are in museums.

5–5       **PLOUGHSHARE TYPE ca. 200–50 B.C.**   ER
Iron Currency Bar

OBV: Similar to Sword Type
Identifying points:
    1) thicker blade
    2) heavier blade

REV: Same as obverse
Identifying points:
    1) same as obverse

CLASSIFICATION: None

NOTES: Not usually found hoarded.
       Iron requires special conservation treat-
       ment.
       Often found along the Thames, and were
       possibly votive offerings.
       Most are in museums.

5–7       **BAY–LEAF TYPE ca. 200–50 B.C.**     ER
Iron Currency Bar

OBV: Similar to Sword Type
Identifying points:
    1) long hilt
    2) hilt has semi-circular section
REV: Same as obverse
Identifying points:
    1) same as obverse

CLASSIFICATION: None

NOTES: Not usually found hoarded.
        Iron requires special conservation treat-
        ment.
        Most are in museums.

## IMPORTED COINAGE

Most of the coins imported into Britain were struck by the Ambiani tribe. The
first imports began about 125 B.C and coins continued to be imported until
the end of the Gallic War.

10-1     LARGE FLAN TYPE 125-100 B.C.                    S
         Ν Stater 7.8 gms. 25 mm

OBV: Celticized head of Apollo right
Identifying points:
        1) naturalistic face

REV: Celticized horse right
Identifying points:
        1) naturalistic charioteer
        2) 'yoke' in front of horse
        3) 'coffee bean' behind horse

CLASSIFICATION: Gallo-Belgic AA1
Notes:—Normally ocurrs in worn condition.
        Forgery known: see 10-1F.
        Standard weight given.
        Ambianic origin.

10-2     LARGE FLAN TYPE 125-100 B.C.                    S
         Ν Stater 7.3-7.8 gms. 22 mm

OBV: Celticized head of Apollo right
Identifying points:
        1) more prominent wreath than on 10-1
        2) face larger than on 10-1

REV: Celticized horse right
Identifying points:
        1) more open space in field than on 10-1

CLASSIFICATION: Gallo-Belgic AC

NOTES: Normally occurs in worn condition.
        Typical weight given.
        Ambianic origin.

12–1     **LARGE FLAN TYPE 125–100 B.C.**     S
Ꭺ́ Stater 7.8 gms. 26 mm

OBV: Celticized head of Apollo left
Identifying points:
     1) naturalistic face

REV: Celticized horse left
Identifying points:
     1) complex flower below horse
     2) stylized charioteer above

CLASSIFICATION: Gallo-Belgic AB1

NOTES: Normally occurs in worn condition.
     Standard weight given.
     Ambianic origin.
     Some in museums.

15–1     **LARGE FLAN TYPE 125–100 B.C.**     VR
Ꭺ́ Quarter Stater 1.4–2.1 gms. 4 mm

OBV: Celticized head of Apollo right
Identifying points
     1) naturalistic face

REV: Celticized horse right
Identifying points:
     1) naturalistic charioteer

CLASSIFICATION: Gallo-Belgic AA2

NOTES: Normally occurs in worn condition.
     Typical weight given.
     Ambianic origin.

17–1     **LARGE FLAN TYPE 125–100 B.C.**     VR
Ꭺ́ Quarter Stater 1.7–2.0 gms. 14 mm

OBV: Celticized head of Apollo right
Identifying points:
     1) more prominent wreath than on 15–1
     2) face larger than on 15–1

REV: Celticized horse right
Identifying points:
     1) more open space in field than on 15–1

CLASSIFICATION: Gallo-Belgic A

NOTES: Normally occurs in worn condition.
     Typical weight given.
     Ambianic origin.

20-1     LARGE FLAN TYPE 125-100 B.C.                  VR
         Ꝟ Quarter Stater 1.4-2.0 gms. 14 mm

OBV: Celticized head left
Identifying points:
    1) naturalistic face

REV: Celticized horse left
Identifying points:
    1) complex flower below horse
    2) stylized charioteer above

CLASSIFICATION: Gallo-Belgic AB2

NOTES:  Normally occurs in worn condition.
        Typical weight given.
        Ambianic origin.
        Many in museums.

30-1     DEFACED DIE TYPE 125-100 B.C.                 ER
         Ꝟ Stater 7.85 gms. 19 mm

OBV: Die defaced with chisel-marks
Identifying points:
    1) remnant of Apollo head visible beneath
       marks

REV: Celticized horse right
Identifying points:
    1) as 10-1

CLASSIFICATION: Gallo-Belgic BA1

NOTES:  Standard weight given.
        This type has been attributed to the Caletes,
        but the original dies appear to be Ambianic
        in origin.
        Many in museums.

33-1     DEFACED DIE TYPE 125-100 B.C.                 ER
         Ꝟ Stater 7.85 gms. 17 mm

OBV: Die defaced with chisel-marks
Identifying points:
    1) no remnants of Apollo head visible beneath
       marks

REV: Celticized horse left
Identifying points:
    1) 'lyre' below horse

CLASSIFICATION: Gallo-Belgic BB1

NOTES: Standard weight given.
Attributed to the Caletes.
Most in museums.
Modern forgery exists—See 33-1F.

35-1     DEFACED DIE TYPE 125-100 B.C.       ER
*N* Quarter Stater 1.8-2.0 gms. 12 mm

OBV: Die defaced with chisel-marks
Identifying points:
    1) remnant of Apollo head visible below marks

REV: Celticized horse left
Identifying points:
    1) as 20-1

CLASSIFICATION: Gallo-Belgic BA2

NOTES: Typical weight given.
Attributed to the Caletes.

37-1     DEFACED DIE TYPE 125-100 B.C.       R
*N* Quarter Stater 1.4-1.9 gms. 12 mm

OBV: Die defaced with chisel-marks
Identifying points:
    1) no remnants of Apollo head visible beneath marks

REV: Two Celticized horses left
Identifying points:
    1) 'lyre' below horses
    2) 'Rider' on horses

CLASSIFICATION: Gallo-Belgic BB2

NOTES: Typical weight given.
Attributed to the Caletes.
Some in museums.

42-1     ABSTRACT DESIGN TYPE 90-80 B.C.     R
*N* Stater 7.00 gms. 19 mm

OBV: abstracted head of Apollo right
Identifying points:
    1) enlarged eye
    2) pellet and two curves for nose

REV: disjointed horse right

Identifying points:
    1) nose made up of pellet and two lines
    2) large pellet below horse

CLASSIFICATION: Gallo-Belgic C

NOTES: Scheers Cl. C–II, Pl. IV, no. 86.
       Standard weight given.
       Ambianic origin.

42-3    ABSTRACT DESIGN TYPE  90–80 B.C.    ER
Æ/Æ Plated Stater 4.24 gms. 17 mm

OBV: abstracted head of Apollo right
Identifying points:
    1) as 42-1
REV: disjointed horse right
Identifying points:
    1) as 42-1

CLASSIFICATION: Gallo-Belgic C

NOTE:  An ancient forgery.
       Weight of illustrated coin given.
       The illustrated coin was found
       during excavations at Danebury.
       An XRF study of the gold coating revealed
       traces of mercury, sugggesting the mercury-
       gilding processs was used—a very early oc-
       currence of this technique.

44-1    ABSTRACT DESIGN TYPE 80–70 B.C.    R
N Stater 6.65 gms. 16 mm

OBV: abstracted head of Apollo right
Identifying points:
    1) face smaller than on 42-1
    2) larger eye than on 42-1
    3) curves of nose spread further apart than on
       42-1
REV: disjointed horse right
Identifying points:
    1) horse more stylized than on 42-1

CLASSIFICATION: Gallo-Belgic C

NOTES: Scheers Cl. C–III, Pl. IV, nos. 87–88.
       Standard weight given.
       Ambianic origin.

46–1     ABSTRACT DESIGN TYPE 80–70 B.C.          R
N Stater 6.45 gms. 17 mm

OBV: abstracted head of Apollo right
Identifying points:
    1) Wreath more dominant than on 44–1
    2) lips missing

REV: disjointed horse right
Identifying points:
    1) exergual line normally visible

CLASSIFICATION: Gallo-Belgic C

NOTES: Scheers Cl. C–IV, Pl. IV, nos. 89–90.
      Standard weight given.
      Ambianic origin.

48–1     ABSTRACT DESIGN TYPE 80–70 B.C.          R
N Stater 6.45 gms. 16 mm

OBV: abstracted head of Apollo right
Identifying points:
    1) head is now unrecognizable
    2) face small compared to 46–1
    3) face less dominant in design compared to
       46–1

REV: disjointed horse right
Identifying points:
    1) horse is thin and lanky

CLASSIFICATION: Gallo-Belgic C

NOTES: Scheers Cl. C–V, Pl. IV, no. 91.
      Standard weight given.
      Ambianic origin.

50–1     GALLIC WAR TYPE ca. 65 B.C.              C
N Stater 6.35 gms. 16 mm

OBV: blank

REV: disjointed horse
Identifying points:
    1) large, tall horse
    2) large space surrounding pellet below
      horse
    3) zig-zag in exergue

CLASSIFICATION: Gallo-Belgic E

NOTES: Scheers Cl. E–I, Pl. VI, nos. 151–152.
Standard weight given.
Ambianic origin.

52–1    GALLIC WAR TYPE ca. 60 B.C.                    C
Æ Stater 6.25 gms. 16 mm

OBV: blank

REV: disjointed horse right
Identifying points:
    1) horse smaller than on 50–1
    2) crescents and pellets in exergue
    3) exergual line is continuous

CLASSIFICATION: Gallo-Belgic E

NOTES: Scheers Cl. E–II, Pl. VI, no. 153.
Standard weight given.
Ambianic origin.
Modern forgery exists—see 52–1F.

52–3    GALLIC WAR TYPE ca. 60 B.C.                   ER
Æ/Æ Plated Stater 16mm

OBV: blank
REV: disjointed horse right
Identifying points:
    1) as 52–1

CLASSIFICATION: Gallo-Belgic E

NOTES: Scheers Cl. E–II, Pl. VI,
    no. 153.
    Silver core.
    Ancient forgery, made by wrapping gold
    sheet around a silver core, and bonding with
    heat.

52–5    GALLIC WAR TYPE ca. 60 B.C.                   ER
Æ/Æ Plated Stater 16mm

OBV: blank
REV: disjointed horse right
Identifying points:
    1) as 52–1

CLASSIFICATION: Gallo-Belgic E

NOTES: Scheers Cl. E–II, Pl. VI,
    no. 153.
    Bronze core.
    Ancient forgery.

54-1    GALLIC WAR TYPE 60–55 B.C.                C

Ν Stater 6.20 gms. 16 mm

OBV: blank

REV: disjointed horse right
Identifying points:
    1) separate pellets and crescents in exergue
    2) exergual line made up of pellets

CLASSIFICATION: Gallo-Belgic E

NOTES: Scheers Cl. E–III, Pl. VI, no. 154.
      See Modern forgery 54–1F.
      Standard weight given.
      Ambianic origin.

56-1    GALLIC WAR TYPE ca. 55 B.C.               C

Ν Stater 6.05 gms. 17 mm

OBV: blank

REV: disjointed horse right
Identifying points:
    1) double exergual line
    2) cruder die-cutting than 54–1

CLASSIFICATION: Gallo-Belgic E

NOTES: Scheers Cl. E–IV, Pl. VI, no. 155.
      Standard weight given.
      Ambianic origin.

Gallic War Quarter Staters are all modern forgeries.

65-1    GEOMETRIC TYPE 65–50 B.C.               ER

Ν Quarter Stater 1.35 gms. 10 mm

OBV: abstracted head of Apollo
Identifying points:
    1) large pellet-in-ring motif in centre

REV: opposed crescents with pellet and
    and 6-pointed stars

CLASSIFICATION: Gallo-Belgic DA

NOTES: Other previously-designated GEOMETRIC
      TYPES are now believed to be derived from
      the Caesarian trophy denarius, and are thus
      catalogued under Kentish tribes, see 144–1
      to 147–1.

Standard weight given.
Mack was uncertain about the Gallo-Belgic
DA attribution.
Most in museums.

67-1    GEOMETRIC TYPE 65–50 B.C.                    ER
Æ Quarter Stater 1.35 gms. 8 mm

OBV: Almost plain
Identifying points:
    1) small flower–like object in centre

REV: Geometric pattern
Identifying points:
    1) tree–like object in centre
    2) lines and curves near tree

CLASSIFICATION: Gallo-Belgic DA

NOTES: Standard weight given.
        Uncertain tribal origin.
        Many in museums.

67-3    GEOMETRIC TYPE 65–50 B.C.                    ER
Æ Quarter Stater 1.35 gms. 8 mm

OBV: Almost plain
Identifying points:
    1) remnants of flower–like object in centre

REV: Geometric pattern
Identifying points:
    1) similar to 67-1
    2) small rings below tree

CLASSIFICATION: Gallo-Belgic D

NOTES: Standard weight given.
        Uncertain tribal origin.

69-1    GEOMETRIC TYPE 65–50 B.C.                    S
Æ Quarter Stater 1.50 gms. 11 mm

OBV: Geometric pattern
Identifying points:
    1) large curve with holes
    2) three irregular shapes below.

For most of the series, the images were scribed freehand into the clay moulds. Traditionally, these images have been used to establish a type sequence widely used in archaeological work. Today however, the coins are seen to be mass-produced items. The stylus work was done as quickly as possible and thus the images provide little basis for establishing the sequence.

A better indicator of types are the marks produced by the different mould-manufacturing processes. These yield a plausable chronological sequence, consequently, the following catalogue is primarily concerned with the mould-manufacturing techniques. The images are taken into account only when major differences in artistic style are noted. For example, at some point the images on the reverse switch from curvilinear forms to boxy ones. The change may indicate the appearance of a new moneyer or a modification to the coining techniques.

The first three periods of manufacture occurred quickly and in rapid succession, as the moneyers sought the best production methods. After the techniques were perfected, an enormous number of coins were produced over a long period. Quantities of hundreds of thousands (perhaps millions) are thought to have been cast and several thousand examples exist today.

## PROTOTYPE PERIOD-ca. 100 B.C.

These were the first coins manufactured in Britain, the images were adapted directly from the cast bronzes of Masillia. At first, the images were produced using mother-coins. This technique was immediately changed to speed up production—the image was then scribed into the mould with a stylus. The coins of the Prototype Period were thick and dumpy, and evidently unacceptable to the Kentish tribes.

## EXPERIMENTAL PERIOD-ca. 100 B.C.

The mould production method was again changed—a smooth dowel was now pressed into the wet clay to produce the cavity. The sprues and the image were then scribed in with a blunt stylus. Manufacturing problems in the Experimental Period were severe. The moulds did not mate very well, allowing metal to squeeze out and produce 'flash'. Misalignment of the moulds during casting produced an offset between the obverses and reverses. Furthermore, the coins still had a thick, dumpy feel because they were thinner only at the edges.

## INNOVATIVE PERIOD-100 TO 90 B.C.

The moneyers worked to eliminate the problems during the Innovative Period. Various techniques of producing the cavity-and-runner system were tried and experiments to create smooth mating-surfaces were carried out—all producing striations in the coins' fields. Four types of striations have been identified: CROSSED, MEDIUM, HEAVY and THIN, each revealing a different technique of mould production.

The Crossed Striations were produced by textile pressed into the clay to form the cavity and runner system. Medium Striations were the result of cutting a block of clay in two with a wire in an attempt to produce perfectly-mating moulds. Heavy Striations were produced by pressing the clay against a wooden surface to smooth it. None of these techniques was particularly successful— either excessive flash resulted or the striations were so severe the stylus image was ruined.

The Thin Striation coins are the commonest, because the technique was more successful and was employed for a longer time. These were produced by smoothing the clay with a flat scraper.


## OPTIMIZATION PERIOD-90 TO 50 B.C.

The transition to the Optimization Period is marked by an extremely rare type with three pellets in the Apollo head. A Thin Striation predecessor with the same pellets may exist. The first coins continue with a bull made up of curved lines, however at some point a change was made. The bull was given a boxy appearance by using straight lines in place of the curved ones.

A suspected transitional issue is known, with a bull having both straight and curved lines. This unusual issue is denoted by a pair of crescents under the exergual line. It is an extremely rare type and the only one displaying crescents. The date of manufacture is difficult to determine—it probably occurred early in the Optimization Period.

Alternatively, a time of overlap in which both curvilinear and boxy bull images were produced is also possible. Recently, the Stansted Airport Hoard appears to have yielded a striated coin with the boxy image, but this has not been confirmed. The relative chronology of the Innovative and Optimization Periods, at the moment quite problematic, may become clearer as more coins are discovered.

The vast majority of the coins in existence today were produced during the Optimization Period using a new mould-making method. The procedure was extremely successful and yielded exquisitely thin and flat coins—probably the most expertly-produced cast coins known. The clay moulds were pressed against a very smooth material, probably sheet bronze. This yielded moulds that had no striations to ruin the image, yet mated well enough to produce minimal flash. The only remaining problems were either one, the coins were so thin they cracked upon separation from the chain, or two, the moulds were so thin they failed to fill during casting.

## ADJUSTMENT PERIOD–50 TO 35 B.C.

These last two problems, incomplete casting and unsuccessful separation, were solved by a change in policy just before the introduction of the Struck Bronze series. The final cast coins were made small and thick—although they were dumpy and unappealing, they could be produced with no separation or mould-filling problems.

Generally, the various types of cast bronzes are extremely rare. However, the optimization period issues were made in vast quantities over a long time and are today very common.

## PROTOTYPE PERIOD

102–1    LIFE-LIKE BULL TYPE ca. 100 B.C.        ER
Cast Bronze ca. 2.2 gms. 18 mm

OBV: Celticized head of Apollo left
Identifying points:
    1) head relatively naturalistic

REV: Celticized bull charging right
Identifying points:
    1) relatively life-like bull charging right
    2) pellet on body of bull

CLASSIFICATION: Cantian A

NOTES: This is the earliest extant coin manufactured in Britain.
The parting line around the edge and the sprues (casting tabs) indicate a casting process was used.
A mother-coin was used to produce the image in the mould.
This type was copied directly from the cast coinage of Masillia.

104–1    ABSTRACT BULL TYPE ca. 100 B.C.        ER
Cast Bronze ca. 2.6 gms. 20 mm

OBV: Celticized head of Apollo left
Identifying points:
    1) head now scribed—in with a stylus, but an attempt made to produce a life-like image

REV: Celticized bull charging right

Identifying points:
    1) same stylus technique used

CLASSIFICATION: Cantian A

NOTES: This type was directly derived from 102–1.

105–1     ABSTRACT BULL TYPE ca. 100 B.C.       ER
Cast Bronze 18 mm

OBV: Celticized head of Apollo left
Identifying points:
    1) as 104–1

REV: Celticized bull charging left
Identifying points:
    1) as 104–1, but bull faces opposite direction

CLASSIFICATION: Cantian A

NOTES: This type was directly derived from 102–1.

## EXPERIMENTAL PERIOD

106–1     CURVED BULL TYPE ca. 100 B.C.       ER
Cast Bronze 18 mm

OBV: Celticized head of Apollo right
Identifying points:
    1) head now comprised of lines, no attempt at
        life–like reproduction

REV: Celticized bull charging right
Identifying points:
    1) same linear style as obverse
    2) lines of bull are curved

CLASSIFICATION: Cantian B

NOTES: The coin is thicker at the edges than at the
       centre because of the scribed edge-circle.
       Occasionally a coin will have an obverse
       cavity of a different diameter than the re-
       verse. The upper surface of the mould is
       then imaged at the edge of the coin on
       the smaller diameter side. This is smooth,
       indicating a scraping motion was not used
       to produce the mating surfaces.

108-1     **CURVED BULL TYPE** ca. 100 B.C.                ER
          Cast Bronze  ca. 1.7 gms. 19 mm

          OBV: Celticized head of Apollo left
          Identifying points:
              1) as 106-1, but head faces opposite direction

          CLASSIFICATION: Cantian B

          REV: Celticized bull charging right
          Identifying points:
              1) as 106-1

          NOTES: AS 106-1

108-3     **CURVED BULL TYPE** ca. 100 B.C.                ER
          Cast Bronze ca. 1.7 gms. 19 mm

          OBV: Celticized head of Apollo left
          Identifying points:
              1) as 106-1, but head faces opposite direction
              2) line runs vertically through neck

          REV: Celticized bull charging right
          Identifying points:
              1) as 106-1

          CLASSIFICATION: Cantian B

          NOTES: as 106-1.

110-1     **SPRUE EXPERIMENT TYPE**                        ER
              ca. 100 B.C.
          Cast Bronze ca. 1.9 gms. 18 mm

          OBV: Crude head of Apollo left
          Identifying points:
              1) head scribed in such a crude manner as to
                 be barely recognizable

          CLASSIFICATION: Cantian B

          REV: Celticized bull
          Identifying points:
              1) bull scribed in such a crude manner as to
                 be unrecognizable

          NOTES: Sprue (casting tab) width only 3.5 mm.
                 Experimental type—attempt to use a smaller
                 sprue to ease the separation of the coins
                 from one another.

110-3     SPRUE EXPERIMENT TYPE ca. 100 B.C.     ER
Cast Bronze ca. 1.9 gms. 18 mm

OBV: Crude head of Apollo left
Identifying points:
  1) head scribed in such a sloppy manner as to
     be barely recognizable
  2) normal sprue width

REV: Celticized bull
Identifying points:
  1) bull scribed in a sloppy manner
  2) normal sprue width

CLASSIFICATION: Cantian B

NOTES: Normal sprue (casting tab) width.
       Experimental type—attempt to use a
       smaller sprue to ease the separation of
       the coins from one another, this coin may
       represent the 'control' for the experiment—
       because it has the normal sprue width, but
       the same style as the thin sprue type.

## INNOVATIVE PERIOD

112-1     CROSSED STRIATIONS TYPE                ER
             ca. 100 B.C.
Cast Bronze ca. 1.7 gms. 18 mm

OBV: Celticized head of Apollo left
Identifying points:
  1) ring-and-pellet motif in centre of head

REV: Celticized bull charging left
Identifying points:
  1) bull made up of curved lines

CLASSIFICATION: Cantian C

NOTES: Equally-thin striations cross at ninety de-
       gree angles in the coin's field.
       The striations may appear on both sides,
       but are normally more pronounced on one
       side.
       These striations were once thought to be the
       result of the use of papyrus, but this has
       been disproved-the pattern is not correct
       for papyrus.
       The pattern was produced by textile, pressed
       into the clay to produce the cavity system.

114–1 MEDIUM STRIATIONS TYPE ER
ca. 100 B.C.

Cast Bronze ca. 1.9 gms. 19 mm

OBV: Celticized head of Apollo right
Identifying points:
    1) outline head, usually marred by striations

REV: Celticized bull charging right
Identifying points:
    1) bull made up of curved lines, image often
       marred by striations

CLASSIFICATION: Cantian C

NOTES: Striations appear on both sides of the coin,
    and those on one side are parallel to those
    on the other side.
    The striations are deep and fairly heavy,
    with blobs of metal interrupting them. They
    are often so severe they ruin the image or
    create a flash problem.
    The striations run into the flash, indicating
    they were produced independently of the
    cavity-formation process.
    The moulds were produced by cutting a block
    of clay in two with a wire—the striations are
    the result of the cutting process.

115–1 MEDIUM STRIATIONS TYPE ER
ca. 100 B.C.

Cast Bronze 19 mm

OBV: Celticized head of Apollo right
Identifying points:
    1) as 114–1, but head faces the opposite
       direction

REV: Celticized bull charging left
Identifying points:
    1) as 114–1, but bull faces the opposite
       direction

CLASSIFICATION: Cantian C

NOTES: AS 114–1

117-1    HEAVY STRIATIONS TYPE ca. 100 B.C.     ER
Cast Bronze ca. 2.1 gms. 19 mm

OBV: Celticized head of Apollo left
Identifying points:
  1) outline head of Apollo

REV: Celticized bull charging left
Identifying points:
  1) bull made up of curved lines

CLASSIFICATION: Cantian C

NOTES: Striations normally appear on only one side
of coin.
Striations are not so deep, but are broad
and not necessarily parallel.
The striations were produced by wood
pressed against the clay to smooth it. This
type vindicates Evans' 1864 assertion that
wood was used in the mould making process.

119-1    THIN STRIATIONS TYPE 100–90 B.C.       VR
Cast Bronze ca. 1.5 gms. 18 mm

OBV: Celticized head of Apollo left
Identifying points:
  1) outline head of Apollo

REV: Celticized bull charging left
Identifying points:
  1) bull made up of curved lines

CLASSIFICATION: Cantian C

NOTES: Thin, parallel striations in the field, on one
side of the coin.
No blobs interrupt the striations.
The moulds were produced by scraping
blocks of clay flat with a knife or other
similar object.
The illustrated coin has only one sprue
because it was the last coin on the runner
system.

119–3    THIN STRIATIONS TYPE 100–90 B.C.        VR
Cast Bronze ca. 1.0 gm 18 mm

OBV: Celticized head of Apollo right
Identifying points:
    1) as 119–1 but head faces right

REV: Celticized bull charging right
Identifying points:
    1) bull made up of curved lines
    2) bull is of a slightly different form than
       119–1

CLASSIFICATION: Cantian C

NOTES: Same manufacturing method as 119–1.

119–5    THIN STRIATION TYPE 100–90 B.C.        ER
Cast Bronze ca. 1.5 gms. 18 mm

OBV: Celticized head of Apollo right
Identifying points:
    1) outline head of Apollo
    2) pellet in eye
    3) line runs vertically through neck

REV: Celticized bull charging left
Identifying points:
    1) bull made up of straight lines

CLASSIFICATION: Cantian C

NOTES: Same manufacturing method as 119–1.

## OPTIMIZATION PERIOD

122–1    THREE DOTS TYPE ca. 90 B.C.        ER
Cast Bronze ca. 1.6 gms. 19 mm

OBV: Celticized head of Apollo left
Identifying points:
    1) outline head of Apollo
    2) three dots inside head

REV: Celticized bull charging left
Identifying points:
    1) bull made up of curved lines

CLASSIFICATION: Cantian D

NOTES: Transitional type.
       Thin striation variety possibly exists, but
       not confirmed.

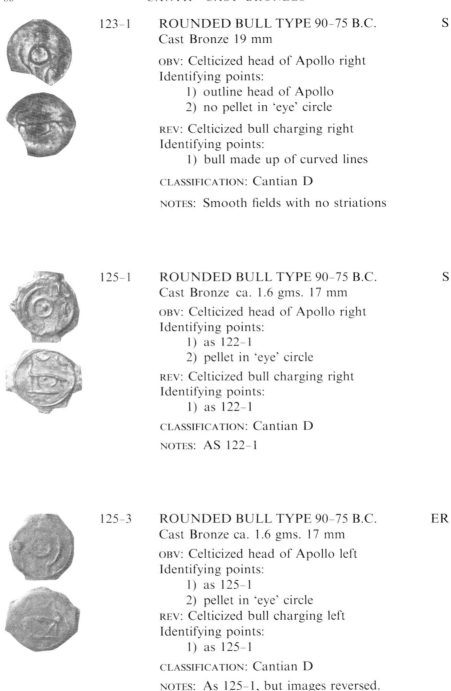

**123-1**     **ROUNDED BULL TYPE 90–75 B.C.**     **S**
Cast Bronze 19 mm

OBV: Celticized head of Apollo right
Identifying points:
     1) outline head of Apollo
     2) no pellet in 'eye' circle

REV: Celticized bull charging right
Identifying points:
     1) bull made up of curved lines

CLASSIFICATION: Cantian D

NOTES: Smooth fields with no striations

**125-1**     **ROUNDED BULL TYPE 90–75 B.C.**     **S**
Cast Bronze ca. 1.6 gms. 17 mm

OBV: Celticized head of Apollo right
Identifying points:
     1) as 122-1
     2) pellet in 'eye' circle

REV: Celticized bull charging right
Identifying points:
     1) as 122-1

CLASSIFICATION: Cantian D

NOTES: AS 122-1

**125-3**     **ROUNDED BULL TYPE 90–75 B.C.**     **ER**
Cast Bronze ca. 1.6 gms. 17 mm

OBV: Celticized head of Apollo left
Identifying points:
     1) as 125-1
     2) pellet in 'eye' circle

REV: Celticized bull charging left
Identifying points:
     1) as 125-1

CLASSIFICATION: Cantian D

NOTES: As 125-1, but images reversed.

127-1     CRESCENT TYPE ca. 85 B.C.        ER
Cast Bronze ca. 1.2 gms. 17 mm

OBV: Celticized head of Apollo left
Identifying points:
    1) outline head of Apollo

REV: Celticized bull charging right
Identifying points:
    1) bull made up of some straight lines
    2) bull's tail curved
    3) two crescents below exergual line

CLASSIFICATION: Cantian D

NOTES: Transitional type.
       Illustrated coin has been gold plated in Iron
       Age times, possibly for fraudulent use as a
       quarter stater.

129-1     ANGULAR BULL TYPE 85–50 B.C.        C
Cast Bronze ca. 1.6 gms. 17 mm

OBV: Celticized head of Apollo right
Identifying points:
    1) outline head of Apollo
    2) pellet in centre

REV: Celticized bull charging left
Identifying points:
    1) bull made up of straight lines
    2) pellet in centre

CLASSIFICATION: Cantian D

NOTES: The illustrated coin has only one sprue
       because it was the last coin on the runner
       system.

131-1     ANGULAR BULL TYPE 85–50 B.C        C
Cast bronze 18 mm

OBV: Celticized head of Apollo left
Identifying points:
    1) as 129-1 but head faces left

REV: Celticized bull charging right
Identifying points:
    1) as 129-1 but bull faces right

CLASSIFICATION: Cantian D

133-1     ANGULAR BULL TYPE 85–50 B.C.          C
Cast Bronze ca. 1.5 gms. 17 mm

OBV: Celticized head of Apollo left
Identifying points:
    1) as 129–1 but head faces left
    2) central pellet

REV: Celticized bull charging left
Identifying points:
    1) as 129–1
    2) central pellet

CLASSIFICATION: Cantian D

## ADJUSTMENT PERIOD

135-1     EARLY DUMP TYPE 50–45 B.C.          VR
Cast Bronze ca. 1.5 gms. 14 mm

OBV: Celticized head of Apollo right
Identifying points:
    1) outline head of Apollo
    2) pronounced pellet in centre of head.

REV: Celticized bull
Identifying points:
    1) bull made up of straight lines
    2) pronounced pellet in centre of bull.
    3) often not possible to determine which way
       bull faces.

CLASSIFICATION: Cantian E

136-1     EARLY DUMP TYPE 50–45 B.C.          VR
Cast Bronze 13 mm

OBV: Celticized head of Apollo left
Identifying points:
    1) as 135–1 but head faces left

REV: Celticized bull
Identifying points:
    1) as 135–1

CLASSIFICATION: Cantian E

137-1     MIDDLE DUMP TYPE 45–40 B.C.      VR
Cast Bronze ca. 1.2 gms. 13 mm

OBV: Crude head of Apollo right
Identifying points:
     1) barely recognizable outline head
     2) pronounced pellet in centre

REV: Crude bull
Identifying points:
     1) barely recognizable bull made up of straight
        lines
     2) pronounced pellet in centre of coin

CLASSIFICATION: Cantian E

138-1     MIDDLE DUMP TYPE 45–40 B.C.      VR
Cast Bronze 13 mm

OBV: Crude head of Apollo left
Identifying points:
     1) as 137–1 but head faces left

REV: Crude bull
Identifying points:
     1) as 137–1

CLASSIFICATION: Cantian E

139-1     LATE DUMP TYPE 40–35 B.C.      VR
Cast Bronze ca. 1.3 gms. 13 mm

OBV: Crude head of Apollo right
Identifying points:
     1) head of Apollo now only a circle with a line
        for the nose
     2) pronounced pellet in centre

REV: Crude bull
Identifying points:
     1) as 137–1

CLASSIFICATION: Cantian E

NOTES: Unconfirmed 'head left' variety, found at
         Rochester, may exist.

## THE FIRST STRUCK COINAGES IN KENT

At the close of the Gallic War, about 50 B.C., imports of gold coins from Gaul would have nearly ceased. The need for coins prompted the Kentish tribes to strike their own. These first pieces had no inscriptions, but within thirty years, dynastic types appeared.

The uninscribed coins have been arranged in two successive issues. The type sequence starts with the ORNAMENTED TYPE staters, which carry on the reverse a horse in an elaborately-ornamented field. These, and the following types have plain obverses. The ORNAMENTED staters are quickly replaced by the WEALD TYPE, a variety that suffers a decline in die-cutting workmanship over time.

The first inscribed variety, the SOUTH THAMES BANDED TYPE, has a wavy pattern in place of the plain obverse. The legends on the staters are almost off the flan on the existing coins, but enough is seen on one to suggest the letters 'IVII'. The succeeding inscribed coins continue the bands on the obverse.

Possibly, several tribes were simultaneously striking the different types. Although this would fit more closely with Caesar's comment that four 'kings' inhabited Kent, a simultaneous-production hypothesis is less likely. The coins appear to form a stylistic progression, hence a chronological order. Alternatively, the distribution of modern findspots does not offer enough support to suggest the different types were used in different parts of Kent.

Gold quarter staters are known for the two types of uninscribed staters. The first are a British version of the Gaulish GEOMETRIC TYPE, called the KENTISH GEOMETRIC TYPE. The design is soon changed to the TROPHY TYPE, which has a Celtic adaptation of the trophy motif seen on some of Caesar's denarii. Uninscribed quarters appear to have the same banded pattern as the 'IVII' SOUTH THAMES BANDED staters.

## KENTISH UNINSCRIBED COINS
## FIRST STRUCK COINAGE

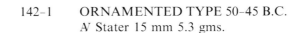

142-1      ORNAMENTED TYPE 50–45 B.C.                    ER
Aʹ Stater 15 mm 5.3 gms.

OBV: Plain
Identifying points:
    1) no evidence of banding at this time

REV: Celticized horse left
Identifying points:
    1) rings and lines in abstract pattern below
       horse

2) horse's right front foreleg made up of two lines

3) pellet-and-elipse motif with 'wings' above horse

CLASSIFICATION: Cantian F

NOTES: Weight of 5.3 grammes is probably too low for period, but inadequate number of coins exists to determine correct standard weight.

143-1    KENTISH GEOMETRIC TYPE                VR
         50-45 B.C.
         Ν Quarter Stater 11 mm 1.3-1.6 gms.

OBV: Large crescent and uncertain shapes
Identifying points:
    1) crescent has voids

REV: Large cross-motif with pellets
Identifying points:
    1) arms of cross touch

CLASSIFICATION: Cantian F

NOTES: Many in museums
    Attribution to Britain is traditional and somewhat arbitrary, type is possibly a Gaulish import.
    Obverse has been described as a wolf-and-twins motif or a boat with three occupants. Type is possibly derived from the Gaulish Monnaies à Croix series. These are all unproven speculations.

## SECOND STRUCK COINAGE

144-1    EARLY WEALD TYPE 45-40 B.C.          ER
         Ν Stater 16 mm 5.6 gms.

OBV: plain
Identifying points:
    1) no evidence of banding at this time

REV: Celticized horse left

Identifying points:
> 1) box with cross-hatching below horse done in neat workmanship
> 2) pellet below tail
> 3) pellet-in-ring motif in front of horse
> 4) S-shape with pellets in arms above horse
> 5) horse's right foreleg made up of a single line

CLASSIFICATION: Cantian G

NOTES: Some in museums
> Typical weight given.

145-1     **EARLY TROPHY TYPE 45–40 B.C.**          ER
N Quarter Stater 13 mm 1.3–1.6 gms.

OBV: plain
Identifying points:
> 1) no evidence of banding at this time

REV: stylized Roman trophy
Identifying points:
> 1) trophy still recognizable
> 2) two rings with cross-hatching at 5 and 7 o'clock engraved with good workmanship
> 3) boxes with cross-hatching at 3 and 9 o'clock engraved with good workmanship

CLASSIFICATION: Cantian G

NOTES: Reverse design adapted from denarius of Caesar, BMC. 3961.
> Traditionally described as a British type; possibly, but unlikely a Gaulish import.
> Most in museums.
> Typical weight given.

146-1     **MIDDLE TROPHY TYPE 45–40 B.C.**          ER
N Quarter Stater 10 mm 1.3–1.6 gms.

OBV: Flower-like ornament in plain field
Identifying points:
> 1) field not ornamented
> 2) flower has four petals

REV: Stylized Roman trophy
Identifying points:
> 1) trophy highly stylized

2) rings at 5 and 7 o'clock replaced by simple pellets

3) boxes at 3 and 9 o'clock replaced by rows of pellets

CLASSIFICATION: Cantian G

NOTES: Traditionally described as Gaulish type, but more likely a part of the Kentish series on the basis of style.
Reverse design adapted from denarius of Caesar, BMC 3961.
Most in museums.
Typical weight given.

147-1     LATE TROPHY TYPE 45–40 B.C.     ER
Æ Quarter Stater 11 mm 1.3–1.6 gms.

OBV: Plain, perhaps banded
Identifying points:
1) Slight evidence for banding as seen on Third Struck Coinage types.

REV: Stylized Roman trophy
Identifying points:
1) Trophy highly stylized
2) Trophy made up of lines and pellets
3) Rings at 2 and 11 o'clock
4) Boxes at 3 and 9 o'clock as on 145–1.

CLASSIFICATION: Cantian G

NOTES: Many in museums
Reverse design adapted from denarius of Caesar, BMC (Spain) 86 or 89.
Traditionally described as a British type; possibly, but unlikely a Gaulish import.
Chronologically, this type may preceed or be contemporary with the MIDDLE TROPHY TYPE.
Typical weight given.

150-1     LATE WEALD TYPE 40–35 B.C.     ER
Æ Stater 15 mm

OBV: Plain
Identifying points:
1) No evidence of banding at this time.

REV: Celticized horse left
Identifying points:
1) box with cross-hatching below horse, engraved with less careful workmanship as 144–1.
2) pellet-in-ring motif on horse's shoulder
3) three pellet-in-ring motifs above horse
4) pellet-in-ring in front of horse
5) horse's right foreleg made up of a single line

CLASSIFICATION: Cantian H

NOTES: Some in museums
        Modern forgery exists–see 150–1F.

151–1     LATE WEALD TYPE 40–35 B.C.        ER
          $\cancel{A}$ Quarter Stater 11 mm

OBV: Plain
Identifying points:
1) No evidence of banding at this time.

REV: Celticized horse left
Identifying points:
1) pellet-in-ring on horse's shoulder
2) pellet-in-ring motifs above horse
3) 'V' made up of one corded arm and one of short, parallel strokes
4) box with cross-hatching below horse, engraved with less careful workmanship as 144–1
5) horse's right foreleg made up of single line

CLASSIFICATION: Cantian H

NOTES: Most are in museums.

## ARBITRARILY ASSIGNED COINS

The following types, for the most part known from only a handful of examples, are traditionally assigned to the Cantii. There is little reason for doing so, other than they have been found in Kent. The types are of unknown date and may be earlier imports from Gaul.

153–1    KENTISH UNCERTAIN ca. 50–30 B.C.    ER
         Æ minim 11 mm 0.4 gms.

OBV: Horseman right
Identifying points:
    1) horseman holds spear or carnyx

REV: Seated man
Identifying points:
    1) man wearing belt
    2) man hold spear or staff to left

CLASSIFICATION: None
NOTES: Not illustrated.

154–1    KENTISH UNCERTAIN ca. 30–50 B.C.    ER
         Æ unit 18 mm 1.6 gms.

OBV: Wolf left
Identifying points:
    1) tree? behind wolf
    2) rings in field

REV: Celticized horse right
Identifying points:
    1) rings in field above horse

CLASSIFICATION: None

NOTES: Possibly earlier import from Gaul

154–3    KENTISH UNCERTAIN ca. 30–50 B.C.    ER
         Æ unit 12 mm 2.1 gms.

OBV: Uncertain animal right
Identifying points:
    1) exergual line made up of pellets

REV: Uncertain animal right
Identifying points:
    1) rings and pellets in field around animal

CLASSIFICATION: None

NOTES: Obverse    possibly    adapted    from    the
       KENTISH GEOMETRIC TYPE, 143–1.

154-5       KENTISH UNCERTAIN ca. 30–50 B.C.          ER
Æ unit 13 mm

OBV: Boar left
Identifying points:
    1) pellet-in-ring motif below boar

REV: Lion right
Identifying points:
    1) pellet-in-ring motifs above lion

CLASSIFICATION: None
NOTES: Not illustrated.

154-7       KENTISH UNCERTAIN ca. 30–50 B.C.          ER
Æ unit ca. 15 mm

OBV: Uncertain animal right
Identifying points:
    1) curved line above animal

REV: Celticized horse left
Identifying points:
    1) pellet border

CLASSIFICATION: None

NOTES: Current whereabouts of coin uncertain, rec-
        orded in Evans, plate G14, in 1864.
        Not illustrated.

154-9       KENTISH UNCERTAIN ca. 30–50 B.C.          ER
Æ unit 11 mm

OBV: Head right
Identifying points:
    1) too poorly preserved to identify

REV: Uncertain animal left
Identifying points:
    1) pellets in field around animal

CLASSIFICATION: None

NOTES: Possibly an earlier import from Gaul.
        Not illustrated.

154-11    KENTISH UNCERTAIN ca. 30–50 B.C.          ER
Æ unit 11 mm

OBV: PELLET-AND-RING MOTIF
Identifying points:
      1) Larger pellet-in-ring motif in center
      2) seven rings surround central ring

REV: Uncertain
Identifying points:
      1) too poorly preserved to identify

CLASSIFICATION: None

NOTES: Not illustrated.


154-13    KENTISH UNCERTAIN ca. 30–50 B.C.          ER
Æ minim 10 mm

OBV: PELLET-IN-RING MOTIFS
Identifying points:
      1) four pellet-in-ring motifs surrounded by a
         ring of pellets

REV: Celticized horse right
Identifying points:
      1) horse surrounded by ring of pellets

CLASSIFICATION: None

NOTES: Not illustrated.


## KENTISH DYNASTIC COINAGES

The first inscribed coins carry an illegible inscription, mostly off the flan on existing pieces. The letters 'IVII' partially appear on one stater, but the reading is uncertain. Hopefully, future finds will enable the full inscription to be read.

The next series of inscribed coins are those of the Kentish Dubnovellaunus, probably a different ruler from the one in Essex. Dubnovellaunus-in-Kent struck coins from about 30 B.C. up to the Trinovantian/Catuvellaunian Interregnum, about 10 B.C. At this point, he was replaced by a short-lived ruler, Vosenos, who was in turn replaced by Eppillus of the Atrebates/Regni. Eppillus, sensing a loss of Trinovantian/Catuvellaunian influence, intervened in Kent only to be later driven out by Cunobeline. Eppillus issued special coins for use in Kent; subsequently, Cunobeline's coinage circulated. Between the death of Cunobeline and the Claudian invasion, the brief issues of Amminius appeared.

All Kentish dynastic coinage is extremely rare, with only a few examples of each type known today. The issues must have been small, and would be relatively unimportant except they identify the names of Kentish rulers. For the most part, the economic influences of the Trinovantes/Catuvellauni, and for a short time the Artebates/Regni were the significant factors in Kent.

## UNCERTAIN RULER—'IVII'

<table>
<tr><td>157–1</td><td>SOUTH THAMES BANDED TYPE</td><td>ER</td></tr>
</table>

157–1    SOUTH THAMES BANDED TYPE          ER
         35–30 B.C.
         PARTIAL INSCRIPTION 'IVII'
         Æ Stater 15 mm 5.6 gms.

OBV: plain, with bands
Identifying points:
    1) Three raised bands extend across field.

REV: Celticized horse right
Identifying points:
    1) pellet-in-ring motif on horse's shoulder
    2) pellet-in-ring below horse
    3) large ring above horse
    4) horse lacks mane
    5) partial inscription above horse, probable reading—'IVII'

CLASSIFICATION: Cantian I

NOTES: Plate coin reappeared in March, 1987 Muenz Zentrum auction, weight recorded in catalogue.
Actual weight of existing coin given.

158–1    SOUTH THAMES BANDED TYPE          ER
         35–30 B.C.
         Æ Quarter Stater 11 mm

OBV: Plain, with bands
Identifying points:
    1) Three raised bands extend across field.

REV: Celticized horse right
Identifying points:
    1) large ring above horse
    2) horse lacks mane
    3) no inscription

CLASSIFICATION: Cantian I

NOTES: Most are in museums.

## DUBNOVELLAUNUS IN KENT

Dubnovellaunus' coinage is broken down into three separate issues, each having gold, silver and bronze coins. The dating of these is problematic, but the order may be identified by the increasing Romanization of the designs and the influence of the Trinovantian/Catuvellaunian coinage on the gold.

The first coinage staters carry a pellet-in-ring motif on the horse's shoulder, but later coins eliminate it. This mirrors the coinage of the Trinovates/ Catuvellauni—Addedomaros' third coinage carries the pellet-in-ring motif, but Dubnovellaunus-in-Essex' and Tasciovanus' coins eliminate it. Dubnovellaunus-in-Kent's second coinage adopts the bucranium above the horse from the staters of Tasciovanus.

Several issues appear to have privy-marks and probably all carry some sort of identification which we are unable to recognize today.

## FIRST COINAGE

This issue carries the most easily-identified privy marks. The key is that the animals all have pellets under their necks, which disappear on the next issue. Some animals have necklaces and belts, or a curious five-pointed outline star beneath them.

162-1    DUBNOVELLAUNUS IN KENT                    ER
         30–23 B.C.
         Ν Stater 17 mm 5.4 gms.

OBV: Plain with slight banding
Identifying points:
  1) Banding slight—only a raised band across centre

REV: Celticized horse right
Identifying points:
  1) pellet under neck
  2) Inscription above horse
  3) eight-spoked wheel with axle under horse
  4) pellet-in-ring on horse's shoulder
  5) Yoke-like object above horse

CLASSIFICATION: Cantian J

NOTES: Coin definitely a Dubnovellaunus in Kent type. The inscription is mostly off the flan on all published examples. Allen, perhaps reacting to Evan's report of an Essex origin, read it as 'DIRAS?', thereby suggesting a

Trinovantian/Catuvellaunian origin. Evans noted it similar to coins of Dubnovellaunus and Vosenos, but felt the coin an Essex type because of a Colchester find. He read the inscription as 'DUBORIG'. However, the slightly banded obverse proves it Kentish, and the privy mark matches up with the other coins in the series. Speculatively, 'DOBORIG' is 'DUBNOVELLAUNUS RIGONIS', abbreviated.

Typical weight given.

163–1     DUBNOVELLAUNUS IN KENT          ER
          30–23 B.C.

A´ Quarter Stater 11 mm 1.3 gms.

OBV: Plain with slight banding
Identifying points:
> 1) Banding slight—only a raised band across centre

REV: Celticized horse right
Identifying points:
> 1) pellet under neck
> 2) horse has necklace
> 3) five-pointed outline star under horse
> 4) pellet-in-ring motif above horse with three pellets near it

CLASSIFICATION: Cantian J

NOTES: Horse possibly has belt.
Typical weight given.

164–1     DUBNOVELLAUNUS IN KENT          ER
          30–23 B.C.

Æ unit 13 mm

OBV: Serpent-pinwheel
Identifying points:
> 1) four-armed pinwheel made of serpents.
> 2) pellet-in-ring in centre
> 3) bucranium in each angle of pinwheel

REV: Celticized horse right

Identifying points:
   1) pellet under neck
   2) pellet-in-ring motif behind horse
   3) horse has necklace and belt
   4) five-point outline star below horse
   5) wavy tail

CLASSIFICATION: Cantian J

NOTES: Allen described this coin as a 'North Thames
       Type' erroneously. The privy marks match
       up with Dubnovellaunus' First Coinage, and
       the coin may be transitional to the Second
       Coinage, with the bucranium and wavy tail
       motifs.
       Most are in museums.

165-1    DUBNOVELLAUNUS IN KENT                    ER
         30-23 B.C.
         Æ unit 12 mm 0.9-1.1 gms.

OBV: Celticized head left
Identifying points:
   1) DVBNO in front of head
   2) head beardless, possibly laureate

REV: Pegasus right
Identifying points:
   1) pellet below neck
   2) pegasus has necklace and belt
   3) box with cross-hatching below pegasus
   4) asterisks above and below pegasus
   5) pellet-in-ring motif behind pegasus

CLASSIFICATION: Cantian J

NOTES: A coin of Cuhobeline copies the reverse type
       of this coin—see 2053-1. Henig's alternate
       suggestion the reverses may copy a gem is
       not problematic, one may be inspired by a
       gem, and the other copied from it, or
       both may be derived from similiar engraved
       stones.
       Most are in museums.

166-1    DUBNOVELLAUNUS IN KENT                    ER
         30-23 B.C.
         Æ unit 15 mm 2.4-2.7 gms.

OBV: Celticized horse right
Identifying points:
    1) horse's head turned to rear
    2) pellet under neck

REV: Lion left
Identifying points:
    1) Box below lion with DVBN

CLASSIFICATION: Cantian J

NOTES: A coin of Cunobeline copies the reverse type
       of this coin—see 2107-1. Henig's alternate
       suggestion the reverses may copy a gem is
       not problematic, one may inspired by a gem,
       and the other copied from it, or both may
       be derived from similiar engraved stones.
       Most are in museums.

167-1    DUBNOVELLAUNUS IN KENT                    ER
         30-23 B.C.
         Æ Unit 2.1 gms. 14 mm

OBV: Celticized boar left
Identifying points:
    1) pellet-in-ring motif below boar
    2) pellet-in-ring motif near boar's tail
    3) pellet near boar's tail
    4) wreath above boar

REV: Celticized horse right
Identifying points:
    1) five-point outline star below horse
    2) horse raises front leg
    3) pellet-in-ring motif above and below raised
       leg
    4) pellet below horse's neck
    5) horse has necklace and belt

CLASSIFICATION: Cantian J

NOTES: Illustrated coin found in Essex in 1979.
       Second coin in Bibliotheque Nationale;
       Paris, De La Tour number 8473.

## SECOND COINAGE

The Second Coinage deletes the pellet from below the neck, and the bucranium now appears on the gold. The horse's raised leg on the silver and bronze may be a privy mark. In general, the horses are slightly more Romanized, less abstract, than on the First Coinage. Coin 164–1, also carrying the bucranium, may be a transitional silver type between the First and Second coinages.

169–1    DUBNOVELLAUNUS IN KENT                    ER
23–17 B.C.

N Stater 20 mm 5.1–5.3 gms.

OBV: Plain with slight banding
Identifying points:
1) banding slight—only a raised band across the centre

REV: Celticized horse right
Identifying points:
1) inscription above horse
2) bucranium between horse and inscription
3) pellet-in-ring motifs above horse's head and behind and below animal

CLASSIFICATION: Cantian K

NOTES: Typical weight given.
The standard weight, which should be about 5.6 gms. is probably not revealed because of the small number of recorded coins.
Inscription DVBNOVELLAUNUS, probably, but uncertain if complete legend actually appears.

170–1    DUBNOVELLAUNUS IN KENT                    ER
23–17 B.C.

N Quarter Stater 12 mm 1.1–1.3 gms.

OBV: Plain with slight banding
Identifying points:
1) banding slight—only a raised band across the centre

REV: Celticized horse right

Identifying points:
>    1) rings above horse's head and tail, and in front of animal
>    2) 'V-shaped' object above horse (disintegrated bucranium)

CLASSIFICATION: Cantian K

NOTES: Typical weight given.

171–1     **DUBNOVELLAUNUS IN KENT**     ER
23–17 B.C.
Æ Unit 13 mm 0.7 gms.

OBV: Uncertain animal right
Identifying points:
>    1) DVBN inscription
>    2) pellet-in-ring motifs above and behind animal
>    3) wavy tail as on 164–1

REV: Celticized horse left
Identifying points:
>    1) pellet-in-ring motifs above, below and in front of horse
>    2) horse's right front leg raised
>    3) DVBNO above horse

CLASSIFICATION: Cantian K

173–1     **DUBNOVELLAUNUS IN KENT**     ER
23–17 B.C.
Æ Unit 15 mm 2.6 gms.

OBV: Boar right
Identifying points:
>    1) DVBNO above boar

REV: Celticized horse left
Identifying points:
>    1) horse's right front leg raised

CLASSIFICATION: Cantian K

NOTES: A Gaulish origin has also been claimed for this coin.

## THIRD COINAGE

The Third Coinage introduces thoroughly Romanized designs to the silver and bronze. No distinguishing privy mark identifies the series consistently, though the gold and silver have a pronounced pellet-in-ring motif in the field. The Third Coinage's quarter stater awaits discovery.

176-1     DUBNOVELLAUNUS IN KENT        ER
                17-10 B.C.
                N Stater 17 mm 5.6 gms.

OBV: Plain with slight banding
Identifying points:
     1) slight banding—only a raised band across the centre

REV: Celticized horse right
Identifying points:
     1) six-spoked wheel with axle below horse
     2) pellet-in-ring above horse
     3) 'sunburst' in front of horse
     4) inscription above horse

CLASSIFICATION: Cantian L

NOTES: Typical weight given, but likely to be the standard weight as well.
Inscription contains at least the letters DVBNOVI.
Modern forgery known, see 176-1F.

178-1     DUBNOVELLAUNUS IN KENT        ER
                17-10 B.C.
                Æ Unit 14 mm 0.9 gms.

OBV: Horned animal left
Identifying points:
     1) fan-like object above animal
     2) pellet-in-ring motifs below animal
     3) pellet border

REV: Seated metalworker
Identifying points:
     1) man seated on cushion left
     2) man holds hammer
     3) pellet-in-ring motif in front of man
     4) inscription DVBNO behind man

CLASSIFICATION: Cantian L

NOTES: A coin of Cunobeline, 2097-1, copies this coin's reverse design.

Henig suggests reverse design is adapted from an engraved gemstone.

180-1 **DUBNOVELLAUNUS IN KENT** ER

17-10 B.C.

Æ Unit 13 mm 1.9 gms.

OBV: Boar right

Identifying points:

    1) inscription DVBNO between two lines below boar

REV: Eagle standing three-quarters right

Identifying points:

    1) Eagle's wings spread

CLASSIFICATION: Cantian L

NOTES: A coin of Cunobeline's, 2105-1, copies this coin's reverse design.

Henig suggests the reverse design is adapted from an engraved gemstone.

Most are in museums.

181-1 **DUBNOVELLAUNUS IN KENT** ER

17-10 B.C.

Æ Unit 15 mm 2.3 gms.

OBV: Boar left

Identifying points:

    1) inscription DVBNO above boar

    2) pellet-in-ring motif below boar

REV: Horseman right

Identifying points:

    1) horseman hold object, possibly carnyx

CLASSIFICATION: Cantian L

NOTES: Most are in museums.

## VOSENOS

Vonenos, a short-lived ruler, issued a single coinage. All his types are known in only a handful of examples. On the gold, the banding, seen only slightly on the coinage of Dubnovellaunus, becomes pronounced.

184–1    VOSENOS 10–5 B.C.                                    ER
A′ Stater 17 mm 5.4 gms.

OBV: Plain with pronounced bands
Identifying points:
    1) three pronounced, raised bands

REV: Celticized horse left
Identifying points:
    1) pellet-in-ring motif on shoulder, above and in front of horse
    2) bucranium above horse
    3) horned serpent below horse
    4) inscription above horse, contains at least the letters NOS, probably VOSENOS

CLASSIFICATION: Cantian M

NOTES: Most in museums.
    Typical weight given, also likely to be the standard weight.

185–1    VOSENOS 10–5 B.C.                                    ER
A′ Quarter Stater 11 mm 1.3 gms.

OBV: Plain with pronounced bands
Identifying points:
    1) three pronounced, raised bands

REV: Celticized horse right
Identifying points:
    1) pellet-in-ring motif above horse's rump
    2) ring with six-pointed star above horse
    3) pellet under neck and tail
    4) inscription under horse VOSII
    5) two pellet-in-ring motifs above horse

CLASSIFICATION: Cantian M

NOTES: Typical weight given.

186-1    VOSENOS 10-5 B.C.                                    ER
AR Unit 16 mm 1.1 gms.

OBV: Horse and griffin
Identifying points:
1) horse and griffin standing on two legs
2) pellet-in-ring motifs between animals in vertical column
3) pellet-in-ring motifs above animals in row
4) pellet border

REV: Celticized horse right
Identifying points:
1) three pellet-in-ring motifs in front of horse
2) pellet-in-ring motifs below exergual line
3) inscription between two lines diagonally above horse, retrograde, reading VODENOS or VODENIOS

CLASSIFICATION: Cantian M

187-1    VOSENOS 10-5 B.C                                     ER
Æ Unit 13 mm 1.9 gms.

OBV: Boar left
Identifying points:
1) meandering wreath above boar
2) probable pellet border

REV: Celticized horse left
Identifying points:
1) horse similiar to one on stater
2) pellet-in-ring motifs in field
3) pellet border

CLASSIFICATION: Cantian M

NOTES: Most in museums.

## POST-VOSENOS COINAGE

Sometime during the Trinovantian/Catuvellaunian Interregnum, Vosenos disappears and the Atrebatic/Regnan ruler Eppillus appears. Eppillus issues a special coinage for use in Kent, including a Victory stater. The coins point to an invasion with a travelling mint following the invaders. Eppillus' occupation of Kent is also short-lived because Cunobeline drives him out. At this point Cunobeline's coins become the normal coins of Kent for the next thirty years.

For the coins of Eppillus in Kent, refer to the coinage of the Atrebates/Regni, 430-1 to 453-1. The coins of Cunobeline which circulated in Kent are the normal Trinovantian/Catuvellaunian issues.

## AMMINIUS

After Cunobeline's death, a local Kentish ruler appears, Amminius, who strikes two small issues of silver and bronze coins prior to the Roman invasion of 43 A.D.

### FIRST COINAGE

The first coinage is made up of coins with Romanized designs. The designs are well-engraved.

192-1     AMMINIUS 35–38 A.D.          ER
Æ Unit 12 mm 0.9 gms.

OBV: Plant in circle
Identifying points:
     1) plant has seven stalks
     2) inscription acound circle AMMINIUS

REV: Pegasus right
Identifying points:
     1) pellet above pegasus
     2) inscription DVN above exergual line

CLASSIFICATION: Cantian N

NOTES: Obverse possibly adapted from an engraved gemstone with a fruiting palm tree design. Reverse adapted from a coin of Tasciovanus 1788-1, in turn adapted from a Roman denarius of P. Petronius Turpilianus, RIC I (Augustus), 115.
Wanborough finds reported, but cannot be confirmed.

193-1     AMMINIUS 35–38 A.D.          ER
Æ Unit 13 mm 2.5 gms.

OBV: Wreath
Identifying points:
     1) box in wreath
     2) inscription AM in wreath

REV: Celticized horse right
Identifying points:
     1) inscription DVNO above exergual line
     2) Horse has left front leg raised

CLASSIFICATION: Cantian N

NOTES: Wanborough finds reported, but cannot be confirmed.

## SECOND COINAGE

Amminius' Second Coinage is cruder in execution than the First. The coins are characterized by a Capricorn on the reverse. These are the last Celtic coins struck in Kent, on the eve of the Claudian invasion. A silver minim with an 'A' in an eight-sided star and bird reverse, traditionally assigned to Amminius is actually a coin of Verica (561–1)—a type-series of these was found in the Wanborough Hoard.

194–1     AMMINIUS 38–40 A.D.                          VR
          Æ Unit 12 mm 0.8 gms.

          OBV: Wreath
          Identifying points:
               1) circle inside wreath
               2) letter A inside circle

          REV: Hippocamp right
          Identifying points:
               1) inscription AM below hippocamp
               2) pellet border

          CLASSIFICATION: Cantian O

          NOTES: design possibly adapted from a gemstone
                 with a hippocamp.
                 Several were found in the Wanborough
                 Hoard.

195–1     AMMINIUS 38–40 A.D.                          ER
          Æ Unit 13 mm 1.5 gms.

          OBV: Head right
          Identifying points:
               1) too poorly preserved to see details

          REV: Hippocamp right
          Identifying points:
               1) as on 194–1

          CLASSIFICATION: Cantian O

          NOTES: Head probably adapted from denarius of
                 Augustus, but exact type not yet identified.
                 Design possibly adapted from a gemstone
                 with a hippocamp.

# THE COINAGE OF THE ATREBATES/REGNI

The Atrebates/Regni occupied the territory that is today Berkshire, Sussex and parts of Hampshire. Whether two distinct tribes occupied separate areas is not known because the Regni are virtually unknown to history until the Roman period. The Atrebates, on the other hand, are mentioned by Caesar-he noted the Gaulish Atrebates had tribal members on both sides of the Channel. Traditionally, the Atrebates/Regni have been treated numismatically as one tribe, and there is no reason to change this approach. Only one coinage circulated in the tribal territory.

Initially, the Atrebates/Regni were one of the most advanced groups in Britain. They had trading contacts with Belgic Gaul in the late second and early first centuries B.C., and were one of the first tribes to strike coins. Their later coins served as prototypes for the Trinovantian/Catuvellaunian coinage during the Gallic War.

After the war, however, their position changed dramatically. They evidently fell out of favour with the Romans because the cross-Channel trading rights were given to the Trinovantes/Catuvellauni instead. The loss of trading rights may be the result of Commius' activities during the War.

Commius, at first a supporter of Caesar, became disillusioned with the Romans and went over to Vercingetorix. After the collapse of Celtic resistance at Alesia, he fled to join the British part of his tribe. Later, the Atrebates/Regni struck coins with his name, and possibly the acceptance of Commius in Britain was the reason the Atrebates/Regni fell out of favour.

The change in trading rights altered the relative fortunes of the two tribes forever. By the end of the millennium, the Trinovantes/Catuvellauni had economic influence throughout southern Britain and had begun to rival the Atrebates/Regni in influence.

The Atrebates/Regni seized the opportunity of the Trinovantian/Catuvellaunian Interregnum to mount a military incursion into Kent under their leader, Eppillus. Eppillus struck a victory stater commemorating the initial success of the expedition. The incursion was cut short, however, by the elevation of Cunobeline to the Trinovantian/Catuvellaunian throne. He drove the Atrebates/Regni out of Kent and Eppillus promptly disappeared. He is replaced on the coins by Verica, a self-styled 'son of Commius'.

Sometime before the Claudian invasion, Verica was in turn overthrown. He probably was the historical Celtic leader 'Bericus' who appeared in Rome seeking aid from Claudius. Verica was replaced on the coins by Epaticcus, who styled himself a 'son of Tasciovanus'. Whether the family–tie was real is not so important, the result was the Atrebatic/Regnan leadership was now held by a Trinovantian/Catuvellaunian sympathizer.

Shortly before the Claudian invasion, Epaticcus was replaced by Caratacus, the famous leader of the British resistance against the Roman invaders. The

Atrebatic/Regnan coinage came to an end during the forties, as Caratacus fled westwards to lead the resistance amongst the tribes in Wales.

One Atrebatic/Regnan leader known to history, Cogidubnus, has not yet been identified on the coinage. It seems he was not elevated to leadership until the coinage had come to an end.

The oppidum of Calleva, Silchester today, was the site of the Atrebatic/Regnan mint, and the name Calleva appears on coins of Eppillus. The other leaders may have had mints elsewhere, but none have been identified.

# THE ATREBATIC/REGNAN UNINSCRIBED COINAGE

Imported Ambiani staters were the first coins used by the Atrebates/Regni. Some Large Flan, Abstract Design and Gallic War Type coins are known from the tribal territory. By 75 B.C, the tribe was striking **WESTERHAM TYPE** staters, amongst the heaviest (and thus earliest) of all British types.

The Westerham Type was replaced by the lighter **ATREBATIC ABSTRACT TYPE** during the Gallic War. The tribe produced an enormous number of these staters and quarters during the War. During the period Commius collaborated with Caesar, the tribe must have been part of the scheme against the Durotriges, and would have received aid from the Romans to obtain war matériel.

# UNINSCRIBED GOLD COINS

200-1     WESTERHAM TYPE 75-60 B.C.          R
A⁄ Stater 6.6 gms. 18 mm

OBV: Abstracted head of Apollo right
Identifying points:
    1) wreath: leaves downwards
    2) spike-with-crescent

REV: Disjointed horse left
Identifying points:
    1) pellet under horse
    2) horse more disjointed than on the imported
       AV staters

CLASSIFICATION: Atrebatic A

NOTES: Many in museums.
       Standard weight given.

202-1     WESTERHAM TYPE 75–60 B.C.          R
Æ Stater 6.5 gms. 19 mm

OBV: Abstracted head of Apollo right
Identifying points:
    1) wreath: leaves upwards
    2) spike-with-curve

REV: Disjointed horse left
Identifying points:
    1) pellet under horse
    2) horse more disjointed than on the imported
       AV staters

CLASSIFICATION: Atrebatic A

NOTES: Many are in museums.
       Standard weight given.

210-1     ATREBATIC ABSTRACT TYPE 55–45 B.C.     R
Æ Stater 5.9 gms. 18 mm

OBV: Abstracted head of Apollo right
Identifying points:
    1) wreath with leaves downwards, curved ar-
       ound face
    2) spike-with-crescent has pellet terminal and
       one additional pellet

REV: Disjointed horse right
Identifying points:
    1) horse has triple–tail with pellet terminals
    2) eight-spoked wheel under horse
    3) horse's ear made of two curves forming oval
    4) curved, zig–zag exergual line

CLASSIFICATION: Atrebatic B

NOTES: Standard weight given.

212-1     ATREBATIC ABSTRACT TYPE 55–45 B.C.     R
Æ Stater 5.9 gms. 18 mm

OBV: Abstracted head of Apollo right
Identifying points:
    1) series of small rings scattered within hair
    2) spike ornamented with three pellets

REV: Disjointed horse right
Identifying points:
1) horse has triple-tail with pellet terminals
2) horse's ear made up of two curves forming oval

CLASSIFICATION: Atrebatic B

NOTES: Standard weight given.

212–3    ATREBATIC ABSTRACT TYPE 55–45 B.C.   ER
N/Æ Plated Stater ca. 3.8 gms. 19 mm

OBV: Abstracted head of Apollo right
Identifying points:
1) as 212-1

REV: Disjointed horse right
Identifying points:
1) as 212-1

CLASSIFICATION: Atrebatic B

NOTES: Actual weight of illustrated coin given.
Ancient forgery.

212–5    ATREBATIC ABSTRACT TYPE 55–45 B.C.    R
N Stater 5.9 gms. 19 mm

OBV: Abstracted head of Apollo right
Identifying points:
1) two lines connect wreath and outline crescent
2) bird-like face hidden above outline crescent

REV: Disjointed horse right
Identifying points:
1) as 212-1
2) zig-zag line below horse

CLASSIFICATION: Atrebatic B

NOTES: Standard weight given.

214-1     ATREBATIC ABSTRACT TYPE              R
          55-45 B.C.
          N Stater 5.9 gms. 18 mm

OBV: Abstracted head of Apollo right
Identifying points:
    1) series of small rings scattered within hair
    2) spike ornamented with three pellets or
       pellet-in-ring motifs

REV: Disjointed horse right
Identifying points:
    1) horse has triple-tail with pellet terminals
    2) horse's ear made up of two curves forming
       oval
    3) six-spoked wheel below horse
    4) pellet below crescent-hand of charioteer

CLASSIFICATION: Atrebatic B

NOTES: Standard weight given.

216-1     ATREBATIC ABSTRACT TYPE              R
          55-45 B.C.
          N Stater 5.9 gms. 18 mm

OBV: Traditionally-styled uniface
Identifying points:
1) well-worn die with abstracted
   head of Apollo

REV: Disjointed horse right
Identifying points:
    1) horse has triple-tail with pellet terminal
    2) eight-spoked wheel below horse

CLASSIFICATION: Atrebatic B

NOTES: Standard weight given.
      Six and seven-spoked wheels also known.

## ATREBATIC ABSTRACT TYPE FRACTIONAL STATERS

These are fractional denominations of which there are a large number of varieties. It is uncertain whether they should be called quarter staters and thus the term 'fractional' is used. The intricate design is struck on a small flan and crucial details may be missing. The weights vary from 1.0 to 1.4 grammes, indicating the heavier coins are actually of Gallic War date, while the lighter issues are probably post-war. The series has been catalogued by three major subtypes: Apollo heads, Apollo head variations, and alternate obverses.

## APOLLO HEAD TYPES

**220-1**     **ATREBATIC ABSTRACT TYPE**          ER
55-45 B.C.

Aʹ Fractional Stater 16 mm

OBV: Abstracted head of Apollo right
Identifying points:
    1) spike is decorated with three pellet-in-ring motifs

REV: Celticized horse right
Identifying points:
    1) horse has triple-tail with pellet terminals
    2) dahlia above horse
    3) spoked wheel below horse
    4) collar around horse's neck, and strap around belly beginning to emerge as distinct elements

CLASSIFICATION: Atrebatic B
NOTES: Many are in museums

**222-1**     **ATREBATIC ABSTRACT TYPE 55-45 B.C.**     R

Aʹ Fractional Stater 14 mm

OBV: Abstracted head of Apollo right
Identifying points:
    1) spike is decorated with three pellet-in-ring motifs

REV: Celticized horse right
Identifying points:
    1) horse has triple-tail with pellet terminals
    2) complex flower with pellet-in-ring motif at centre
    3) spoked wheel with axle
    4) collar around horse's neck
    5) strap around horse's belly

CLASSIFICATION: Atrebatic B
NOTES: Many are in museums

224-1 ATREBATIC ABSTRACT TYPE ER
55–45 B.C.
A′ Fractional Stater 15 mm

OBV: Abstracted head of Apollo right
Identifying points:
1) seven or eight-spoked wheel with axle
2) spike ornamented with three pellet-in-ring motifs

REV: Celticized horse right
Identifying points:
1) horse has triple–tail with pellet terminals
2) collar around horse's neck
3) strap around horse's belly
4) eight-spoked wheel with axle above and below horse

CLASSIFICATION: Atrebatic B

NOTES: Many are in museums

226-1 ATREBATIC ABSTRACT TYPE VR
55–45 B.C.
A′ Fractional Stater 12 mm

OBV: Abstracted head of Apollo right
Identifying points:
1) spike ornamented with four pellets

REV: Celticized horse right
Identifying points:
1) horse has triple–tail with pellet terminals
2) three solid crescents above horse
3) strap around horse's belly
4) dahlia above horse
5) cog wheel below horse

CLASSIFICATION: Atrebatic B

NOTES: Most are in museums

228-1 ATREBATIC ABSTRACT TYPE VR
55–45 B.C.
A′ Fractional Stater 12 mm

OBV: Abstracted head of Apollo right
Identifying points:
1) spike ornamented with three pellets or pellet-in-ring motifs

REV: Celticized horse right
Identifying points:
1) horse has triple-tail probably with pellet terminals
2) eleven-petalled flower with uncertain centre
3) cog wheel without central pellet below horse

CLASSIFICATION: Atrebatic B

230-1       ATREBATIC ABSTRACT TYPE                ER
55-45 B.C.
N Fractional Stater 12 mm

OBV: Abstracted head of Apollo right
Identifying points:
1) spike ornamented with three pellets

REV: Celticized horse left
Identifying points:
1) horse has triple-tail
2) strap around horse's belly
3) dahlia above horse
4) anemone below horse

CLASSIFICATION: Atrebatic B

NOTES: Most are in museums

232-1       ATREBATIC ABSTRACT TYPE                ER
55-45 B.C.
N Fractional Stater 11 mm

OBV: Abstracted head of Apollo right
Identifying points:
1) spike replaced by two parallel lines with pellet-in-ring terminals

REV: Celticized horse left
Identifying points:
1) horse has triple-tail
2) collar around horse's neck
3) strap around horse's belly
4) uncertaim complex flower with small pellets

CLASSIFICATION: Atrebatic B

## APOLLO HEAD VARIATIONS

234-1      ATREBATIC ABSTRACT TYPE                    ER
           55–45 B.C.
N Quarter Stater 12 mm

OBV: Degraded head of Apollo
Identifying points:
1) laurel leaves downwards
2) spike made up of lines with pellet-in-ring motifs
3) pellet-in-ring motifs in vestiges of hair

REV: Celticized horse right
Identifying points:
1) eight-spoked wheel with axle above horse
2) anemone below horse
3) pellet-in-ring motifs near tail

CLASSIFICATION: Atrebatic B

NOTES: Though the type appears to be Atrebatic/Regnan, a Trinovantian/Catuvellaunian origin is also possible.

236-1      ATREBATIC ABSTRACT TYPE                    ER
           55–45 B.C.
N Fractional Stater 14 mm

OBV: Apollo head variation
Identifying points:
1) symmetrical design diagonally arranged
2) centre occupied by two multi-spoked wheels
3) wreath split in two and placed on either side of wheels
4) curls of hair beyond wreath on both sides of wreath

REV: Celticized horse left
Identifying points:
1) horse has triple-tail
2) strap around horse's belly
3) cog wheel within circle above horse
4) bird with curved bill right below horse

CLASSIFICATION: Atrebatic B
NOTES: Some are in museums
Modern forgery exists—see 236–1F.

242-1     ATREBATIC ABSTRACT TYPE          ER
          55-45 B.C.

N Fractional Stater 10 mm

OBV: Apollo head variation
Identifying points:
    1) pellet-in-ring surrounded by circle of pellets,
       the whole inserted into central portion of
       wreath

REV: Celticized horse left
Identifying points:
    1) pellet-in-ring below horse

CLASSIFICATION: Atrebatic B

NOTES: Some are in museums

244-1     ATREBATIC ABSTRACT TYPE          ER
          55-45 B.C.

N Fractional Stater 11 mm

OBV: Crossed wreath of Apollo
Identifying points:
    1) large pellet-in ring motif in centre, almost
       flower-like

REV: Celticized horse right
Identifying points:
    1) horse prances right
    2) flower made up of large pellet with three
       petals around it below horse

CLASSIFICATION: Atrebatic B

NOTES: Many in museums.

244-3     ATREBATIC ABSTRACT TYPE          ER
          55-45 B.C.

N/Æ Plated Fractional Stater ca. 0.7 gms.
10 mm

OBV: Crossed wreath of Apollo
Identifying points:
    1) as 244-1

REV: Celticized horse right
Identifying points:
>1) similiar to 250–1, but dahlia above as well as below horse

CLASSIFICATION: Atrebatic B

NOTES: Likely struck from an ancient forger's dies.

246–1      ATREBATIC ABSTRACT TYPE          ER
           55–45 B.C.
N Fractional Stater 9 mm
OBV: Apollo head variation
Identifying points:
>1) faint traces of Apollo head

REV: Celticized horse right
Identifying points:
>1) horse has double–tail
>2) strap around horse's belly
>3) pellet-in-ring motifs on horse's shoulder and haunch
>4) seven-spoked wheel below horse

CLASSIFICATION: Atrebatic B

NOTES: Most are in museums

250–1      ATREBATIC ABSTRACT TYPE          ER
           55–45 B.C.
N Fractional Stater 11 mm

OBV: Wreath and crescents
Identifying points:
>1) two outline crescents, back–to–back
>2) wreath runs between crescents

REV: Celticized horse right
Identifying points:
>1) dahlia below horse
>2) pellet-in-ring motif on horse's rump
>3) pellet-in-ring motifs in front of and behind horse
>4) uncertain ring–like object above horse

CLASSIFICATION: Atrebatic B

NOTES: Most in museums.

254-1     ATREBATIC ABSTRACT TYPE                    ER
          55–45 B.C.

N Fractional Stater 10 mm

OBV: Floral pattern
Identifying points:
  1) pattern of crossed wreaths
  2) pattern made up of small rings and pellet-in-ring motifs
  3) pellet-in-ring motif in centre

REV: Celticized horse left
Identifying points:
  1) pellet-in-ring motif above horse
  2) two small rings in front of horse

CLASSIFICATION: Atrebatic B

NOTES: Most in museums.

## ALTERNATE OBVERSES

256-1     ATREBATIC ABSTRACT TYPE                    ER
          55–45 B.C.

N Fractional Stater 12 mm

OBV: Cross with curved arms
Identifying points:
  1) each arm of cross terminates in a different animal head

REV: Celticized horse left
Identifying points:
  1) horse has triple–tail
  2) collar on horse's neck
  3) strap around horse's belly
  4) dahlia above horse
  5) anemone below horse

CLASSIFICATION: Atrebatic B

NOTES: Most are in museums.

## UNINSCRIBED SILVER

260-1     EARLY ATREBATIC TYPE 50–45 B.C.          ER

Æ Unit 12 mm

OBV: Abstracted head of Apollo right
Identifying points:
  1) laurel leaves inwards

2) spike made up of lines and pellet-in-ring motifs

3) pellet-in-ring motifs in vestiges of hair

REV: Celticized horse right
Identifying points:
1) wheel below horse
2) horse appears to have triple–tail

CLASSIFICATION: Atrebatic B

NOTES: This is a silver version of 222–1.

262–1      EARLY ATREBATIC TYPE 50–45 B.C.       ER
Æ Unit 1.1 gms. 11 mm

OBV: Celticized head right
Identifying points:
1) large pellet in front of forehead, small ring above the pellet
2) large pellet below chin
3) hair made up of long curves

REV: Celticized horse left
Identifying points:
1) flower above horse made up of a ring with fifteen arms, each ending in a pellet
2) small ring above and below horse's head
3) two small rings and two pellets below horse
4) curved line in front of horse

CLASSIFICATION: Atrebatic B

NOTES: Typical weight is given

264–1      EARLY ATREBATIC TYPE 50–45 B.C.       VR
Æ Unit 1.2 gms. 11 mm

OBV: Celticized head right
Identifying points:
1) oval eye
2) helmet with crest

REV: Celticized horse right
Identifying points:
1) Wheel below horse
2) pellet-in-ring motifs on horse's breast and rump
3) small ring below horse

4) uncertain object above horse made up of a line and small rings

CLASSIFICATION: Atrebatic B

NOTES: Most are in museums.
Typical weight is given.
The prototype for the next two types.

268-1     EARLY ATREBATIC TYPE 50–45 B.C.     ER
Æ Minim 0.2–0.3 gms. 8 mm

OBV: Celticized head right
Identifying points:
1) degraded version of 264-1
2) eye now elongated pellet

REV: Celticized horse right
Identifying points:
1) as 264-1, but wheel below horse is now a ring

CLASSIFICATION: Atrebatic B

NOTES: Most are in museums.
Typical weight is given.
Derived from 264-1.

270-1     EARLY ATREBATIC TYPE 50–45 B.C.     ER
Æ Minim 8 mm

OBV: Celticized head right
Identifying points:
1) as 268-1

REV: Celticized horse right
Identifying points:
1) as 268-1, but no object below horse

CLASSIFICATION: Atrebatic B

NOTES: Most are in museums.
Derived from 264-1.

280-1     DANEBURY TYPE 50–45 B.C.     ER
Æ Unit 11 mm

OBV: Celticized head right
Identifying points:
1) elliptical eye
2) hair made up of elliptical pellets
3) face outlined

REV: Celticized horse right
Identifying points:
    1) pellet-in-ring motif on breast
    2) eight-spoked wheel with axle below horse
    3) wavy-armed star above horse
    4) right foreleg of horse made up of two lines

CLASSIFICATION: Atrebatic B

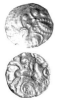

282-1    DANEBURY TYPE 50–45 B.C.       ER
         Æ Unit 12 mm

OBV: Celticized face right
Identifying points:
    1) head made up of a triangle with curved sides
    2) large, ornate coffee bean in front of face
    3) pellet-in-ring motifs below and in front of
       face

REV: Celticized horse right
Identifying points:
    1) elliptical eye
    2) ornate ring below horse
    3) elliptical ear
    4) two pellets and an uncertain object above
       horse

CLASSIFICATION: Atrebatic B

NOTES: The horse has similarities to those on later
       types of Commius and Tincommius.
       The obverse possibly inspired a Dubunnic
       coin—see 1170-1.

284-1    DANEBURY TYPE 50–45 B.C.       ER
         Æ Unit 11 mm

OBV: Celticized head left
Identifying points:
    1) pellet-in-ring motif for eye
    2) two concentric rings in front of nose and
       near chin
    3) large pellet for chin
    4) pellet-in-ring motif encircled by two rings
       of pellets in front of face

REV: Celticized horse left
Identifying points:
1) seven-spoked wheel below horse
2) ring behind horse
3) pellet-in-ring motif above horse
4) two concentric rings above horse

CLASSIFICATION: Atrebatic B

NOTES: Most in museums

286-1    DANEBURY TYPE 50-45 B.C.    ER
Æ Unit 14 mm

OBV: Celticized dragon right
Identifying points:
1) dragon surrounded by pellet-in-ring motifs and crescents
2) pellet-in-ring motif for head
3) curved, serpent-like neck

REV: Celticized horse left
Identifying points:
1) pellet-in-ring motif in front of horse
2) rings near head
3) dahlia above horse
4) cog wheel and two pellets below horse

CLASSIFICATION: Atrebatic B

288-1    DANEBURY TYPE 50-45 B.C.    ER
Æ Unit 14 mm

OBV: Celticized boar left
Identifying points:
1) three crescents above boar
2) lines of pellets above boar
3) large pellet inside ring of pellets below boar

REV: Celticized horse left
Identifying points:
1) small rings around horse
2) pellet-in-ring motif behind horse
3) wheel above horse

CLASSIFICATION: Atrebatic B

NOTES: Most are in museums

290-1        DANEBURY TYPE 50–45 B.C.                        ER
Æ Unit 12 mm

OBV: Crossed wreaths
Identifying points:
    1) pellet-in-ring motif in centre
    2) crescents and pellets in angles of wreath

REV: Celticized horse left
Identifying points:
    1) dahlia above horse
    2) pellet below tail

CLASSIFICATION: Atrebatic B

292-1        DANEBURY TYPE 50–45 B.C.                        ER
Æ Unit 12 mm

OBV: Celticized head left
Identifying points:
    1) head in outline form

REV: Celticized horse right
Identifying points:
    1) horse rears on hind legs
    2) ring below horse
    3) ring below neck
    4) uncertain curves below horse

CLASSIFICATION: Atrebatic B

NOTES: Existing example too poorly preserved to describe in detail.

## COINS DELETED FROM CATALOGUE

Several coins have been deleted from the uninscribed types catalogued in this section. Three coins in Mack's *Coinage of Ancient Britain*, numbers 86, 87 and 87a, have been removed. Both M86 and M87 have been described as 'British or Gaulish' in the past.

M87 is now suspected to be a Gaulish type. Similiar coins with a boar under a horse have been found during excavations at Fanum de Chilly, France. The only example of M87 published was found at Richborough, Kent and a Kentish Cast Bronze coin was found at Fanum de Chilly, suggesting trade may have brought the Gaulish coin to Kent. M87a is a definite Fanum de Chilly type. M86, possibly carrying an image of Cernunnos, is also probably Gaulish. The long-legged horse is unusual for southern British coinage, but is completely at home amongst Gaulish types.

Several new types found in southern Britain, especially Sussex and Hampshire, have not been added to the catalogue. Silver units with pairs of animals back-to-back are similiar to ones from Fanum de Chilly and are thus believed to be Gaulish. One has opposed birds above a boar on the obverse and a boar above a deer on the reverse. Another has opposed horses on the obverse and a triple-tailed horse on the reverse. This one, having a triple-tailed horse, is the most likely of these coins to be British. A silver unit with a facing Cernunnos on the obverse awaits authentication via metallurgical analysis.

## THE ATREBATIC/REGNAN DYNASTIC COINAGE
## THE COINAGE OF COMMIUS

Commius came to Britain after the battle of Alesia to join the British Atrebates. He quickly became their leader because his name soon appears on the Atrebatic/Regnan staters. These are like the Early Atrebatic Type, but have COMMIOS inscribed below the horse. Two types are known, one has an 'E symbol' that also appears on some rare silver units, and this symbol has been used to identify Commius' silver coinage.

Commius' quarter staters have also been identified. These had previously been attributed as 'Gallo-Belgic XC2', but one variety has the same upright 'E' symbol as found on the silver units. A partial inscription, 'CO', appears in front of the horse. The mane of the horse, and the double-stranded tail also link the silver and gold quarters. The quarter staters are almost always found in Britain, in Atrebatic territory, they do not occur on the Continent.

A silver unit with a wheel, and a quarter stater with an anemone are identical in style to the 'E' symbol types, and are undoubtedly part of the same coinage. Thus the coinage of Commius is now seen to be made up of gold staters, quarter staters and silver units, all linked by stylistic details and privy marks.

350-1      COMMIUS 45-30 B.C.                                VR
Æ Stater 5.45 gms. 17 mm

OBV: Celticized head of Apollo right
Identifying points:
    1) wreath: leaves downwards
    2) spike made up of lines and large pellets
    3) two lines connect wreath to curl above hook of spike
    4) ring or pellet near hook
    5) pellet between curls

REV: Celticized horse right
Identifying points:
    1) five-spoked wheel with axle below horse

2) COMMIOS below horse
3) triple–tail on horse
4) three-ringed object, similar to Llyn Cerrig Bach gang-chain
5) vestige of charioteer's arms reduced to a thick line with a curve and pellet at the end

CLASSIFICATION: Atrebatic C

NOTES: Standard weight given, however too few coins are known to estimate it accurately, the true standard is probably 0.1 to 0.2 grammes heavier.
Some in museums.
The alternate use of the ring or pellet near hook may constitute a privy mark.

352-1      COMMIUS 45–30 B.C.                          ER
Ν STATER 5.45 gms. 17 mm

OBV: Celticized head of Apollo right
Identifying points:
    1) as 350–1

REV: Celticized horse right
Identifying points:
    1) similar to 350–1
    2) six-spoked wheel with axle below horse
    3) 'E symbol' above horse

CLASSIFICATION: Atrebatic C

NOTES: Standard weight given, same comment as 350–1.
Change from five to six-spoked wheel with axle may be a privy mark.

353-1      UPRIGHT E TYPE 45–30 B.C.                   VR
Ν Quarter Stater 1.35 gms. 8 mm

OBV: Digamma on blank field
REV: Celticized horse left
Identifying points:
    1) below horse, figure-of-eight with ring in lower loop
    2) 'E' symbol above horse, with arms of E pointing right
    3) middle arm of E is bent downwards
    4) mane made up of curve with lines

5) CO in front of horse
6) double-stranded tail

CLASSIFICATION: Atrebatic C

NOTES: Standard weight given.
Continental type, possibly of of Commius exists, see 87-1.
Many in museums.

353-5        ANEMONE TYPE 45-30 B.C.                    VR
N Quarter Stater 1.35 gms. 9 mm

OBV: Digamma on blank field

REV: Celticized horse left
Identifying points:
1) below horse, figure-of-eight with ring in lower loop
2) anemone above horse
3) mane made up of curve with lines
4) double-stranded tail

CLASSIFICATION: Atrebatic C

NOTES: Standard weight given.
Continental type, possibly of Commius, exists, see 87-1,

355-1        COMMIUS UPRIGHT E TYPE 30-45 B.C.
Æ Unit 0.9 gms. 11 mm                               ER

OBV: Celticized head left
Identifying points:
1) 'curved ladder' for hair
2) eye is crudely-engraved pellet-in-ring motif
3) scroll in front of face

REV: Celticized horse left
Identifying points:
1) backwards 'S' shape below horse
2) 'E symbol' above horse, with arms of E pointing right
3) middle arm of E is bent downwards

CLASSIFICATION: Atrebatic C

NOTES: Some in museums.

355–3    COMMIUS LAZY E TYPE 45–30 B.C.               ER
Æ Unit 1.0 gm 12 mm

OBV: Celticized head left
Identifying points:
1) as 355–1

REV: Celticized horse left
Identifying points:
1) as 355–1
2) arms of 'E symbol' point downwards.

CLASSIFICATION: Atrebatic C

355–5    COMMIUS WHEEL TYPE 30–45 B.C.             ER
Æ Unit 11 mm

OBV: Celticized head left
Identifying points:
1) 'curved ladder' for hair
2) eye is crudely-engraved pellet-in-ring motif
3) two pellet-in-ring motifs in front of face

REV: Celticized horse left
Identifying points:
1) backwards 'S' shape below horse
2) eight (?)-spoked wheel above horse
3) mane made up of curve with lines
4) double-stranded tail

CLASSIFICATION: Atrebatic C

NOTES: Most are in museums

## THE COINAGE OF TINCOMMIUS

The next name appearing on the coins is Tincommius. His rule, lasting about twenty years, ended around the beginning of the Trinovantian/Catuvellaunian Interregnum. Tincommius afterwards appears in Rome seeking assistance from Augustus—evidently he had been deposed. The historical Tincommius, mentioned on the Monumentum Ancyranum (constructed about 7 A.D.) must be the man on the Atrebatic/Regnan coins.

Tincommius' coinage is divided into three periods; based on the stater types. The corresponding quarter staters and silver coins are assigned according to their inscriptions and on typological grounds. The more Romanized designs on the silver are assigned to the later periods.

## TINCOMMIUS FIRST COINAGE

362-1     TINCOMMIUS FIRST COINAGE          ER
          30–25 B.C.
          N Stater 5.45 gms. 17 mm

OBV: Celticized head of Apollo right
Identifying points:
    1) similar to 350–1

REV: Celticized horse right
Identifying points:
    1) pellet-in-ringmotif below and behind horse
    2) TINC COMMI F around horse
    3) triple tail

CLASSIFICATION: Atrebatic D

NOTES: Standard weight given, same comment as
    350–1.

363-1     TINCOMMIUS FIRST COINAGE          ER
          30–25 B.C.
          N Stater 5.45 gms. 17 mm

OBV: Celticized head of Apollo right
Identifying points:
    1) similar to 350–1
REV: Celticized horse right
Identifying points:
    1) TIN DV around horse
    2) triple tail
    3) six-spoked wheel with axle below horse

CLASSIFICATION: Atrebatic D

NOTES: Standard weight given, same comment as
    350–1.
    Many in museums.

365-1     TINCOMMIUS FIRST COINAGE          VR
          30–25 B.C.
          N Quarter Stater 1.2 gms. 10 mm

OBV: Inscribed tablet
Identifying points:
    1) TIN COM in two lines in tablet
    2) zig-zag line in field

REV: Celticized horse left
Identifying points:
    1) wheel and ring above horse
    2) hook below horse
    3) three rings in front of horse

CLASSIFICATION: Atrebatic D

NOTES: Typical weight given.
        Most in museums.

366-1    TINCOMMIUS FIRST COINAGE    C
         30–25 B.C.

A′ Quarter Stater 1.2 gms. 10 mm

OBV: Spiral
Identifying points:
    1) multi-armed spiral with large pellet in centre

REV: Celticized horse right
Identifying points:
    1) 'T' above horse
    2) pellet below horse

CLASSIFICATION: Atrebatic D

NOTES: Many found at Wanborough.

370-1    TINCOMMIUS FIRST COINAGE    S
         30–25 B.C.

ÆR Unit 1.1 gms. 12 mm

OBV: Celticized head facing
Identifying points:
    1) rounded face
    2) thick hair

REV: Bull left
Identifying points:
    1) TIN above bull
    2) C below bull
    3) pellet below tail

CLASSIFICATION: Atrebatic D

NOTES: Many found at Wanborough.

371–1    TINCOMMIUS FIRST COINAGE          C
30–25 B.C.
Æ Unit 1.2–1.3 gms. 12 mm

OBV: Wind flower
Identifying points:
    1) six petals on wind flower
    2) central pellet

REV: Boy riding dolphin right
Identifying points:
    1) TINC in field

CLASSIFICATION: Atrebatic D

NOTES: Many found at Wanborough.
    Seldom well-struck, the reverse is usually difficult to see.
    Reverse adapted from a denarius of L. Lucretius Trio.
    Letters, weakly-struck, have been reported on the obverse.

372–1    TINCOMMIUS FIRST COINAGE          ER
30–25 B.C.
Æ Unit 13 mm

OBV: Inscription in cross
Identifying points:
    1) cross made up of two lines
    2) TINC in angles

REV: Lion left
Identifying points:
    1) S—shaped tail

CLASSIFICATION: Atrebatic D

NOTES: Type possibly found at Wanborough, may be commoner than indicated.
    Not authenticated via metallurgical analysis, but type appears plausible.

## TINCOMMIUS SECOND COINAGE

Mack indicated the mounted warrior theme on the following staters is probably adapted from Roman denarii of the Crepusia family. The C.F. inscription stands for Commius Filius.

375-1     TINCOMMIUS SECOND COINAGE          VR
          25–20 B.C.
          A' Stater 5.3 gms. 16 mm

OBV: Inscribed tablet
Identifying points:
    1) TINC in tablet

REV: Celtic warrior on horse right
Identifying points:
    1) warrior holds spear
    2) six pointed star above horse's head
    3) C F with pellets below horse
    4) exergual line below horse

CLASSIFICATION: Atrebatic E

NOTES: Typical weight given.
        Most in museums.
        Reverse adapted from a denarius of P.
        Crepusius.
        Rarity provided via trade survey.

376-1     TINCOMMIUS SECOND COINAGE          VR
          25–20 B.C.
          A' Stater 4.9 gms.

OBV: Inscribed tablet
Identifying points:
    1) TINC in tablet

REV: Celtic warrior on horse right
Identifying points:
    1) as 375-1 but no star above horse's head
    2) large C in C F

CLASSIFICATION: Atrebatic E

NOTES: Weight of one example given.
        Rarity provided via trade survey.

376-3     TINCOMMIUS SECOND COINAGE          ER
          25–20 B.C.
          A' Stater 17 mm

OBV: Inscribed tablet
Identifying points:
    1) as 376-1, but TINCO in tablet

REV: Celtic warrior on horse right
Identifying points:
    1) as 376-1, but no inscription

CLASSIFICATION: Atrebatic E

NOTES: Existing example in British Museum.

378-1    **TINCOMMIUS MEDUSA TYPE 25-20 B.C.**   S
Aʹ Quarter Stater 1.0 gm 10 mm

OBV: Inscribed tablet
Identifying points:
    1) TINC on tablet
    2) C above tablet
    3) A below tablet
    4) pellet border

REV: Medusa head
Identifying points:
    1) head faces viewer
    2) pellet border

CLASSIFICATION: Atrebatic E

NOTES: Some in museums.
    Typical weight given.
    Many found at Wanborough.
    Mack suggested variety with B below the
    tablet may exist.
    'C A' may indicate Calleva mint.
    Reverse adapted from a denarius of L.
    Aquilius Florus.

379-1    **TINCOMMIUS SECOND COINAGE**   R
    25-20 B.C.
Aʹ Quarter Stater 1.1 gms. 9 mm

OBV: Inscribed tablet
Identifying points:
    1) TIN on tablet

REV: Celticized horse left
Identifying points:
    1) three pointed star above horse

CLASSIFICATION: Atrebatic E

NOTES: Some in museums.
    Some found at Wanborough.
    Typical weight given.
    Rarity provided via trade survey.

381-1    TINCOMMIUS SECOND COINAGE        ER
         25-20 B.C.
         Æ Unit 12 mm

OBV: Celticized head right
Identifying points:
    1) head has laurel wreath
    2) short lines for hair

REV: Celticized bull right
Identifying points:
    1) Bull rears on hind legs
    2) TIN above bull
    3) pellet-in-ring motif below bull
    4) bull's head faces

CLASSIFICATION: Atrebatic E

NOTE: Most in museums.

381-3    TINCOMMIUS SECOND COINAGE        ER
         25-20 B.C.
         Æ Unit 12 mm

OBV: Celticized head right
Identifying points:
    1) as 381-1, but cruder head

REV: Celticized bull right
Identifying points:
    1) Bull butting
    2) TI above bull
    3) NC below bull

CLASSIFICATION: Atrebatic E.

NOTES: Type possibly from Wanborough, could be
       commoner than indicated.
       Not authenticated via metallurgical analysis,
       but appears genuine.

382-1    TINCOMMIUS SECOND COINAGE         C
         25-20 B.C.
         Æ Unit 13 mm

OBV: Inscription
Identifying points:
    1) TINC around central pellet

REV: Animal left
Identifying points:
    1) animal prancing

CLASSIFICATION: Atrebatic E

NOTES: Many found at Wanborough.
Rarity provided via trade survey.

383-1    TINCOMMIUS SECOND COINAGE    R
25-20 B.C.
Æ Minim 0.4 gms. 9 mm

OBV: Geometric pattern
Identifying points:
    1) two interlocking squares
    2) squares have inwardly-curved sides
    3) 'C.F' in centre

REV: Animal right
Identifying points:
    1) animal probably a boar or dog
    2) T I above animal
    3) N C below animal

CLASSIFICATION: Atrebatic E

NOTES: Some found at Wanborough.
Rarity provided via trade survey.

383-5    TINCOMMIUS SECOND COINAGE    ER
25-20 B.C.
Æ Minim 0.4 gms. 9 mm

OBV: Geometric pattern
Identifying points:
    1) two interlocking squares
    2) C O inside squares
    3) pellet border
    4) pellets in angles

REV: Bull right
Identifying points:
    1) bull butting right
    2) TI above bull

CLASSIFICATION: Atrebatic E

383-7    TINCOMMIUS SECOND COINAGE    ER
25-20 B.C.
Æ Minim 8 mm

OBV: Letter C in box
Identifying points:
    1) C with pellet to right, all inside box

2) box has curved sides
3) box-with-pellet above and below central box
4) pellet on each side of central box

REV: Bull right
Identifying points:
1) bull butting
2) TIN above bull

CLASSIFICATION: Atrebatic E

384-1    TINCOMMIUS SECOND COINAGE      ER
25-20 B.C.
Æ Minim 0.24 gms. 7 mm

OBV: Box
Identifying points:
1) C and F separated by pellet-in-ring motif inside box
2) pellet on either side of box
3) pellet-in-ring motif above and below box
4) pellet border

REV: Facing Medusa
Identifying points:
1) straight hair
2) legend, illegible below head

CLASSIFICATION: Atrebatic E

NOTES: Most in museums.
Coin has not been authenticated via metallurgical analysis but appears to be a plausible type.

TINCOMMIUS THIRD COINAGE

385-1    TINCOMMIUS THIRD COINAGE      ER
20-10 B.C.
Ν Stater 5.40 gms. 18 mm

OBV: Inscribed tablet
Identifying points:
1) COM.F in tablet

REV: Celtic warrior on horse right
Identifying points:
1) warrior holds spear

2) star and three pellets behind horse and rider
3) TIN below horse
4) pellet  border

CLASSIFICATION: Atrebatic F

NOTES: Standard weight given, same comment as for 350–1.
Most in museums.
Reverse adapted from a denarius of P. Crepusius.

387–1    TINCOMMIUS THIRD COINAGE                R
20–10 B.C.
Æ Quarter Stater 1.2 gms. 8 mm

OBV: Inscribed tablet
Identifying points:
    1) COMF in tablet

REV: Celticized bull right
Identifying points:
    1) TI below bull
    2) N above bull

CLASSIFICATION: Atrebatic F

NOTES: Some in museums.
Typical weight given.
Some found at Wanborough.
Rarity provided via trade survey.

388–1    TINCOMMIUS THIRD COINAGE                C
20–10 B.C.
Æ Quarter Stater 1.2 gms. 8 mm

OBV: Inscribed tablet
Identifying points:
    1) COMF in tablet

REV: Celticized horse left
Identifying points:
    1) TI above horse
    2) C below horse

CLASSIFICATION: Atrebatic F

NOTES: Typical weight given.
Many found at Wanborough.
Rarity provided via trade survey.

389-1 TINCOMMIUS THIRD COINAGE VR
20-10 B.C.
*N* Quarter Stater 1.2 gms.

OBV: Inscribed tablet
Identifying points:
    1) COM in tablet

REV: Celticized horse left
Identifying points:
    1) T above horse

CLASSIFICATION: Atrebatic F

NOTES: Most in museums.
    Typical weight given.
    Some reported from Wanborough.
    Rarity provided via trade survey.

390-1 TINCOMMIUS THIRD COINAGE R
20-10 B.C.
*N* Quarter Stater 1.1 gms. 10 mm

OBV: Inscribed tablet
Identifying points:
    1) COMF in tablet

REV: Celticized horse right
Identifying points:
    1) TIN above horse
    2) C below horse

CLASSIFICATION: Atrebatic F

NOTES: Some in museums.
    Typical weight given.
    Some found at Wanborough, may be com-
    moner than indicated.

396-1 TINCOMMIUS THIRD COINAGE C
20-10 B.C.
*R* Unit 1.3 gms. 11 mm

OBV: Romanized head left
Identifying points:
    1) head beardless, laureate

REV: Bull charging left
Identifying points:
    1) TIN above bull
    2) C below bull

CLASSIFICATION: Atrebatic F

NOTES: Some found at Wanborough.
Rarity provided via trade survey.

397–1    TINCOMMIUS THIRD COINAGE          C
20–10 B.C.
Æ Unit 1.0–1.3 gms. 10 mm

OBV: Romanized head right
Identifying points:
  1) TINCOM in front of face
  2) head laureate and beardless

REV: Eagle
Identifying points:
  1) eagle stands with spread wings

CLASSIFICATION: Atrebatic F

NOTES: Many found at Wanborough.
Mack indicated the coin was copied from a coin of Augustus.
Both obverse and reverse adapted from denarii of Augustus.
Rarity provided via trade survey.

## THE COINAGE OF EPPILLUS

Eppillus' coins are divided into two distinct issues, the Calleva types and the Kentish types. Eppillus assumed the Atrebatic/Regnan leadership after Tincommius had been deposed and exiled about the time of the Trinovantian/Catuvellaunian Interregnum. Sometime after 10 B.C., Trinovantian/Catuvelluanian power was rendered ineffective by the tribe's internal problems and Eppillus decided to test its strength by invading Kent.

The Cantii had used Trinovantian/Catuvellaunian coins for some time, issuing few of their own. Now, a new series appeared carrying the name Eppillus. Eppillus also issued a victory stater in Kent, supporting the idea of a military incursion. By 10 A.D., Cunobeline assumed leadership of the Trinovantes/Catuvellauni and proceeded to drive Eppillus from Kent. Eppillus disappeared about this time, he was probably killed during the incursion in Cantian territory.

The Calleva types, all struck at Silchester, are the normal Atrebatic/Regnan coins of Eppillus. The Kentish types constitute an emergency coinage struck to finance military operations.

## EPPILLUS CALLEVA TYPES

405-1    EPPILLUS EARLY TYPE                    ER
10 B.C.–10 A.D.
Aʹ Stater 5.2 gms. 17 mm

OBV: Celticized head of Apollo right
Identifying points:
> 1) spike made up of lines and pellets
> 2) wreath: leaves downwards

REV: Celticized horse right
Identifying points:
> 1) EPPI above horse
> 2) COMMI F below horse
> 3) three ringed object above horse reminiscent of the Llyn Cerrig Bach gang-chain
> 4) four-spoked wheel below horse
> 5) triple tail on horse

CLASSIFICATION: Atrebatic G

NOTES:  Weight of recorded example given.
A most exceptional coin. The die-cutting and striking appear to be correct for Atrebatic/Regnan work of the time, and the colour appears correct.
Metallurgical data recently confirms authenticity of this coin.

407-1    EPPILLUS 10 B.C.–10 A.D.                    C
Aʹ Quarter stater 1.0–1.2 gms. 9 mm

OBV: Inscription in pellet border
Identifying points:
> 1) CALLEVA
> 2) six pointed star above and below inscription

REV: Celticized horse right
Identifying points:
> 1) EPPI above horse
> 2) daisy below horse

CLASSIFICATION: Atrebatic G

NOTES:  Many found at Wanborough.
Typical weight given.
Modern forgery exists—see 407-1F.

408-1     EPPILLUS 10 B.C.-10 A.D.                    R
N Quarter stater 1.2 gms. 10 mm

OBV: Inscription in pellet border
Identifying points:
    1) as 407-1

REV: Celticized horse right
Identifying points:
    1) as 407-1
    2) ring above horse

CLASSIFICATION: Atrebatic G

NOTES: Some found at Wanborough, may be com-
        moner than indicated.
        Typical weight given.

409-1     EPPILLUS 10 B.C.-10 A.D.                    R
N Quarter Stater 1.2 gms. 9 mm

OBV: Crescent with inscription
Identifying points:
    1) crescent in centre
    2) COMM.F.EPPILLV. around crescent

REV: Celticized horse right
Identifying points:
    1) six pointed star above and below horse

CLASSIFICATION: Atrebatic G

NOTES: Typical weight given.
        Some found at Wanborough.
        Rarity provided via trade survey.

415-1     EPPILLUS 10 B.C.-10 A.D.                    C
AR Unit 1.2 gms. 13 mm

OBV: Crescent with inscription
Identifying points:
    1) outline crescent, points upwards, in centre
    2) REX above crescent
    3) CALLE below crescent
    4) daisy on either side of crescent
    5) pellet border

REV: Eagle right
Identifying points:
    1) eagle's wing spread

2) EPP above eagle's tail
3) pellet border

CLASSIFICATION: Atrebatic G

NOTES: Many found at Wanborough.

Mack transposed the obverse and reverse designations. The crescent is on the convex side and the eagle on the concave.

Variety with obverse legend REX CALL awaits metallurgical analysis to verify authenticity. Catalogue number 416-3 reserved for the REX CALL type.

Obverse adapted from a denarius of L. Lucretius Trio.

Reverse adapted from a denarius of Cn. Nerius or Augustus—Turpilianus.

416-1    EPPILLUS 10 B.C.-10 A.D.                    C
Æ Unit 12 mm

OBV: Celticized head right
Identifying points:
    1) beard made up of pellets
    2) vine border

REV: Boar right
Identifying points:
    1) EPPI above boar
    2) three pellets after EPPI
    3) COM below boar
    4) F above COM
    5) pellet border

CLASSIFICATION: Atrebatic G

NOTES: Many found at Wanborough.

417-1    EPPILLUS 10 B.C.-10 A.D.                    C
Æ Unit 1.2 gms. 13 mm

OBV: Celticized head right
Identifying points:
    1) similar head to that on 416-1
    2) beard made up of strokes
    3) pellet border

REV: Lion right
Identifying points:
  1) lion stands on exergual line
  2) EPP above lion
  3) COM below exergual line
  4) F in front of lion

CLASSIFICATION: Atrebatic G

NOTES: Many found at Wanborough.
       Previously, this type was listed by Mack as a Kentish type, but many of these and similar types have recently been found in the normal tribal area.
       Reverse adapted from a denarius of Mark Anthony.


## SILVER MINIMS

The following types are just appearing as this text is being written. Undoubtedly, there will be many more types appearing in the next few years. This represents an opportunity for original research.

420–1     EPPILLUS 10 B.C.–10 A.D.                    R
          Æ Minim 0.3 gms. 8 mm

OBV: Floral pattern
Identifying points:
  1) pellet-in-ring motif in centre
  2) U's with line in centre, pointing outwards around edge
  3) pellet between U's
  4) pellet border

REV: Eagle right
Identifying points:
  1) eagle as on 415–1
  2) EPPI in front of eagle
  3) pellet border

CLASSIFICATION: Atrebatic G

NOTES: Some found at Wanborough.
       Type appears genuine, awaits metallurgical analysis to establish authenticity.
       Rarity provided via trade survey.

421-1    EPPILLUS 10 B.C.-10 A.D.                    R
Æ Minim 0.3 gms. 9 mm

OBV: Spiral pattern
Identifying points:
1) four armed spiral
2) four pellets in each angle
3) pellet-in-ring motif in centre
4) pellet border

REV: Celticized horse right
Identifying points:
1) EPP above horse

CLASSIFICATION: Atrebatic G

NOTES: Some found at Wanborough.
Type appears genuine, awaits metallurgical
analysis to establish authenticity.
Rarity provided via trade survey.

422-1    EPPILLUS 10 B.C.—10 A.D.                    ER
Æ Minim 8 mm

OBV: Bull's head facing
Identifying points:
1) pellet above and on each side of bull's head
2) pellet border

REV: Ram right
Identifying points:
1) EPP above ram

CLASSIFICATION: Atrebatic G

NOTES: Some found at Wanborough, may
be commoner than indicated.
Type appears genuine, awaits metallurgical
analysis to establish authenticity.

423-1    EPPILLUS 10 B.C.—10 A.D.                    ER
Æ Minim 8 mm

OBV: Wreath-like pattern
Identifying points:
1) pattern made up of a line with curves
crossing it

REV: Boar right
Identifying points:
1) ring below boar
2) boar stands on exergual line
3) uncertain object above boar, possibly vestiges of inscription EPP

CLASSIFICATION: Atrebatic G

NOTES: Some found at Wanborough, may be commoner than indicated.
Type appears genuine, awaits metallurgical analysis to establish authenticity.

## EPPILLUS KENTISH TYPES

430-1    EPPILLUS 10 B.C.–10 A.D.      ER
Æ Stater 5.40 gms. 17 mm

OBV: Inscription in wreath
Identifying points:
1) COMF in wreath
2) wreath has leaves pointing in the clockwise direction

REV: Celtic warrior on horse left
Identifying points:
1) flower below horse
2) pellet-in-ring motifs in field
3) six pointed star above horse
4) EPPILLVS above rider

CLASSIFICATION: Atrebatic H

NOTES: Standard weight given.
Most in museums.

431-1    EPPILLUS VICTORY TYPE      ER
10 B.C.–10 A.D.
Æ Stater 5.40 gms. 18 mm

OBV: Victory left
Identifying points:
1) victory hold wreath in left hand
2) wreath border has leaves pointing in counter-clockwise direction

REV: Chariot right
Identifying points:
    1) chariot has two horses
    2) C.F. below chariot

CLASSIFICATION: Atrebatic H

NOTES: Many in museums.

## THE COINAGE OF VERICA

Verica replaced Eppillus as leader of Atrebates/Regni around 10 A.D.

Cunobeline, after his accession to the Trinovantian/Catuvellaunian leadership, had driven Eppillus and the Atrebates/Regni from Kent. Once Eppillus was deposed—he disappeared completely—peace was restored between the tribes.

Initially, Verica must have been accepted by his more powerful neighbour. By the mid 30's however, he evidently lost the support of Cunobeline. Coins began to appear in the northern part of Atrebatic/Regnan territory carrying the name Epaticcus, who styled himself a son of Tasciovanus. This leader, a Trinovantian/Catuvellaunian sympathizer if not actually a relative of Cunobeline's, soon expanded his influence in Verica's territory. Verica was ultimately deposed by the encroacher and undoubtedly was the Berikos who fled to Rome on the eve of 43 A.D. Verica's appeal for Roman military intervention prompted the Claudian invasion the following year.

Verica struck three successive coinages, distinguished by the types of the staters. The First Coinage staters show a tablet with COMF on the obverse and a mounted warrior with the inscription VIR on the reverse. The Second Coinage staters are almost identical, but add the title REX to the reverse. The third coinage introduces a new design to the obverse, a vine leaf with VI RI on the sides. All three coinages include quarter staters, silver units and silver minims. No bronze coins have been identified and it is likely Verica struck only gold and silver.

## VERICA FIRST COINAGE

460-1    VERICA FIRST COINAGE 10–20 A.D.    ER
    Aʹ Stater 5.40 gms. 16 mm

OBV: Inscription in Tablet
Identifying points:
    1) COMF in incuse tablet
    2) plain field

REV: Celtic warrior on horse right
Identifying points:
    1) warrior holds spear
    2) VIR below horse
    3) five-pointed star above horse
    4) ring behind horse
    5) pellet border

CLASSIFICATION: Atrebatic I

NOTES: Standard weight given.
            Reverse adapted from a denarius of P. Crepusius.

461-1     **VERICA FIRST COINAGE 10-20 A.D.**      ER
         N Stater 5.40 gms. 17 mm

OBV: Inscription in Tablet
Identifying points:
    1) similar to 460-1
    2) pellet-in-ring motif above and below tablet

REV: Celtic warrior on horse right
Identifying points:
    1) similiar to 460-1
    2) daisy behind horse
    3) exergual line below horse
    4) VIR below exergual line
    5) pellet border

CLASSIFICATION: Atrebatic I

NOTES: Standard weight given.

465-1     **VERICA FIRST COINAGE 10-20 A.D.**      ER
         N Quarter Stater 1.0 gms. 8 mm

OBV: Inscription in tablet
Identifying points:
    1) COMF in incuse tablet
    2) solid crescent above and below

REV: Celticized horse left
Identifying points:
    1) VIR above horse
    2) eight-spoked wheel below horse

CLASSIFICATION: Atrebatic I

NOTES: Typical weight given.
        Most in museums.

466-1    **VERICA FIRST COINAGE 10–20 A.D.**          C
AV Quarter Stater 1.2 gms. 9 mm

OBV: Inscription in tablet
Identifying points:
    1) COMF in tablet
    2) pellet border

REV: Celticized horse right
Identifying points:
    1) horse rears on back legs
    2) exergual line
    3) VI above horse
    4) pellet border

CLASSIFICATION: Atrebatic I

NOTES: Typical weight given.
        Many found at Wanborough.

467-1    **VERICA FIRST COINAGE 10–20 A.D.**          C
AV Quarter Stater 1.2 gms. 10 mm

OBV: Inscription in tablet
Identifying points:
    1) COMF in incuse tablet
    2) pellet border

REV: Celticized horse right
Identifying points:
    1) horse stands on exergual line
    2) VI above
    3) horse's left front leg raised
    4) pellet border

CLASSIFICATION: Atrebatic I

NOTES: Typical weight given.
        Many found at Wanborough.
        Rarity provided via trade survey.
        Modern forgery exist—see 467–1F.

468-1    **VERICA FIRST COINAGE 10–20 A.D.**          C
AV Quarter Stater 1.3 gms. 10 mm

OBV: Inscription and scroll pattern
Identifying points:
    1) pellet-in-ring motif in centre
    2) horizontal line runs to right and left from
       pellet-in-ring motif

3) two curved lines run right and left from pellet-in-ring motif
4) COM above
5) FILI below
6) pellet border

REV: Celticized horse right
Identifying points:
1) VIR above horse
2) pellet-in-ring motif below horse
3) pellet border

CLASSIFICATION: Atrebatic I

NOTES: Typical weight given.
Many found at Wanborough.
Rarity provided via trade survey.

470-1    VERICA FIRST COINAGE 10-20 A.D.          C
Æ Unit 1.2 gms. 12 mm

OBV: Inscription in scroll pattern
Identifying points:
1) COMF in centre
2) outline crescent and two pellet-in-ring motifs above and below COMF
3) pellet border

REV: Boar right
Identifying points:
1) boar stands on exergual line
2) VIRI below exergual line
3) six-pointed star above boar

CLASSIFICATION: Atrebatic I

NOTES: Many found at Wanborough.
Reverse adapted from a denarius of M. Voteius.

470-3    VERICA FIRST COINAGE 10-20 A.D.          C
Æ Unit 1.2 gms. 12 mm

OBV: Inscription in scroll pattern
Identifying points:
1) as 470-1, but no pellet-in-ring motifs
REV: Boar right
Identifying points:
1) no exergual line

2) VIRI below boar
3) six-pointed star above boar

CLASSIFICATION: Atrebatic I

NOTES: Many found at Wanborough.
Reverse adapted from a denarius of M.
Voteius.

470–5    VERICA FIRST COINAGE 10–20 A.D.        C
Æ Unit 1.2 gms. 13 mm

OBV: Inscription in scroll pattern
Identifying points:
1) as 470–3

REV: Boar right
Identifying points:
1) boar stands on exergual line
2) VI and pellet below exergual line
3) six-pointed star above boar

CLASSIFICATION: Atrebatic I

NOTES: Many found at Wanborough.
Reverse adapted from a denarius of M.
Voteius.

470–7    VERICA FIRST COINAGE 10–20 A.D.        C
Æ Unit 1.2 gms. 12 mm

OBV: Inscription in scroll pattern
Identifying points:
1) as 470–3

REV: Boar right
Identifying points:
1) as 470–3, but VIR below boar

CLASSIFICATION: Atrebatic I

NOTES: Many found at Wanborough.
Reverse adapted from a denarius of M.
Voteius.

471–1    VERICA FIRST COINAGE 10–20 A.D.        C
Æ Unit 0.6–1.0 gms. 12 mm

OBV: Inscription in tablet and scroll
Identifying points:
1) COMF in tablet
2) solid crescent with pellet and two rings
above and below tablet

3) large circle around entire image
4) pellet border outside circle

REV: Eagle
Identifying points:
    1) eagle faces with wings spread
    2) head turned left
    3) pellet border
    4) VI RI above eagle

CLASSIFICATION: Atrebatic I

NOTES: Many found at Wanborough.

472-1     VERICA FIRST COINAGE 10–20 A.D.            R
Æ Unit 13 mm

OBV: Inscription in scroll pattern
Identifying points:
    1) COMF in centre
    2) pellet above and below COMF
    3) outline crescent with two pellet-in-ring
       motifs above and below COMF
    4) pellet border

REV: Bull right
Identifying points:
    1) bull stands on exergual line
    2) VIR below exergual line
    3) pellet border

CLASSIFICATION: Atrebatic I

NOTES: Some found at Wanborough.
       Rarity provided via trade survey.

473-1     VERICA FIRST COINAGE 10–20 A.D.           ER
Æ Unit 15 mm

OBV: Celticized head left
Identifying points:
    1) pellet-in-ring motif for eye
    2) diadem made up of a line
    3) inscription around head, probably VERIC

REV: Celticized horse left
Identifying points:
    1) outline crescent above horse with three lines
       rising above it

CLASSIFICATION: Atrebatic I

NOTES: Traditionally attributed to Verica,
but possibly an earlier type.

474–1      VERICA FIRST COINAGE 10–20 A.D.          ER
Æ Unit 0.5 gms. 11 mm

OBV: Celticized horse left
Identifying points:
1) pellet-in-ring motifs around horse
2) anemone behind horse
3) outline crescent above horse with lines and
pellets rising from it

REV: Celticized horse right
Identifying points:
1) horse highly stylized
2) pellet-in-ring motifs around horse
3) two wavy lines rise above pellet-in-ring motif
above horse

CLASSIFICATION: Atrebatic I

NOTES: Some in museums.
Traditionally described as a North Thames
Type LX14 by Allen, but now attributed
to Verica. The type is related to 473–1
stylistically. One design element the coins
have in common is the crescent-with-lines
above the horse.
Possibly this and 473–1 are earlier types.

480–1      VERICA FIRST COINAGE 10–20 A.D.          VR
Æ Minim

OBV: Head right
Identifying points:
1) head bare

REV: Horse right
Identifying points:
1) VIRI above horse
2) CO below horse

CLASSIFICATION: Atrebatic I

NOTES: No illustration.
Reports of many finds at Wanborough, but
cannot be confirmed.
Rarity provided via trade survey.

482-1     **VERICA FIRST COINAGE 10-20 A.D.**          S
Æ Minim 0.3 gms. 8 mm

OBV: Geometric pattern
Identifying points:
    1) square with concave sides
    2) central pellet-in-ring motif
    3) pellet-in-ring motif to each side of square

REV: Celticized horse left
Identifying points:
    1) pellet-in-ring motif below horse
    2) wheel above horse, probably has six spokes

CLASSIFICATION: Atrebatic I

NOTES: Many found at Wanborough.
      Rarity provided via trade survey.
      Traditionally attributed to Verica, but possibly an earlier type.

483-1     **VERICA FIRST COINAGE 10-20 A.D.**          VR
Æ Minim 0.3 gms. 9 mm

OBV: Cross
Identifying points:
    1) irregular objects in angles

REV: Irregular object
Identifying points:
    1) possibly an animal, object has irregular outline

CLASSIFICATION: Atrebatic I

NOTES: Some in museums.
      Published example poorly preserved, images not clear, but type is different from other minims.
      Rarity provided via trade survey.

484-1     **VERICA FIRST COINAGE 10-20 A.D.**          R
Æ Minim 9 mm

OBV: Pellet and ring pattern
Identifying points:
    1) pellet-in-ring motif in centre
    2) four groups of three pellets around central pellet-in-ring motif
    3) pellet border

REV: Celticized horse right
Identifying points:
    1) VIR above horse
    2) pellet-in-ring motif below horse

CLASSIFICATION: Atrebatic I

NOTES: Most in museums.
    Mack listed type twice as M120a and 120c
    to illustrate more of image.
    Reports of many finds at Wanborough, but
    cannot be confirmed.
    Rarity provided via trade survey.

485-1    VERICA FIRST COINAGE 10-20 A.D.    VR
    Æ Minim 0.3 gms. 9 mm

OBV: Inscription in plain field
Identifying points:
    1) VIRIC in mirror-image

REV: Boar right
Identifying points:
    1) C above boar
    2) O below boar
    3) pellet border

CLASSIFICATION: Atrebatic I

NOTES: Some found at Wanborough.
    New variety has not been analyzed metal-
    lurgically, but type appears genuine.
    Rarity provided via trade survey.

486-1    VERICA FIRST COINAGE 10-20 A.D.    ER
    Æ Minim 7 mm

OBV: Cross and floral pattern
Identifying points:
    1) two lines form cross
    2) three pellets in each angle
    3) pellet border

REV: Trident
Identifying points:
    1) trident in plain field
    2) pellet border

CLASSIFICATION: Atrebatic I

NOTES: This coin, first shown to Derek Allen in the British Museum during the Second World War, was reported in his 1958 PPS article as a find during excavations at West Harting, Sussex in 1941. The coin (or an identical one) reappeared in New York City in September, 1986.

Reports of many finds at Wanborough, but cannot be confirmed.

Trade survey indicates 'VR', but cannot be confirmed.

487-1      VERICA FIRST COINAGE 10-20 A.D.          ER
Æ Minim 8 mm

OBV: Geometric pattern
Identifying points:
    1) pellet-in-ring motif in centre
    2) four crescents around pellet-in-ring motif
    3) line inside each crescent
    4) three pellets between crescents

REV: Hand holding trident
Identifying points:
    1) V R on sides of hand
    2) EX below hand
    3) crescent above hand

CLASSIFICATION: Atrebatic I

NOTES: Most in museums.
Coin has not been authenticated via metallurgical analysis but appears to be plausible type.

## VERICA SECOND COINAGE

500-1      VERICA SECOND COINAGE 20-25 A.D.         S
Æ Stater 5.40 gms. 16 mm

OBV: Inscription in tablet
Identifying points:
    1) COM.F in incuse tablet
    2) plain field

REV: Celtic warrior on horse right
Identifying points:
    1) warrior brandishes spear

2) VIR above horse
3) REX below horse
4) pellet border

CLASSIFICATION: Atrebatic J

NOTES: Standard weight given.

500-3     VERICA SECOND COINAGE 20–25 A.D.     ER
N/Æ Plated Stater 3.0 gms. 8 mm

OBV: Inscription in tablet
Identifying points:
    1) as 500–1

REV: Celtic warrior on horse right
Identifying points:
    1) as 500–1
    2) blundered legend 'RIX'

CLASSIFICATION: Atrebatic J

NOTES: Struck from ancient forger's dies.
       Example illustrated found at Danebury dur-
       ing excavations.

501-1     VERICA SECOND COINAGE 20–25 A.D.     R
N Quarter Stater 1.3 gms. 12 mm

OBV: Inscription, crescent and star
Identifying points:
    1) VERIC COMF in two lines
    2) solid crescent above inscription
    3) six-pointed star below inscription

REV: Celticized horse right
Identifying points:
    1) seven-pointed star above horse
    2) REX below horse
    3) pellet border

CLASSIFICATION: Atrebatic J

NOTES: Typical weight given.
       Some in museums.
       Some found at Wanborough.

Mack indicated a six-pointed star above the horse, but the published example actually has seven.

Rarity provided via trade survey.

505-1     **VERICA SECOND COINAGE 20-25 A.D.     C**
Æ Unit 1.1 gms. 14 mm

OBV: Inscription in circle
Identifying points:
    1) pellet-in-ring motif in centre
    2) large ring around central pellet-in-ring motif
    3) VERICA COMMI F around large ring
    4) pellet border

REV: Lion right
Identifying points:
    1) solid crescent above lion
    2) REX below lion
    3) pellet border

CLASSIFICATION: Atrebatic J

NOTES: Many found at Wanborough.
        Reverse copied from a coin of Augustus.

506-1     **VERICA SECOND COINAGE 20-25 A.D.     C**
Æ Unit 1.3 gms. 13 mm

OBV: Bull right
Identifying points:
    1) bull lowers head to butt
    2) bull stands on exergual line
    3) VERICA inverted above bull
    4) REX below exergual line
    5) pellet border

REV: Figure standing left
Identifying points:
    1) figure hold branch in right hand
    2) figure holds bust on lance in left hand
    3) COM MI F around figure
    4) exergual line below figure
    5) pellet border

CLASSIFICATION: Atrebatic J

NOTES: Many found at Wanborough.

510-1     VERICA SECOND COINAGE 20–25 A.D.     ER
          Æ Minim 8 mm

OBV: Uncertain figure
Identifying points:
    1) figure possibly a Celtic warrior on horse right
    2) pellet border

REV: Boar right
Identifying points:
    1) O below boar
    2) possibly C above boar
    3) pellet border

CLASSIFICATION: Atrebatic J

NOTES: Type not reported amongst Wanborough finds yet.

510-5     VERICA SECOND COINAGE 20–25 A.D.     ER
          Æ Minim 9 mm

OBV: Geometric pattern
Identifying points:
    1) pellet-in-ring motif in centre
    2) four lines extend from pellet-in-ring motif
    3) crescents with lines in angles

REV: Boar right
Identifying points:
    1) boar charging right
    2) R below boar
    3) pellet border

CLASSIFICATION: Atrebatic J

NOTES: Most are in museums.
    Coin has not been authenticated via metallurgical analysis but appears to be a plausible type.

511-1     VERICA SECOND COINAGE 20–25 A.D.     ER
          Æ Minim 8 mm

OBV: Inscription in tablet
Identifying points:
    1) VIR VAR in two lines inside tablet
    2) pellet border

REV: Pegasus right
Identifying points:
    1) Pegasus rears on hind legs
    2) CO below pegasus
    3) pellet border

CLASSIFICATION: Atrebatic J

NOTES: Many in museums.
      Type not reported amongst Wanborough finds yet.

512-1    **VERICA SECOND COINAGE 20-25 A.D.**    **R**
Æ Minim 0.2 gms. 8 mm

OBV: Bull right
Identifying points:
    1) similiar to 506-1
    2) bull lowers head to butt
    3) exergual line below bull
    4) pellet border

REV: Eagle standing left
Identifying points:
    1) eagle spreads wing
    2) eagle stands on branch

CLASSIFICATION: Atrebatic J

NOTES: Some found at Wanborough.
      Not yet authenticated via metallurgical analysis, the type appears genuine, however. This is the minim corresponding to 506-1. Rarity provided via trade survey.

## VERICA THIRD COINAGE

520-1    **VERICA THIRD COINAGE 25-35 A.D.**    **S**
N Stater 5.40 gms. 17 mm

OBV: Vine leaf
Identifying points:
    1) VI to left of leaf
    2) RI to right of leaf

REV: Celtic warrior on horse right
Identifying points:
    1) warrior holds shield and spear

2) C O F in field: C behind rider, O above horse's head and F below horse
3) horse stands on incomplete 'boxes'
4) pellet border

CLASSIFICATION: Atrebatic K

NOTES: Standard weight given.
Some in museums.
Vine leaf motif possible adapted from ancient intaglios.

520-5     **VERICA THIRD COINAGE 25-35 A.D.**     ER
Ꞵ Stater 5.40 gms. 17 mm

OBV: Vine leaf
Identifying points:
1) as 520-1, but VE to left of leaf

REV: Celtic warrior on horse right
Identifying points:
1) as 520-1

CLASSIFICATION: Atrebatic K

NOTES: Standard weight given.
Most in museums.

520-7     **VERICA SECOND COINAGE 20-25 A.D.**     ER
Ꞵ Stater 5.4 gms. 17 mm

OBV: Vine leaf
Identifying points:
1) as 520-5

REV: Celtic warrior on horse right
Identifying points:
1) as 520-5, but retrograde F below horse

CLASSIFICATION: Atrebatic K

NOTES: Standard weight given.
Most in museums.

525-1     **VERICA THIRD COINAGE 25-35 A.D.**     ER
Ꞵ Quarter Stater 1.0 gms. 10 mm

OBV: Vine leaf
Identifying points:
1) VERI below leaf

REV: Celtic warrior on horse right
Identifying points:
1) warrior holds sword and small round shield
2) horse stands on exergual line
3) F RX in field, probably intended as 'REX'
4) pellet border

CLASSIFICATION: Atrebatic K

NOTES: Typical weight given.
Most in museums.
Obverse possible adapted from ancient intaglios.

526-1    VERICA THIRD COINAGE 25-35 A.D.          ER
Aʹ Quarter Stater 0.9 gms. 9 mm

OBV: Celtic warrior on horse right
Identifying points:
1) warrior holds sword and small round shield
2) COM above horse
3) pellet border

REV: Seated figure right
Identifying points:
1) figure holds spear
2) VERICA around figure
3) exergual line below figure
4) pellet border

CLASSIFICATION: Atrebatic K

NOTES: Typical weight given.
Most in museums.
There is some question which is the obverse, Mack indicated the seated figure. It appears the rider occupies the convex side, which is normally the obverse.
Coin may share obverse die with 527-1.

527-1    VERICA THIRD COINAGE 25-35 A.D.          ER
Aʹ Quarter Stater 0.7 gms. 9 mm

OBV: Celtic warrior on horse right
Identifying points:
1) warrior holds sword and small round shield
2) COM above horse
3) pellet border

REV: Bust right
Identifying points:
1) head is laureate
2) VIRI in front of face

CLASSIFICATION: Atrebatic K

NOTES: Typical weight given.
Most in museums
Mack noted the obverse was copied from a coin of Tiberius.
There is some question which is the obverse, Mack indicated the bust side. It appears the the rider occupies the convex side which is normally the obverse.
Coin may share ovberse die with 526-1.

530-1    VERICA THIRD COINAGE 25-35 A.D.    C
Æ Unit 1.2 gms. 12 mm

OBV: Celtic warrior on horse right
Identifying points:
1) warrior carries oval shield
2) COMMI F below horse
3) pellet border

REV: Celtic warrior on horse right
Identifying points:
1) warrior brandishes spear
2) VERI above horse
3) CA below horse
4) pellet border

CLASSIFICATION: Atrebatic K

NOTES: Many found at Wanborough.
There is some question which is the obverse, Mack indicated the VERICA side. It appears the COMMI F occupies the convex side which is normally the obverse.
Reverse copied from a Roman Rubublican denarius of Q. Pilipus.

531-1    VERICA THIRD COINAGE 25-35 A.D.    C
Æ Unit 1.1 gms. 11 mm

OBV: Two cornucopiae
Identifying points:
1) sceptre between cornucopiae

2) vase below sceptre
3) COMMI F around cornucopiae

REV: Seated figure right
Identifying points:
    1) VERI in front of figure
    2) CA behind figure
    3) figure holds spear
    4) oval shield behind figure
    5) pellet border

CLASSIFICATION: Atrebatic K

NOTES: Many found at Wanborough.
There is some question which is the obverse,
Mack indicated the seated figure side. It
appears the cornucopia side occupies the
convex side which is normally the obverse.
Mack noted obverse (cornucopia side) was
copied from a denarius of Mark Anthony.

532-1      VERICA THIRD COINAGE 25-35 A.D.      C
Æ Unit 13 mm

OBV: Bust right
Identifying points:
    1) bust draped and diademed
    2) VIRI in front of face
    3) pellet border

REV: Seated figure left
Identifying points:
    1) figure wears helmet
    2) figure holds branch in left hand, spear in
       right
    3) pellet on either side of branch

CLASSIFICATION: Atrebatic K

NOTES: Some found at Wanborough.
Reverse copied from a coin of Tiberius.
Rarity provided via trade survey.

533-1      VERICA THIRD COINAGE 25-35 A.D.      C
Æ Unit 1.1 gms. 12 mm

OBV: Male figure standing left
Identifying points:
    1) figure, naked, holds left arm above head
    2) figure holds lituus in right hand

3) COM to left of figure
4) MI F to right of figure
5) pellet border

REV: Bust right
Identifying points:
    1) bust of Tiberius, laureate
    2) VERI behind bust
    3) CA in front of face
    4) pellet border

CLASSIFICATION: Atrebatic K

NOTES: Many found at Wanborough.
    There is some question which is the obverse,
    Mack indicated the bust side. It appears the
    bust occupies the concave side which is
    normally the reverse.
    Reverse (bust side) copied from a coin of
    Tiberius.

534-1    VERICA THIRD COINAGE 25-35 A.D.    VR
Æ Unit

OBV: Head right
Identifying points:
    1) head 'Augustan' according to Mack
    2) VERICA in field

REV: Eagle left
Identifying points:
    1) COMMI F in field

CLASSIFICATION: Atrebatic K

NOTES: Photograph, metrological data not available.
    Rarity provided via trade survey.

550-1    VERICA THIRD COINAGE 25-35 A.D.    R
Æ Minim 0.3 gms. 8 mm

OBV: Vine leaf
Identifying points:
    1) C to left of leaf
    2) F to right of leaf
    3) pellet border

REV: Celticized horse right
Identifying points:
1) horse rears on hind legs
2) VERI above horse
3) CA below horse
4) pellet border

CLASSIFICATION: Atrebatic K

NOTES: Some found at Wanborough.
Not yet authenticated via metallurgical analysis, the type appears genuine, however. This is the minim corresponding to 520-1 and 525-1.
Rarity provided via trade survey.

551-1      **VERICA THIRD COINAGE 25-35 A.D.**      R
Æ Minim 0.2 gms. 8 mm

OBV: Torc
Identifying points:
1) C.F inside torc
2) torc has pellet terminals

REV: Bust right
Identifying points:
1) VERI in front of face

CLASSIFICATION: Atrebatic K

NOTES: Some found at Wanborough, may be commoner than indicated.
There is some question which side is the obverse, Mack indicated the bust side. This side is concave, however, and would normally be the reverse.
Reverse (bust side) copied from a denarius of Tiberius.

552-1      **VERICA THIRD COINAGE 25-35 A.D.**      R
Æ Minim 9 mm

OBV: Altar
Identifying points:
1) altar made up of lines and pellets, top is curved
2) C to left of altar
3) F to right of altar
4) pellet border

REV: Facing bull's head
Identifying points:
1) V, up-side-down above head
2) ERICA below head

CLASSIFICATION: Atrebatic K

NOTES: Most in museums.
Not yet authenticated via metallurgical analysis, the type appears genuine, however. Reports of many finds from Wanborough, but cannot be confirmed.
Rarity provided via trade survey.

553–1    VERICA THIRD COINAGE 25–35 A.D.        R
ÆR Minim 0.3 gms. 8 mm

OBV: Temple
Identifying points:
1) temple with peaked roof
2) C and F, upside-down on sides
3) indistinct figure in temple appears to hold spear
4) pellet border

REV: Bull right
Identifying points:
1) bull butting right
2) VER upside-down above bull
3) REX below bull
4) pellet border
5) exergual line below bull

CLASSIFICATION: Atrebatic K

NOTES: Some found at Wanborough.
Later version of 552–1.
Not yet authenticated via metallurgical analysis, the type appears genuine, however. Obverse adapted from denarius of Augustus with temple of Jupiter Tonans, B.M.C. 4415. Reverse adapted from a denarius of Augustus.
The suggestion a Celtic temple is depicted is unlikely.
Rarity provided via trade survey.

554-1 **VERICA THIRD COINAGE 25-35 A.D.** R
Æ Minim 0.3 gms. 7 mm

OBV: Cornucopia
Identifying points:
1) three pellets at open end of cornucopia
2) COM to left of cornucopia
3) probably MI F to right of cornucopia, but partially off-flan on only published example
4) pellet border

REV: Celticized lion right
Identifying points:
1) lion has reversed-S tail
2) pellet border

CLASSIFICATION: Atrebatic K

NOTES: Some found at Wanborough, may be commoner than indicated.
Not yet authenticated via metallurgical analysis, the type appears genuine, however.

555-1 **VERICA THIRD COINAGE 25-35 A.D.** S
Æ Minim 0.2 gms. 8 mm

OBV: Two cornucopiae
Identifying points:
1) similiar to 531-1
2) standard between two cornucopiae
3) pellet border

REV: Eagle flying left
Identifying points:
1) eagle's head turned back to right
2) pellet border

CLASSIFICATION: Atrebatic K

NOTES: Some found at Wanborough, possible commoner than indicated.
Not yet authenticated via metallurgical analysis, the type appears genuine, however. Obverse copied from a coin of Mark Anthony.
This is the minim corresponding to 531-1.

556-1   VERICA THIRD COINAGE 25–35 A.D.   R
Æ Minim 0.3 gms. 9 mm

OBV: Floral pattern
Identifying points:
1) two leaved, or flowered plant
2) C F above plant
3) pellet border

REV: Hippocamp right
Identifying points:
1) VER, up-side-down, above hippocamp
2) CA below hippocamp, no crossbar to A
3) I in VERICA does not appear
4) pellet border

CLASSIFICATION: Atrebatic K

NOTES: Some found at Wanborough.
Not yet authenticated via metallurgical analysis, the type appears genuine, however. Rarity provided via trade survey.

557-1   VERICA THIRD COINAGE 25–35 A.D.   R
Æ Minim

OBV: Sphinx right
Identifying points:
1) sphinx crouches
2) C below sphinx
3) F in front of sphinx
4) exergual line below sphinx
5) pellet border

REV: Animal, curled up right
Identifying points:
1) VERI inverted above animal
2) animal appears to be a hound sleeping

CLASSIFICATION: Atrebatic K

NOTES: Some found at Wanborough.
Metrological data not available.
Not yet authenticated via metallurgical analysis, the type appears genuine, however. Rarity provided via trade survey.

558-1     VERICA THIRD COINAGE 25-35 A.D.          R
AR Minim 0.2 gms. 8 mm

OBV: Bust right
Identifying points:
    1) bust laureate
    2) pellet-in-ring motif in front of bust
    3) pellet border
REV: Celtized dog right
Identifying points:
    1) dog very stylized
    2) exergual line below
    3) pellet-in-ring motif above dog

CLASSIFICATION: Atrebatic K

NOTES: Some found at Wanborough.
      Not yet authenticated via metallurgical
      analysis, the type appears genuine, however.
      Bust undoubtedly derived from a Roman
      denarius.
      Rarity provided via trade survey.

559-1     VERICA THIRD COINAGE 25-35 A.D.          R
AR Minim 6 mm

OBV: Inscription in plain field
Identifying points:
    1) VERI in centre
    2) pellet border
REV: Urn
Identifying points:
    1) urn has two handles
    2) pellet-in-oval motif for lid
    3) COM to left of urn
    4) MI F to right of urn
    5) pellet border

CLASSIFICATION: Atrebatic K

NOTES: Some found at Wanborough.
      Not yet authenticated via metallurgical
      analysis, the type appears genuine, however.
      Rarity provided via trade survey.

560-1    VERICA THIRD COINAGE 25–35 A.D.        R
Æ Minim 0.3 gms. 8 mm

OBV: Geometric pattern
Identifying points:
1) two squares form eight-pointed star
2) VI in centre, or possibly TA
3) pellet in arms of V
4) pellet border

REV: Pegasus right
Identifying points:
1) Pegasus prancing
2) exergual line below
3) V above pegasus, REX, almost illegible, below
4) pellet border

CLASSIFICATION: Atrebatic K

NOTES: Some found at Wanborough.
Not yet authenticated via metallurgical analysis, the type appears genuine, however. Rarity provided via trade survey.

561-1    VERICA THIRD COINAGE 25–35 A.D.        R
Æ Minim 0.2 gms. 9 mm

OBV: Geometric pattern
Identifying points:
1) as 560-1
2) A in centre

REV: Bird right
Identifying points:
1) bird stands on branch
2) pellet border

CLASSIFICATION: Atrebatic K

NOTES: Some found at Wanborough.
Reverse possibly adapted from an intaglio, a pre-Flavian plasma intaglio from Fishbourne is similiar.
Previously attributed to Amminius.
Rarity provided via trade survey.

562-1    VERICA THIRD COINAGE 25-35 A.D.          ER
ÆR Minim

OBV: Geometric pattern
Identifying points:
    1) as 560-1
    2) B in centre

REV: Bird right
Identifying points:
    1) as 561-1

CLASSIFICATION: Atrebatic K

NOTES: Some found at Wanborough.
    Traditionally attributed to Amminius, but
    now reassigned to Verica. The type is the
    successor to 560-1 and 561-1.
    Metrological data not available.
    Not yet authenticated via metallurgical
    analysis, the type appears genuine, however.
    May share reverse die with 561-1.
    Reverse possibly adapted from an intaglio,
    a pre-Flavian plasma intaglio from Fish-
    bourne is similiar.
    Not illustrated.

563-1    VERICA THIRD COINAGE 25-43 A.D.          ER
ÆR Minim ca. 7-8 mm

OBV: Urn
Identifying points:
    1) urn has base and two handles
    2) REX above
    3) pellet border

REV: Eagle flying right
Identifying points:
    1) eagle wears 'necktie'
    2) VERICA COMMI F around eagle
    3) pellet border

CLASSIFICATION: Atrebatic K

NOTES: Some found at Wanborough,
    Possibly more common than indicated.

564-1    VERICA THIRD COINAGE 25-43 A.D.          ER
         Æ Minim ca. 7-8 mm

OBV: Inscription in tablet
Identifying points:
    1) VIR in concave-sided box
    2) daisy above and below box
    3) pellet border

REV: Boar's head right
Identifying points:
    1) boar's head in plain field

CLASSIFICATION: Atrebatic K

NOTES: Coin not yet authenticated via metallurgical
    analysis, but type appears genuine.

## THE COINAGE OF EPATICCUS

The coins of Epaticcus appear shortly before the Claudian invasion in the northern part of Atrebatic/Regnan territory. Epaticcus evidently was a Trinovantian/Catuvellaunian sympathizer, or perhaps a member of Cunobeline's family, who gradually encroached on Verica's territory. By 42 A.D., Verica was deposed, and fled to Rome seeking military aid to regain his throne. Epaticcus' rule was short-lived, curtailed by the Roman invasion of 43. His coins are followed by those of Caratacus.

There is no question the coinage of Epaticcus is Atrebatic/Regnan, it follows the typical pattern of gold and silver, with no bronze. The types of the gold staters, however, are derived from Trinovantian/Catuvellaunian motifs.

575-1    EPATICCUS 35-43 A.D.                     ER
         Æ Stater 5.40 gms. 16 mm

OBV: Corn ear
Identifying points:
    1) corn ear has central stalk
    2) TAS to left of ear
    3) CIF to right of ear

REV: Celtic warrior on horse right
Identifying points:
    1) warrior brandishes spear in right hand
    2) warrior holds oval shield in left hand
    3) EPATI below horse, C above, V behind
    4) horse's tail may furnish the missing S

CLASSIFICATION: Atrebatic L

NOTES: Standard weight given.
    Many in museums.

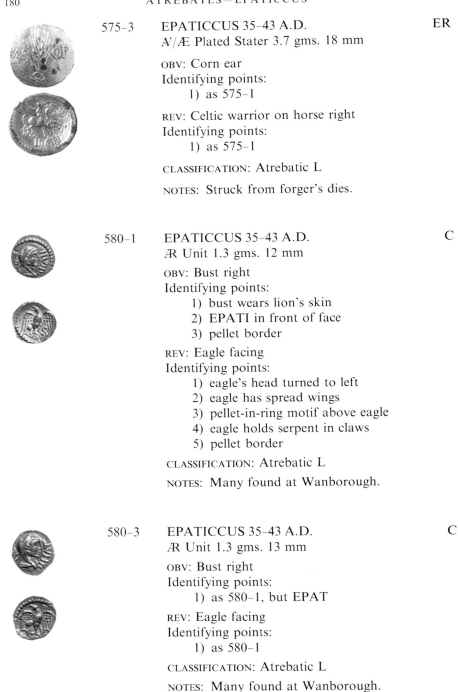

575–3    EPATICCUS 35–43 A.D.                                    ER
         AV/Æ Plated Stater 3.7 gms. 18 mm

OBV: Corn ear
Identifying points:
   1) as 575–1

REV: Celtic warrior on horse right
Identifying points:
   1) as 575–1

CLASSIFICATION: Atrebatic L

NOTES: Struck from forger's dies.


580–1    EPATICCUS 35–43 A.D.                                    C
         ÆR Unit 1.3 gms. 12 mm

OBV: Bust right
Identifying points:
      1) bust wears lion's skin
      2) EPATI in front of face
      3) pellet border

REV: Eagle facing
Identifying points:
      1) eagle's head turned to left
      2) eagle has spread wings
      3) pellet-in-ring motif above eagle
      4) eagle holds serpent in claws
      5) pellet border

CLASSIFICATION: Atrebatic L

NOTES: Many found at Wanborough.


580–3    EPATICCUS 35–43 A.D.                                    C
         ÆR Unit 1.3 gms. 13 mm

OBV: Bust right
Identifying points:
      1) as 580–1, but EPAT

REV: Eagle facing
Identifying points:
      1) as 580–1

CLASSIFICATION: Atrebatic L

NOTES: Many found at Wanborough.

581-1     EPATICCUS 35–43 A.D.                                C
          Æ Unit 1.3 gms. 12 mm

OBV: Seated victory right
Identifying points:
    1) victory sits on box with X
    2) victory holds wreath
    3) TASCIOV around victory
    4) pellet border

REV: Boar right
Identifying points:
    1) branch above boar
    2) boar stands on exergual line
    3) EPAT on exergual line
    4) row of pellets below exergual line
    5) pellet border

CLASSIFICATION: Atrebatic L

NOTES:  Many found at Wanborough.
Obverse copied from a denarius of M. Volteius.
Reverse copied from a denarius of M. Porcius Cato or M. Porcius Cato Uticensis, or alternatively a jasper intaglio from Figsbury Rings.

582-1     EPATICCUS 35–43 A.D.                               ER
          Æ Unit 12 mm

OBV: Bust left
Identifying points:
    1) bust is bare-headed and bearded
    2) TASC in front of face
    3) IO behind head
    4) pellet border

REV: Lion right
Identifying points:
    1) EPATI below lion
    2) flower with four petals above lion
    3) lion turns head to face viewer

CLASSIFICATION: Atrebatic L

NOTES: Some found at Wanborough, trade survey indicated commoner, but cannot be confirmed.

Coin has not been authenticated via metallurgical analysis, but type appears authentic.

583-1     EPATICCUS 35-43 A.D.                    R

Æ Unit 14 mm

OBV: Inscription in tablet

Identifying points:

1) EPATI in box
2) two vertical lines extend above and below tablet
3) row of pellets between lines

REV: Lion right

Identifying points:

1) three exergual lines

CLASSIFICATION: Atrebatic L

NOTES: Some found at Wanborough.

Rarity provided via trade-survey.

No weight data available.

Coin seen December 1984, is no longer available for inspection.

Coin has not been authenticated via metallurgical analysis, but type appears genuine.

585-1     EPATICCUS 35-43 A.D.                    S

Æ Minim 9 mm

OBV: Inscription in pellet ring

Identifying points:

1) EPATI in centre
2) pellet-in-ring motif above and below EPATI
3) pellet border

REV: Boar's head right

Identifying points:

1) TA below boar's head
2) pellet border

CLASSIFICATION: Atrebatic L

NOTES: Some found at Wanborough.

Rarity provided via trade survey.

## THE COINAGE OF CARATACUS

The historical Caratacus is represented by two coins, a silver Unit and a Minim.
The Unit is a direct descendant of the bust/eagle type of Epaticcus, the Minim
is a new type. The coinage was probably short-lived, though could have been
struck up to Caratacus's capture in 51 A.D.

593-1    CARATACUS 43-51 A.D.                          C
AR Unit 1.3 gms. 12 mm

OBV: Bust right
Identifying points:
   1) bust wears lion's skin
   2) CARA in front of face
   3) pellet border

REV: Eagle facing
Identifying points:
   1) eagle's head turned to left
   2) eagle has spread wings
   3) pellet-in-ring motif above eagle
   4) eagle holds serpent in claws
   5) pellet border

CLASSIFICATION: Atrebatic M

NOTES: Many found at Wanborough.
       Type is direct descendant of 580-1.

595-1    CARATACUS 43-51 A.D.                          C
AR Minim

OBV: CARA around pellet-in-ring motif
Identifying points:
   1) pellet-in-ring in centre
   2) C A R A around pellet-in-ring motif
   3) pellet border

REV: Pegasus right
Identifying points:
   1) Pegasus stands on exergual line
   2) pellet border

CLASSIFICATION: Atrebatic M

NOTES: The rarity of this type is almost impossible
       to judge. Reports of many finds at Wan-
       borough cannot be confirmed. The trade
       survey yielded ratings of R to C. On balance,
       the type is likely to prove common.

## THE COINAGE OF THE ICENI

The Iceni occupied the area that is today Norfolk, Suffolk and parts of Cambridgeshire. Until the time of the Gallic War, the tribe seems economically isolated. Large Flan, Defaced Die and Abstract Design Type staters are not found in Icenian territory, and presumably were not imported. Locally-made coins, the NORFOLK WOLF TYPE staters, were first produced just prior to the Gallic War, though in small quantities.

This earliest Icenian coinage comprises gold staters with the abstracted head of Apollo on the obverse and a disjointed wolf on the reverse. The heavy weight indicates the series began some time before the war. With the onset of the war, the coins become quite debased and bronze cores of plated staters occur with some frequency.

Apparently, extensive trading contacts developed during the war, initiated by the Trinovantes/Catuvellauni. A small number of Gallic War Type staters are found and uninscribed staters of the Trinovantes/Catuvellauni also appear. After the war, the coins of Addedomaros circulated, though a short-lived issue of gold staters was produced locally—the FRECKENHAM TYPE.

About 45 B.C., the gold content of the Icenian coinage was restored, with the introduction of the FRECKENHAM TYPE. Staters and quarters were struck lighter in weight to conform with the coinages of the other British tribes. The staters had a flower pattern or cross of pellets on the obverse and a Celticized horse on the reverse. Three major types occured, described as EARLY, MIDDLE and LATE, based on style and the progressive damage to one particular die linked with several others. Since all three types occurred in the Freckenham Hoard, it is likely they were contemporary. The Iceni struck very few of these coins, existing examples are known primarily from the one hoard and single finds are unusual. Generally, Icenian gold is very rare.

About 35 B.C., an extensive Icenian silver coinage began, which continued until the final supression of the tribe after the Boudiccan Rebellion. The silver units were produced to a standard weight of 1.25g. for nearly 100 years, a remarkable economic and technological achievement. They had a bewildering succession of types, subtypes and minor die varieties, which probably served as die-control marks. However, the minor varieties have not been systematically analyzed and still offer an opportunity for original research.

The first Icenian silver coinage, the BOAR TYPE, appears to be stylistically based on the Corieltauvian South Ferriby Type, carrying a boar on the obverse and a horse on the reverse. One late variety of the Boar Type carries an inscription: CAN DURO. The Boar Type was replaced by the CELTIC HEAD TYPE, in turn replaced by the CRESCENT TYPE. The rarity of the Celtic Head type may suggest it was only a local issue and the Crescent Type succeeded the Boar Type directly.

The Freckenham Type disappeared by 40 B.C. and the uninscribed silver coins were superceded by the dynastic issues at the turn of the millennium.

Very few inscribed gold coins are known. It is possible the gold coinage was discontinued and the Iceni used silver coins and Trinovantian/Catuvellaunian gold exclusively after 40 B.C. The Icenian dynastic period is largely one of a prolific silver coinage, beginning with the addition of an inscription to the Crescent Type.

All major types and subtypes are delineated in the catalogue, but no attempt is made to list minor die varieties. The dating of the various issues is controversial and that offered is somewhat arbitrary, based on typological sequences and statistical analyses of coin hoards deposited during the rebellion of 61 A.D.

## UNINSCRIBED GOLD COINS

610-1    NORFOLK WOLF TYPE 65-45 B.C.                    S
N Stater 5.7-6.2 gms. 16 mm

OBV: Abstracted head of Apollo right
Identifying points:
    1) laurel leaves upwards

REV: Wolf right
Identifying points:
    1) pellet and solid crescent below wolf

CLASSIFICATION: Icenian A

NOTES: See modern forgery 610-1F.
        Typical weight given.
        Most are in museums.

610-2    NORFOLK WOLF TYPE 65-45 B.C.                    ER
N Stater 5.7-6.2 gms. 17mm

OBV: Abstracted head of Apollo right
Identifying points:
    1) Laurel leaves downwards

REV: Wolf left
Identifying points:
    1) pellet and solid crescent below wolf

CLASSIFICATION: Icenian A

NOTES: Typical weight given.
        Change in laurel leaves' direction may indi-
        cate a change in weight or metal content.

610-3     **NORFOLK WOLF TYPE 65-45 B.C.**          ER
          Æ Stater 5.7-6.2 gms. 17 mm

          OBV: Abstracted head of Apollo right
          Identifying points:
              1) laurel leaves downwards

          REV: Wolf left
          Identifying points:
              1) large pellet and triangular arrangement of
                 three pellets below wolf

          CLASSIFICATION: Icenian A

          NOTES: Typical weight given.
                 Change in laurel leaves' direction may indi-
                 cate a change in weight or metallic content.

610-5     **NORFOLK WOLF TYPE 65-45 B.C.**          ER
          Æ/Æ Plated Stater ca. 4.4 gms. 21 mm

          OBV: Abstracted head of Apollo right
          Identifying points:
              1) as 610-3

          REV: Wolf left
          Identifying points:
              1) as 610-3

          CLASSIFICATION: Icenian A

          NOTES: Actual weight of illustrated coin given.
                 Ancient forgery.

620-1     **EARLY FRECKENHAM TYPE**                ER
          45-40 B.C.
          Æ Stater 5.25-5.55 gms. 17 mm

          OBV: Opposed crescents
          Identifying points:
              1) symmetrical design with opposed crescents
                 as dominant element
              2) crescents superimposed on cross of pellets
              3) ring and pellet motifs at the four points of
                 the crescents

          REV: Celticized horse right
          Identifying points:
              1) daisy above and below horse
              2) ring and pellet motif above horse's tail

          CLASSIFICATION: Icenian B

NOTES: Relative dates in this series determined by worn condition of this type in Freckenham hoard.

Typical weight given, not enough Early Freckenham Type staters exist to identify standard weight.

Some are in museums.

620-4 EARLY FRECKENHAM TYPE ER
45-40 B.C.
Æ Stater 5.25-5.55 gms. 16 mm

OBV: Opposed crescents with stars
Identifying points:
  1) symmetrical design with opposed crescents as dominant element
  2) two large five-pointed stars
  3) triangular arrangement of three pellets

REV: Celticized horse right
Identifying points:
  1) cog wheel below horse

CLASSIFICATION: Icenian B

NOTES: As 620-1.
  Typical weight given.
  Some are in museums.

620-5 EARLY FRECKENHAM TYPE ER
45-40 B.C.
Æ/Æ Plated Stater 5.3 gms. 19 mm

OBV: Opposed crescents with stars
Identifying points:
  1) as 620-1

REV: Celticized horse right
Identifying points:
  1) as 620-1

CLASSIFICATION: Icenian B

NOTES: Ancient forgery of 620-4.
  Actual weight of illustrated coin given.
  Some are in museums.

620-7     EARLY FRECKENHAM TYPE                    ER
45–40 B.C.
N Stater 5.25–5.55 gms. 17 mm

OBV: Opposed crescents with triple pellets
Identifying points:
1) symmetrical design with opposed crescents as dominant element
2) crescents superimposed on single line of pellets
3) triangular arrangement of three pellets below crescents

REV: Celticized horse right
Identifying points:
1) ring of pellets enclosing triangular arrangement of three pellets all above horse
2) another triangular arrangement of pellets above horse

CLASSIFICATION: Icenian B

NOTES: As 620–1.
        Typical weight given.
        Some are in museums.

620-9     EARLY FRECKENHAM TYPE                    ER
45–40 B.C.
N Stater 5.25–5.55 gms. 17 mm

OBV: Opposed crescents with pellets
Identifying points:
1) symmetrical design with opposed crescents as dominant element
2) minimal ornamentation in field
3) pellets at ends of crescents

REV: Celticized horse right
Identifying points:
1) daisy above horse
2) six-pointed star below horse

CLASSIFICATION: Icenian B

NOTES: As 620–1.
        Typical weight given.
        Some are in museums.

624-1    MIDDLE FRECKENHAM TYPE                    ER
45-40 B.C.
*N* Stater 5.70 gms. 16 mm

OBV: Cross of pellets
Identifying points:
    1) field plain except for pellets

REV: Celticized horse right
Identifying points:
    1) four-spoked wheel above horse
    2) eight-spoked wheel below horse

CLASSIFICATION: Icenian B

NOTES: Obverse die shows faint traces of other
        design elements.
        Relative dating based on die-linking within
        the hoard.
        Standard weight given.
        Some are in museums.
        Modern forgery exists—see 624-1F.

624-4    MIDDLE FRECKENHAM TYPE                    ER
45-40 B.C.
*N* Stater 5.70 gms. 16 mm

OBV: Cross of pellets
Identifying points:
    1) pellet-in-ring motif in centre

REV: Celticized horse right
Identifying points:
    1) three pellets in triangular arrangement
       below horse
    2) above horse: arch with two lobes, each of
       which contains two pellets

CLASSIFICATION: Icenian B

NOTES: As 624-1.
        Standard weight given.
        Some are in museums.

624-7    MIDDLE FRECKENHAM TYPE                    ER
45-40 B.C.
*N* Stater 5.70 gms. 16 mm

OBV: Cross of pellets
Identifying points:
    1) pellet-in-ring motif in centre

REV: Celticized horse right
Identifying points:
>1) three pellets in triangular arrangement above horse
>2) eight-spoked wheel below horse

CLASSIFICATION: Icenian B

NOTES: Standard weight given.
>Most are in museums.

626-1　LATE FRECKENHAN TYPE 45–40 B.C.　　R
Æ Stater 5.70 gms. 18 mm

OBV: Floral pattern
Identifying points:
>1) flower superimposed on cross of pellets
>2) stylized three-petal flower with central pellet, surrounded by circle
>3) curved lines in angles of pellet-cross

REV: Celticized horse right
Identifying points:
>1) seven or eight-spoked wheel below horse
>2) large outline crescent decorated with zig-zag line and pellets
>3) three pellets in triangular pattern below outline crescent

CLASSIFICATION: Icenian B

NOTES: Relative dating based on die-linking within the hoard.
>Reverse die often worn.
>Modern forgery known, see 626–1F.
>Standard weight given.
>Many are in museums.

626-4　LATE FRECKENHAM TYPE 45–40 B.C.　　ER
Æ Stater 5.70 gms. 18 mm

OBV: Floral pattern
Identifying points:
>1) flower superimposed on cross of pellets
>2) flower and surrounding circle larger than on 626–1

REV: Celticized horse right

Identifying points:
1) four-spoked wheel below horse
2) daisy surrounded by circle above horse

CLASSIFICATION: Icenian B

NOTES: Dating as 626-1.
Standard weight given.
Many are in museums.

626-7    LATE FRECKENHAM TYPE 45-40 B.C.        ER
N Stater 5.70 gms. 18 mm

OBV: Floral pattern
Identifying points:
1) flower superimposed on cross of pellets
2) flower and surrounding circle larger than on 626-1

REV: Celticized horse right
Identifying points:
1) four-spoked wheel below horse
2) five or six-spoked wheel with pellets around above horse

CLASSIFICATION: Icenian B

NOTES: Dating as 626-1.
Type die-linked to 626-4.
Standard weight given.
Many are in museums.

626-9    LATE FRECKENHAM TYPE 45-40 B.C.        ER
N Stater 5.70 gms. 18 mm

OBV: Floral pattern
Identifying points:
1) flower superimposed on cross of pellets
2) flower and surrounding circle larger than on 626-4 and 626-7

REV: Celticized horse right
Identifying points:
1) large wheel with more than four spokes above horse
2) daisy below horse

CLASSIFICATION: Icenian B

NOTES: Dating as 626-1.
Standard weight given.
Many are in museums.

626–12     LATE FRECKENHAM TYPE 45–40 B.C.          ER
Ṉ Stater 5.70 gms. 17 mm

OBV: Floral pattern
Identifying points:
    1) flower superimposed on cross of pellets

REV: Celticized horse right
Identifying points:
    1) six-spoked wheel above horse
    2) circle with line across centre below horse

CLASSIFICATION: Icenian B

NOTES: Dating as 626–1.
       Die-break on obverse die.
       Type die-linked to 626–4.
       Standard weight given.
       Many are in museums.

628–1     LATE FRECKENHAM TYPE 45–40 B.C.          ER
Ṉ Quarter Stater ca. 0.9 gms. 12 mm

OBV: Elaborate wreath motif
Identifying points:
    1) box comprising of lines in centre
    2) branched wreaths at sides of box

REV: Celticized horse right
Identifying points:
    1) ring-and-pellet motif below horse
    2) pellet below horse's tail
    3) possible ring above horse

CLASSIFICATION: Icenian B

NOTES: The coin in the Mack collection is the one
       recorded in Stukeley's 1762 manuscript for
       *Twenty-three Plates of the Coins of the*
       *Ancient British Kings.*
       Typical weight given.

After 40 B.C., Trinovantian/Catuvellaunian gold coins circulated in Icenian territory.

## UNINSCRIBED SILVER COINS

Initially, Trinovantian/Catuvellaunian silver coins circulated in Icenian territory. The first Icenian issue, the BOAR TYPE, is similiar to Corieltauvian coins of the period. The Corieltauvian coinage predates the Icenian, indicating the Iceni were influenced by the Corieltauvi.

The standard weight of the Icenian silver unit, throughout its issue, was 1.25 grammes.

655-1    BOAR TYPE ca. 35–25 B.C.                    VR
Æ Unit ca. 1.0 gm. 13 mm

OBV: Boar right
Identifying points:
    1) ring of pellets above boar
    2) three pellets below boar
    3) upper portion of boar's front leg comprised of two lines
    4) pellet on boar's shoulder

REV: Celticized horse right
Identifying points:
    1) ring of pellets above horse
    2) three pellets above horse
    3) horse stands on exergual line with pellets below
    4) horse's tail made up of a single line with shorter lines coming off at an angle

CLASSIFICATION: Icenian C

NOTES: This type is potentially common, because records of extant specimens are not accurate.

657-1    BOAR TYPE ca. 35–25 B.C.                    VR
Æ Unit ca. 1.1 gms. 14 mm

OBV: Boar right
Identifying points:
    1) pellets in front of boar, possibly in a ring
    2) four pellets below boar
    3) upper portion of boar's front leg comprised of two lines
    4) no pellet on boar's shoulder
    5) boar stands on a double exergual line with a row of pellets between the two lines

REV: Celticized horse right

Identifying points:

    1) three pellets and large crescent above horse

    2) six-pointed star below horse

    3) horse has 'necklace' and 'belt'

    4) horse's tail made up of a single line with shorter lines coming off at an angle

    5) horse has eye comprised of a large pellet

CLASSIFICATION: Icenian C

NOTES: This type is potentially common, because records of extant specimens are not accurate. Many are in museums.

**657-3**    BOAR TYPE ca. 35–25 B.C.        VR

Æ Unit ca. 1.1 gms. 12 mm

OBV: Boar right

Identifying points:

    1) as 657–1, but pellet on boar's shoulder

REV: Celticized horse right

Identifying points:

    1) as 657–1

CLASSIFICATION: Icenian C

NOTES: Many are in museums.

**659-1**    BOAR TYPE ca. 35–25 B.C.       S

Æ Unit ca. 1.1 gms. 14 mm

OBV: Boar right

Identifying points:

    1) pellets above and in front of boar

    2) pellet below boar's tail

    3) upper portion of boar's front leg comprised of two lines

    4) no pellet on boar's shoulder

    5) single pellet below boar

    6) ring-and-pellet motif behind boar

REV: Celticized horse right

Identifying points:

    1) three pellets and four-spoked wheel above horse

    2) five pellets and a cotter-pin shaped line below horse

    3) horse has eye comprised of a large pellet

CLASSIFICATION: Icenian C

NOTES: This type is potentially common, because records of extant specimens are not accurate. Many are in museums.

659–2    BOAR TYPE ca. 35–25 B.C.    ER
Æ/Æ Plated Unit ca. 0.9 gm 14 mm

OBV: Boar right
Identifying points:
   1) as 659–1

REV: Celticized horse right
Identifying points:
   1) as 659–1

CLASSIFICATION: Icenian C

NOTES: An ancient forgery of 659–1, comprised of a bronze core covered with silver.
The field ornaments are the same, and the style similiar, but the coin is not an exact duplicate.

659–3    BOAR TYPE ca. 35–25 B.C.    ER
Æ Unit 13 mm

OBV: Boar right
Identifying points:
   1) as 659–1, but pellet on boar's shoulder

REV: Celticized horse right
Identifying points:
   1) as 659–1

CLASSIFICATION: Icenian C

NOTES: Most are in museums.

661–1    BOAR TYPE ca. 35–25 B.C.    ER
Æ Half Unit ca. 0.5 gm. ca. 11 mm

OBV: Boar right
Identifying points:
   1) two or three pellets below boar
   2) upper portion of boar's front leg comprised of two lines

REV: Celticized horse right
Identifying points:
    1) horse has bridle
    2) ring-and-pellet motif above horse

CLASSIFICATION: Icenian C

NOTES: Flan may be elongated.

663-1    BOAR TYPE-CAN DURO 25-20 B.C.      ER
             Æ Unit 1.25 gms. 12-15 mm

OBV: Celticized Boar right
Identifying points:
    1) Ring of pellets around boar
    2) Boar's tail S-shaped
    3) two pellets near tail
    4) 'A' below boar with pellet for cross-bar, and small ring above

REV: Celticized Horse right
Identifying points:
    1) CAN above horse
    2) DVRO below horse
    3) horse has necklace and belt
    4) pellet below tail and above letter V
    5) exergual line made up of a row of pellets

CLASSIFICATION: Icenian D

NOTES: Earliest inscribed Icenian issue.
        Not necessarily a dynastic issue, possibly a local issue.
        Dating less certain than other coins in this series.

665-1    CELTIC HEAD TYPE ca. 20-15 B.C.      ER
             Æ Unit ca. 0.9 gm. 13 mm

OBV: Celticized head left
Identifying points:
    1) Head much larger than flan
    2) 'coffee bean' for eye
    3) representational ear
    4) elaborately coiled hair

REV: Celticized horse right

Identifying points:
1) three pellets below tail
2) ring-and-pellet motif below horse
3) upper portion of horse's front legs comprised of two lines

CLASSIFICATION: Icenian E

NOTES: This coin is the earliest variety of the Celtic Head Type, Commander Mack felt it was a link to the earlier Boar Type. Later varieties have a less representational ear.

665-3    CELTIC HEAD TYPE ca. 20-15 B.C.          ER
Æ Unit 16 mm

OBV: Celticized head right
Identifying points:
1) Head about the same size as the flan
2) 'coffee bean' for eye
3) outline crescent for ear
4) elaborately coiled hair

REV: Celticized horse right
Identifying points:
1) eight-spoked wheel with axle above horse
2) ring-and-pellet motif above horse
3) curved lines run tangentially upwards from wheel

CLASSIFICATION: Icenian E

665-5    CELTIC HEAD TYPE ca. 20-15 B.C.          ER
Æ Unit 14 mm

OBV: Celticized head right
Identifying points:
1) Head about the same size as the flan
2) oval shape for eye
3) outline crescent for ear
4) hair comprised of parallel lines, ending with pellets

REV: Celticized horse right
Identifying points:
1) ring of pellets above horse
2) pellet below horse's tail
3) probable ring-and-pellet motif below horse

CLASSIFICATION: Icenian E

665–7  CELTIC HEAD TYPE ca. 20–15 B.C.          ER
Æ Unit 13 mm

OBV: Celticized head right
Identifying points:
1) eye comprised of rectangular box with line in centre
2) no ear
3) 'coffe bean' for mouth
4) hair comprised of herring-bone pattern of lines

REV: Celticized horse right
Identifying points:
1) ring-and-pellet motifs above, below and in front of horse
2) pellet below horse's tail

CLASSIFICATION: Icenian E

665–9  CELTIC HEAD TYPE ca. 20–15 B.C.          ER
Æ Unit 14 mm

OBV: Celticized head right
Identifying points:
1) head indistinct, with little detail

REV: Celticized horse right
Identifying points:
1) eight-spoked wheel above horse
2) three pellets above horse's head
3) ring, possibly with several pellets inside, below horse

CLASSIFICATION: Icenian E

675–1  CRESCENT TYPE 15–1 B.C.          R
Æ Unit ca. 1.2 gms. 12 mm

OBV: Crossed wreath and crescent motif
Identifying points:
1) wreath from abstracted head of Apollo transformed into a crossed pattern
2) two outline crescents, back to back in centre
3) two rings near crescents
4) pellets in angles formed by crossed wreaths

REV: Celticized horse left
Identifying points:
    1) six-spoked wheel above horse
    2) pellets on horse's shoulder

CLASSIFICATION: Icenian F

NOTES: A variant type, possibly a local issue.
       Dating less certain than for other coins in
       this series.
       Most are in museums.

679-1    CRESCENT TYPE 15–1 B.C.       ER
         Æ Unit ca. 1.2 gms. 12 mm

OBV: Wreath and crescent motif
Identifying points:
    1) wreath from abstracted head of Apollo
       transformed into rows of pellets
    2) two outline crescents, back to back in centre
    3) two pellets near crescents

REV: Celticized horse right
Identifying points:
    1) pellets above horse

CLASSIFICATION: Icenian F

681-1    CRESCENT TYPE 15–1 B.C.       ER
         Æ Half Unit ca. 0.6 gm. 12mm

OBV: Crossed wreath and crescent motif
Identifying points:
    1) wreath from abstracted head of Apollo
       transformed into a crossed pattern
    2) two solid crescents, back to back in centre
    3) three pellets and a solid crescent near first
       set of crescents
    4) pellets in angles formed by crossed wreaths

REV: Celticized horse right
Identifying points:
    1) pellets surround horse

CLASSIFICATION: Icenian F

683-1     **CRESCENT TYPE 15-1 B.C.**        ER
Æ Half Unit ca. 0.6 gm. 11 mm

OBV: Wreath and crescent motif
Identifying points:
1) wreath from abstracted head of Apollo transformed into rows of pellets with thin lines attached
2) two outline crescents, back to back in centre
3) two pellets near crescents

REV: Celticized horse right
Identifying points:
1) pellet in front of horse
2) horse's mane comprised of pellets with thin line attached

CLASSIFICATION: Icenian F

## ICENIAN DYNASTIC COINAGES

The departure of Tasciovanus from the Trinovantian/Catuvellaunian leadership and the turmoil of the ensuing Interregnum, enabled the Icenian nobility to place their names on the coins. The Trinovantes/Catuvellauni previously had enough influence over the Iceni to prevent this. The first dynastic coins were inscribed ANTED, the name of a tribal leader. Both gold staters and silver units are known. The staters are considered to be the last gold coins of the Iceni.

The ANTED silver units are replaced with coins inscribed ECEN, thought to be the name of the tribe, rather than a specific leader. The removal of the leader's name may indicate Cunobeline extended his influence over the Iceni after establishing control in Trinovantian/Catuvellaunian territory. For a time, the ECEN disappears entirely, replaced by a series of symbols, these in turn replaced by the inscription ECE. Coins inscribed SAENU or SAEHU, AESU and SUBRIIPRASTO ESICO FECIT follow, the last of these undoubtedly the coins of the historical Pratsutagus. A final group of uninscribed silver units is the coinage of Queen Boudicca, struck to finance the Icenian revolt of 61 A.D.

## COINAGE OF ANTED

Both gold and silver coins are known for this leader.

705-1    ANTED 1-25 A.D.                                 ER
         N Stater 5.4 gms. 18 mm

OBV: Triple-crescent pattern
Identifying points:
   1) three outline crescents in centre with points facing outwards
   2) pellet between points of adjacent points
   3) curved lines and pellets design at border

REV: Celticized horse right
Identifying points:
   1) anemone motif in ring above horse
   2) pellet above and below horse, and below tail
   3) ANTED monogram below horse

CLASSIFICATION: Icenian G

NOTES: Only one obverse and one reverse die recorded.
       Typical weight given, this is the likely standard weight, also.

710-1    ANTED 1-25 A.D.                                  C
         Æ UNIT 1.25 gms. 12-15 mm

OBV: Double crescent emblem
Identifying points:
   1) two outline crescents back to back
   2) two pellet between crescents
   3) crescents lie between two parallel lines
   4) lines and rows of pellets extend perpendicularly from the two parallel lines

REV: Celticized horse right
Identifying points:
   1) daisy above horse
   2) ring around daisy
   3) pellets below horse
   4) ANTED monogram below horse

CLASSIFICATION: Icenian G

711-1    ANTED 1–25 A.D.                                        C
ÆR Unit 1.25 gms. 12–15 mm

OBV: Double crescent emblem
Identifying points:
    1) as 710-1

REV: Celticized horse right
Identifying points:
    1) as 710-1, except for form of monogram
    2) ANTD monogram below horse

CLASSIFICATION: Icenian G

NOTES: Many retained in museums

715-1    ANTED 1–25 A.D.                                       VR
ÆR Unit 1.25 gms. 12mm

OBV: Double crescent emblem
Identifying points:
    1) as 710-1

REV: Celticized horse right
Identifying points:
    1) as 710-1, except for form of monogram
    2) monogram below horse simplified to the
       letter T

CLASSIFICATION: Icenian G

NOTES: Rarity provided via trade survey.

720-1    ANTED 1–25 A.D.                                       VR
ÆR Minim 0.5 gm. 11 mm

OBV: Double crescent emblem
Identifying points:
    1) two outline crescents back to back
    2) points of crescents connected by rows of
       pellets and lines to form a triangles
    3) pellets in triangles

REV: Celticized horse right
Identifying points:
    1) pellets around horse
    2) pellet below tail
    3) ANTD monogram below horse

CLASSIFICATION: Icenian G

NOTES: Rarity provided via trade survey.

## COINAGE INSCRIBED ECEN

The inscription ECEN, which appears in various forms, is thought to be the name of the tribe, not a leader. One of the front legs of the horse may supply the missing letter 'I', completing the spelling 'ECENI'. At least one minor die variety is known, on which an added line may actually be the missing letter. An extensive series, on which the inscription is replaced by a symbol, occurs within the ECEN type. The chronological placement of the symbol-coins is determined by the typological sequence—the reverses belong to the ECEN period, and the stylistic details of the horse indicate they were struck between the coins inscribed ECEN and those inscribed ECE.

The number of pellets under the horse's tail may be a privy mark of some sort because the number varies. The correlation between the number of pellets and a chronological sequence has not been discovered.

The chronology of the types is particularly difficult to determine. The relative chronology appears to follow the form of the horse's head on the reverse. The early coins have an 'outline head' similiar to the coins of ANTED. The head is an outline oval with a stroke for an eye. Later coins have a 'facing head', suggested as an adaptation from a bronze coin of Cunobeline, the Facing Horse Type. On the last issues the horse's head is made up of lines in the form of an up-side-down Y, the 'linear head'. There may be some chronological overlap between the facing and linear head types.

Currently, all ECEN coins accepted as genuine are either silver units or minims. A plated coin made from a bronze core covered with a yellow metal, presumably gold, was offered for sale in 1980. This had a design similiar to an ANTED stater but carried the inscription ECEN, instead. Unfortunately, known Haslemere forgeries were offered simultaneously and although the coin in question has not been condemned, such an important type cannot be accepted until properly authenticated. The catalogue number 725-2 has been reserved for the plated core, and 725-1 for a stater with proper gold content, should one be discovered.

A comment must be made about the rarity estimates for ECEN. In general, the coins are common, but there are some extremely rare types. Unfortunately, the records for these coins often fail to identify the exact variety, and opinion in the numismatic trade is divided—as a result the ratings in this section are provisional.

730-1     ECEN 25–38 A.D.                              C
          Æ Unit 1.25 gms. 14 mm

          OBV: Double crescent emblem
          Identifying points:
              1) two outline crescents back to back
              2) two pellets between crescents
              3) crescents between two parallel lines
              4) lines and rows of pellets extend perpendicu-
                 larly from the two lines

          REV: Celticized horse right
          Identifying points:
              1) horse has outline head
              2) daisy above horse
              3) pellets below horse and under the tail
              2) ECEN monogram under horse

          CLASSIFICATION: Icenian H

          NOTES: Many in museums.

732-1     ECEN 25–38 A.D.                              ER
          Æ Unit 1.25 gms. 13 mm

          OBV: Double crescent emblem
          Identifying points:
              1) as 730-1

          REV: Celticized horse right
          Identifying points:
              1) As 730-1 except for monogram under horse
              2) monogram under horse simplified to just
                 the letter E

          CLASSIFICATION: Icenian H

          NOTES: Inaccurate records for this type, possibly
                 commoner than indicated.
                 Many in museums.

734-1     ECEN 25–38 A.D.                              ER
          Æ Unit 1.25 gms. 12 mm

          OBV: Double crescent emblem
          Identifying points:
              1) as 730-1

REV: Celticized horse right
Identifying points:
    1)  As 730-1 except for monogram under horse
    2)  EDN monogram under horse

CLASSIFICATION: Icenian H

NOTES: Inaccurate records for this type, possibly
        commoner than indicated.
        Many in museums.

736-1    ECEN 25-38 A.D.                        ER
          ÆR Minim 0.4 gms. 11 mm

OBV: Double crescent emblem
Identifying points:
    1)  two crescents back-to-back
    2)  two pellets between crescents
    3)  points of crescents connected by lines and
        rows of pellets to form triangles

REV: Celticized horse right
Identifying points:
    1)  horse has outline head
    2)  pellets around horse and below tail
    3)  ECE monogram below horse (letter N pos-
        sibly off the flan on published examples)

CLASSIFICATION: Icenian H

NOTES: Inaccurate records for this type, possibly
        commoner than indicated.
        Many in museums.

738-1    ECEN 25-38 A.D.                        ER
          ÆR Minim 0.5 gms. 11 mm

OBV: Double crescent emblem
Identifying points:
    1)  as 736-1

REV: Celticized horse right
Identifying points:
    1)  as 736-1, except for monogram
    2)  ECN monogram under horse

CLASSIFICATION: Icenian H

NOTES: Inaccurate records for this type, possibly commoner than indicated.
Many in museums.
Published examples do not show the horse's head—presumed to be the outline head type.

740-1    ECEN 38–40 A.D.                                    ER
Æ Unit 1.25 gms. 14 mm

OBV: Double crescent emblem
Identifying points:
    1) as 730–1

REV: Celticized horse right
Identifying points:
    1) As 730–1 except for monogram under horse
    2) ED monogram under horse

CLASSIFICATION: Icenian I

NOTES: Inaccurate records for this type, possibly commoner than indicated.
Many in museums.

742-1    ECEN 38–40 A.D.                                    ER
Æ Minim 0.4 gms. 11 mm

OBV: Double crescent emblem
Identifying points:
    1) as 736–1

REV: Celticized horse right
Identifying points:
    1) as 736–1, except for monogram under horse
    2) EC monogram under horse

CLASSIFICATION: Icenian I

NOTES: Inaccurate records for this type, possibly commoner than indicated.
Many in museums.

744-1    ECEN 38–40 A.D.                                    ER
Æ Minim 0.55 gms. 11 mm

OBV: Double crescent emblem
Identifying points:
    1) as 736–1

REV: Celticized horse right
Identifying points:
1) similiar to 736-1
2) horse has linear head
3) No monogram under horse on published examples

CLASSIFICATION: Icenian I

NOTES: Inaccurate records for this type, possibly commoner than indicated.
Many in museums.

750-1     ECEN SYMBOL TYPE 40-45 A.D.     ER
Æ Unit 1.25 gms. 14 mm

OBV: Double crescent emblem
Identifying points:
1) as 730-1

REV: Celticized horse right
Identifying points:
1) As 730-1 except for monogram under horse
2) monogram under horse replaced by a triangle

CLASSIFICATION: Icenian J

NOTES: Inaccurate records for this type, possibly commoner than indicated.
Many in museums.

752-1     ECEN SYMBOL TYPE 40-45 A.D.     ER
Æ Unit 1.25 gms. 14 mm

OBV: Double crescent emblem
Identifying points:
1) as 730-1

REV: Celticized horse right
Identifying points:
1) As 730-1 except for monogram under horse
2) monogram under horse replaced by a Y made of three lines and a pellet

CLASSIFICATION: Icenian J

NOTES: Inaccurate records for this type, possibly commoner than indicated.
Many in museums.

754–1    ECEN SYMBOL TYPE 40–45 A.D.                    ER
AR Unit 1.25 gms. 14 mm

OBV: Double crescent emblem
Identifying points:
  1) as 730–1

REV: Celticized horse right
Identifying points:
  1) As 730–1 except for monogram under horse
  2) monogram under horse replaced by three pellets in a line

CLASSIFICATION: Icenian J

NOTES: Inaccurate records for this type, possibly commoner than indicated.
Many in museums.

756–1    ECEN SYMBOL TYPE 40–45 A.D.                    ER
AR Unit 1.25 gms. 14 mm

OBV: Double crescent emblem
Identifying points:
  1) as 730–1

REV: Celticized horse right
Identifying points:
  1) As 730–1 except for monogram under horse
  2) monogram under horse replaced by an up-side-down V

CLASSIFICATION: Icenian J

NOTES: Inaccurate records for this type, possibly commoner than indicated.
Many in museums.

758–1    ECEN SYMBOL TYPE 40–45 A.D.                    ER
AR Unit 1.25 gms. 14 mm

OBV: Double crescent emblem
Identifying points:
  1) as 730–1

REV: Celticized horse right
Identifying points:
  1) As 730–1 except for monogram under horse
  2) monogram under horse replaced by a line with a pellet at the top

CLASSIFICATION: Icenian J

NOTES: Inaccurate records for this type, possibly commoner than indicated.
Many in museums.

760–1      ECEN 45–50 A.D.                          C
Æ Unit 1.25 gms. 13 mm

OBV: Double crescent emblem
Identifying points:
    1) as 730–1

REV: Celticized horse right
Identifying points:
    1) similiar to 730–1
    2) horse has facing head
    3) horse's forelegs extend back through body of horse
    4) ECE monogram under horse

CLASSIFICATION: Icenian K

NOTES: Many in museums.
The extension of the forelegs through the body of the horse is to reappear on Queen Boudicca's coins—see 790–1, 792–1 and 794–1.
The horse is adapted from an Æ Unit of Cunobeline, see 2101–1.

761–1      ECEN 45–50 A.D.                          ER
Æ Unit 1.06 gms. 15 mm

OBV: Double crescent emblem
Identifying points:
    1) as 730–1

REV: Celticized horse left
Identifying points:
    1) similiar to 730–1
    2) horse probably has linear head
    3) uncertain legend under horse

CLASSIFICATION: Icenian K

NOTES: Inaccurate records for this type, possibly
commoner than indicated.
Legend on reverse not completely certain,
Mack read it as 'ECE', oriented vertically,
Allen read it as 'AHFB?'.

762–1     ECEN 45–50 A.D.                                    S
AR Unit 1.25 gms. 12 mm

OBV: Double crescent emblem
Identifying points:
   1) as 730–1

REV: Celticized horse right
Identifying points:
   1) similiar to 730–1
   2) horse has linear head
   3) six pellets on horse's shoulder
   4) ECE monogram under horse

CLASSIFICATION: Icenian K

NOTES: Inaccurate records for this type, possibly
commoner than indicated.
Many in museums.

764–1     ECEN 45–50 A.D.                                   ER
AR Unit 1.25 gms. 12 mm

OBV: Double crescent emblem
Identifying points:
   1) as 730–1

REV: Celticized horse right
Identifying points:
   1) similiar to 730–1
   2) horse has linear head
   3) horse's forelegs made up of two lines
   3) three pellets on horse's shoulder
   4) ECE monogram under horse

CLASSIFICATION: Icenian K

NOTES: Inaccurate records for this type, possibly
commoner than indicated.
Many in museums.

766-1        ECEN 45-50 A.D.                              S
             Æ Unit 1.25 gms. 13 mm

             OBV: Double crescent emblem
             Identifying points:
                 1) as 730-1

             REV: Celticized horse left
             Identifying points:
                 1) similiar to 730-1
                 2) horse has linear head
                 3) six pellets on horse's shoulder
                 4) ECE monogram inverted under horse

             CLASSIFICATION: Icenian K

             NOTES: Inaccurate records for this type, possibly
                    commoner than indicated.
                    Many in museums.


## COINAGE OF PRATSUTAGUS

Sometime between the Claudian invasion of 43 A.D., and the Boudiccan
rebellion of 61, a disturbance in Icenian territory was suppressed by the
Romans. The Iceni were forced to surrender their arms and it is at this time
Pratsutagus is thought to have come to the Icenian throne.

The chronology of the late ECEN coins and the successive SAENU and
AESU types is problematic. Arbitrarily, only the SAENU and AESU silver
units have been assigned to Pratsutagus. Some of the later ECEN issues may
be coins of Pratsutagus also. The attribution of the SUBRIIPRASTO ESICO
FECIT minims to him is certain.

770-1        SAENU 50-55 A.D.                            ER
             Æ Fraction 1.25 gms. 13–14 mm

             OBV: Double crescent emblem
             Identifying points:
                 1) as 730-1

             REV: Celticized horse right
             Identifying points:
                 1) horse has linear head
                 2) daisy above horse
                 3) six pellets on horse's shoulder
                 4) SAENV under horse (inscription blundered
                    and somewhat uncertain, could also read
                    SAEHU)

CLASSIFICATION: Icenian L

NOTES: Many in museums.
Unknown quantity of this type reported in the Stonea Hoard, 1982, all now in museums, thus possibly much commoner than noted.

775-1     AESU 55-60 A.D.                              VR
Æ Unit 1.25 gms. 12-14 mm

OBV: Double crescent emblem
Identifying points:
    1) as 730-1

REV: Celticized horse right
Identifying points:
    1) as 770-1
    2) AESV under horse

CLASSIFICATION: Icenian N

NOTES: Many in museums.

780-1     SUBRIIPRATSO ESICO FECIT              ER
50-60 A.D.
Æ Fraction 0.95 gms. 13 mm

OBV: Romanized head left
Identifying points:
    1) ring and pellet motif in front of head
    2) SUBRIIPRASTO inscription around head

REV: Celticized horse right
Identifying points:
    1) ring and pellet motif above horse
    2) ESICO FECIT inscription around horse

CLASSIFICATION: Icenian M

NOTES: Most extant examples are broken and chipped, explaining the light weight reported.

REV: Disjointed horse right
Identifying points:
    1) as 800–5

CLASSIFICATION: Corieltauvian A

NOTES: Most in museums.

800–11    NORTH EAST COAST TYPE 70–55 B.C.    ER
*N* Stater 5.7–6.4 gms. 18 mm

OBV: Abstracted head of Apollo right
Identifying points:
    1) as 800–7

REV: Disjointed horse right
Identifying points:
    1) as 800–7, but has four-armed spiral below
       horse's neck

CLASSIFICATION: Corieltauvian A

NOTES: Most in museums.

## REDUCED WEIGHT TYPE

About the middle of the Gallic War, economic pressures caused a debasement in the value of the Celtic Stater throughout Britain. Some tribes debased the gold content of the coins, others reduced the weight and some produced a sophisticated combination of the two. The Corieltauvi reduced the weight of the stater in one step and marked this by changing the direction of the horse on the reverse. Future metallurgical studies may show they changed the gold/silver/copper relationship simultaneously, but this is not known at present.

804–1    REDUCED WEIGHT TYPE 55–45 B.C.    ER
*N* Stater 5.6–6.1 gms. 22 mm

OBV: Abstracted head of Apollo right
Identifying points:
    1) spike with two crescents
    2) curls oval-shaped, rather than crescents
    3) wreath: leaves inwards
    4) wreath leaves made up of small rectangles

REV: Disjointed horse left
Identifying points:
    1) pellet below horse
    2) horse's neck made up of two curves

3) 'coffee bean' behind and in front of horse
4) curved exergual lines with zig-zag-and-pellets pattern between

CLASSIFICATION: Corieltauvian B

NOTES: Many in museums.
Sometimes struck on a pronounced oval-shaped flan.

804–3    REDUCED WEIGHT TYPE 55–45 B.C.    ER
Ν Stater 5.6–6.1 gms. 20 mm

OBV: Abstracted head of Apollo right
Identifying points:
   1) spike with two crescents
   2) diagonal linear depression to right of curls
   3) curls almost circles, as opposed to crescents
   4) stylized 'yoke' to right of linear depression
   5) wreath: leaves inwards
   6) wreath leaves made up of larger rectangles than on 804–1

REV: Disjointed horse left
Identifying points:
   1) Pellet below horse
   2) horse's neck made up of two curves
   3) 'coffee bean' behind and in front of horse
   4) two curved exergual lines with zig-zag-and-pellets pattern between

CLASSIFICATION: Corieltauvian B

NOTES: Many in museums.
Sometimes struck on a pronounced oval-shaped flan.

804–4    REDUCED WEIGHT TYPE 55–45 B.C.    ER
Ν/Æ Plated Stater 4.9 gms. 19 mm

OBV: Abstracted head of Apollo right
Identifying points:
   1) as 804–3

REV: Disjointed horse right
Identifying points:
   1) as 804–3

CLASSIFICATION: Corieltauvian B

NOTES: Ancient Forgery of 804-3.
Bronze core covered with gold foil or plated.
Possibly struck from 'official' dies.

804-5    REDUCED WEIGHT TYPE 55-45 B.C.        ER
Æ Stater 5.6–6.1 gms. 18 mm

OBV: Abstracted head of Apollo right
Identifying points:
1) spike with two crescents
2) diagonal linear depression to right of curls
3) curls almost circles, as opposed to crescents
4) stylized 'yoke' to right of linear depression
5) wreath: leaves inwards
6) wreath leaves made up of small rectangles as on 804-1

REV: Disjointed horse left
Identifying points:
1) pellet below horse
2) horse's neck made up of two curves
3) 'coffee bean' in front of horse
4) slightly curved exergual line
5) crescents-and-pellets motif below exergual line, instead of normal zig-zag-and-pellets

CLASSIFICATION: Corieltauvian B

NOTES: Recorded specimen in British Museum is holed.
Crescent-and-ring motif in exergue is likely copied from a Gallo-Belgic E Stater—see 52-1.

805-7    REDUCED WEIGHT TYPE 55-45 B.C.        ER
Æ Stater 5.6–6.1 gms. 18 mm

OBV: Abstracted head of Apollo right
Identifying points:
1) spike with two crescents
2) diagonal linear depression to right of curls
3) stylized 'yoke' to right of curls
4) curls almost circles as opposed to crescents
5) small pellets near crescents and spike
6) wreath: leaves inwards

REV: Disjointed horse left
Identifying points:
1) sunflower below horse
2) horse's neck made up of two curves
3) 'coffee bean' in front of horse
4) stylized wreath-like motifs above horse
5) curved exergual line

CLASSIFICATION: Corieltauvian B

NOTES: Many in museums.

805-9     REDUCED WEIGHT TYPE 55–45 B.C.     ER
N̸ Stater 5.6–6.1 gms. 20 mm

OBV: Abstracted head of Apollo right
Identifying points:
1) crude die-cutting compared to 805-7
2) 'U'-shaped curls
3) crude 'yoke', made up of rectangle and small crescents

REV: Disjointed horse left
Identifying points:
1) sunflower below horse made up of central pellet surrounded by large pellets as opposed to the usual small ones
2) two curves of horse's neck not well-distinguished, and may appear as one if the coin is lightly-struck

CLASSIFICATION: Corieltauvian B

NOTES: Many in museums.

805-11     REDUCED WEIGHT TYPE ca. 45 B.C.     ER
N̸ Stater 5.6–6.1 gms. 18 mm

OBV: Abstracted head of Apollo right
Identifying points:
1) spike with two crescents
2) small pellets near crescents and spike
3) wreath: leaves inwards

REV: Disjointed horse left
Identifying points:
1) later-style horse as on 807–1
2) sunflower below horse
3) pellet with rays emanating from it in front of horse
4) two parallel exergual lines
5) vertical lines apend from lower exergual line

CLASSIFICATION: Corieltauvian B

NOTES: Many in museums.
Modern 'Haslemere' forgery see 805–11F.

807–1    TRANSITIONAL TYPE ONE ca. 45 B.C.    ER
Aʹ Stater 5.6–6.1 gms. 17 mm

OBV: Abstracted head of Apollo right
Identifying points:
1) spike with two crescents
2) diagonal linear depression with curls on either side
3) curls on right side of depression are combined with the stylized 'yoke'
4) short, parallel lines below curls run diagonally in same direction as linear depression

REV: Disjointed horse left
Identifying points:
1) later-style horse, as on 805–11
2) Wavy-armed spiral below horse

CLASSIFICATION: Corieltauvian B

NOTES: Most in museums.

## SOUTH FERRIBY TYPE STATERS

In the past, several different varieties of coins were included under the South Ferriby Type. All had a highly stylized horse on the reverse, with variations in the ornaments in the field. The series is one of bewildering complexity and to make it more understandable, the term 'South Ferriby Type' is now limited to only one variety, number 811. The other varieties have been renamed, basically according to the field ornaments.

The ornaments above the horse include variations of an anchor-like object; a rectangle with dots, which is now called a domino; and a lozenge-shaped box with pellets, which is now called a kite. Below the horse appear a six- or eight-pointed star, a wavy-armed star, a sunflower, or a spiral. The upper portions of the horse's front legs are either made up of a single line (the normal type); or two lines, either both straight, or one straight and one curved.

To add to the complexity, the obverse dies were often used until they were almost completely obliterated, yielding almost-uniface varieties. Coins made of bronze cores wrapped in gold foil are known for many types and the dies from which they were struck are competently engraved.

Consequently, when all these variations are combined, a tremendous number of types may be postulated. Many of these are not known to exist today; but many do, and others will probably appear in the future. Consequently, the following catalogue section has been constructed to accommodate the potential varieties. The following table gives the catalogue numbers and descriptions, along with an indication of those types known to exist today.

| Cat. Number | Exists ? | Type | Object Above Horse | Object Below Horse | Fore Legs | Oblit Die | Æ Core |
|---|---|---|---|---|---|---|---|
| 809–1 | Y | Sunflower | Anchor, Form? | Sunflower | Normal | | |
| 809–2 | | ,, | ,, | ,, | ,, | | X |
| 809–3 | | ,, | ,, | ,, | ,, | X | |
| 809–4 | | ,, | ,, | ,, | ,, | X | X |
| 811–1 | Y | S. Ferriby | Anchor | 6-pt Star | ,, | | |
| 811–2 | Y | ,, | ,, | ,, | ,, | | X |
| 811–3 | Y | ,, | ,, | ,, | ,, | X | |
| 811–4 | | ,, | ,, | ,, | ,, | X | X |
| 811–5 | Y | ,, | ,, | 8-pt Star | ,, | | |
| 811–6 | Y | ,, | ,, | ,, | ,, | | X |
| 811–7 | Y | ,, | ,, | ,, | ,, | X | |
| 811–8 | | ,, | ,, | ,, | ,, | X | X |
| 811–9 | Y | ,, | ,, | Wavy-Armed | ,, | | |
| 811–10 | | ,, | ,, | Star | ,, | | X |
| 811–11 | | ,, | ,, | ,, | ,, | X | |
| 811–12 | | ,, | ,, | ,, | ,, | X | X |
| 811–13 | | ,, | Drooping | 6-pt Star | ,, | | |
| 811–14 | | ,, | Arms Anchor | ,, | ,, | | X |
| 811–15 | | ,, | ,, | ,, | ,, | X | |
| 811–16 | | ,, | ,, | ,, | ,, | X | X |
| 811–17 | Y | ,, | ,, | 8-pt Star | ,, | | |
| 811–18 | | ,, | ,, | ,, | ,, | | X |
| 811–19 | | ,, | ,, | ,, | ,, | X | |
| 811–20 | | ,, | ,, | ,, | ,, | X | X |
| 811–21 | Y | ,, | Spiral | 6-pt Star | ,, | | |
| 811–22 | | ,, | Anchor | ,, | ,, | | X |
| 811–23 | Y | ,, | ,, | ,, | ,, | X | |

| Cat. Number | Exists ? | Type | Object Above Horse | Object Below Horse | Fore Legs | Oblit Die | Æ Core |
|---|---|---|---|---|---|---|---|
| 811–24 | | S. Ferriby | ,, | ,, | Normal | X | X |
| 811–25 | | ,, | ,, | 8-pt Star | ,, | | |
| 811–26 | | ,, | ,, | ,, | ,, | | X |
| 811–27 | | ,, | ,, | ,, | ,, | X | |
| 811–28 | | ,, | Anchor | 8-pt Star | ,, | X | X |
| 811–29 | Y | ,, | Spread-Arms | 6-pt Star | ,, | | |
| 811–30 | | ,, | Anchor | ,, | ,, | | X |
| 811–31 | | ,, | ,, | ,, | ,, | X | |
| 811–32 | | ,, | ,, | ,, | ,, | X | X |
| 811–33 | | ,, | ,, | 8-pt Star | ,, | | |
| 811–34 | | ,, | ,, | ,, | ,, | | X |
| 811–35 | | ,, | ,, | ,, | ,, | X | |
| 811–36 | | ,, | ,, | ,, | ,, | X | X |
| 815–1 | Y | Transitional | Spread-Arms | 6-pt Star | 2 Lines | | |
| 815–2 | | Type Two | Anchor? | ,, | Straight | | X |
| 815–3 | | ,, | ,, | ,, | ,, | X | |
| 815–4 | | ,, | ,, | ,, | ,, | X | X |
| 815–5 | Y | ,, | ,, | ,, | 1 Straight | | |
| 815–6 | | ,, | ,, | ,, | 1 Curved | | X |
| 815–7 | | ,, | ,, | ,, | Line | X | |
| 815–8 | | ,, | ,, | ,, | ,, | X | X |
| 815–9 | Y | ,, | ,, | 8-pt Star | 2 Lines | | |
| 815–10 | | ,, | ,, | ,, | Straight | | X |
| 815–10 | | ,, | ,, | ,, | Straight | | X |
| 815–11 | | ,, | ,, | ,, | ,, | X | |
| 815–12 | | ,, | ,, | ,, | ,, | X | X |
| 815–13 | | ,, | ,, | ,, | 1 Straight | | |
| 815–14 | | ,, | ,, | ,, | 1 Curved | | X |
| 815–15 | | ,, | ,, | ,, | Line | X | |
| 815–16 | | ,, | ,, | ,, | ,, | X | X |
| 817–1 | Y | Wheel | Spread-Arms | Wheel | 2 Lines | | |
| 817–2 | | Type | Anchor | ,, | Straight | | X |
| 817–3 | | ,, | ,, | ,, | ,, | X | |
| 817–4 | | ,, | ,, | ,, | ,, | X | X |
| 817–5 | | ,, | ,, | ,, | 1 Straight | | |
| 817–6 | | ,, | ,, | ,, | 1 Curved | · | X |
| 817–7 | | ,, | ,, | ,, | Line | X | |
| 817–8 | | ,, | ,, | ,, | ,, | X | X |
| 819–1 | | Transitional | Spiral | 6-pt Star | Normal | | |
| 819–2 | | Type Three | Anchor | ,, | ,, | | X |
| 819–3 | Y | ,, | W/Boot | ,, | ,, | X | |
| 819–4 | | ,, | ,, | ,, | ,, | X | X |
| 821–1 | Y | Trefoil | ,, | ,, | ,, | | |
| 821–2 | | ,, | ,, | ,, | ,, | | X |

| Cat. Number | Exists ? | Type | Object Above Horse | Object Below Horse | Fore Legs | Oblit Die | Æ Core |
|---|---|---|---|---|---|---|---|
| 825–1 | Y | Kite | Kite/4 Dots | Spiral | ,, | | |
| 825–2 | | ,, | ,, | ,, | ,, | | X |
| 825–3 | | ,, | ,, | ,, | ,, | X | |
| 825–4 | | Kite | Kite/4 Dots | Spiral | Normal | X | X |
| 825–5 | | ,, | Kite/3 Dots | ,, | ,, | | |
| 825–6 | | ,, | ,, | ,, | ,, | | X |
| 825–7 | | ,, | ,, | ,, | ,, | X | |
| 825–8 | Y | ,, | ,, | ,, | ,, | X | X |
| 825–9 | Y | ,, | Open-End Kite | ,, | ,, | | |
| 825–10 | | ,, | 3 Dots | ,, | ,, | | X |
| 825–11 | | ,, | ,, | ,, | ,, | X | |
| 825–12 | | ,, | ,, | ,, | ,, | X | X |
| | | | | | | | |
| 829–1 | Y | Domino | Domino/4 Dots | ,, | ,, | | |
| 829–2 | | ,, | ,, | ,, | ,, | | X |
| 829–3 | Y | ,, | ,, | ,, | ,, | X | |
| 829–4 | Y | ,, | ,, | ,, | ,, | X | X |
| 829–5 | | ,, | Domino/3 Dots | ,, | ,, | | |
| 829–16 | | ,, | ,, | ,, | ,, | | X |
| 829–7 | | ,, | ,, | ,, | ,, | X | |
| 829–8 | | ,, | ,, | ,, | ,, | X | X |

809–1    SUNFLOWER TYPE ca. 45–10 B.C.    ER
Æ Stater 5.2–5.7 gms. 19 mm

OBV: Abstracted head of Apollo right
Identifying points:
    1) spike with one crescent, end of spike may
      be bent to form two-pronged hook
    2) wreath: leaves inwards

REV: Disjointed horse left
Identifying points:
    1) sunflower below horse

CLASSIFICATION: Corieltauvian C

811–1    SOUTH FERRIBY TYPE ca. 45–10 B.C.    S
Æ Stater 5.2–5.7 gms. 18 mm

OBV: Abstracted head of Apollo right
Identifying points:
    1) spike with one crescent, end of spike may
      be bent to form two-pronged hook
    2) wreath: leaves inwards

REV: Disjointed horse left
Identifying points:
    1) pointed 'anchor' above horse
    2) six-pointed star below horse

CLASSIFICATION: Corieltauvian D

NOTES: A variety with a four-pointed star is known,
    see 835–1.

811–2    SOUTH FERRIBY TYPE ca. 45–10 B.C.    ER
Aʹ/Æ Plated Stater ca. 4.7 gms. 19 mm

OBV: Abstracted head of Apollo right
Identifying points:
    1) spike with one crescent, end of spike may
        be bent to form two-pronged hook
    2) wreath: leaves inwards

REV: Disjointed horse left
Identifying points:
    1) pointed 'anchor' above horse
    2) six-pointed star below horse

CLASSIFICATION: Corieltauvian D

NOTES: Æ core of plated stater.

811–3    SOUTH FERRIBY TYPE ca. 45–10 B.C.    ER
Aʹ Stater 5.2–5.7 gms. 18 mm

OBV: Abstracted head of Apollo right
Identifying points:
    1) almost obliterated obverse die

REV: Disjointed horse left
Identifying points:
    1) pointed 'anchor' above horse
    2) six-pointed star below horse

CLASSIFICATION: Corieltauvian D

NOTES: Obverse die of 811–1 used until almost
    completely obliterated, some examples show
    almost a plain obverse.

811–5     SOUTH FERRIBY TYPE ca. 45–10 B.C.     S
A′ Stater 5.2–5.7 gms. 18 mm

OBV: Abstracted head of Apollo right
Identifying points:
    1) spike with one crescent, end of spike may
       be bent to form two-pronged hook
    2) wreath: leaves inwards

REV: Disjointed horse left
Identifying points:
    1) pointed 'anchor' above horse
    2) eight-pointed star below horse

CLASSIFICATION: Corieltauvian D

811–6     SOUTH FERRIBY TYPE ca. 45–10 B.C.     ER
A′/Æ Plated Stater ca. 4.1 gms. 18 mm

OBV: Abstracted head of Apollo right
Identifying points:
    1) spike with one crescent, end of spike may
       be bent to form two-pronged hook
    2) wreath: leaves inwards

REV: Disjointed horse left
Identifying points:
    1) pointed 'anchor' above horse
    2) eight-pointed star below horse

CLASSIFICATION: Corieltauvian D

NOTES: Æ core of plated stater.

811–7     SOUTH FERRIBY TYPE ca. 45–10 B.C.     ER
A′ Stater 5.2–5.7 gms. 19 mm

OBV: Abstracted head of Apollo right
Identifying points:
    1) almost obliterated obverse die

REV: Disjointed horse left
Identifying points:
    1) pointed 'anchor' above horse
    2) eight-pointed star below horse

CLASSIFICATION: Corieltauvian D

NOTES: Obverse die of 811–5 used until almost completely obliterated, some examples show almost a plain obverse.

Allen'63 Coritani Sylloge number 65 has seven-pointed star, but this is considered to be a die–cutting error, see 837–3.

811–9     SOUTH FERRIBY TYPE ca. 45–10 B.C.     S
*N* Stater 5.2–5.7 gms. 18 mm

OBV: Abstracted head of Apollo right
Identifying points:
  1) spike with one crescent, end of spike may be bent to form two-pronged hook
  2) wreath: leaves inwards

REV: Disjointed horse left
Identifying points:
  1) pointed 'anchor' above horse
  2) wavy-armed star below horse

CLASSIFICATION: Corieltauvian D

811–17     SOUTH FERRIBY TYPE ca. 45–10 B.C.     ER
*N* Stater 5.2–5.7 gms. 20 mm

OBV: Abstracted head of Apollo right
Identifying points:
  1) spike with one crescent, end of spike may be bent to form two-pronged hook
  2) wreath: leaves inwards

REV: Disjointed horse left
Identifying points:
  1) arms of 'anchor' droop downwards and do not encircle pellets

CLASSIFICATION: Corieltauvian D

811–21     SOUTH FERRIBY TYPE ca. 45–10 B.C.     ER
*N* Stater 5.2–5.7 gms. 19 mm

OBV: Abstracted head of Apollo right
Identifying points:
  1) spike with one crescent, end of spike may be bent to form two-pronged hook
  2) wreath: leaves inwards

REV: Disjointed horse left
Identifying points:
1) 'anchor' above horse transformed into two spirals encompassing pellets
2) six-pointed star below horse

CLASSIFICATION: Corieltauvian D

811–23    SOUTH FERRIBY TYPE ca. 45–10 B.C.    ER
Æ Stater 5.2–5.7 gms. 18 mm

OBV: Abstracted head of Apollo right
Identifying points:
1) almost obliterated obverse die

REV: Disjointed horse left
Identifying points:
1) 'anchor' above horse transformed into two spirals encompassing pellets
2) six-pointed star below horse

CLASSIFICATION: Corieltauvian D

NOTES: Obverse die of 811–21 used until almost completely obliterated, some examples show almost a plain obverse.

811–29    SOUTH FERRIBY TYPE ca. 45–10 B.C.    ER
Æ Stater 5.2–5.7 gms. 18 mm

OBV: Abstracted head of Apollo right
Identifying points:
1) spike with one crescent, end of spike may be bent to form two-pronged hook
2) wreath: leaves inwards

REV: Disjointed horse left
Identifying points:
1) 'anchor' has spread arms curling upwards
2) six-pointed star below horse

CLASSIFICATION: Corieltauvian D

815–1    TRANSITIONAL TYPE TWO    ER
ca. 45–10 B.C.
Æ Stater 5.2–5.7 gms. 17 mm

OBV: Abstracted head of Apollo right
Identifying points:
1) spike with one crescent, end of spike may be bent to form two-pronged hook

2) wreath: leaves inwards

REV: Disjointed horse left
Identifying points:
    1) front forelegs of horse are made up of two
       straight lines
    2) six-pointed star below horse

CLASSIFICATION: Corieltauvian D

815-5    TRANSITIONAL TYPE TWO        ER
          ca. 45-10 B.C.
          Aʹ Stater 5.2-5.7 gms. 18 mm

OBV: Abstracted head of Apollo right
Identifying points:
    1) spike with one crescent, end of spike may
       be bent to form two-pronged hook
    2) wreath: leaves inwards

REV: Disjointed horse left
Identifying points:
    1) front forelegs of horse are made up of one
       curved and one straight line
    2) six-pointed star below horse

CLASSIFICATION: Corieltauvian D

815-9    TRANSITIONAL TYPE TWO        ER
          ca. 45-10 B.C.
          Aʹ Stater 5.2-5.7 gms. 18 mm

OBV: Abstracted head of Apollo right
Identifying points:
    1) spike with one crescent, end of spike may
       be bent to form two-pronged hook
    2) wreath: leaves inwards

REV: Disjointed horse left
Identifying points:
    1) front forelegs of horse are made up of two
       straight lines
    2) eight-pointed star below horse

CLASSIFICATION: Corieltauvian D

817-1    **WHEEL TYPE** ca. 45–10 B.C.                    ER
Æ Stater 5.2–5.7 gms. 18 mm

OBV: Abstracted head of Apollo right
Identifying points:
    1) spike with one crescent, end of spike may be bent to form two-pronged hook
    2) wreath: leaves inwards

REV: Disjointed horse left
Identifying points:
    1) front forelegs of horse are made up of two straight lines
    2) four-spoked wheel below horse

CLASSIFICATION: Corieltauvian E

819-3    **TRANSITIONAL TYPE THREE**              ER
ca. 45–10 B.C.
Æ Stater 5.2–5.7 gms. 18 mm

OBV: Abstracted head of Apollo right
Identifying points:
    1) obverse die almost obliterated

REV: Disjointed horse left
Identifying points:
    1) 'anchor' above horse transformed into two spirals encompassing pellets
    2) boot-like object in centre of horse
    3) six-pointed star below horse

CLASSIFICATION: Corieltauvian E

NOTES: Obverse die used until almost completely obliterated, some examples show almost a plain obverse.

821-1    **TREFOIL TYPE** ca. 45–10 B.C.              ER
Æ Stater 5.2–5.7 gms. 20 mm

OBV: Elaborate trefoil
Identifying points:
    1) six pellets encircling a single pellet, all within a circle
    2) three large leaves extend from circle
    3) field of coin has raised striations as if die was smoothed off with a file

NOTES: This is the earliest extant Corieltauvian type because it conforms closest to the denarii of C. f. Hostidius Geta.

The reversed 'S' object below the boar is the vestige of the dog on the Roman prototype. The reverse die was used until severely damaged, a large die-break is often seen in front of the horse's nose.

Reverse adapted from 80–1.

855–5    HOSTIDIUS TYPE 55–45 B.C.                    ER

Æ Unit ca. 1.0 gm. 14 mm

OBV: Boar right

Identifying points:
1) spear piercing boar is missing
2) ring and pellet motifs surround boar
3) vestiges of reversed 'S' object below boar

REV: Celticized horse left

Identifying points:
1) elaborate anemone above horse
2) ring and pellet motifs in front of and behind horse

CLASSIFICATION: Corieltauvian B

855–7    HOSTIDIUS TYPE 55–45 B.C.                    ER

Æ Unit 14 mm

OBV: Boar right

Identifying points:
1) as 855–5

REV: Celticized horse left

Identifying points:
1) as 855–5, but no pellet-in-ring motif in front of horse

CLASSIFICATION: Corieltauvian B

855–8    HOSTIDIUS TYPE 55–45 B.C.                    ER

Æ Unit 14–15 mm

OBV: Boar right

Identifying points:
1) as 855-3, but no reversed 'S' below boar

REV: Celticized horse left
Identifying points:
    1) similar to 855-3
    2) pellet-in-ring inside ring of pellets above horse
    3) pellet-in-ring motif in front of horse
    4) ring, or pellet-in-ring motif below horse

CLASSIFICATION: Corieltauvian B

NOTES: A later variety than 855-3, because the reversed 'S' has been deleted.

857-1    **HOSTIDIUS TYPE 55–45 B.C.**    ER
Æ Unit ca. 1.4 gms. 16 mm

OBV: Boar right
Identifying points:
    1) large ring of pellets above boar
    2) ring-and-pellet motifs above, below and in front of boar
    3) upper portion of boar's front leg made up of two lines

REV: Celticized horse left
Identifying points:
    1) large ring of pellets above horse
    2) ring-and-pellet motifs above, below and in front of horse

CLASSIFICATION: Corieltauvian B

NOTES: A later variety, because reversed 'S' object has been replaced with a ring-and-pellet motif.

857-3    **HOSTIDIUS TYPE 55–45 B.C.**    ER
Æ Unit 15 mm

OBV: Boar right
Identifying points:
    1) as 857-1

REV: Celticized horse left
Identifying points:
    1) as 875-1, but no ring-and-pellet motif below horse

CLASSIFICATION: Corieltauvian B

NOTES: Most are in museums.

857-5    HOSTIDIUS TYPE 55-45 B.C.                    ER
Æ Unit 15 mm

OBV: Boar right
Identifying points:
  1) as 857-1, but ring-in-pellet motif in ring of
     pellets above boar
REV: Celticized horse left
Identifying points:
  1) as 857-1, but ring-in-pellet motif in ring of
     pellets above horse

CLASSIFICATION: Corieltauvian B

NOTES: Most are in museums.

860-1    HOSTIDIUS TYPE 55-45 B.C.                    ER
Æ Unit ca. 1.3 gms. 14 mm

OBV: Boar right
Identifying points:
  1) boar stands on exergual line made up of
     two rows of pellets
  2) wheel in front of and behind boar
OBV: Celticized horse right
Identifying points:
  1) eight-spoked wheel above horse
  2) Ring in front of horse

CLASSIFICATION: Corieltauvian B

862-1    HOSTIDIUS TYPE 55-45 B.C.                    ER
Æ Fractional Unit ca. 0.5 gms. 12 mm

OBV: Boar right
Identifying points:
  1) four-spoked wheel above boar
  2) ring-and-pellet motif behind boar
OBV: Celticized horse right
Identifying points:
  1) four-spoked wheel above horse

CLASSIFICATION: Corieltauvian B

NOTES: This coin is a fractional denomination of
       860-1.

864-1     HOSTIDIUS TYPE 55–45 B.C.                    ER
Æ Unit ca. 1.2–1.4 gms. 13 mm

OBV: Boar right
Identifying points:
    1) ring-and-double-pellet motif behind boar
    2) two elaborate curves above boar

REV: Celticized horse left
Identifying points:
    1) ring-and-double-pellet motif above horse
    2) elaborate curve above ring-and-double-pellet motif

CLASSIFICATION: Corieltauvian B

866-1     HOSTIDIUS TYPE 55–45 B.C.                    ER
Æ Fractional Unit ca. 0.3 gms. 0.9 mm

OBV: Boar right
Identifying points:
    1) pellet below boar

REV: Celticized horse left
Identifying points:
    1) pellets above and below horse

CLASSIFICATION: Corieltauvian B

NOTES: Possibly a fractional denomination of 864-1.

867-1     HOSTIDIUS TYPE 55–45 B.C.                    ER
Æ Unit ca. 1.1–1.2 gms. 15 mm

OBV: Boar left
Identifying points:
    1) ring-and-pellet motif behind boar
    2) large pellet on boar's shoulder
    3) four elaborate curves above boar

REV: Celticized horse left
Identifying points:
    1) large ring of pellets enclosing a ring-and-pellet motif in front of horse
    2) same object above horse, but large ring comprised of a greater number of pellets
    3) two ring-and-pellet motifs below horse with a row of pellets in between running vertically

CLASSIFICATION: Corieltauvian B

875–1    SOUTH FERRIBY TYPE ca. 45–10 B.C.         ER
Æ Unit 17 mm

OBV: Stylized boar right
Identifying points:
  1) ring-and-pellet motif above, below and in front of boar
  2) upper portion of boar's front leg comprised of two lines

REV: Celticized horse right
Identifying points:
  1) horse more stylized than on Hostidius type
  2) ring of pellets above horse
  3) ring-and-pellet motif below horse
  4) upper portion of horse's front legs comprised of two lines
  5) horse has 'belt'

CLASSIFICATION: Corieltauvian D

875–2    SOUTH FERRIBY TYPE ca. 45–10 B.C.         ER
Æ Unit ca. 1.4 gms. 15 mm

OBV: Stylized boar right
Identifying points:
  1) ring-and-pellet motifs below and behind boar
  2) large ring of pellets with large central pellet above boar
  3) upper portion of boar's front leg comprised of two lines

REV: Celticized horse right
Identifying points:
  1) horse more stylized than on Hostidius type
  2) ring of pellets above horse
  3) ring-and-pellet motifs below and in front of horse
  4) upper portion of horse's front legs comprised of two lines
  5) horse has 'necklace'

CLASSIFICATION: Corieltauvian D

**877-1**     SOUTH FERRIBY TYPE ca. 45–10 B.C.          ER
Æ Unit ca. 1.4 gm. 15 mm

OBV: Stylized boar right
Identifying points:
   1) pellet below boar's tail
   2) large ring of pellets above boar
   3) upper portion of boar's front leg comprised
      of two lines
   4) no object below boar

REV: Celticized horse right
Identifying points:
   1) horse more stylized than on Hostidius type
   2) ring of pellets above horse
   3) pellet below horse's tail
   4) upper portion of horse's front legs com-
      prised of two lines
   5) horse has 'necklace' and 'belt'
   6) no object below horse

CLASSIFICATION: Corieltauvian D

NOTES: Pellet below horse's tail may be a privy mark
       denoting date or issue.

**877-3**     SOUTH FERRIBY TYPE ca. 45–10 B.C.          VR
Æ Unit ca. 1.1 gms. 15 mm

OBV: Almost plain
Identifying points:
   1) vestiges of boar may be visible

REV: Celticized horse right
Identifying points:
   1) horse more stylized than on Hostidius type
   2) ring of pellets with large central pellet above
      horse
   3) two pellets below horse's tail
   4) upper portion of horse's front legs com-
      prised of two lines
   5) horse has 'necklace' and 'belt'
   6) no object below horse

CLASSIFICATION: Corieltauvian D

NOTES: Pellets below horse's tail may be a privy
       mark denoting date or issue.
       Obverse die used until almost completely
       obliterated.

877–5     SOUTH FERRIBY TYPE ca. 45–10 B.C.       ER
Æ Unit 16 mm

OBV: Almost plain
Identifying points:
    1) vestiges of boar may be visible

REV: Celticized horse right
Identifying points:
    1) horse more stylized than on Hostidius type
    2) large ring with large central pellet above horse
    3) no pellets below horse's tail
    4) upper portion of horse's front legs comprised of two lines
    5) horse has 'necklace'
    6) horse has a mane
    7) no object below horse

CLASSIFICATION: Corieltauvian D

NOTES: Obverse die used until almost completely obliterated.

877–7     SOUTH FERRIBY TYPE ca. 45–10 B.C.       R
Æ Unit ca. 1.2 gms. 13mm

OBV: Almost plain
Identifying points:
    1) vestiges of boar may be visible

REV: Celticized horse right
Identifying points:
    1) horse more stylized than on Hostidius type
    2) large ring of pellets above horse
    3) one or more pellets below horse's tail
    4) upper portion of horse's front legs comprised of two lines
    5) no object below horse

CLASSIFICATION: Corieltauvian D

NOTES: Pellets below horse's tail may be a privy mark denoting date or issue.
Obverse die used until almost completely obliterated.

879-1    SOUTH FERRIBY TYPE ca. 45–10 B.C.    VR
Æ Fractional Unit 0.4–0.6 gms. 11 mm

OBV: Almost plain
Identifying points:
  1) vestiges of boar may be visible

REV: Celticized horse right
Identifying points:
  1) horse more stylized than on Hostidius type
  2) large ring of pellets above horse, possibly
     with large central pellet
  3) one or more pellets below horse's tail
  4) upper portion of horse's front legs com-
     prised of two lines
  5) three pellets below horse

CLASSIFICATION: Corieltauvian D

NOTES: Pellets below horse's tail may be a privy
       mark denoting date or issue.
       Obverse die used until almost completely
       obliterated.
       Fractional denomination, possibly an Æ
       Half Unit.

881-1    SOUTH FERRIBY TYPE ca. 45–10 B.C.    ER
Æ Fractional Unit ca. 0.2 gms. 1.0 mm

OBV: Almost plain
Identifying points:
  1) vestiges of boar may be visible

REV: Celticized horse right
Identifying points:
  1) horse more stylized than on Hostidius type
  2) probably a large ring of pellets above horse,
     possibly with a large central pellet
  3) upper portion of horse's front legs com-
     prised of two lines
  5) no object below horse

CLASSIFICATION: Corieltauvian D

NOTES: Obverse die used until almost completely
       obliterated.
       Fractional denomination, possibly of 877–3
       or 877–7.

# COINS INSCRIBED AVN AST OR AVN COST

Gold staters, plated staters, silver units and half units are known. The heaviest inscribed gold staters occur in this series, dating them earliest. A pellet in the centre of the horse on the stater sets this type apart from all other inscribed types, but it is reminiscent of the boot-like object in the Trefoil Type, number 821–1.

910–1  AVN AST 5–1 B.C.                                    ER
Aʹ Stater 5.55 gms. 19 mm

OBV: Corieltauvian Apollo-Wreath
Identifying points:
1) Wreath from head of Apollo now fills field of coin
2) crossbar with crescents bisects wreath
3) ornate ring and pellet motifs at ends of crossbar

REV: Celticized horse left
Identifying points:
1) horse has pellet in ring for a head
2) AVN above horse
3) uncertain legend, probably OST below horse
4) letter 'A' has no crossbars
5) question-mark shaped object below tail
6) pellet in centre of body

CLASSIFICATION: Corieltauvian J

NOTES: Estimated standard weight given.
Existing coins weigh as much as 5.55 gms.

910–2  AVN AST 5–1 B.C.                                    ER
Aʹ/Æ Plated Stater 3.4–5.5 gms. 19 mm

OBV: Corieltauvian Apollo-Wreath
Identifying points:
1) as 910–1

REV: Celticized horse left
Identifying points:
1) as 910–1

CLASSIFICATION: Corieltauvian J

NOTES: Possibly struck from official dies.
Obverse die may be obliterated.
Typical weight given.

914-1     AVN AST 5-1 B.C.                                    VR
Æ Unit ca. 1.1 gm. 12 mm

OBV: Plain
Identifying points:
    1) some traces of Apollo-Wreath may appear
       on some coins

REV: Celticized horse left
Identifying points:
    1) AVN above horse, no crossbar on letter 'A'
    2) pellet above horse
    3) question-mark shaped object below tail

CLASSIFICATION: Corieltauvian J

NOTES: 'AST' may appear below horse, or 'OST'

914-3     AVN AST 5-1 B.C.                                    ER
Æ Unit 12 mm

OBV: Plain
Identifying points:
    1) no traces of Apollo-Wreath

REV: Celticized horse left
Identifying points:
    1) AVN above horse
    2) pellet above horse
    3) floral pattern below horse

CLASSIFICATION: Corieltauvian J

918-1     AVN AST 5-1 B.C.                                    ER
Æ Half Unit ca. 0.5 gms. 11 mm

OBV: Plain
Identifying points:
    1) traces of Apollo-Wreath may appear on
       some coins

REV: Celticized horse left
Identifying points:
    1) AVN above horse, no crossbar on letter 'A'

CLASSIFICATION: Corieltauvian J

NOTES: 'AST' may appear below horse, or 'OST'
       Many are in museums.

918–3     AVN AST 5–1 B.C.                                      ER
          Æ Half Unit ca. 0.5 gms. 11 mm

OBV: Plain
Identifying points:
   1) as 914–3

REV: Celticized horse left
Identifying points:
   1) as 914–3

CLASSIFICATION: Corieltauvian I

## COINS INSCRIBED ESVP ASV

Gold staters, plated staters and silver units are known. The crosses in the Apollo-Wreath and the star below the horse's tail on the stater links this type to the First Coinage of VEP CORF. The catalogue number 928–1 is reserved for a silver half unit, should one be discovered.

920–1     ESVP ASV 1–5 A.D.                                    ER
          Ꞥ Stater 5.40 gms. 19 mm

OBV: Corieltauvian Apollo-Wreath
Identifying points:
   1) as 910–1
   2) two crosses in wreath

REV: Celticized horse left
Identifying points:
   1) star below tail
   2) ESVP above horse, first letter usually uncertain
   3) ASV below horse
   4) pellet in centre of body

CLASSIFICATION: Corieltauvian K

NOTES: Star below horse's tail and crosses in the wreath link ESVP ASV and VEP CORF First Coinage chronologically.
Some are in museums.
Estimated standard weight given, since too few coins exist to determine standard with certainty.

920-3        ESVP ASV 1–5 A.D.                        ER
             Æ/Æ Plated Stater 3.9–4.9 gms. 18 mm
             OBV: Corieltauvian Apollo-Wreath
             Identifying points:
                 1) as 920–1
             REV: Celticized horse left
             Identifying points:
                 1) as  920–1
             CLASSIFICATION: Corieltauvian K
             NOTES: Possibly struck from official dies.

924-1        ESVP ASV 1–5 A.D.                        ER
             ÆR Unit ca. 1.1 gms. 14 mm
             OBV: Enlarged Apollo-Wreath
             Identifying points:
                 1) Apollo-Wreath fills field of coin
                 2) pellet on either side of wreath
                 3) crosses in wreath
             REV: Celticized horse right
             Identifying points:
                 1) ESVP above horse
                 2) ASV below horse
             CLASSIFICATION: Corieltauvian K
             NOTES: Crosses and pellets in the wreath link this
                    type to the First Coinage of VEP CORF.
                    Not illustrated.

## COINS INSCRIBED VEP CORF

Three distinct coinages are known: the First Coinage, with a star below the horse's tail; the Second Coinage, with a pellet-in-ring motif below the tail; and the Third Coinage, with three pellets below the tail.

The chronological relationship of ESVP ASV, the three coinages of VEP CORF and DVMNOC TIGIR SENO is well-established by a typological analysis. The crosses in the Apollo-wreath staters and the star below the horse's tail links the First Coinage to its predecessor ESVP ASV. The silver units of ESVP ASV and VEP CORF First Coinage both have pellets and crosses in the wreaths. The three pellets on the Third Coinage reappear under the horse's neck on the succeeding type, DVMNOC TIGIR SENO.

The large number of varieties, and the extensive use of privy marks by VEP CORF argues for a relatively long coinage, compared to other Corieltauvian inscribed issues. The estimated ten-year span has been divided amongst the three coinages arbitrarily.

The spelling of VEP CORF varies widely and somewhat depends on the available space in the field. Possibly, the CORF should be read COR F, indicating a 'son of COR' construction, though the lack of a stop between the R and F argues against this. One silver variety, with finer die-cutting overall, gives a reading VEPOC COMES or VEPOC OMES.

Gold staters, silver units and half units are known for all three coinages. Plated staters are known for the Third Coinage, though off-centre striking and the poor state of preservation of most cores often make it difficult to determine the object below the tail. Plated staters probably exist undetected for the other two coinages. Catalogue numbers 930-2 and 940-2 are reserved for the cores corresponding to 930-1 and 940-1, should they be discovered.

The obverse dies for the silver units were generally used until completely obliterated. No attempt has been made to list the obliterated die states under separate catalogue numbers because insufficient information exists.

Although VEP CORF coins are extremely rare by individual varieties, an example of a silver unit is usually not too difficult to obtain. The three varieties of staters rate a 'VR', taken together, but most are held in museums.

## VEP CORF FIRST COINAGE

930-1     VEP CORF FIRST COINAGE 5–8 A.D.            ER
          A′ Stater 5.40 gms. 20 mm

          OBV: Corieltauvian Apollo-Wreath
          Identifying points:
              1) Apollo-wreath fills field
              2) two crosses in wreath

          REV: Celticized horse left
          Identifying points:
              1) VEP, retrograde, above horse
              2) CORF below horse
              3) crude eight-pointed star below horse's tail

          CLASSIFICATION: Corieltauvian L

          NOTES: The crosses in the wreath and the star below
                  the horse's tail link this type to the coinage
                  of ESVP ASV.
                  Standard weight given.
                  Most are in museums.

934-1     VEP CORF FIRST COINAGE 5-8 A.D.     ER
Æ Unit ca. 1.1 gm 14 mm

OBV: Enlarged Apollo-Wreath
Identifying points:
1) Apollo-Wreath fills the field
2) pellet on either side of wreath
3) crosses in wreath

REV: Celticized horse right
Identifying points:
1) star below horse's tail
2) VEP above horse
3) CO below horse

CLASSIFICATION: Corieltauvian L

NOTES: Crosses and pellets in the wreath link this
type with the coinage of ESVP ASV chronologically.

938-1     VEP CORF FIRST COINAGE 5-8 A.D.     ER
Æ Half Unit ca. 0.5 gms. 11-12 mm

OBV: Enlarged Apollo-Wreath
Identifying points:
1) wreath fills field

REV: Celticized horse right
Identifying points:
1) star below tail
2) VEP above horse
3) CO below horse

CLASSIFICATION: Corieltauvian L

## VEP CORF SECOND COINAGE

940-1     VEP CORF SECOND COINAGE     ER
8-12 A.D.
Ả Stater 5.4 gms. 20 mm

OBV: Corieltauvian Apollo-Wreath
Identifying points:
1) wreath fills field
2) large question-mark objects around wreath

REV: Celticized horse left
Identifying points:
    1) pellet-in-ring below tail
    2) VEP above horse
    3) CORF below horse

CLASSIFICATION: Corieltauvian M

NOTES: Many are in museums.
        Modern forgeries exist—see 940–1F.
        Standard weight given.


943–1    **VEP CORF SECOND COINAGE**    ER
        **8–12 A.D.**
        Æ Unit ca. 1.1 gms. 14 mm

OBV: Enlarged Apollo-Wreath
Identifying points:
    1) wreath fills field

REV: Celticized horse right
Identifying points:
    1) pellet-in-ring below tail
    2) VEP above horse
    3) CORF below horse

CLASSIFICATION: Corieltauvian M
NOTES: Not illustrated.


945–1    **VEP CORF SECOND COINAGE**    ER
        **8–12 A.D.**
        Æ Unit ca. 1.1 gms. 14 mm

OBV: Enlarged Apollo-Wreath
Identifying points:
    1) wreath fills field

REV: Celticized horse right
Identifying points:
    1) pellet-in-ring below tail
    2) VEP, retrograde above horse
    3) CORF below horse

CLASSIFICATION: Corieltauvian M
NOTES: Not illustrated.

947-1     **VEP CORF SECOND COINAGE**                    ER
8-12 A.D.
Æ Half Unit ca. 0.5 gms. 11–12 mm

OBV: Enlarged Apollo-Wreath
Identifying points:
1) wreath fills field

REV: Celticized horse left
Identifying points:
1) pellet-in-ring below tail
2) VEP above horse

CLASSIFICATION: Corieltauvian M
NOTES: Not illustrated

950-1     **VEP CORF SECOND COINAGE**                    ER
8-12 A.D.
Æ Unit ca. 1.1 gms. 14 mm

OBV: Enlarged Apollo-Wreath
Identifying points:
1) wreath fills field

REV: Celticized horse right
Identifying points:
1) pellet-in-ring below tail
2) VEP above horse
3) CO below horse

CLASSIFICATION: Corieltauvian M

952-1     **VEP CORF SECOND COINAGE**                    ER
8-12 A.D.
Æ Half Unit ca. 0.5 gms. 11–12 mm

OBV: Enlarged Apollo-Wreath
Identifying points:
1) wreath fills field

REV: Celticized horse right
Identifying points:
1) pellet-in-ring below tail
2) VEP above horse
3) CO below horse

CLASSIFICATION: Corieltauvian M
NOTES: Not illustrated.

REV: Celticized horse right
Identifying points:
1) three pellets below horse's neck
2) TIGIR above horse
3) SENO below horse

CLASSIFICATION: Corieltauvian O

NOTES: No accurate weight available because most existing coins are chipped or broken.
Obverse die apparently used for some time before horizontal lines and DVMNOC were engraved because wreath is almost obliterated, but inscription is clearly visible.
Some are in museums.

## COINS INSCRIBED VOLISIOS DVMNOCOVEROS

Gold staters, plated staters, silver units and half units are known. The three pellets below the horse's neck are repeated from the coinage inscribed DVMNOC TIGIR SENO. The VOLISIOS DVMNOVELLAUNUS coinage that follows contines the triple-pellet motif below the neck, but the staters are of greatly reduced weight.

978–1    VOLISIOS DVMNOCOVEROS 20–35 A.D.    R
Ν Stater 5.40 gms. 20 mm

OBV: Corieltauvian Apollo-Wreath
Identifying points:
1) wreath fills field
2) three horizontal lines run across wreath
3) VO LI between top lines
4) SI OS between bottom lines

REV: Celticized horse left
Identifying points:
1) three pellets below horse's neck
2) DVM NOCO VER OS around horse

CLASSIFICATION: Corieltauvian P

NOTES: Some are in museums.
Standard weight given.

978-2     VOLISIOS DVMNOCOVEROS                           ER
20-35 A.D.
N/Æ Plated Stater ca. 3.0 gms. 18 mm
OBV: Corieltauvian Apollo-Wreath
Identifying points:
   1) as 978-1
REV: Celticized horse left
Identifying points:
   1) as 978-1
CLASSIFICATION: Corieltauvian P
NOTES: Ancient forgery of 978-1.


980-1     VOLISIOS DVMNOCOVEROS                           ER
20-35 A.D.
Æ Unit ca. 1.3 gms. 16 mm
OBV: Enlarged Apollo-Wreath
Identifying points:
   1) wreath fills field
   2) three horizontal lines across wreath
   3) VOLI between top lines
   4) SIOS between bottom lines
REV: Celticized horse right
Identifying points:
   1) three pellets below horse's neck
   2) DVMNOCOVEROS around horse
CLASSIFICATION: Corieltauvian P
NOTES: Not illustrated.

984-1     VOLISIOS DVMNOCOVEROS                           ER
20-35 A.D.
Æ Half Unit ca. 0.8 gms. 15 mm
OBV: Enlarged Apollo-Wreath
Identifying points:
   1) wreath fills field
   2) three horizontal lines across wreath
   3) VOLI between top lines
   4) SOIS between bottom lines

REV: Celticized horse right
Identifying points:
1) pellets below horse's neck
2) DVMNOCO around horse

CLASSIFICATION: Corieltauvian P

NOTES: Uncertain if the complete 'DVMNOCO-VEROS' appears around the horse.
Many are in museums.


# COINS INSCRIBED VOLISIOS DVMNOVELLAVNOS

Gold staters, plated staters and silver units are all known. The type continues the style of **VOLISIOS DVMNOCOVEROS** but the stater's weight is drastically reduced. The coinage was probably produced during the emergency of the Roman Invasion.

988–1     VOLISIOS DVMNOVELLAVNOS     ER
35–45 A.D.
$N$ Stater 19 mm

OBV: Corieltauvian Apollo-Wreath
Identifying points:
1) wreath fills field
2) three horizontal lines across wreath
3) VO LI between top lines
4) SI OS between bottom lines

REV: Celticized horse left
Identifying points:
1) three pellets below horse's neck
2) DVMNOVELLAVNOS around horse

CLASSIFICATION: Corieltauvian Q

NOTES: Typical weight uncertain, thought to be around 5.0 gms.
Some are in museums.

988–2     VOLISIOS DVMNOVELLAVNOS     ER
35–45 A.D.
$N$/Æ Plated Stater 3.9–4.8 gms. 20 mm

OBV: Corieltauvian Apollo-Wreath
Identifying points:
1) as 988–1

REV: Celticized horse left
Identifying points:
    1) 988–1

CLASSIFICATION: Corieltauvian Q

NOTES: Ancient forgery of 988–1.

992–1    VOLISIOS DVMNOVELLAVNOS    ER
35–45 A.D.
Æ Unit ca. 0.5 gms. 13 mm

OBV: Enlarged Apollo-Wreath
Identifying points:
    1) wreath fills field
    2) three lines across wreath
    3) VO LI between top lines
    4) SI OS between bottom lines

REV: Celticized horse right
Identifying points:
    1) pellets below horse's neck
    2) DVMNOVE around horse

CLASSIFICATION: Corieltauvian Q

NOTES: Uncertain if the complete 'DVNMOVEL-
    LAVNOS' appears around the horse.
    Most are in museums.

## COINS INSCRIBED VOLISIOS CARTIVEL

A core of a plated stater has been reported with the inscription CARTIVEL,
and another with a blundered legend DANINLIR (?). Catalogue number 993–1
is reserved for a gold stater of CARTIVEL, and 993–2 for a plated variety.

994–1    VOLISIOS CARTIVEL 45–55 A.D.    ER
Æ Unit ca. 0.5 gms. 15 mm

OBV: Enlarged Apollo-Wreath
Identifying points:
    1) wreath fill the field
    2) three horizontal lines across wreath
    3) VO LI between top lines
    4) SI OS between bottom lines

REV: Celticized horse right
Identifying points:
    1) pellets below horse's neck
    2) CARTIVEL around horse

CLASSIFICATION: Corieltauvian R

NOTES: The type was once believed to be the coinage of Queen Cartimandua, but this is now thought unlikely.
Some are in museums.

## UNCERTAIN TYPES OF THE CORIELTAUVI

The following two coins appear to be Corieltauvian, but do not fit in the normal series, typologically. They may represent irregular issues struck at the time of the Trinovantian/Catuvellaunian Interregnum. Alternatively, it is possible they are Icenian, but this is less likely.

996-1    ALE SCA 10 B.C.–10 A.D.?          ER
             Æ Unit ca. 1.8 gms. 15 mm

OBV: Boar right
Identifying points:
    1) pellet-in-ring motifs above boar
    2) ALE below boar

REV: Celticized horse right
Identifying points:
    1) pellet-in-ring motifs above horse
    2) SCA below horse, no crossbar on letter 'A'

CLASSIFICATION: None

NOTES: Modern forgeries are believed to exist.

998-1    IAT ISO 10 B.C.–10 A.D.?          ER
             Æ Unit ca. 1.0 gm 13 mm

OBV: Line with legend
Identifying points:
    1) uncertain legend, possibly IAT
    2) possibly IAT is actually the legs of an animal which is off the flan

REV: Celticized horse right
Identifying points:
    1) E above horse

CLASSIFICATION: None

NOTES: The type was recorded in Stukeley 1762, plate IV, number 1.

# THE COINAGE OF THE DOBUNNI

The Dobunni occupied Gloucestershire and Avon, parts of Hereford and Worcestershire, Somerset, Oxfordshire and Wiltshire. Their coinage comprises a small number of gold coins, mostly inscribed, and an extensive series of silver units, largely without inscriptions.

The gold staters are almost identical in appearance, making it difficult to organize and date them. The following catalogue lists them in a new order— according to their weight and metallic content. The Dobunni gradually reduced the weight and gold content of the staters, and this reveals the chronological sequence.

An analysis of the intrinsic value of the staters gives the chronological order of the inscriptions. This is, in order of decreasing standard weight and gold content: CORIO, BODVOC, ANTEDRIG, COMUX, EISV and CATTI. CORIO and BODVOC's staters contain a standard 2.6 grammes of fine gold. This drops to 2.3 grammes for ANTEDRIG and COMUX, and finally to 2.2 grammes for EISV and CATTI. Metrologically and metallurgically, the Dobunnic coinage suffered the same debasement as the coins of the other British tribes. It seems, the Dobunni were under the same pressures to devalue their coinage.

The silver coins are related to the gold issues by the objects in the fields. Those near the horse's tail seem to give the best indicators as to ruler-of-origin in many cases. Three types are inscribed and carry the names BODVOC, ANTED and EISV. The units inscribed ANTED and EISV are accompanied by uninscribed coins of a similar type.

Three clues provide fixed points to construct an absolute chronology for the coinage, as a whole. First, the silver units of BODVOC typologically date to the end of the First Century B.C. The horse on the reverse is a mirror-image of one on a quarter stater of Tasciovanus—the die cutters may have simply copied it directly onto their dies. Similarly, a Tasciovanus bronze may supply the prototype for the obverse, again in mirror-image. Previously, workers have dated BODVOC's coinage last because of the legend on the stater. The lettering need not be dated mid-First Century A.D., because similiar letters do appear on earlier coins. Generally, BODVOC's coinage should be dated about the end of Tasciovanus' reign.

The second clue is the dramatic reduction in the gold content for ANTE-DRIG—probably a reaction to the events of the Trinovantian/Catuvellaunian Interregnum. When the other tribes reduced the intrinsic value of their staters, the Dobunni reacted by debasing the gold content.

Finally, the Dobunnic coinage would have come to an end during the middle of the 40's A.D., as the Romans overran the Dobunnic territory. The plated stater with the blundered legend 'INAM' probably dates from this disturbed time.

Using the chronology of the gold staters, the following interpretation of the

Dobunnic coinage is suggested. During the Gallic War, contacts with the Dobunni were organized by the Atrebates/Regni to obtain war matériel, perhaps iron, for the Continental trade. Atrebatic Abstract Type staters are found in Dobunnic territory attesting to the trade. After the war, the tribe eventually felt the need to produce its own coins, and uninscribed gold and silver pieces were first struck about 35 B.C.

The Atrebates/Regni and Trinovantes/Catuvellauni were already striking inscribed coins by this time. The Dobunni quickly followed their lead, adding the name CORIO to their staters, around 30 B.C. Later, at the end of Tasciovanus' reign, BODVOC succeeded CORIO. He removed the Dobunnic emblem from the staters and emblazoned his name across the field. He also changed the silver coins as well, by placing a more life-like head on the obverses.

BODVOC soon disappeared during the Trinovantian/Catuvellaunian Inter-regnum, replaced by ANTEDRIG. The Dobunnic emblem was immediately restored to the staters and it was maintained by all subsequent rulers. Possibly, BODVOC's removal of the emblem had been an unpopular change. A series of inscriptions occurs after ANTEDRIG—COMUX, EISV, and CATTI—leading up to the Claudian invasion, when the coinage ends.

This chronological sequence, derived from metallurgy and metrology, is unlike that proposed by earlier scholars. Consequently, it must be viewed as a hypothesis, not proven fact. Normally in a catalogue such as this, the traditionally accepted chronologies would be used, but those proposed by Allen over twenty-five years ago are clearly unworkable today. Because the chronological interpretation here is greatly different from Allen's, the reasons for the change should be discussed.

There are two problems with Allen's interpretations. The first is the order of the inscriptions—it requires the staters to increase in intrinsic value. This is unlikely because the neighbouring tribes were reducing the value of their coins. Secondly, there is inadequate pairing of the silver units with the gold staters. The tribe used silver coins extensively and probably there were silver coins corresponding to each of the gold types.

Hoard analysis has supplied the dating evidence for many tribal coinages, the best example is the relative dating of the Icenian silver. Unfortunately, the small number of Dobunnic hoards has hampered study here since most Dobunnic coins have been single finds. Two hoards contained coins of ANTEDRIG, EISV and CATTI, and one of them had uninscribed silver, as well. This does not provide much information to construct a relative chronology.

A historical retrospective points out some additional areas of controversy. Evans, in 1864, identified the BODVOC staters as heavier than the rest and accordingly dated them earliest. Evans' argument—heavier coins are earlier—should not be taken so lightly. Additional coins have come to light since Evans wrote, so the BODVOC staters are no longer the heaviest.

The Interregnum dating for ANTEDRIG's coinage places him roughly at the time of ANTED of the Iceni. Evans' assertion—the coinages of ANTEDRIG

and the Icenian ANTED represented the unified output of a single ruler—
should be reconsidered.

Brooke, in 1933, gave a list with ANTEDRIG first and BODVOC last, but
offered no explanation, leaving it to Allen to supply the missing interpretation.
The coins seemed to have different findspot distributions, Allen noted, offering
this as evidence for paired rulers in sequence: ANTEDRIG/EISV first and
CORIO/BODVOC last. The inscribed silver coins of ANTEDRIG and EISV
were almost identical to some stylistically late uninscribed types, but BODVOC's
inscriptions looked Roman. Thus, Allen argued, ANTEDRIG and EISV must
be first, BODVOC last. He placed CATTI and COMUX in between these,
unpaired.

The argument for paired rulers is tenuous today; additional findspots have
been added to the maps and the distributions now show no statistically valid
differences. This is particularly true for CORIO and BODVOC, the two rulers
whose coinages previously had shown a good example of mutual exclusivity.

A final problem is posed by a small number of uninscribed silver coins,
described by Allen as the IRREGULAR SERIES. These have an unusual style
that does not fit in well with the rest of the Dobunnic silver. Previously, the
coins had been found only in Wiltshire, and a separate tribal group had been
suggested as its source. Today, while still unusual, the coins cannot be seen
as coming solely from Wiltshire, because recent finds have come from
Gloucestershire. The distribution may ultimately be similar to the rest of the
Dobunnic coinage. The irregular series may indeed be local issues, but there is
no strong evidence they come from a separate tribe or sub group.

The arrangement of the catalogue is as follows: The early uninscribed coins
are listed first. The Dobunni evidently used Atrebatic/Regnan coins after the
Gallic War, striking their own for the first time around 35 B.C. Then the series
of inscribed coins is given, using the order suggested by the metrology and
metallurgy. The later uninscribed silver types are listed under the most likely
ruler, based on stylistic similarities.

Allen's system of naming the silver coins by classes has been retained for the
type nomenclature because it is still a useful guide to the typology. New
classifications have been given, however, linking the gold and silver issues.

The site of a Dobunnic mint has been found at Bagendon, a large oppidum
near Cirencester. Clay 'coin-moulds', two pairs of tongs, a bronze ladle and a clay
spoon for handling molten metal were found on the site during archaeological
excavations. Several bronze lumps were found, which appeared to be the
remains of coin dies. Of interest was a number of plated forgeries of Dobunnic
coins found in the vicinity. The mint could have been turning out plated coins,
or alternatively the finds represent coins taken to the mint for authentication,
only to be discarded when the forgery was exposed by the mint workers.

## THE EARLY UNINSCRIBED COINS

Prior to the introduction of a tribal coinage, the Dobunni used the coins of the Atrebates/Regni. Sometime after 55 B.C., Atrebatic Abstract staters and quarters began to appear. Within twenty years, the tribe bagan to strike their own coins.

1005–1    DOBUNNIC EMBLEM TYPE 35–30 B.C.      ER
Æ Stater 5.55 gms. 19 mm

OBV: Dobunnic emblem
Identifying points:
1) plain, except for emblem
2) emblem in form of tree–like object with ten branches
3) ring at bottom of emblem

REV: Celticized horse right
Identifying points:
1) three tail strands with pellets
2) ear in form of ellipse
3) coffee-bean in front of and behind horse
4) six-spoked wheel below horse
5) three large pellets above tail

CLASSIFICATION: Dobunnic A

NOTES: Standard weight given, future finds may prove a slightly higher weight was used, however.
Many in museums.
Modern forgery exists—see 1005–1F.

1010–2    DOBUNNIC ABSTRACT TYPE      ER
35–30 B.C.
Æ/Æ Plater ¼ Stater ca. 1.0 gm. 12–13 mm

OBV: Celticized head of Apollo right
Identifying points:
1) spike made up of line with three pellets
2) sunburst at lower end of spike
3) wreath made up of line of pellets on left, heavy solid line in centre, and thin solid line at right
4) spike cuts wreath

REV: Celticized horse right
Identifying points:
    1) three tail strands with pellets
    2) outline crescents, probably four, around horse
    3) reversed 'S' with ring below horse
    4) tiny ring and pellet motifs around horse
    5) Sunburst with central pellet all in large ring above horse

CLASSIFICATION: Dobunnic A

NOTES: Many in museums.
        The reverse of this coin is similiar to that of 1039–1.
        The corresponding quarter stater, 1010–1, awaits discovery.

1010–3    DOBUNNIC ABSTRACT TYPE          ER
          35–30 B.C.
          N Quarter Stater 1.0–1.3 gms. 13–15 mm

OBV: Plain
Identifying points:
    1) May show traces of Celticized head of Apollo

REV: Celticized horse right
Identifying points:
    1) as 1010–2

CLASSIFICATION: Dobunnic A

NOTES: Many in museums.
        The obverse die for this coin was used until completely obliterated.

1015–1    DOBUNNIC ABSTRACT TYPE          ER
          35–30 B.C.
          N Quarter Stater 0.7–0.8 gms. 8 mm

OBV: Celticized head of Apollo right
Identifying points:
    1) spike made up of line with two pellets, ring at top and sunburst at bottom
    2) wreath made up of two lines of pellets with row of oblique dashes in between
    3) wreath continues through spike

REV: Celticized horse left

Identifying points:
1) probably three stranded tail
2) pellet in ring motif on horse's breast and rump
3) large sunburst below horse
4) large sunburst in ring above horse, possibly with central pellet

CLASSIFICATION: Dobunnic A

NOTES: Many in museums.
Previously thought to be Atrebatic/Regnan, Robinson (1977) has argued convincingly it should be re-attributed to the Dobunni.

1020-1    HEAD TYPE CLASS A 35–30 B.C.                    ER

Æ Unit ca. 1.25 gms. 15 mm

OBV: Celticized head right

Identifying points:
1) face still recognizable
2) pellet in ring for eye
3) two reversed 'S' forms in front of face
4) crescents for hair
5) additional solid crescents behind head

REV: Celticized horse left

Identifying points:
1) tail has three strands
2) bird's head above and below horse
3) six-spoked wheel above tail
4) small sunburst and reversed 'S' form in front of horse

CLASSIFICATION: Dobunnic A

NOTES: Some in museums.
'S' forms on obverse may be vestiges of Dolphins from a prototype coin as yet not identified.
Several coins exist which appear to be earlier varieties, but these have not been formally authenticated.

# THE DOBUNNIC DYNASTIC COINAGE

1035–1    CORIO 30–15 B.C.                                S
A' Stater 5.60 gms. 18 mm

OBV: Dobunnic Emblem
Identifying points:
1) plain except for emblem
2) emblem in form of tree-like object with three branches
3) pellet at bottom of emblem

REV: Celticized horse right
Identifying points:
1) tail has three strands with pellets
2) six-spoked wheel below horse
3) ear has elliptical shape
4) 'V' form with pellet in angle and three pellets below tail
5) CORIO above horse

CLASSIFICATION: Dobunnic B

NOTES: Standard Weight given, the heaviest of the dynastic series.
Most in museums.
Modern forgery exists see 1035–1F.

1039–1    CORIO 30–15 B.C.                               ER
A' Quarter stater ca. 1.15 gms. 12 mm

OBV: Plain with Inscription
Identifying points:
1) plain except for incription
2) COR in centre of field

REV: Celticized horse right
Identifying points:
1) tail has three strands with pellets
2) pellet in ring above horse
3) large pellet in ring above horse
4) 'S' formed object below horse

CLASSIFICATION: Dobunnic B

NOTES: The reverse of this coin is similiar to that of 1010–2.

1042-1     CORIO HEAD TYPE CLASS B 30-15 B.C.        S
Æ Unit ca. 1.15 gms. 14mm

OBV: Celticized head right
Identifying points:
1) more stylized head than on 1020-1
2) large pellet on chin
3) pellet and ring motif below chin
4) crescents for hair

REV: Celticized horse left
Identifying points:
1) triple strand tail
2) bird head above horse very stylized
3) flower below horse

CLASSIFICATION: Dobunnic B

NOTES: Weight given is typical, standard weight is
not yet identified.
Some in museums.
Flower below horse is a disintegrated bird's
head.

1045-1     CORIO HEAD TYPE CLASS C 30-15 B.C.        R
Æ Unit ca. 1.15 gms. 13 mm

OBV: Celticized head right
Identifying points:
1) similiar to 1042-1
2) 'X' in ring on chin
3) crescents for hair

REV: Celticized horse left
Identifying points:
1) similiar to 1042-1
2) flower below horse shows further stylization
3) pellet in ring below tail

CLASSIFICATION: Dobunnic B

NOTES: Weight given is typical, standard weight is
not yet identified.
Flower below horse is a disintegrated bird's
head.

1049-1 CORIO HEAD TYPE CLASS D 30-15 B.C.    R
Æ Unit ca. 1.15 gms. 14 mm

OBV: Celticized head left
Identifying points:
    1) similiar to 1042-1
    2) triple pellets for hair
    3) 'X' on chin (without ring)

REV: Celticized horse right
Identifying points:
    1) similiar to 1042-1
    2) pellet in ring below tail
    3) bird head above horse is almost completely
       disintegrated
    4) flower below horse

CLASSIFICATION: Dobunnic B

NOTES: Weight given is typical, standard weight is
       not yet identified.
       Flower below horse is a disintegrated bird's
       head.
       Some in museums.

1052-1 BODVOC 15-10 B.C.                      ER
N Stater 5.55 gms. 18 mm

OBV: Plain with inscription
Identifying points:
    1) plain, except for inscription
    2) BODVOC in centre of field

REV: Celticized horse right
Identifying points:
    1) tail has three strands with pellets
    2) eight-spoked wheel with axle below horse
    3) two pellet in ring motifs, a crescent and a
       small 'X' above horse
    4) three large pellets below tail
    5) elliptical ear

CLASSIFICATION: Dobunnic C

NOTES: Weight given is standard weight for type.
       Some in museums.
       Modern forgery exists, see 1052-1F.
       BODVOC is a fairly common Celtic name.

1057-1   BODVOC 15-10 B.C.                          ER
         Æ Unit ca. 1.05 gms. 12 mm

OBV: Celticized head left
Identifying points:
  1) BODVOC in front of head

REV: Celticized horse right
Identifying points:
  1) pellet in ring motif above horse
  2) tail has single strand
  3) pellet in ring motif, all in a ring of pellets below horse

CLASSIFICATION: Dobunnic C

NOTES: Weight given is typical, standard weight is not yet identified.
       Many in museums.
       Modern forgery exists, see 1057-1F.
       Obverse possibly adapted from a bronze of Tasciovanus, see 1790-1.
       Reverse probably adapted from gold quarter stater of Tasciovanus, see 1660-1.
       BODVOC is a fairly common Celtic name.

1062-1   ANTED MONOGRAM TYPE                       ER
         10 B.C.-10 A.D.
         Æ Stater 5.40 gms. 17 mm

OBV: Dobunnic Emblem
Identifying points:
  1) emblem made up of tree-like object with ten branches
  2) ring at bottom of emblem

REV: Celticized horse right
Identifying points:
  1) tail has three strands with pellets
  2) ANTED monogram above horse
  3) 'RIG', found on other staters of ANTE-DRIG probably missing on this type
  4) wheel, probably with six spokes below horse
  5) crescent above horse
  6) elliptical ear is spread open at top

CLASSIFICATION: Dobunnic D

NOTES: Ring at bottom of emblem, as found on
uninscribed staters poses dating problems—
this type is possibly earlier than indicated,
or this particular coin is not part of the
ANTEDRIG series.
The style of the coin is unusual, possibly
not a product of the official mint.
Recorded example in BM.
Weight given is that of one recorded
example.

1066-1    ANTEDRIG 10 B.C.–10 A.D.                    VR
N Stater 5.50 gms. 19 mm

OBV: Dobunnic Emblem
Identifying points:
    1) Emblem made up of tree-like object with
       ten branches.

REV: Celticized horse right
Identifying points:
    1) tail has three strands with pellets
    2) elliptical ear
    3) six-spoked wheel below horse
    4) 'V' form below tail
    5) ANTED above horse 'D' is in form of
       Greek theta
    6) RIG in front of horse and around front legs

CLASSIFICATION: Dobunnic D

NOTES: Weight given is standard weight for type.
Some in museums.
RIG is possibly the title 'King'.
Modern forgery exists—see 1066–1F.

1066-3    ANTEDRIG 10 B.C.–10 A.D.                    ER
N Stater 5.50 gms. 19 mm

OBV: Dobunnic Emblem
Identifying points:
    1) as 1066-1

REV: Celticized horse right
Identifying points:
    1) as 1066-1, but legend reads ANED, without
       the letter T

CLASSIFICATION: Dobunnic D

NOTES  Weight given is standard weight for type.
        Most in museums.
        RIG is possibly the title 'King'.

1069–1     ANTEDRIG 10 B.C.–10 A.D.                    VR
           N Stater 5.50 gms. 19 mm

OBV: Dobunnic Emblem
Identifying points:
        1) as 1066–1
REV: Celticized horse right
Identifying points:
        1) as 1066–1
        2) ANTED has 'D' in Roman letter form

CLASSIFICATION: Dobunnic D

NOTES: Weight given is standard weight for type.
        Some in museums.

1074–1     ANTEDRIG HEAD TYPE 10 B.C.–10 A.D.     C
           CLASS E
           Æ Unit  ca. 1.15 gms. 13 mm

OBV: Celticized head right
Identifying points:
        1) Head more stylized than on CORIO HEAD
           TYPE
        2) face has O–X–O pattern made up of two
           pellet in ring motifs with an 'X' in between
        3) Hair made up of triple pellets, but pellets
           are smaller than on CORIO HEAD TYPE

REV: Celticized horse left
Identifying points:
        1) triple stranded tail
        2) pellet in ring motif behind and in front of
           horse
        3) bird head above horse is very stylized, has
           crescent below it
        4) flower below horse
        5) two pellets above tail

CLASSIFICATION: Dobunnic D

NOTES: Weight given is typical, standard weight is not yet identified.
Modern forgery exists, see 1074-1F.

1078-1    ANTEDRIG HEAD TYPE 10 B.C.–10 A.D.    C
CLASS F
Æ Unit ca. 1.15 gms. 13 mm

OBV: Celticized head right
Identifying points:
    1) as 1074-1
    2) two pellet in ring motifs in front of face

REV: Celticized horse left
Identifying points:
    1) as 1074-1
    2) bird head above horse has small 'X' below
       it instead of crescent
    3) single pellet above tail

CLASSIFICATION: Dobunnic D

NOTES: Weight given is typical, standard weight is not yet identified.
Modern forgery exists, see 1078-1F.

1082-1    ANTEDRIG 10 B.C.–10 A.D.    VR
Æ Unit ca. 1.15 gms. 15 mm

OBV: Celticized head right
Identifying points:
    1) as 1078-1

REV: Celticized horse left
Identifying points:
    1) as 1078-1
    2) AN below horse
    3) TED above horse, 'D' in form of Greek
       letter theta

CLASSIFICATION: Dobunnic D

NOTES: Weight given is typical, standard weight is not yet identified.
Some in museums.
Coin was designated 'Class G' by Allen.

1085–1    ANTEDRIG 10 B.C.–10 A.D.                     VR
Æ Unit ca. 1.15 gms. 13 mm

OBV: Celticized head right
Identifying points:
    1) as 1078–1

REV: Celticized horse left
Identifying points:
    1) as 1082–1
    2) 'D' in form of Roman letter

CLASSIFICATION: Dobunnic D

NOTES: Weight given is typical, standard weight is
    not yet identified.
    Some in museums.

1092–1    COMUX 10–15 A.D.                             ER
N Stater 5.45 gms. 19 mm

OBV: Dobunnic Emblem
Identifying points:
    1) Emblem made up of tree-like object with
      ten branches

REV: Celticized horse right
Identifying points:
    1) tail has three strands with pellets
    2) elliptical ear
    3) COMUX up-side-down above horse
    4) three pellets below tail
    5) six-spoked wheel below horse

CLASSIFICATION: Dobunnic E

NOTES: Weight given is standard weight for type.
    Some in museums.
    Modern forgery exists, see 1092–1F.
    COMUX is a variant spelling of the Celtic
    name Commius.

1095–1    COMUX HEAD TYPE CLASS MX              ER
10–15 A.D.
Æ Unit ca. 1.15 gms. 14 mm

OBV: Celticized head right
Identifying points:
    1) head more stylized than on 1082–1

2) O–X–O pattern on Class F is here replaced
   with a six-pointed star
3) six-pointed star near nose
4) five-pointed star near mouth
5) pellet in ring motif below mouth

REV: Celticized horse left
Identifying points:
1) triple stranded tail
2) flower below horse
3) five-pointed star below tail
4) pellet in ring motif and crescent above tail

CLASSIFICATION: Dobunnic E

NOTES: Weight given is typical, standard weight is
   not yet identified.
   Most in museums.
   This type was traditionally considered part
   of the Dobunnic Irregular Series, however
   horse has triple tail and flower below.
   Typologically it is similiar to Classes I and
   J, assigned to CATTI.
   This coin has been assigned to COMUX
   arbitrarily, but may belong to another ruler.

1105-1     EISV 15–30 A.D.                                ER
           Aʹ Stater 5.40 gms. 19 mm

OBV: Dobunnic Emblem
Identifying points:
1) emblem made up of tree-like object with ten
   branches

REV: Celticized horse right
Identifying points:
1) tail has three strands with pellets
2) elliptical ear
3) six-spoked wheel below horse
4) hook-like object in front of horse
5) three pellets below tail
6) EISV above horse

CLASSIFICATION: Dobunnic F

NOTES: Weight given is standard weight for type.
   Some in museums.
   Hook-like object in front of horse may be

REV: Celticized horse left
Identifying points:
    1) similar to 1170–1, but has a six-spoked
       wheel above the horse

CLASSIFICATION: None

NOTES Weight given is typical, standard weight is
       not yet identified.
       Most are in museums.

1175–1    IRREGULAR SERIES 15 B.C.–30 A.D.      ER
           CLASS M
           Æ Unit 0.9–1.0 gm. 12 mm

OBV: Celticized head right
Identifying points:
    1) similiar to 1170–1
    2) coffee beans missing
    3) hair made up of smaller lines

REV: Celticized horse left
Identifying points:
    1) pellet in ring motif below, behind and in
       front of horse
    2) tail has two strands
    3) large wheel made up of six spokes with
       pellet-ring above horse

CLASSIFICATION: None

NOTES: Weight range is typical, standard weight is
       not yet identified.
       Most are in museums.

1180–1    IRREGULAR SERIES 15 B.C.–30 A.D.      ER
           CLASS N
           Æ Unit 0.3–1.0 gm 11 mm

OBV: Abstract Design
Identifying points:
    1) two large curves
    2) smaller crescents and curves

REV: Celticized horse left
Identifying points:

1) tail has two strands
2) pellet in ring motifs below and behind horse
3) pellet in ring motif surrounded by pellet ring above horse
4) horse's neck made up of two lines

CLASSIFICATION: None

NOTES: Weight range is typical; standard weight is not known.
Fractional denominations may exist.

1185-1    IRREGULAR SERIES 15 B.C.-30 A.D.         ER
CLASS O
Æ Unit  ca. 0.6 gms.  16 mm

OBV: Abstract Design
Identifying points:

1) two lines of pellets in centre
2) large curve intersects pellet-line
3) other curves, lines and ellipses in field

REV: Celticized horse left
Identifying points:

1) tail has two strands
2) small crescent in front of horse
3) large pellet below horse
4) large pellet in ring motif above horse

CLASSIFICATION: None

NOTES: Weight given is typical, standard weight is not yet identified.
Most are in museums.

## THE COINAGE OF THE DUROTRIGES

The Durotriges occupied all of Dorset, parts of Somerset, Wiltshire and Hampshire. They had extensive trading contacts with the Armorican peninsula and consequently their coinage was unlike that of the other British tribes. Armorican coins were primarily silver and billon, and the bulk of the Durotrigan coinage was made of these metals instead of gold.

After their first issues, the Durotriges ignored the mainstream of British coinage, suggesting they were economically isolated. Moreover, their coins circulated less and less beyond the tribal boundaries as time went on, and as the tribe's isolation increased.

Initially however, the Durotrigan coinage was an integral part of the economy of southern Britain. Their first coins were inspired by those of the Atrebates/Regni and these did circulate beyond the tribal borders. The CHUTE TYPE, a gold stater first struck about 65 B.C., was adapted from the Westerham Type of the Atrebates/Regni. The Durotrigan moneyers evidently struck the staters using the correct alloy and standard weight at the outset. The Atrebatic/Regnan influence was short lived, however, for the tribe had converted to an Armorican-style silver coinage by the middle of the Gallic War.

At the beginning of the Gallic War, the Durotriges did two divergent things to their gold coinage. First, they struck a series of gold staters of increasingly lighter weight and lower gold content. The Chute Type was replaced by the CHUTE–CHERITON TRANSITIONAL TYPE and finally the CHERITON TYPE.

One Cheriton Type Stater has been analyzed metallurgically, and has been found to have a high tin content. This suggests the Durotriges were debasing their gold staters with addition of bronze to the alloy.

The Cheriton staters perhaps represented an emergency attempt to maintain a gold coinage for trade with the other British tribes. If this was the case, the attempt failed because production soon stopped.

The second change to the coinage was the introduction of a Westerham Type copy in white gold, which rapidly became debased to silver, billon and ultimately bronze. These coins, although occasionally found outside the tribe's territory, were primarily used in the Durotrigan economy since no other tribe used such coins. The series was long-lived, with many types issued in succession. The silver stater and its billon descendants are accompanied by fractional denominations.

Whether the Durotriges went to a silver standard because of the preferences of their Armorican partners, or because they simply ran out of gold bullion, is uncertain. Their trading contacts used mostly silver coins, and by the time of the Gallic War were using them exclusively. After the defeat of the Venetic Fleet and conquest of Armorica by the Romans, the Durotriges ran out of bullion of all types, because their trade with the continent was cut off. They had already been excluded from the British trading network by strong competition from the Atrebates/Regni and Trinovantes/Catuvellauni. Durotrigan silver coins ceased about 30 B.C., and were replaced by struck bronze staters of increasingly crude style. The silver fractional denominations disappeared entirely.

A series of cast bronzes follows, starting probably in the first century A.D., and known mostly from two large hoards. A small number of extremely rare silver coins carrying the inscription CRAB are found in Durotrigan territory. Although these pieces appear Atrebatic/Regnan in style, they have been attributed traditionally to the Durotriges because of the findspots.

The Durotrigan coinage would have come to an end in the mid-forties A.D. as Vespasian's legions overran the tribal territory. The tribe offered difficult resistance to the Roman invasion and their coinage would have been ruthlessly suppressed. Durotrigan coins are sometimes found in surprisingly late hoards of Roman pieces, but probably these represented curiosities at the time of deposit.

The site of the Durotrigan mint has never been located with certainty, and several mints may have been in operation. One likely place was the trading port at Hengistbury. Some of the rare varieties of billon staters may have been irregular issues, struck by local authorities.

The moneyers produced flans by the 'Flat Rock' method, pouring molten metal directly on a smooth surface. Some of the coins display splash appendages produced during the flan pouring operation. The Durotriges learned the technique from Armorican moneyers, whose coins also show the appendages. The early gold and silver coins were well-struck, but the later billon ones were hastily produced in enormous numbers and were consequently less well made. The manufacturing methods for the cast coins have never been studied, and represent an opportunity for original research.

A number of plated forgeries of silver staters are known and sometimes it is difficult to distinguish between plated cores and struck bronzes. Conceivably, all struck bronzes may originally have been silver coated.

## DUROTRIGAN GOLD COINS

The first gold coins were struck after the appearance of the Westerham Type of the Atrebates. The Durotrigan adaptation replaced the pellet below the horse with a crab-like object, and placed a 'bug' above the animal. These coins were gradually replaced with more debased types, probably intended for external trade in Britain. The tribe's internal coinage became entirely silver around the middle of the Gallic War.

The earliest gold pieces are reasonably common today, not because they were struck in large quantities, but rather because of several hoards found this century, one near Chute.

1227–1 EARLY GEOMETRIC TYPE 65–58 B.C. ER
Aʼ Quarter Stater 10 mm

OBV: Almost plain
Identifying points:
    1) portions of geometric pattern may appear

REV: Geometric pattern
Identifying points:
    1) similar to 1225–1

CLASSIFICATION: Durotrigan A

NOTES: Most are in museums.

1229–1 EARLY GEOMETRIC TYPE 65–58 B.C. ER
Aʼ Quarter Stater 11 mm

OBV: Almost plain
Identifying points:
    1) portions of geometric pattern may appear

REV: Geometric pattern
Identifying points:
    1) pattern indistinct
    2) pattern made up of lines

CLASSIFICATION: Durotrigan A

NOTES: Most are in museums.

1231–1 UNCERTAIN GEOMETRIC TYPE ER
    65–58 B.C.
Aʼ and Æ mixed Quarter Stater 1.3 gms.
14 mm

OBV: Almost plain
Identifying points:
    1) possibly remains of design appear

REV: Geometric pattern
Identifying points:
    1) pattern indistinct
    2) pattern made up of lines and pellets

CLASSIFICATION: None

NOTES: Most are in museums.
    Typical weight given.
    Possibly Gaulish, see similar type in Scheers
    pl. 5 number 113.
    May have been derived from the Gaulish
    type.

In the past, this coin has been described as Dobunnic or possibly Silurian, based on an Ariconium findspot. The most likely suggestion is that it it Durotrigan, but this is not certain.

## WHITE GOLD, SILVER AND BILLON COINAGES

The transition from gold to silver coins is indistinct. The Quarter staters become white gold, silver and then billon all with no apparent changes in style or privy marks. The silver staters actually begin as white gold coins, but rapidly degrade to silver and finally billon. The billon types have many varieties, some possibly the products of local or irregular mints. A new series of quarters, the starfish type, is entirely within the billon series. Two major varieties of starfish quarters, distinguished by the thickness of the flan, are known. Most of these types are common today, because a hoard of well over 800 pieces was discovered in the vicinity of Badbury Rings hillfort.

The metallurgical and typological sequences of the coins are problematic and the dating uncertain—the following treatment is somewhat arbitrary. An alternative interpretation, not used here, is that several mints were striking coins without centralized control.

## EARLIEST WHITE GOLD, SILVER AND BILLON COINAGES

1235-1    ABSTRACT TYPE 58-45 B.C.      C
White GOLD, Æ, or Billon Stater
4.9-5.8 gms. 19 mm

OBV: Abstract head of Apollo right
Identifying points:
    1) wreath: leaves up

REV: Disjointed horse left
Identifying points:
    1) pellet below horse
    2) tiny elliptical pellet above horse
    3) tail has three strands and points upwards
    4) coffee bean above tail

CLASSIFICATION: Durotrigan E

NOTES: Some in museums.
    The type starts as a white gold coin, but immediately degrades to silver, then billon. White gold coins, and those of good silver

are uncommon, most extant pieces are billon.

Similiar to the Westerham Type of the Atrebates/Regni.

Modern forgery exists—see 1235–1F.

**1235–3    ABSTRACT TYPE 58–45 B.C.**          ER
Æ/Æ Plated Stater 4.7 gms. 19 mm

OBV: Abstract head of Apollo right
Identifying points:
    1) as 1235–1, but a bit cruder

REV: Disjointed horse left
Identifying points:
    1) as 1235–1, but a bit cruder

CLASSIFICATION: Durotrigan E

NOTES: Ancient forgery, struck from forger's dies. Laurel leaf filled in on die, not struck up on coin.

**1235–7    ABSTRACT TYPE 58–45 B.C.**          ER
Æ/Æ Plated Stater 3.2 gms. 17 mm

OBV: Abstract head of Apollo right
Identifying points:
    1) as 1235–1, but cruder
    2) wreath: leaves down

REV: Disjointed horse left
Identifying points:
    1) as 1235–1 but cruder

CLASSIFICATION: Durotrigan E

NOTES: Ancient forgery struck from forger's dies. Forger blundered direction of laurel leaves, which was always carefully oriented on genuine dies.

**1238–1    SPREAD-TAIL TYPE 58–45 B.C.**          VR
Billon Stater 4.0–5.6 gms. 20 mm

OBV: Abstract head or Apollo right
Identifying points:
    1) as 1235–1
    2) sometimes two pellets above curve of spike, but not on all examples

REV: Disjointed horse left
Identifying points:
1) as 1235-1 except three strands of tail spread apart as they extend to right
2) sometimes pellets between strands of tail, but not on all examples

CLASSIFICATION: Durotrigan F

NOTES: Type may exist in good silver variety.
Sometimes the tail strands meet at a pellet on the left, sometimes not.
Rarity provided via trade survey.

1242-1    LATER GEOMETRIC TYPE 58-45 B.C.        C
WHITE GOLD, Æ or BILLON Quarter Stater
1.1 gms. 11 mm

OBV: Pattern
Identifying points:
1) large crescent with one end squared off
2) three appendages hang from crescent
3) daisy to right of appendages

REV: Geometric Pattern
Identifying points:
1) vertically-oriented zigzag across field
2) 'bird' to right
3) six-sided irregular object to left
4) Y-like object on either side of zigzag

CLASSIFICATION: Durotrigan E

NOTES: It has been suggested the obverse design, oriented upside-down, is a boat with three occupants.
The type is derived from the Ambiani Geometric Type.
The typical weight is given.
The metal is gradually reduced from gold to white gold, silver and ultimately billon. It is difficult to separate the issues without metallurgical analysis.
Silver pieces have been chemically treated to look like the white gold variety by modern forgers. These have a dark reddish appearance and porous surfaces—*caveat emptor*!

## LATER SILVER AND BILLON COINS

1246-1    PELLET AND RING TYPE 45–40 B.C.            C
ÆR or Billon Stater  ca. 5.5 gms. 19 mm

OBV: Abstract head of Apollo right
Identifying points:
> 1) as 1235-1, but two pellets below lowest curl of hair

REV: Disjointed horse left
Identifying points:
> 1) similiar to 1235-1
> 2) pellet-in-ring motifs above and behind horse
> 3) tail extends downwards and has pellets between strands
> 4) crescent to left of coffee bean
> 5) pellet with two attached crescents to right of coffee bean

CLASSIFICATION: Durotrigan G

NOTES: The type was known to Evans, see his plate F2.
One of these coins per every ten Abstract Type Staters appears in hoards, apparently a consistent average.
Rarity provided via trade survey.

1249-1    SECOND GEOMETRIC TYPE 45–40 B.C.         S
ÆR or Billon Quarter Stater
1.2 gms. 11 mm

OBV: Pattern
Identifying points:
> 1) similiar to 1242-1, but image is larger and cruder
> 2) long spikes with pellet-ends above the truncated crescent

REV: Geometric pattern
Identifying points:
> 1) similiar to 1242-1 but cruder
> 2) 'bird', irregular six-sided figure and Y-like objects all almost unrecognizable
> 3) ring added to left of field
> 4) zigzag decorated with line of pellets

CLASSIFICATION: Durotrigan G

NOTES: Some in museums.
Rarity provided via trade survey.

## FINAL SILVER AND BILLON COINAGES

One of the following three stater types was known to Evans, see his plate F3.

1252-1    TWO BRANCH TYPE 40–35 B.C.         ER
Billon Stater ca. 4.1 gms. 19 mm

OBV: Abstract head of Apollo right
Identifying points:
    1) similiar to 1235-1 but head larger and cruder
    2) Two pellets above curve of spike
    3) hair to left made up of two-branched objects

REV: Disjointed horse left
Identifying points:
    1) Similiar to 1235-1 but horse larger and cruder

CLASSIFICATION: Durotrigan H

NOTES: Most in museums.

1254-1    THREE BRANCH TYPE 40–35 B.C.       ER
Billon Stater ca. 4.3 gms. 17 mm

OBV: Abstract head of Apollo right
Identifying points:
    1) similiar to 1235-1 but head larger and cruder
    2) two pellets above curve of spike
    3) hair to left made up of three-branched objects

REV: Disjointed horse left
Identifying points:
    1) similiar to 1235-1 but horse larger and cruder

CLASSIFICATION: Durotrigan H

NOTES: Most in museums.

1255-1    FOUR BRANCH TYPE 40–35 B.C.        ER
Billon Stater ca. 4.5 gms. 19 mm

OBV: Abstract head of Apollo right
Identifying points:
    1) similiar to 1235-1 but head larger and cruder

2) two pellets above curve of spike
3) hair to left made up of four-branched objects

REV: Disjointed horse left
Identifying points:

1) similiar to 1235-1 but horse larger and cruder

CLASSIFICATION: Durotrigan H

1260-1    THIRD GEOMETRIC TYPE 40–35 B.C.        S
Æ or Billon Quarter Stater
0.8–1.0 gms. 14 mm

OBV: Pattern, almost plain
Identifying points:

1) as 1249-1, but obverse die used until almost obliterated

REV: Geometric Pattern
Identifying points:

1) similiar to 1249-1 but cruder
2) all objects in field almost unrecognizable
3) 'clamshell' object in upper right

CLASSIFICATION: Durotrigan H

NOTES: Rarity provided via trade survey.

## STARFISH TYPE

The starfish type appears to follow the geometric types, because it continues the zigzag pattern decorated with lines of pellets.

1270-1    STARFISH TYPE 35–30 B.C.               S
Billon Unit ca. 1.2 gms. 13 mm

OBV: Starfish
Identifying points:

1) five armed starfish with pellet in centre
2) lines of pellets between arms
3) pellet-in-ring motifs in field

REV: zigzag and spider pattern
Identifying points:

1) zigzag with lines of pellets
2) 'spider' on either side with eight arms
3) pellet-in-ring motifs in field

CLASSIFICATION: Durotrigan I

NOTES: Possibly commoner than indicated, Badbury/Shapwick hoard contents not adequately recorded.

1273-1    THICK STARFISH TYPE 35-30 B.C.        S
Billon Unit ca. 1.1 gms. 12 mm

OBV: Starfish
Identifying points:
    1) similiar to 1270-1 but starfish has thicker arms

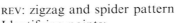

REV: zigzag and spider pattern
Identifying points:
    1) similiar to 1270-1 but spiders have six arms

CLASSIFICATION: Durotrigan I

NOTES: This type normally found struck from a damaged reverse die, with a cud forming at one of the spiders.
Rarity provided via trade survey.

1276-1    ELEGANT STARFISH TYPE 35-30 B.C.        ER
Billon Unit ca. 0.8 gms. 14 mm

OBV: Starfish
Identifying points:
    1) similiar to 1270-1 but the starfish is thin and elegant
    2) the arms of the starfish split into two ends

REV: zigzag and spider pattern
Identifying points:
    1) similiar to 1270-1 but the arms of the spiders are long and thin
    2) the field has fewer objects

CLASSIFICATION: Durotrigan I

NOTES: Possibly commoner than indicated, Badbury/Shapwick hoard contents not adequately recorded.

1278-1    ELEGANT STARFISH TYPE 35-30 B.C.        ER
Billon Fractional Unit ca. 0.6 gms. 12 mm

OBV: Starfish
Identifying points:
    1) as 1276-1

REV: zigzag and spider pattern
Identifying points:
    1) as 1276-1, but objects added to field
    2) ring and 'V' objects near spiders

CLASSIFICATION: Durotrigan I

NOTES: The relationship of this type to the previous
    is uncertain, not enough examples exist to
    determine the standard weights.
    The additional objects near the spiders may
    indicate a change in denomination.

1280-1    THIN SILVER TYPE 65-45 B.C.    ER
    Æ Unit 0.8 gms. 15 mm

OBV: Pattern of pellets
Identifying points:
    1) crude pattern of pellets possibly forming a
    man

REV: Celticized horse left
Identifying points:
    1) crude horse in field of pellets

CLASSIFICATION: None

NOTES: Some in museums.

1285-1    CRAB TYPE 10-45 A.D.    ER
    Æ Unit 1.1 gms. 13 mm

OBV: Cross with inscription
Identifying points:
    1) cross of pellets
    2) large pellet and ring in centre
    3) CRAB in angles

REV: Eagle
Identifying points:
    1) eagle faces left with head turned to face
    right

CLASSIFICATION: None

NOTES: Most in museums.
    Possibly Atrebatic/Regnan in origin, or
    influence.

1286-1     CRAB TYPE 10–45 A.D.                          ER
ÆR Minim 0.3 gms. ca. 0.9 mm

OBV: Tablet with inscription
Identifying points:
    1) CRAB in tablet
    2) 'O' above
    3) 'S' below

REV: Pattern
Identifying points:
    1) pellet-in-ring motif in centre
    2) six crescents around central motif to form star pattern
    3) triple pellets inside crescents
    4) pellet border

CLASSIFICATION: None

NOTES: Most in museums.
    The type was recorded by Evans, see plate on page 214 of his book.

## STRUCK BRONZE COINAGE

The struck bronzes apparently follow the billon coins, but the sequence and dating are difficult to identify. The bronzes were probably struck for a long time, because they degrade in style until the head and horse are almost unrecognizable.

1290-1     STRUCK BRONZE TYPE 30 B.C.–10 A.D.     C
Æ Bronze Stater ca. 3.4 gms. 19 mm

OBV: Abstract head of Apollo right
Identifying points:
    1) similiar to 1235-1 but head larger and cruder

REV: Disjointed horse left
Identifying points:
    1) similiar to 1235-1 but horse larger and cruder

CLASSIFICATION: Durotrigan J

NOTES: Many in museums.
    The style of these becomes increasingly cruder over time.
    Often confused with plated forgeries of 1235-1.
    The trend-surface map suggests a date 58–

45 B.C. for the earlier types, but the records of findspots must include some plated forgeries mistaken for bronzes. The dating for this type needs more investigation, and the one given above is provisional, at best.

## CAST BRONZE COINAGE

The earliest cast bronzes copy the Apollo head and the horse from the struck coins. Consequently, they probably followed the struck coinage without great delay. The weights are constant enough for cast coins and different denominations cannot be identified.

The best method of arranging these coins is somewhat controversial, because a simple sequence of 'evolving' images may be misleading. As a comparison, the images on the Kentish Cast Bronze series have been shown to be a poor indicator of type. Instead, the sequence of marks left by the different mould production methods yielded a better understanding.

Unfortunately, an analysis of the Durotrigan cast coinage carried out at the Institute of Archaeology, Oxford was not published in time to include the findings in this book. In 1953, Mack listed the coins according to the number of pellets in the field. Although this ultimately may not produce the most revealing sequence, it has been reproduced in the following catalogue. To aid students of the series, Mack's numbering system has been embedded in the one used here—the catalogue number is Mack's plus 1000. Thus Mack number 344 becomes 1344 here.

1322-1    CAST BRONZE 10–45 A.D.          R
Æ Unit 17 mm

OBV: Disintegrated head of Apollo right
Identifying points:
    1) remnants of Apollo head

REV: Disjointed horse left
Identifying points:
    1) remnants of horse

CLASSIFICATION: Durotrigan K

1323-1    CAST BRONZE 10–45 A.D.          R
Æ Unit 2.5–3.0 gms. 16 mm

OBV: Disintegrated head of Apollo right
Identifying points:
    1) remnants of Apollo head

REV: Disjointed horse left
Identifying points:
    1) twelve pellets in field
    2) some remnants of horse's legs

CLASSIFICATION: Durotrigan K

1324-1    CAST BRONZE 10–45 A.D.        R
            Æ Unit 16 mm

OBV: Disintegrated head of Apollo right
Identifying points:
    1) remnants of Apollo head

REV: Disjointed horse left
Identifying points:
    1) remnants of horse

CLASSIFICATION: Durotrigan K

1325-1    CAST BRONZE 10–45 A.D.        R
            Æ Unit 16 mm

OBV: Disintegrated head of Apollo right
Identifying points:
    1) large 'Y' remains from Apollo head
    2) two pellets on one side of the Y
    3) three pellets and a crescent on the other side

REV: Pellets
Identifying points:
    1) nine pellets in field

CLASSIFICATION: Durotrigan K

1326-1    CAST BRONZE 10–45 A.D.        R
            Æ Unit 16 mm

OBV: Disintegrated head of Apollo right
Identifying points:
    1) large 'Y' remains from Apollo head
    2) two pellets on one side of the Y
    3) two pellets on the other side
    4) crescent in fork of Y

REV: Pellets
Identifying points:
    1) seven pellets in field

CLASSIFICATION: Durotrigan K

1327-1    CAST BRONZE 10–45 A.D.          R
Æ Unit

OBV: Disintegrated head of Apollo right
Identifying points:
    1) large 'Y' remains from Apollo head
    2) two pellets on one side of the Y
    3) two pellets on the other side
    4) pellets arranged diagonally

REV: Pellets
Identifying points:
    1) seven pellets in field
    2) two pellets connected by line

CLASSIFICATION: Durotrigan K

1328-1    CAST BRONZE 10–45 A.D.          R
Æ Unit 1.6–2.1 gms. 16 mm

OBV: Disintegrated head of Apollo right
Identifying points:
    1) large 'Y' remains from Apollo head
    2) two pellets on one side of the Y
    3) two pellets on the other side
    4) pellets arranged vertically

REV: Pellets
Identifying points:
    1) seven pellets in field
    2) two pellets connected by line

CLASSIFICATION: Durotrigan K

1329-1    CAST BRONZE 10–45 A.D.          R
Æ Unit 2.2–2.6 gms. 16 mm

OBV: Disintegrated head of Apollo right
Identifying points:
    1) large 'Y' remains from Apollo head
    2) three pellets on one side of the Y
    3) three pellets on the other side
    4) two crescents near fork of Y

REV: Pellets
Identifying points:
    1) four pellets in field
    2) crescent and branch-like object in field

CLASSIFICATION: Durotrigan K

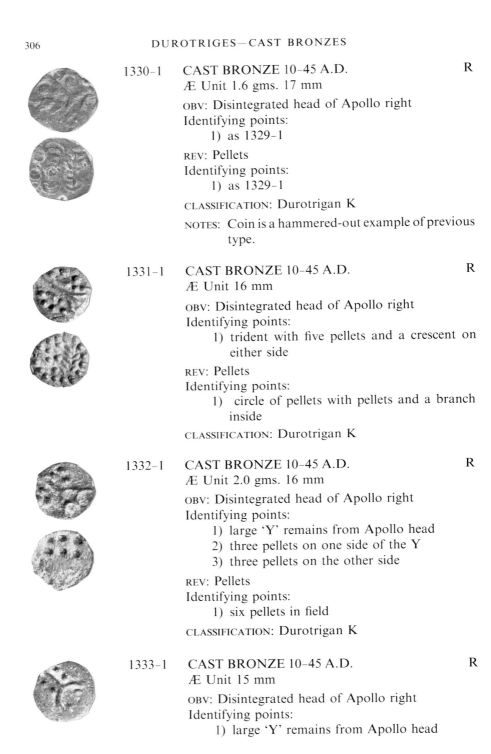

**1330-1**    CAST BRONZE 10-45 A.D.            R
Æ Unit 1.6 gms. 17 mm

OBV: Disintegrated head of Apollo right
Identifying points:
     1) as 1329-1

REV: Pellets
Identifying points:
     1) as 1329-1

CLASSIFICATION: Durotrigan K

NOTES: Coin is a hammered-out example of previous type.

**1331-1**    CAST BRONZE 10-45 A.D.            R
Æ Unit 16 mm

OBV: Disintegrated head of Apollo right
Identifying points:
     1) trident with five pellets and a crescent on either side

REV: Pellets
Identifying points:
     1) circle of pellets with pellets and a branch inside

CLASSIFICATION: Durotrigan K

**1332-1**    CAST BRONZE 10-45 A.D.            R
Æ Unit 2.0 gms. 16 mm

OBV: Disintegrated head of Apollo right
Identifying points:
     1) large 'Y' remains from Apollo head
     2) three pellets on one side of the Y
     3) three pellets on the other side

REV: Pellets
Identifying points:
     1) six pellets in field

CLASSIFICATION: Durotrigan K

**1333-1**    CAST BRONZE 10-45 A.D.            R
Æ Unit 15 mm

OBV: Disintegrated head of Apollo right
Identifying points:
     1) large 'Y' remains from Apollo head

2) two pellets on one side of the Y
3) two pellets on the other side
4) two pellets in fork of 'Y'

REV: Pellets
Identifying points:
    1) six pellets in field

CLASSIFICATION: Durotrigan K

1334-1   CAST BRONZE 10-45 A.D.                    R
         Æ Unit 2.4 gms. 16 mm

OBV: Disintegrated head of Apollo right
Identifying points:
    1) large 'Y' remains from Apollo head
    2) two pellets on one side of the Y
    3) two pellets on the other side

REV: Pellets
Identifying points:
    1) three pellets in field
    2) large crescent in field

CLASSIFICATION: Durotrigan K

1335-1   CAST BRONZE 10-45 A.D.                    R
         Æ Unit 16 mm

OBV: Disintegrated head of Apollo right
Identifying points:
    1) large 'Y' remains from Apollo head
    2) one pellet on one side of the Y
    3) one pellet on the other side
    4) pellet-in-crescent on either side of Y

REV: Pellets
Identifying points:
    1) five pellets in field
    2) some coins have a crescent in the field

CLASSIFICATION: Durotrigan K

1336-1   CAST BRONZE 10-45 A.D.                    R
         Æ Unit 18 mm

OBV: Disintegrated head of Apollo right
Identifying points:
    1) large 'Y' remains from Apollo head
    2) three pellets on one side of the Y
    3) three pellets on the other side

REV: Pellets
Identifying points:
    1) crescent in field
    2) two pellets above crescent
    3) three pellets below crescent

CLASSIFICATION: Durotrigan K

1337-1    **CAST BRONZE 10–45 A.D.**    R
    Æ Unit

OBV: Disintegrated head of Apollo right
Identifying points:
    1) large 'Y' remains from Apollo head
    2) two pellets on one side of the Y
    3) two pellets on the other side

REV: Pellets
Identifying points:
    1) ten pellets in field

CLASSIFICATION: Durotrigan K

NOTES: No illustration available.

1338-1    **CAST BRONZE 10–45 A.D.**    R
    Æ Unit 17 mm

OBV: Disintegrated head of Apollo right
Identifying points:
    1) large 'Y' remains from Apollo head
    2) three pellets on one side of the Y
    3) three pellets on the other side
    4) two short lines on either side of Y

REV: Pellets
Identifying points:
    1) eight pellets in field

CLASSIFICATION: Durotrigan K

1339-1    **CAST BRONZE 10–45 A.D.**    R
    Æ Unit 2.7 gms. 15 mm

OBV: Disintegrated head of Apollo right
Identifying points:
    1) large 'Y' remains from Apollo head
    2) five pellets on one side of the Y
    3) five pellets on the other side
    4) crescent on either side of Y

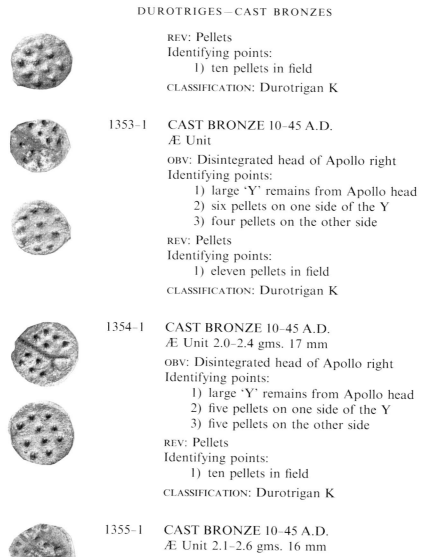

REV: Pellets
Identifying points:
    1) ten pellets in field

CLASSIFICATION: Durotrigan K

1353-1    CAST BRONZE 10–45 A.D.        R
    Æ Unit

OBV: Disintegrated head of Apollo right
Identifying points:
    1) large 'Y' remains from Apollo head
    2) six pellets on one side of the Y
    3) four pellets on the other side

REV: Pellets
Identifying points:
    1) eleven pellets in field

CLASSIFICATION: Durotrigan K

1354-1    CAST BRONZE 10–45 A.D.        R
    Æ Unit 2.0–2.4 gms. 17 mm

OBV: Disintegrated head of Apollo right
Identifying points:
    1) large 'Y' remains from Apollo head
    2) five pellets on one side of the Y
    3) five pellets on the other side

REV: Pellets
Identifying points:
    1) ten pellets in field

CLASSIFICATION: Durotrigan K

1355-1    CAST BRONZE 10–45 A.D.        R
    Æ Unit 2.1–2.6 gms. 16 mm

OBV: Disintegrated head of Apollo right
Identifying points:
    1) large 'Y' remains from Apollo head
    2) five pellets on one side of the Y
    3) five pellets on the other side

REV: Pellets
Identifying points:
    1) nine pellets in field

CLASSIFICATION: Durotrigan K

1356-1   CAST BRONZE 10–45 A.D.                          R
ÆUnit 16 mm

OBV: Disintegrated head of Apollo right
Identifying points:
    1) as 1355–1, but pellets arranged differently

REV: Pellets
Identifying points:
    1) as 1355–1, but pellets arranged differently

CLASSIFICATION: Durotrigan K

1357-1   CAST BRONZE 10–45 A.D.                          R
ÆUnit 2.2 gms. 16 mm

OBV: Disintegrated head of Apollo right
Identifying points:
    1) large 'Y' remains from Apollo head
    2) five pellets on one side of the Y
    3) five pellets on the other side

REV: Pellets
Identifying points:
    1) seven pellets in field

CLASSIFICATION: Durotrigan K

1358-1   CAST BRONZE 10–45 A.D.                          R
ÆUnit 2.0–2.8 gms. 16 mm

OBV: Disintegrated head of Apollo right
Identifying points:
    1) large 'Y' remains from Apollo head
    2) four pellets on one side of the Y
    3) four pellets on the other side

REV: Pellets
Identifying points:
    1) ten pellets in field

CLASSIFICATION: Durotrigan K
NOTES: Mack indicated five and four pellets on the
        obverse, but four and four appears to be
        correct.

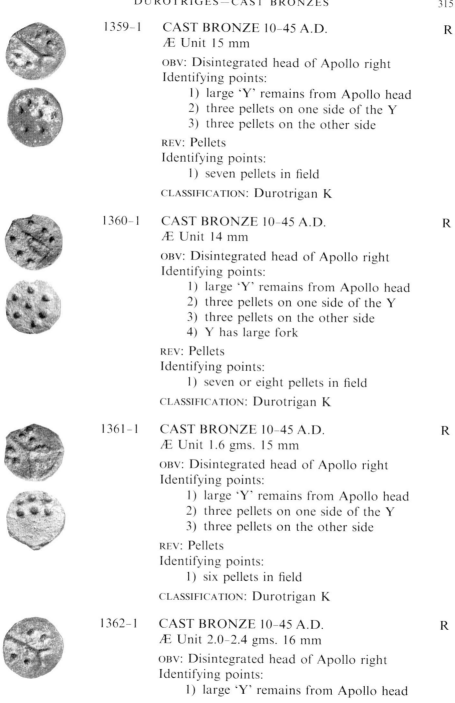

1359-1    CAST BRONZE 10-45 A.D.                    R
          Æ Unit 15 mm

          OBV: Disintegrated head of Apollo right
          Identifying points:
              1) large 'Y' remains from Apollo head
              2) three pellets on one side of the Y
              3) three pellets on the other side
          REV: Pellets
          Identifying points:
              1) seven pellets in field
          CLASSIFICATION: Durotrigan K

1360-1    CAST BRONZE 10-45 A.D.                    R
          Æ Unit 14 mm

          OBV: Disintegrated head of Apollo right
          Identifying points:
              1) large 'Y' remains from Apollo head
              2) three pellets on one side of the Y
              3) three pellets on the other side
              4) Y has large fork
          REV: Pellets
          Identifying points:
              1) seven or eight pellets in field
          CLASSIFICATION: Durotrigan K

1361-1    CAST BRONZE 10-45 A.D.                    R
          Æ Unit 1.6 gms. 15 mm

          OBV: Disintegrated head of Apollo right
          Identifying points:
              1) large 'Y' remains from Apollo head
              2) three pellets on one side of the Y
              3) three pellets on the other side
          REV: Pellets
          Identifying points:
              1) six pellets in field
          CLASSIFICATION: Durotrigan K

1362-1    CAST BRONZE 10-45 A.D.                    R
          Æ Unit 2.0-2.4 gms. 16 mm

          OBV: Disintegrated head of Apollo right
          Identifying points:
              1) large 'Y' remains from Apollo head

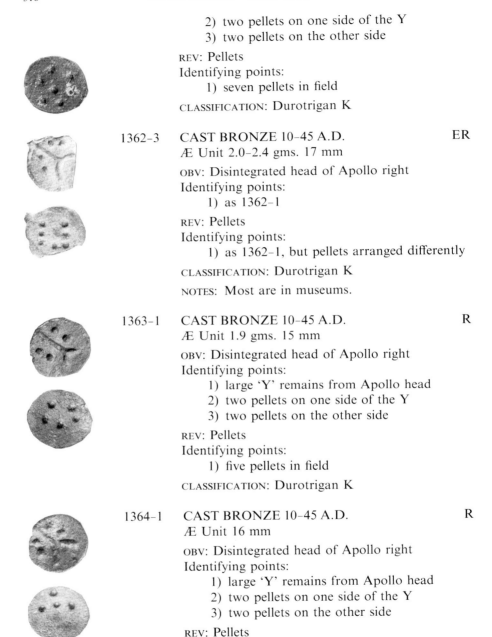

2) two pellets on one side of the Y
3) two pellets on the other side

REV: Pellets
Identifying points:
1) seven pellets in field

CLASSIFICATION: Durotrigan K

1362–3    CAST BRONZE 10–45 A.D.                    ER
Æ Unit 2.0–2.4 gms. 17 mm

OBV: Disintegrated head of Apollo right
Identifying points:
1) as 1362–1

REV: Pellets
Identifying points:
1) as 1362–1, but pellets arranged differently

CLASSIFICATION: Durotrigan K

NOTES: Most are in museums.

1363–1    CAST BRONZE 10–45 A.D.                    R
Æ Unit 1.9 gms. 15 mm

OBV: Disintegrated head of Apollo right
Identifying points:
1) large 'Y' remains from Apollo head
2) two pellets on one side of the Y
3) two pellets on the other side

REV: Pellets
Identifying points:
1) five pellets in field

CLASSIFICATION: Durotrigan K

1364–1    CAST BRONZE 10–45 A.D.                    R
Æ Unit 16 mm

OBV: Disintegrated head of Apollo right
Identifying points:
1) large 'Y' remains from Apollo head
2) two pellets on one side of the Y
3) two pellets on the other side

REV: Pellets
Identifying points:
1) four pellets in field

CLASSIFICATION: Durotrigan K

1365–1    CAST BRONZE 10–45 A.D.                              R
Æ Unit 15 mm

OBV: Disintegrated head of Apollo right
Identifying points:
    1) large 'Y' remains from Apollo head
    2) one pellet on one side of the Y
    3) one pellet on the other side

REV: Pellets
Identifying points:
    1) seven pellets in field

CLASSIFICATION: Durotrigan K

1366–1    CAST BRONZE 10–45 A.D.                              R
Æ Unit 16 mm

OBV: Disintegrated head of Apollo right
Identifying points:
    1) large 'Y' remains from Apollo head
    2) one pellet on one side of the Y
    3) one pellet on the other side

REV: Pellets
Identifying points:
    1) five or seven pellets in field

CLASSIFICATION: Durotrigan K

1367–1    CAST BRONZE 10–45 A.D.                              R
Æ Unit

OBV: Disintegrated head of Apollo right
Identifying points:
    1) large 'Y' remains from Apollo head
    2) crescent on either side of Y

REV: Pellets
Identifying points:
    1) seven pellets in field

CLASSIFICATION: Durotrigan K

1368–1    CAST BRONZE 10–45 A.D.                              R
Æ Unit

OBV: Disintegrated head of Apollo right
Identifying points:
    1) large 'Y' remains from Apollo head
    2) one pellet on one side of the Y
    3) one pellet on the other side

REV: Plain
Identifying points:
     1) no pellets

CLASSIFICATION: Durotrigan K

1369-1    CAST BRONZE 10-45 A.D.                          R
          Æ Unit 15 mm

OBV: Disintegrated head of Apollo right
Identifying points:
     1) large 'Y' remains from Apollo head
     2) no pellets

REV: Pellets
Identifying points:
     1) five pellets in field

CLASSIFICATION: Durotrigan K

1369-3    CAST BRONZE 10-45 A.D.                         ER
          Æ Unit 16 mm

OBV: Disintegrated head of Apollo right
Identifying points:
     1) as 1369-1

REV: Pellets
Identifying points:
     1) as 1369-1, but four pellets in field

CLASSIFICATION: Durotrigan K

NOTES: Most are in museums.

1370-1    CAST BRONZE 10-45 A.D.                          R
          Æ Unit

OBV: Plain
Identifying points:
     1) no 'Y' nor pellets

REV: Pellets
Identifying points:
     1) five pellets in field

CLASSIFICATION: Durotrigan K

NOTES: No illustration available.

## THE COINAGE OF THE
## TRINOVANTES/CATUVELLAUNI

Traditionally, the Trinovantes and Catuvellauni were considered distinct tribes, each with its own coinage. An elaborate history, written from the coin inscriptions, described a long intertribal warfare. The Trinovantes received blow after devastating blow from the warlike Catuvellauni and lost Camulodunum, their tribal capital, several times in the process.

The evidence was founded partially on Caesar's writings—the ruler of the Trinovantes had been killed by Cassivellaunus. Cassivellaunus was assumed to be a ruler of the Catuvellauni, though Caesar never stated so. The rest of the support came from an analysis of the findspots of the Dynastic coins.

Today, this history is considered a myth—the coin evidence no longer supports continual internecine warfare north of the Thames. Cassivellaunus' tribal origin is not mentioned by any contemporary writer and there is no indication he was the ruler of the Catuvellauni. The similarity of the tribal and personal names is coincidence, not a link between the two. Furthermore, recent analyses of the findspot distributions indicate the coins circulated farther afield than previously thought. The territory north of the Thames can no longer be separated into two distinct coin-using zones.

Instead, the coinage is seen today as that of a single economic group— coin types appear in succession and circulate not only throughout the area immediately north of the Thames, but into Icenian and Cantian territory as well. Metrology and typology show the inscriptions on the dynastic issues are those of successive rulers, not contemporary adversaries.

In general, the picture today is of a powerful, united tribe occupying the area north of the Thames. This unified tribe had economic influence beyond its borders which increased throughout the period of the coinage. The tribal group ultimately controlled the economy of the Cantii, and to a lesser extent the economies of the Iceni and Atrebates/Regni.

## BUT WHAT WAS THIS TRIBAL GROUP?

That two tribes existed is not in doubt. Caesar mentions the Trinovantes in his Gallic War commentaries, stating they were probably the most powerful tribe in southern Britain. The Catuvellauni are mentioned on an inscribed Roman stone from Hadrian's wall. There were two minting centres in the territory, at the tribal oppida of Verulamium and Camulodunum, suggesting two political centres existed. However, the coinage is a unified one since the two tribal groups must have merged into a single economic unit before they started producing coins.

As a result, the tribes cannot be distinguished numismatically, and they are referred to as the Trinovantes/Catuvellauni. For all practical purposes, by the introduction of the Whaddon Chase Type about 55 B.C., they had come to act as one economically, and perhaps had been doing so as early as 125 B.C.

The inscribed coinage argues in addition for political unity by 40 B.C. The dynastic coins show an orderly succession of rulers, except for a brief period around the turn of the millenium. This appears to have been an Interregnum, during which the succession was disputed.

The Trinovantes/Catuvellauni occupied the entire territory immediately north of the Thames. They were bounded on the north-east by the Iceni, on the south by the Cantii and Atrebates/Regni, on the north the by the Corieltauvi, and on the west, probably, by the Dobunni. Thus, they were in physical contact with all the tribes of the south-east, and in a position to exert influence.

By 125 B.C., they were importing coins from the Ambiani on the Continent, and shared the cross-Channel trade with the Cantii and Atrebates/Regni. Large Flan, Defaced Die and Abstract Type gold coins are found throughout their territory in quantity.

When the Cantii began casting bronze coins about 100 B.C., the Trinovantes/Catuvellauni followed this lead and produced their own cast coinage for a brief period. In the early 1980s a small hoard of unusual cast bronze coins was dispersed in Europe, about 100 to 300 pieces with an alleged 'Folkestone findspot'. At first this was dismissed as incorrect, and the coins branded Gaulish. However, during the late summer of 1987 a hoard of about 2,000 cast bronzes, including the unusual type, were found in a pit in the vicinity of West Thurrock, Essex.

The coins occurred in at least sixteen varieties, with a reasonable typological progression. One coin had a large protrusion of flash which would have broken off had the coin been moved any great distance. In general, the hoard appeared to be made up of coins collected by a mint, perhaps for remelting. No other evidence of minting activity was noted at the site, but it appears the mint cannot have been far away.

THURROCK TYPE cast bronzes are seldom found singly in Kent, but a few have been found in the Thames. The coins cannot have been used over a very wide area, nor for a very long time. Two interpretations are likely: either they have a Gaulish origin and were briefly imported, or they have a British one and represent the first coinage of the Trinovantes/Catuvellauni. Although similar coins are reported from the Continent (Castelin, 1978, numbers 477 to 485), they are not sufficiently alike to have a common Gaulish origin. Thus, of the two interpretations, the Trinovantian/Catuvellaunian origin appears the most likely.

Thurrock Types appear to have been influenced by the Prototype Period cast bronzes of the Cantii, dating them about 100 to 90 B.C. Within twenty years, the tribe was striking its own gold coinage.

The Trinovantes/Catuvellauni were one of the earliest tribes to begin striking gold staters, with the introduction of the CLACTON TYPE about 70 B.C. A hoard of these was found with Ambiani Abstract Type staters at Clacton beach.

NOTES: All known specimens are from the Clacton
hoard—see Hill, G. F., 1919, pp. 172–178,
Pl. VII.
1455-1, 1455-3 and 1455-7 are obverse die-
linked with Clacton hoard coins in the
British Museum.
Most are in museums.
Typical weight given.

1455-3    EARLY CLACTON TYPE 70–65 B.C.          ER
*A'* Stater ca. 6.4 gms. 19 mm

OBV: Abstracted head right
Identifying points:
    1) similiar to 46-1
    2) wreath: leaves upwards

REV: Disjointed horse right
Identifying points:
    1) similar to 1455-1
    2) 'coffee bean' above horse's tail

CLASSIFICATION: Trinovantian B

NOTES: As 1455-1.
    Typical weight given.

1455-7    EARLY CLACTON TYPE 70–65 B.C.          ER
*A'* Stater ca. 6.4 gms. 19 mm

OBV: Abstracted head right
Identifying points:
    1) similiar to 46-1
    2) wreath: leaves upwards

REV: Disjointed horse right
Identifying points:
    1) below pellet with four short rays and two
       curved arms
    2) shaggy mane on horse
    3) 'coffee bean' below horse's tail

CLASSIFICATION: Trinovantian B

NOTES: As 1455-1.
    Typical weight given.

1458-1     LATE CLACTON TYPE 70-65 B.C.          ER
N Stater ca. 6.4 gms. 18 mm

OBV: Abstracted head of Apollo right
Identifying points:
    1) wreath: leaves downwards
    2) ring beneath lower end of wreath
    3) stylized garment (lower portion of coin) is
       now represented by inverted 'V' with single
       line of pellets

REV: Disjointed horse left
Identifying points:
    1) three broad crescents form horse's neck and
       body
    2) 'star' made up of large pellet with ten rays
       ending in pellets
    3) row of pellets beneath 'star'

CLASSIFICATION: Trinovantian B

NOTES: All known specimens from Clacton hoard.
       Most in museums.
       All specimens of type 1458-1 to 1458-9 are
       struck from the same obverse die.
       Type designated 'LATE' because further
       removed from Continental prototype 46-1.
       Typical weight given.

1458-3     LATE CLACTON TYPE 70-65 B.C.          ER
N Stater ca. 6.4 gms. 20 mm

OBV: Abstracted head of Apollo right
Identifying points:
    1) struck from same die as 1458-1

REV: Disjointed horse left
Identifying points:
    1) As 1458-1
    2) 'star' made up of large pellet with seven rays
       ending in pellets

CLASSIFICATION: Trinovantian B

NOTES: As 1458-1.
       Typical weight given.

1458–5    LATE CLACTON TYPE 70–65 B.C.                    ER
Æ Stater ca. 6.4 gms. 20 mm

OBV: Abstracted head of Apollo right
Identifying points:
    1) struck from same die as 1458–1

REV: Disjointed horse left
Identifying points:
    1) As 1458–1
    2) 'star' made up of large pellet with six rays
       ending in pellets
    3) curved exergual line

CLASSIFICATION: Trinovantian B

NOTES: As 1458–1.
      Typical weight given.

1458–7    LATE CLACTON TYPE 70–65 B.C.                    ER
Æ Stater ca. 6.4 gms. 19 mm

OBV: Abstracted head of Apollo right
Identifying points:
    1) struck from same die as 1458–1

REV: Disjointed horse left
Identifying points:
    1) As 1458–1
    2) 'star' made up of large pellet with six rays
       ending in pellets
    3) almost straight exergual line

CLASSIFICATION: Trinovantian B

NOTES: As 1458–1.
      Typical weight given.

1458–9    LATE CLACTON TYPE 70–65 B.C.                    ER
Æ Stater ca. 6.4 gms. 20 mm

OBV: Abstracted head of Apollo right
Identifying points:
    1) struck from same die as 1458–1

REV: Disjointed horse left
Identifying points:
    1) As 1458–1
    2) 'star' made up of large pellet with six rays
       ending in pellets

3) ring in front of horse
4) ring at junction of horse's neck and body
5) rings in angles of horse's body and legs

CLASSIFICATION: Trinovantian B

NOTES: As 1458-1.
Typical weight given.

1460-1    LATE CLACTON TYPE 70-65 B.C.                    ER
Ą Quarter Stater 1.4-1.8 gms. 14 mm

OBV: Plain
Identifying points:
1) almost obliterated pattern, possibly Apollo head

REV: Cross
Identifying points:
1) outline cross, pellets in angles

CLASSIFICATION: Trinovantian B

NOTES: Five specimens, from Clacton hoard, all struck from same reverse die, are currently in museums.
See modern forgery 1460-1F.
Typical weight given.

1462-1    WALDINGFIELD TYPE 65-60 B.C.                    ER
Ą Stater 6.2 gms. 20 mm

OBV: Abstracted head of Apollo right

REV: Disjointed horse left
Identifying points:
1) three broad strokes form neck and body of horse
2) beaded mane on horse
3) large pellet and two rings below horse

CLASSIFICATION: Trinovantian C

NOTES: Most are in museums.
Typical weight given.

A new style of stater was introduced during or after Caesar's invasion of Britain in 55 B.C. The WHADDON CHASE TYPE was struck in several varieties, eventually leading to the first dynastic issue of the Trinovantes/Catuvellauni.

1470–1    WHADDON CHASE TYPE 55–45 B.C.        S
Æ Stater 5.90 gms. 18 mm

OBV: Abstracted head of Apollo right
Identifying points:
    1) spike made up of line with a pellet at either end
    2) two wing-like objects on either side of spike to left of wreath

REV: Romanized horse right
Identifying points:
    1) cog wheel with teeth of unequal length below horse
    2) same cog wheel in front of horse's head
    3) winged object above horse
    4) ellipse in front of and behind horse
    5) 'X' behind horse
    6) horse has oversized ear

CLASSIFICATION: Trinovantian D

NOTES: Winged object and 'X' near the horse are copied directly from the winged-head Roma type denarius of the Roman Republic. Standard weight given.

1472–1    WHADDON CHASE TYPE 55–45 B.C.        C
Æ Stater 5.90 gms. 19 mm

OBV: Abstracted head of Apollo right
Identifying points:
    1) spike made up of line with a pellet at either end
    2) two wing-like objects on either side of spike to left of wreath

REV: Romanized horse right
Identifying points:
    1) sunflower below horse
    2) winged object above horse
    3) row of pellets enclosed in two parallel lines near winged object

4) ellipse with row of pellets in front of and behind horse
6) 'X' behind horse
7) horse has oversized ear

CLASSIFICATION: Trinovantian D

NOTES: Winged object and 'X' near the horse are copied directly from the winged-head Roma type denarius of the Roman Republic. Standard weight given.

1474-1     WHADDON CHASE TYPE 55–45 B.C.     ER
AV Quarter Stater ca. 1.25 gms. 14 mm

OBV: Abstracted head of Apollo right
Identifying points:
   1) spike made up of line and pellet
   2) two wing-like objects on either side of spike to left of wreath

REV: Romanized horse right
Identifying points:
   1) sunflower above horse
   2) sunflower below horse
   3) horse has oversized ear

CLASSIFICATION: Trinovantian D

NOTES: Typical weight given.

1476-1     WHADDON CHASE TYPE 55–45 B.C.     C
AV Stater 5.90 gms. 17–18 mm

OBV: Abstracted head of Apollo right
Identifying points:
   1) spike made up of line with a pellet at either end
   2) two wing-like objects on either side of spike to left of wreath

REV: Romanized horse right
Identifying points:
   1) ring-and-large-pellet motif below horse
   2) winged object above horse
   3) ellipse with row of pellets in front of horse
   4) ellipse behind horse
   5) horse has oversized ear

CLASSIFICATION: Trinovantian D

NOTES: Winged object near the horse is copied directly from the winged-head Roma type denarius of the Roman Republic.
Modern forgeries exist, see 1476-1F.
Standard weight given.

1476-3    WHADDON CHASE TYPE 55–45 B.C.            C
N Stater 5.90 gms. 17–18 mm

OBV: Abstracted head of Apollo right
Identifying points:
    1) spike made up of line with a pellet at either end
    2) two wing-like objects on either side of spike to left of wreath

REV: Romanized horse right
Identifying points:
    1) ring-and-large-pellet motif below horse
    2) winged object above horse
    3) ellipse with meandering line in front of horse
    4) ellipse behind horse
    5) horse has oversized ear

CLASSIFICATION: Trinovantian D

NOTES: Winged object near the horse is copied directly from the winged-head Roma type denarius of the Roman Republic.
Standard weight given.

1476-5    WHADDON CHASE TYPE 55–45 B.C.            C
N Stater 5.90 gms. 17–18 mm

OBV: Abstracted head of Apollo right
Identifying points:
    1) spike made up of line with a pellet at either end
    2) two wing-like objects on either side of spike to left of wreath

REV: Romanized horse right
Identifying points:
    1) ring-and-large-pellet motif below horse
    3) uncertain animal or fish head with row of pellets in front of horse
    2) winged object above horse
    4) ellipse behind horse
    5) horse has oversized ear

CLASSIFICATION: Trinovantian D

NOTES: Winged object near the horse is copied directly from the winged-head Roma type denarius of the Roman Republic. Standard weight given.

1478-1     WHADDON CHASE TYPE 55–45 B.C.          ER
AV Quarter Stater 14 mm

OBV: Abstracted head of Apollo right
Identifying points:
   1) spike made up of line and pellets
   2) two wing-like objects on either side of spike to left of wreath
   3) wreath is bent at an angle at the point it intersects the spike

REV: Romanized horse right
Identifying points:
   1) ring-and-large-pellet motif below horse
   2) Maltese cross-like object above horse
   3) horse has oversized ear

CLASSIFICATION: Trinovantian D

1478-3     WHADDON CHASE TYPE 55–45 B.C.          ER
AV Quarter Stater 13 mm

OBV: Abstracted head of Apollo right
Identifying points:
   1) spike made up of line and pellets
   2) two wing-like objects on either side of spike to left of wreath
   3) wreath is bent at an angle at the point it intersects the spike

REV: Romanized horse right
Identifying points:
   1) large pellet below horse
   2) flower made up of lines above horse
   3) horse has oversized ear

CLASSIFICATION: Trinovantian D

1478-5 WHADDON CHASE TYPE 55–45 B.C. ER

*N*/Æ Quarter Stater 14 mm

OBV: Abstracted head of Apollo right
Identifying points:
    1) spike made up of line and pellets
    2) two wing-like objects on either side of spike to left of wreath
    3) wreath is bent at an angle at the point it intersects the spike

REV: Romanized horse right
Identifying points:
    1) large pellet below horse
    2) flower made up of lines above horse
    3) horse has oversized ear

CLASSIFICATION: Trinovantian D

NOTES: Æ core of plated quarter stater of 1478–3.

1478-7 WHADDON CHASE TYPE 55–45 B.C. ER

*N* Quarter Stater 13 mm

OBV: Abstracted head of Apollo right
Identifying points:
    1) as 1478–3

REV: Romanized horse right
Identifying points:
    1) as 1478–3, but two pellets below horse

CLASSIFICATION: Trinovantian D

NOTES: Most are in museums.

Later varieties of the Whaddon Chase Type, distinguished by a new obverse style in which the wreath is now shown as two wreaths crossed at a ninety degree angle.

1485-1 MIDDLE WHADDON CHASE TYPE ER
45–40 B.C.

*N* Stater 5.9–5.4 gms. 16 mm

OBV: Abstracted head of Apollo right
Identifying points:
    1) wreath now forms 'X' pattern
    2) two outline crescents back-to-back in centre
    3) no spike

REV: Romanized horse right
Identifying points:
1) sunflower below horse
2) crescent, points downward, above horse
3) horse's tail made up of a single line
4) three diagonal lines extend downwards from horse's tail

CLASSIFICATION: Trinovantian E

NOTES: Typical weight given.

1487-1    MIDDLE WHADDON CHASE TYPE        ER
45-40 B.C.
Æ Stater 5.9-5.4 gms. 17 mm

OBV: Abstracted head of Apollo right
Identifying points:
1) wreath now forms 'X' pattern
2) two outline crescents back-to-back in centre
3) no spike
4) wing-like objects in angles of crossed wreaths

REV: Romanized horse right
Identifying points:
1) six-spoked wheel with axle below horse
2) wing-like object above horse
3) wreath in place of exergual line
4) ellipse behind horse
5) horse's tail made up of a single line

CLASSIFICATION: Trinovantian E

NOTES: Typical weight given.
        Modern forgery exists—see 1487-1F.

1487-3    MIDDLE WHADDON CHASE TYPE        ER
45-40 B.C.
Æ/Æ Plated Stater 18 mm

OBV: Abstracted head of Apollo right
Identifying points:
1) as 1487-1

REV: Romanized horse right
Identifying points:
1) as 1487-1

CLASSIFICATION: Trinovantian E

NOTES: Ancient forgery of 1487–1.
Most are in museums.

1488–1     MIDDLE WHADDON CHASE TYPE          ER
45–40 B.C.
*N* Quarter Stater 10 mm

OBV: Crossed wreaths
Identifying points:
  1) wreaths made up of pellets
  2) two back-to-back crescents in centre
  3) two pellets near crescents

REV: Celticized horse right
Identifying points:
  1) small ring above horse
  2) pellet below horse
  3) six(?)-spoked wheel with axle below horse
  4) dahlia in front of horse

CLASSIFICATION: Trinovantian E

1491–1     MIDDLE WHADDON CHASE TYPE          ER
45–40 B.C.
*N* Stater 5.9–5.4 gms. 18 mm

OBV: Abstracted head of Apollo right
Identifying points:
  1) wreath now forms 'X' pattern
  2) two outline crescents back-to-back in centre
  3) no spike
  4) circle with pellet in each angle of crossed wreath

REV: Romanized horse right
Identifying points:
  1) circle with pellet on breast and rump of horse
  2) circle with pellet in front of horse
  3) horse's tail made up of a single line

CLASSIFICATION: Trinovantian E

NOTES: Typical weight given.

1493-1    MIDDLE WHADDON CHASE TYPE          ER
45-40 B.C.

N Stater 5.9–5.4 gms. 19 mm

OBV: Abstracted head of Apollo right
Identifying points:
    1) wreath now forms 'X' pattern
    2) two outline crescents back-to-back in centre
    3) no spike
    4) one wreath now curved

REV: Romanized horse right
Identifying points:
    1) circle with large pellet below horse
    2) crescent, points to right, above horse
    3) 'coffee bean' behind horse
    4) horse's tail made up of a single line

CLASSIFICATION: Trinovantian E

NOTES: This obverse die-type is the prototype for
    the dynastic coinage of Tasciovanus.
    Typical weight given.

1493-3    MIDDLE WHADDON CHASE TYPE          ER
45-40 B.C.

N/Æ Plated Stater 17 mm

OBV: Abstracted head of Apollo right
Identifying points:
    1) as 1493-1

REV: Romanized horse right
Identifying points:
    1) as 1493-1

CLASSIFICATION: Trinovantian E

NOTES: Ancient forgery of 1493-1.
    Most are in museums.

The following varieties are distinguished from the Middle Whaddon Chase
Type by the obliteration of the obverse dies through over-use.

1498-1    LATE WHADDON CHASE TYPE          ER
45-40 B.C.

N Stater 5.9–5.4 gms. 16 mm

OBV: Almost plain
Identifying points:
    1) slight traces of crossed wreaths from Middle
    Whaddon Chase Type

REV: Romanized horse right
Identifying points:
    1) winged object above horse
    2) large pellet below horse
    3) 'coffee bean' behind horse
    4) horse's tail made up of a single line

CLASSIFICATION: Trinovantian F

NOTES: Typical weight given.

1500-1    LATE WHADDON CHASE TYPE    ER
            45–40 B.C.
            $N$ Stater 5.9–5.4 gms. 16 mm

OBV: Almost plain
Identifying points:
    1) slight traces of crossed wreaths from Middle
       Whaddon Chase Type

REV: Romanized horse right
Identifying points:
    1) winged object above horse
    2) multi-armed spiral with large central pellet
       below horse
    4) horse's tail made up of two lines

CLASSIFICATION: Trinovantian F

NOTES: Typical weight given.

1502-1    LATE WHADDON CHASE TYPE    ER
            45–40 B.C.
            $N$ Stater 5.9–5.4 gms. 16 mm

OBV: Almost plain
Identifying points:
    1) slight traces of crossed wreaths from Middle
       Whaddon Chase Type

REV: Romanized horse right
Identifying points:
    1) two concentric circles with central pellet
       below horse
    2) large pellet below horse's neck
    3) horse's tail made up of two lines

CLASSIFICATION: Trinovantian F

NOTES: Typical weight given.

1505-1     LATE WHADDON CHASE TYPE          VR
45-40 B.C.
N Stater 5.9-5.4 gms. 16 mm

OBV: Almost plain
Identifying points:
    1) slight traces of crossed wreaths from Middle
       Whaddon Chase Type

REV: Romanized horse right
Identifying points:
    1) circle with pellet above horse
    2) circle with pellet below horse
    3) horse's tail made up of two lines

CLASSIFICATION: Trinovantian F

NOTES: Typical weight given.
       Most are in museums.

1507-1     LATE WHADDON CHASE TYPE          ER
45-40 B.C.
N Stater 5.9-5.4 gms. 16 mm

OBV: Almost plain
Identifying points:
    1) slight traces of crossed wreaths from Middle
       Whaddon Chase Type

REV: Romanized horse right
Identifying points:
    1) two concentric circles on horse's breast
    2) large wheel below horse made up of a small
       circle at the centre, with a large circle for
       the rim, connected by four sets of double-
       spokes
    3) horse's tail made up of a single line
    4) object above horse appears to be a hand

CLASSIFICATION: Trinovantian F

NOTES: Typical weight given.

1509-1     LATE WHADDON CHASE TYPE          ER
45-40 B.C.
N Stater 5.9-5.4 gms. 16 mm

OBV: Almost plain
Identifying points:
    1) slight traces of crossed wreaths from Middle
       Whaddon Chase Type
    2) two reversed 'S' motifs in field

REV: Romanized horse right
Identifying points:
  1) pellet-in-ring motif on horse's breast
  2) large wheel below horse made up of a small circle at the centre, with a large circle for the rim, connected by four sets of double-spokes
  3) horse's tail made up of three lines, ending in a circle with pellet

CLASSIFICATION: Trinovantian F

NOTES: Typical weight given.

The following WONERSH TYPE is similiar in style to some of the Middle Whaddon Chase staters. Lighter than the standard weight for the period, it is often found outside the normal tribal area. It may be a coin used for external trade, or may be a copy produced by a different tribe.

1520–1    WONERSH TYPE 45–40 B.C.                    VR
N Stater ca. 5.4–5.3 gms. 19 mm

OBV: Abstracted head of Apollo right
Identifying points:
  1) wreath now forms 'X' pattern
  2) two outline crescents back-to-back in centre
  3) no spike

REV: Romanized horse right
Identifying points:
  1) eight-spoked wheel with axle below horse
  2) eight-armed spiral above horse
  3) horse's ear shaped like an ellipse, as on Whaddon Chase staters
  4) small rings in field around horse
  5) anemone in front of horse

CLASSIFICATION: Trinovantian G

NOTES: Typical weight given.
       Some varieties have a six-spoked wheel.

1520–5    WONERSH TYPE 45–40 B.C.                    ER
N Stater 18 mm

OBV: Abstracted head of Apollo right
Identifying points:
  1) as 1520–1

REV: Romanized horse right
Identifying points:
    1) as 1520-1, but rows of pellets between arms
       of spiral

CLASSIFICATION: Trinovantian G

NOTES: Most are in museums.

1522-1     WONERSH TYPE 45-40 B.C.          VR
Æ Stater ca. 5.4-5.2 gms. 16 mm

OBV: Abstracted head of Apollo right
Identifying points:
    1) wreath now forms 'X' pattern
    2) two outline crescents back-to-back in centre
    3) no spike

REV: Celticized horse right
Identifying points:
    1) five-spoked wheel below horse
    2) six-armed spiral above horse
    3) horse's tail made up of a single line

CLASSIFICATION: Trinovantian G

NOTES: Previously, this type was thought to be a
      link between the Whaddon Chase Type and
      the Wonersh Type. However, stylistically it
      is a link between the Wonersh and Savernake
      Forest Types.
      Typical weight given.

1522-5     WONERSH TYPE 45-40 B.C.          ER
Æ Stater 18 mm

OBV: Almost plain
Identifying points:
    1) obverse die almost obliterated

REV: Celticized horse right
Identifying points:
    1) similar to 1522-1
    2) arms of spiral turn in opposite direction,
       compared to 1522-1
    3) six-spoked wheel with axle below horse
    4) pellet-in-ring motif in field

CLASSIFICATION: Trinovantian G

NOTES: Most are in museums.

REV: Celticized horse right
Identifying points:
    1) pellet near tail
    2) horse looks back to left
    3) uncertain objects, possibly rings below horse

CLASSIFICATION: Trinovantian I

NOTES: Some are in museums.

1613-1    **ADDEDOMAROS FIRST COINAGE**    **ER**
        40–37 B.C.
        Æ Unit 1.14 gms. 14 mm

OBV: Celticized head right
Identifying points:
    1) similar to the Æ Unit 1615-1, but the head
        faces the opposite direction
    2) corded hair
    3) pointed nose

REV: Celticized horse left
Identifying points:
    1) pellet-in-ring motif above and below horse
    2) pellet near horse's tail

CLASSIFICATION: Trinovantian I

NOTES: From Harlow Temple excavations.

1615-1    **ADDEDOMAROS FIRST COINAGE**    **VR**
        40–37 B.C.
        Æ Unit 1.3–1.5 gms. 14 mm

OBV: Celticized head left
Identifying points:
    1) similar to the AR Unit 1613-1, but the head
        faces the opposite direction
    2) corded, streaming hair
    3) eye formed by pellet in inverted and curved
        line

REV: Celticized horse right
Identifying points:
    1) pellet below tail
    2) pellet-in-ring motif below horse made into
        flower by addition of rays

CLASSIFICATION: Trinovantian I

NOTES: Some are in museums.

## ADDEDOMAROS SECOND COINAGE

The second coinage is distinguished by a new style stater in which the crossed wreaths become a six-armed spiral, and the back-to-back crescents become three. The privy mark linking the gold, silver and bronze coins is a pellet-in-ring motif near the tail.

1620–1     **ADDEDOMAROS SECOND COINAGE**     VR
37–33 B.C.
Aʹ Stater 5.6 gms. 19 mm

OBV: Six-armed spiral
Identifying points:
    1) three back-to-back crescents in centre
    2) spiral points clockwise

REV: Celticized horse right
Identifying points:
    1) pellet-in-ring motif below tail
    2) cornucopia below horse
    3) ADDIIDOM above horse, first two Ds in form of Greek letter Θ

CLASSIFICATION: Trinovantian J

NOTES: Some are in museums.
        Standard weight given.

1620–3     **ADDEDOMAROS SECOND COINAGE**     ER
37–33 B.C.
Aʹ/Æ Plated Stater 3.9 gms. 18 mm

OBV: Six-armed spiral
Identifying points:
    1) as 1620–1

REV: Celticized horse right
Identifying points:
    1) as 1620–1

CLASSIFICATION: Trinovantian J

NOTES: Possibly struck from official dies.

1623–1     **ADDEDOMAROS SECOND COINAGE**     ER
37–33 B.C.
Aʹ Quarter Stater 1.4 gms. 11 mm

OBV: Flower pattern
Identifying points:
    1) pellet-in-ring in centre

2) four ellipses form petals
3) four 'arms', straightened varieties of those on 1620-1, form additional petals

REV: Celticized horse right
Identifying points:
    1) ring under tail (too small to fit pellet)
    2) pellet-in-ring motif under horse

CLASSIFICATION: Trinovantian J

NOTES: Many are in museums.
       Typical weight given.

1626-1    **ADDEDOMAROS SECOND COINAGE**    ER
          37–33 B.C.
          Æ Unit 11 mm

OBV: Celticized horse right
Identifying points:
    1) pellet-in-ring motif near tail
    2) pellet-in-ring motif under horse

REV: Celticized horse left
Identifying points:
    1) pellet-in-ring motif under horse

CLASSIFICATION: Trinovantian J

NOTES: Some are in museums.
       The attribution is somewhat arbitrary, the coins may be part of the earlier uninscribed coinage.

1629-1    **ADDEDOMAROS SECOND COINAGE**    ER
          37–33 B.C.
          Æ Unit 1.7 gms. 13 mm

OBV: Pegasus left
Identifying points:
    1) pellet-in-ring motif near tail

REV: Pegasus left
Identifying points:
    1) rings below animal

CLASSIFICATION: Trinovantian J

NOTES: Most are in museums.
       The attribution is somewhat arbitrary, and the coin may be part of the earlier uninscribed coinage.

## ADDEDOMAROS THIRD COINAGE

The third coinage is distinguished by another change in the stater in which all vestiges of the wreath disappear and only the crescents remain. The gold, silver and bronze coins are linked by a pellet-in-ring privy mark in front of the horse. The attribution of the silver and bronze to this coinage is less arbitrary than the Second Coinage. The pellet-in-ring motif on the silver coin is not absolutely certain, since on published examples it is struck partially off the flan.

1635-1     **ADDEDOMAROS THIRD COINAGE**     ER
33–30 B.C.
N Stater 5.6 gms. 19 mm

OBV: Crescent design
Identifying points:
     1) two crescents back-to-back
     2) pellets between crescent arms
     3) pellets and lines in crescents

REV: Celticized horse right
Identifying points:
     1) pellet-in-ring motif in front of horse
     2) branch below horse
     3) outline pinwheel above horse
     4) ADDEDOMAROS around horse, first two
        Ds in form of Greek letter $\Theta$

CLASSIFICATION: Trinovantian K

NOTES: Most are in museums.
        Standard weight is given.
        Modern forgery exists, see 1635–1F.

1638-1     **ADDEDOMAROS THIRD COINAGE**     ER
33–30 B.C.
N Quarter Stater 1.3 gms. 13 mm

OBV: Crescent design
Identifying points:
     1) similar to 1635–1, but less detail owing to
        small size of coin

REV: Celticized horse right
Identifying points:
     1) pellet-in-ring motif in front of horse
     2) box with X inside below horse

3) ADDEDOMAROS around horse, first two
Ds in form of Greek letter $\Theta$

CLASSIFICATION: Trinovantian K

NOTES: Typical weight is given.

1643–1    ADDEDOMAROS THIRD COINAGE          ER
33–30 B.C.
Æ Unit 0.3 gms. 11 mm

OBV: Celticized horse right
Identifying points:
    1) Possible pellet-in-ring motif in front of horse
    2) pellet-in-ring motif above horse
    3) corded line above horse

REV: Celticized horse right
Identifying points:
    1) large-pellet-in-ring motif above horse
    2) pellet below horse

CLASSIFICATION: Trinovantian K

NOTES: In the 1953 edition of Mack's *Coinage of
       Ancient Britain*, number 444 shows a pos-
       sible pellet-in-ring motif in front of the horse.
       This coin was dropped from subsequent
       editions because it was the same as number
       272. The plate coin here is number 272,
       which shows less of the area in front of the
       horse.

1644–1    ADDEDOMAROS THIRD COINAGE          ER
33–30 B.C.
Æ Unit 12 mm

OBV: Coiled serpent right
Identifying points:
    1) pellet-in-ring motif inside of serpent's coil

REV: Celticized horse right
Identifying points:
    1) pellet-in-ring motif in front of horse
    2) pellet-in-ring  motif  for  horse's  head,
       shoulder and rump

CLASSIFICATION: Trinovantian K

1646-1    ADDEDOMAROS THIRD COINAGE    VR
33-30 B.C.
Æ Unit 13 mm

OBV: Celticized head left
Identifying points:
    1) corded hair similar to 1615-1

REV: Celticized horse left
Identifying points:
    1) pellet-in-ring motif in front of horse
    2) pellet-in-ring motif near head

CLASSIFICATION: Trinovantian K

NOTES: Some are in museums.


## COINAGE OF DUBNOVELLAUNUS IN ESSEX

Addededomaros is followed by a short-lived ruler who inscribed his coins 'Dubnovellaunus'. Dubnovellaunus 'in Essex' has traditionally been dated to the earlier part of the Interregnum, about 10 B.C., and thus was thought to be the ruler who assumed power after Tasciovanus. He is not the same ruler who stuck coins in Kent, the two Dubnovellaunus's on the coins are different people.

Dubnovellaunus' coinage lasts about five years, with only one major variety of stater. There is a problem with dating it, however. The coin looks earlier than the issues of Tasciovanus, stylistically. The Marks Tey hoard contained staters of Addedomaros and Dubnovellaunus together in a pot. Furthermore, the bronzes of Dubnovellaunus appear to follow those of Addedomaros in style. Thus, it is probable Dubnovellaunus ruled after Addedomaros and before Tasciovanus.

However, a statistical analysis of Dubnovellaunus' staters shows they were less worn, on average, when deposited than those of the other two rulers. Furthermore, the staters of all three are struck to about the same standard (the 0.05 gramme lower weight for Tasciovanus is not significant), so coins of Addedomaros could have circulated right up to the time of the Interregnum and be deposited in the hoard with ones of Dubnovellaunus.

Consequently, some contrary evidence seems to indicate Dubnovellaunus followed Tasciovanus. He might have issued heavy staters, at the beginning of the Interregnum, but used an antiquated style—perhaps to appeal to traditions and consolidate his rule. Thus, it should be kept in mind there is the alternate interpretation of Dubnovellaunus' coins—that they postdate Tasciovanus'.

On balance, however, the early-date interpretation best fits the data available today, and this places Dubnovellaunus between Addedomaros and Tasciovanus.

1650–1     **DUBNOVELLAUNUS IN ESSEX**      VR
30–25 B.C.
Æ Stater 5.60 gms. 17 mm

OBV: Crescents and wreath
Identifying points:
    1) two small outline crescents back-to-back
    2) wreath extends from cresents in both direc-
       tions
    3) pellet-in-ring motif on either side of cres-
       cents

REV: Celticized horse right
Identifying points:
    1) branch below horse
    2) pellet-in-ring motif above horse
    3) pellet in front of horse
    4) **DVBNOVELLAVN** around horse

CLASSIFICATION: Trinovantian L

NOTES: Standard weight given.
       Many in museums.

1650–3     **DUBNOVELLAUNUS IN ESSEX**      ER
30–25 B.C.
Æ/Æ Plated Stater 4.2 gms. 18 mm

OBV: Crescents and wreath
Identifying points:
    1) as 1650–1

REV: Celticized horse right
Identifying points:
    1) as 1650–1

CLASSIFICATION: Trinovantian L

NOTES: Ancient forgery probably from forger's dies.

1650–5     **DUBNOVELLAUNUS IN ESSEX**      VR
30–25 B.C.
Æ Stater 5.60 gms. 18 mm

OBV: Crescents and wreath
Identifying points:
    1) as 1650–1

REV: Celticized horse right
Identifying points:
    1) as 1650-1, but **DVBNOVALLAVN** around
       horse

CLASSIFICATION: Trinovantian L

NOTES: Standard weight given.
       Many in museums.

1655-1    DUBNOVELLAUNUS IN ESSEX        ER
30-25 B.C.
Aʹ Stater 5.60 gms. 17 mm

OBV: Crescents and wreath
Identifying points:
    1) as 1650-1

REV: Celticized horse right
Identifying points:
    1) similiar to 1650-1
    2) legend reads **DVBNOVILLA**
    3) star below horse's tail

CLASSIFICATION: Trinovantian L

NOTES: Standard weight given.

1655-5    DUBNOVELLAUNUS IN ESSEX        ER
30-25 B.C.
Aʹ Stater 5.60 gms. 18 mm

OBV: Crescents and wreath
Identifying points:
    1) as 1655-1

REV: Celticized horse right
Identifying points:
    1) similiar to 1655-1
    2) legend reads **DVBNOVILLA**
    3) pellet below horse's tail

CLASSIFICATION: Trinovantian L

NOTES: Standard weight given.
       Most are in museums.

1655–9     DUBNOVELLAUNUS IN ESSEX          ER
30–25 B.C.
N Stater 5.60 gms. 18 mm

OBV: Crescents and wreath
Identifying points:
 1) as 1655–1

REV: Celticized horse right
Identifying points:
 1) similiar to 1655–5
 2) no pellet below horse's tail

CLASSIFICATION: Trinovantian L

NOTES: Standard weight given.
   Most are museums.

1660–1     DUBNOVELLAUNUS IN ESSEX          ER
30–25 B.C.
N Quarter Stater 1.3 gms. 11 mm

OBV: Crescents and wreath
Identifying points:
 1) as 1650–1

REV: Celticized horse left
Identifying points:
 1) branch below horse
 2) pellet in front of horse

CLASSIFICATION: Trinovantian L

NOTES: Typical weight given.

1662–1     DUBNOVELLAUNUS IN ESSEX          ER
30–25 B.C.
Æ Unit 10 mm

OBV: Crescents and wreath
Identifying points:
 1) similar to design on the stater 1650–1
 2) two pellet-in-ring motifs on either side of
  wreath

REV: Celticized horse right
Identifying points:
 1) pellet with two concentric rings above horse
 2) two concentric rings, possibly with a central
  pellet below horse

CLASSIFICATION: Trinovantian L

1663-1     **DUBNOVELLAUNUS IN ESSEX**                    ER
30–25 B.C.
Æ Unit 1.3 gms. 13 mm

OBV: Celticized head right
Identifying points:
    1) pellet-in-ring motif for eye
    2) crescents for hair
    3) two pellets for lips
    4) line of pellets to indicate hairline

REV: Celticized horse left
Identifying points:
    1) pellet-in-ring motif for head and on shoulder
    2) ring below tail
    3) pellet near tail
    4) two pellets under head
    5) elliptical ear
    6) two lines with ellipse ends and corded line
       ending in pellet-in-ring motif above horse
    7) [DVBNOVE]LLAUNOS around horse

CLASSIFICATION: Trinovantian L

NOTES: Silver version of Æ unit 1665–1.
      Existing example does not show area below
      horse, a branch probably appears there.

1665-1     **DUBNOVELLAUNUS IN ESSEX**                    VR
30–25 B.C.
Æ Unit 15 mm

OBV: Celticized head right
Identifying points:
    1) same as 1663-1
    2) head appears to have necklace or torc
    3) pellet-in-ring motif for eye
    4) crescents for hair
    4) two pellets for lips
    5) line of pellets to indicate hairline

REV: Celticized horse left
Identifying points:
    1) branch below horse
    2) pellet under horse's tail
    3) DV above horse

CLASSIFICATION: Trinovantian L

NOTES: Some in museums.

1667–1   DUBNOVELLAUNUS IN ESSEX               ER
30–25 B.C.
Æ Unit 1.8 gms. 14 mm

OBV: Celticized head left
Identifying points:
1) headband retains hair
2) hair indicated by vertical lines rising from headband
3) Possible inscription **DVBNOV** in front of face

REV: Celticized horse right
Identifying points:
1) horse's head turns back to left
2) pellet above horse
3) pellet-in-ring motif in front of horse
4) uncertain legend, possibly **DVB** below horse

CLASSIFICATION: Trinovantian L

NOTES: Published examples too poorly preserved to identify details.

1669–1   DUBNOVELLAUNUS IN ESSEX               ER
30–25 B.C.
Æ Unit 1.7 gms. 17 mm

OBV: Celticized head left
Identifying points:
1) pellet-in-ring motif above brow
2) pellet-in-ring motif behind head
3) hair indicated by curves

REV: Celticized horse left
Identifying points:
1) pellet-in-ring motifs above and below horse
2) pellet below tail
3) branch below horse
4) **DVBNO** above horse

CLASSIFICATION: Trinovantian L

## THE COINAGE OF TASCIOVANUS

Dubnovellaunus-in-Essex is followed by Tasciovanus, who adds his name to the silver and bronze coins, as well as the gold. Tasciovanus' coins show a bewildering variety of types, with increasingly Romanized images.

At the end of the reign, Tasciovanus' name was linked with others and there was a period in which several new names appeared alone. The departure of Tasciovanus from the throne, evidently without a strong successor, resulted in a contest for the tribal leadership. A turbulent Interregnum ensued, creating a power vacuum and unsettled conditions throughout the south-east of Britain. Several rulers of neighbouring tribes disappeared at the time and there was military activity in Kent involving the Atrebates/Regni, during which Trinovantian/Catuvellaunian coins ceased to circulate amongst the Cantii. Peace was restored upon the elevation of Cunobeline to the throne about 10 A.D.

Two mints were in operation during Tasciovanus' reign, with Verulamium and Camulodunum both striking gold coins with mint names. The coinage is divided into three issues, distinguished by the increasing Romanization of the staters. Privy-marking, if used during this period, is difficult to identify because of the wide variety of types. The sequence of issues is not completely proven and represents an opportunity for original research.

Tasciovanus managed to maintain the weight of the stater near the 5.6 gramme standard of his predecessor, but during the Interregnum this drops to 5.4. Some of the participants in the struggle for the throne had to issue light-weight staters and others were unable to issue gold coins at all. Some of the coins may represent local issues struck in emergencies, signalling the temporary absence of a central coin-producing authority.

It was once thought the coins inscribed ANDOCO were those of a western ruler, and those inscribed DUBNOVELLAUNOS an eastern one, proving the existence of two tribes, the Catuvellauni and the Trinovantes. However, the findspot distributions of these coins are now seen to be more dispersed than initially thought, and it is probably too much to read a political division from them. Andoco and Dubnovellaunus-in-Essex are almost certainly sequential rulers.

The Trinovantian/Catuvellaunian coinage displayed a great diversity of types under Tasciovanus. The use of bronze coinage came into extensive use as the tribe's fortune steadily improved and a thriving market economy demanded increasing quantities of small change. Although Cunobeline is credited with the great prosperity of the next century, clearly this has its roots in the reign of Tasciovanus, and probably earlier.

The tribe's influence had begun to expand in southern Britain during the rule of Addedomaros and this grows under Dubnovellaunus and Tasciovanus. It appears the time from 55 B.C. to 43 A.D is one of those episodes in British history in which a succession of strong, capable rulers created flourishing growth and prosperity. The reigns of Addedomaros, Dubnovellaunus, Tasciovanus and Cunobeline deserve recognition as one of the great dynasties.

## TASCIOVANUS FIRST COINAGE

Tasciovanus' first coins are distinguished by staters with Celticized horses and the crossed wreath motif. These have their inspiration in the Middle Whaddon Chase Types.

An innovation on the obverse, however, gives us one of the few examples seen on coins of the 'Celtic joke'. In many examples of Celtic decorative art, a face is hidden in what is otherwise an abstract pattern. The viewer is challenged to find it, and once he does, he never fails to see it on subsequent viewings having become privy to the joke. The first coinage staters all have a pair of faces hidden in the crossed Apollo wreath, made up of a pair of pellet-in-ring motifs for eyes, a pellet for a nose, and a small crescent for a mouth.

The silver and bronze issues of the First Coinage have been defined as the Celticized types, with the Romanized coins assigned to the Second and Third Coinages.

1680–1    TASCIOVANUS FIRST COINAGE          ER
25–20 B.C.
A′ Stater 5.55 gms. 16 mm

OBV: Crossed wreaths
Identifying points:
1) two curves back-to-back in centre
2) four pellet-in-ring motifs near curves
3) outline crescents at edge
4) two hidden faces (see preceding text)

REV: Celticized horse right
Identifying points:
1) bucranium above horse
2) anemone above horse's head
3) hook-like object below horse
4) TASCIAV above horse

CLASSIFICATION: Trinovantian M

NOTES: Standard weight given.
Verulamium mint.
This coin type was copied many years later by Andoco during the Interregnum. The coin must have been worn, and the die-cutter unfamiliar with the design details. He blundered the bucranium above the horse, see 1860–1. Possibly Andoco wanted to legitimize himself by appealing to conservatism and tradition by copying an obsolete coin type.

1680-3    **TASCIOVANUS FIRST COINAGE**      ER
25–20 B.C.
Æ'/Æ Plated Stater 3.5 gms. 18 mm

OBV: Crossed wreaths
Identifying points:
     1) as 1680-1

REV: Celticized horse right
Identifying points:
     1) as 1680-1

CLASSIFICATION: Trinovantian M

NOTES: Struck from forger's dies.
         Die cutting considerably cruder than on
         coins of the official mint.

1682-1    **TASCIOVANUS FIRST COINAGE**      ER
25–20 B.C.
Æ' Stater 5.55 gms. 19 mm

OBV: Crossed wreaths
Identifying points:
     1) as 1680-1

REV: Celticized horse right
Identifying points:
     1) as 1680-1, but different inscription
     2) TAXCIAV above horse

CLASSIFICATION: Trinovantian M

NOTES: Standard weight given.
         Verulamium mint.
         Modern forgeries may exist.

1684-1    **TASCIOVANUS FIRST COINAGE**      ER
25–20 B.C.
Æ' Stater 5.55 gms. 17 mm

OBV: Crossed wreaths
Identifying points:
     1) as 1680-1

REV: Celticized horse right
Identifying points:
    1) as 1680-1, but different inscription
    2) pellet-in-ring motif below horse instead of
       hook-like object
    3) TASCIOVAN above horse
    4) CAM monogram below horse

CLASSIFICATION: Trinovantian M

NOTES: Standard weight given.
        Camulodunum mint.
        Die cutting on this coin is generally better-
        executed than on Verulamium issues.

1688-1     TASCIOVANUS FIRST COINAGE       ER
           25–20 B.C.
           $N$ Quarter Stater 1.3 gms. 11 mm

OBV: Crossed wreaths
Identifying points:
    1) circular ornament in angles

REV: Celticized horse left
Identifying points:
    1) uncertain object, possibly degraded bucran-
       ium below horse

CLASSIFICATION: Trinovantian M

NOTES: Typical weight given.
        Many in museums.
        Verulamium mint.
        Coin is uninscribed, but is almost identical
        to next three inscribed types.

1690-1     TASCIOVANUS FIRST COINAGE       ER
           25–20 B.C.
           $N$ Quarter Stater 1.4 gms. 11 mm

OBV: Crossed wreaths
Identifying points:
    1) VERO in angles

REV: Celticized horse left
Identifying points:
    1) bucranium above horse
    2) TAS below horse

CLASSIFICATION: Trinovantian M

NOTES: Typical weight given.
Many in museums.
Verulamium mint.
Modern forgery exists, see 1690–1F.

1692–1    TASCIOVANUS FIRST COINAGE              ER
25–20 B.C.
A′ Quarter Stater 1.3 gms. 11 mm

OBV: Crossed wreaths
Identifying points:
    1) TASCI in angles
    2) wreaths end in pellet-in-ring motifs

REV: Celticized horse right
Identifying points:
    1) TASC below horse
    2) bucranium above horse

CLASSIFICATION: Trinovantian M

NOTES: Typical weight given.
Most in museums.
Verulamium mint.

1694–1    TASCIOVANUS FIRST COINAGE              ER
25–20 B.C.
A′ Quarter Stater 1.4 gms. 11 mm

OBV: Crossed wreaths
Identifying points:
    1) circular ornaments in angles

REV: Celticized horse left
Identifying points:
    1) CAM monogram above horse
    2) anemone above horse

CLASSIFICATION: Trinovantian M

NOTES: Typical weight given.
Many in museums.
Camulodunum mint.
Although Tasciovanus' name does not
appear, typologically this is the quarter
stater of 1684–1.

1698-1 **TASCIOVANUS FIRST COINAGE** ER
25-20 B.C.
ÆR Unit 13 mm

OBV: Celticized head left
Identifying points:
1) corded hair
2) hook for ear
3) pellet for eye

REV: Celticized horse right
Identifying points:
1) bucranium above horse
2) pellet-in-ring motif for head and shoulder of horse
3) pellet-in-ring motifs in field

CLASSIFICATION: Trinovantian M

NOTES: This coin provides a 'bridge' between the coins of Addedomaros and other coins of Tasciovanus (see the obverse of 1613-1 and the reverse of 1688-1).

1699-1 **TASCIOVANUS FIRST COINAGE** ER
25-20 B.C.
ÆR Unit 1.4 gms. 13 mm

OBV: Inscription in pellet ring
Identifying points:
1) VER in pellet-ring

REV: Celticized horse right
Identifying points:
1) TASCIA around horse
2) exergual line below

CLASSIFICATION: Trinovantian M

NOTES: Verulamium mint.
Modern forgery exists, see 1699-1F.

1705-1 **TASCIOVANUS FIRST COINAGE** ER
25-20 B.C.
Æ Unit 1.9 gms. 15 mm

OBV: Celticized heads right, jugate
Identifying points:
1) hair made up of short curves
2) pellets for mouth
3) hook for ear

REV: Celticized ram left

Identifying points:

    1) wild flowers around ram

    2) TASC above ram

    3) pellet-in-ring motif above ram

CLASSIFICATION: Trinovantian M

NOTES: Mint is not identified, but is probably Verulamium.

    Many in museums.

1707-1    TASCIOVANUS FIRST COINAGE    ER

25-20 B.C.

Æ Unit 2.3-2.6 gms. 15 mm

OBV: Celticized head right

Identifying points:

    1) similar to 1705-1

    2) head somewhat more lifelike

    3) VERL in front of face

REV: Celticized horse left

Identifying points:

    1) pellet-in-ring motif above horse

    2) sunflower in front of horse

    3) VIIR below horse

    4) exergual line below

CLASSIFICATION: Trinovantian M

NOTES: Verulamium mint.

    Many in museums.

    The reverse design is adapted from a Roman denarius of L. Rusticus.

1707-3    TASCIOVANUS FIRST COINAGE    ER

25-20 B.C.

Æ Unit 2.3 gms. 17 mm

OBV: Celticized head right

Identifying points:

    1) as 1707-1, but inscription is VER (instead of VERL)

REV: Celticized horse left

Identifying points:

    1) as 1707-1, but inscription is VER (instead of VIIR)

CLASSIFICATION: Trinovantian M

NOTES: Verulamium mint.
The reverse design is adapted from a Roman denarius of L. Rusticus.

1709-1 TASCIOVANUS FIRST COINAGE ER
25-20 B.C.
Æ Unit 2.4 gms. 14 mm

OBV: Celticized head right
Identifying points:
1) as 1707-3

REV: Celticized horse left
Identifying points:
1) pellet-in-ring motif above horse
2) probable sunflower in front of horse
3) TAS below horse
4) exergual line below

CLASSIFICATION: Trinovantian M

NOTES: Verulamium mint.
Many in museums.
Mack declined to identify animal as a horse.

1711-1 TASCIOVANUS FIRST COINAGE ER
25-20 B.C.
Æ Unit 2.3 gms. 14 mm

OBV: Celticized head right
Identifying points:
1) as 1707-1 but different inscription
2) TASC in front of face

REV: Celticized Pegasus left
Identifying points:
1) pellet-in-ring motifs above and in front of Pegasus
2) three elongated pellets above Pegasus appear to be disintegrated bucranium

CLASSIFICATION: Trinovantian M

NOTES: Verulamium mint.
Some in museums.

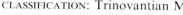

1713-1    TASCIOVANUS FIRST COINAGE    ER
25-20 B.C.
Æ Unit 2.3 gms. 16 mm

OBV: Pattern of crossed lines
Identifying points:
1) cruciform pattern made up of lines, pellets and rings
2) pellets in field

REV: Boar right
Identifying points:
1) crescent above boar
2) VER below boar

CLASSIFICATION: Trinovantian M

NOTES: Verulamium mint.
Some in museums.

1715-1    TASCIOVANUS FIRST COINAGE    ER
25-20 B.C.
Æ Unit 13 mm

OBV: Celticized head left
Identifying points:
1) head similar to that on 1705-1, but faces opposite direction
2) VER in front of face

REV: Celticized goat right
Identifying points:
1) pellet-in-ring motif below animal
2) wind flower above animal

CLASSIFICATION: Trinovantian M

NOTES: Verulamium mint.
Some in museums.

1717-1    TASCIOVANUS FIRST COINAGE    ER
25-20 B.C.
Æ Unit 1.3 gms. 15 mm

OBV: Inscription and uncertain objects
Identifying points:
1) VER or VERL below line

REV: Celticized horse right
Identifying points:
1) horse is grazing
2) crescent above horse
3) ring above horse, may actually be a pellet-in-ring motif

CLASSIFICATION: Trinovantian M

NOTES: Coin is too poorly preserved to identify obverse image.
Verulamium mint.
The reverse design may be adapted from Ptolemaic seals. Also, an intaglio from Corbridge, and seals from Edfu and Cyrene carry similar devices.

## TASCIOVANUS SECOND COINAGE

Tasciovanus' Second Coinage begins with a dramatic change on the gold staters: the Celticized horse is replaced with a spirited scene—a mounted Celtic Warrior brandishing a carnyx. There are no quarter staters for this coinage, and only a few silver and bronze coins. The issue must have been of short duration.

1730-1 TASCIOVANUS SECOND COINAGE ER
20-15 B.C.
N Stater 5.55 gms. 16 mm

OBV: Crossed wreaths
Identifying points:
1) as 1680-1
2) three pellets between crescents

REV: Celtic warrior on horse right
Identifying points:
1) warrior brandishes carnyx
2) four-spoked wheel above and behind horse
3) TASC in field
4) T of TASC below tail and A is below horse

CLASSIFICATION: Trinovantian N

NOTES: Many in museums.
Standard weight given.

1730–5      TASCIOVANUS SECOND COINAGE          ER
20–15 B.C.
N Stater 5.55 gms. 17 mm

OBV: Crossed wreaths
Identifying points:
    1) as 1730–1

REV: Celtic warrior on horse right
Identifying points:
    1) as 1730–1, but AS below horse

CLASSIFICATION: Trinovantian N

NOTES: Most are in museums.
       Standard weight given.

1732–1      TASCIOVANUS SECOND COINAGE          ER
20–15 B.C.
N Stater 5.55 gms. 16 mm

OBV: Crossed wreaths
Identifying points:
    1) as 1680–1
    2) three pellets between crescents

REV: Celtic warrior on horse right
Identifying points:
    1) as 1730–1, but T of TASC above tail and
       A is below the tail

CLASSIFICATION: Trinovantian N

NOTES: Many in museums.
       Standard weight given.

1732–5      TASCIOVANUS SECOND COINAGE          ER
20–15 B.C.
N Stater 5.55 gms. 18 mm

OBV: Crossed wreaths
Identifying points:
    1) as 1732–1

REV: Celtic warrior on horse right
Identifying points:
    1) as 1732–1, but A behind the horse lacks a
       crossbar

CLASSIFICATION: Trinovantian N

NOTES: Most in museums.
       Standard weight given.

REV: Celtic warrior on horse left
Identifying points:
    1) as 1780-1

CLASSIFICATION: Trinovantian O

NOTES: Ancient plated forgery, struck from forger's
      dies.

1780-5    TASCIOVANUS THIRD COINAGE    ER
           15-10 B.C.
           N Stater 5.55 gms. 17 mm

OBV: Inscription on vertical wreath
Identifying points:
    1) as 1780-1, but inscribed TASCIO

REV: Celtic warrior on horse left
Identifying points:
    1) as 1780-1

CLASSIFICATION: Trinovantian O

NOTES: Most in museums.
      Standard weight given.
      This coin provides evidence for use of chain
      mail by Celtic warriors.

1780-9    TASCIOVANUS THIRD COINAGE    ER
           15-10 B.C.
           N Stater 5.55 gms. 18 mm

OBV: Inscription on vertical wreath
Identifying points:
    1) as 1780-1, but inscribed TASCI

REV: Celtic warrior on horse left
Identifying points:
    1) as 1780-1

CLASSIFICATION: Trinovantian O

NOTES: Most in museums.
      Standard weight given.
      This coin provides evidence for use of chain
      mail by Celtic warriors.

1786-1    TASCIOVANUS THIRD COINAGE          ER
15-10 B.C.
Nʹ Quarter Stater 1.4 gms. 11 mm

OBV: Wreath with inscribed tablet
Identifying points:
    1) TASC in tablet
    2) pellet-in-ring motifs to left and right of
       tablet

REV: Celticized Pegasus left
Identifying points:
    1) pellet-in-ring motif in front of Pegasus

CLASSIFICATION: Trinovantian O

NOTES: Many in museums.
       Typical weight given.
       Horse is possibly Pegasus.
       The reverse is adapted from a Roman de-
       narius of Q. Titius.

1790-1    TASCIOVANUS THIRD COINAGE          ER
15-10 B.C.
Æ Unit 1.3 gms. 12 mm

OBV: Pegasus left
Identifying points:
    1) Pegasus walking
    2) TAS below

REV: Winged griffin right
Identifying points:
    1) griffin rears back
    2) griffin in three rings, the middle one of
       pellets

CLASSIFICATION: Trinovantian O

1792-1    TASCIOVANUS THIRD COINAGE          ER
15-10 B.C.
Æ Unit 1.0 gms. 11 mm

OBV: Eagle left
Identifying points:
    1) eagle looks back to right
    2) TASCIO around eagle

REV: Winged griffin right
Identifying points:
1) three pellets below griffin
2) loop and pellet in front of griffin form its left wing

CLASSIFICATION: Trinovantian O

NOTES: Many in museums.

1794-1    TASCIOVANUS THIRD COINAGE              ER
15–10 B.C.
Æ Unit 1.2 gms. 12 mm

OBV: Romanized head right
Identifying points:
1) TASCIA in front of head
2) pellet border

REV: Bull left
Identifying points:
1) bull butting downwards
2) pellet border

CLASSIFICATION: Trinovantian O

NOTES: Most in museums.
Head is that of Augustus, adapted from a Roman denarius. Bull on reverse is adapted from the same denarius.

1796-1    TASCIOVANUS THIRD COINAGE              ER
15–10 B.C.
Æ Unit 1.3 gms. 13 mm

OBV: Stylized crossed wreaths
Identifying points:
1) box with X in centre
2) VERL in angles of wreath

REV: Boar right
Identifying points:
1) TAS above boar
2) star below

CLASSIFICATION: Trinovantian O

NOTES: Many in museums.
Verulamium mint.

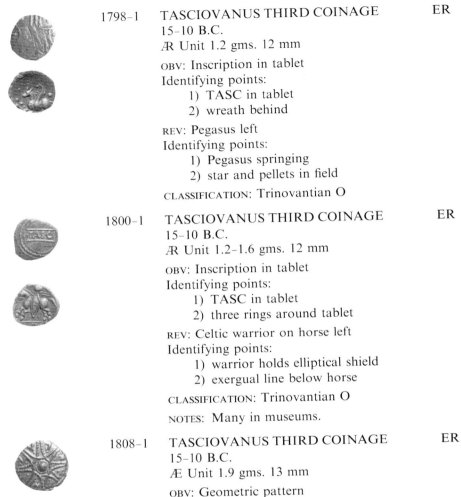

**1798-1    TASCIOVANUS THIRD COINAGE          ER**
15-10 B.C.
Æ Unit 1.2 gms. 12 mm

OBV: Inscription in tablet
Identifying points:
    1) TASC in tablet
    2) wreath behind

REV: Pegasus left
Identifying points:
    1) Pegasus springing
    2) star and pellets in field

CLASSIFICATION: Trinovantian O

**1800-1    TASCIOVANUS THIRD COINAGE          ER**
15-10 B.C.
Æ Unit 1.2-1.6 gms. 12 mm

OBV: Inscription in tablet
Identifying points:
    1) TASC in tablet
    2) three rings around tablet

REV: Celtic warrior on horse left
Identifying points:
    1) warrior holds elliptical shield
    2) exergual line below horse

CLASSIFICATION: Trinovantian O

NOTES: Many in museums.

**1808-1    TASCIOVANUS THIRD COINAGE          ER**
15-10 B.C.
Æ Unit 1.9 gms. 13 mm

OBV: Geometric pattern
Identifying points:
    1) large pellet in centre
    2) geometric pattern forms eight pointed star
    3) VERLAMIO in between points of star

REV: Bull left
Identifying points:
    1) branch below bull
    2) tail curves over bull's back

CLASSIFICATION: Trinovantian O

NOTES: Some in museums.
       Verulamium mint.

1810-1    TASCIOVANUS THIRD COINAGE          ER
15–10 B.C.
Æ Unit 2.1 gms. 13 mm

OBV: Geometric pattern
Identifying points:
    1) pellet-in-ring motif in centre
    2) geometric pattern forms eight-pointed star

REV: Bull right
Identifying points:
    1) bull's tail extends to right
    2) exergual line below bull

CLASSIFICATION: Trinovantian O

NOTES: Many in museums.

1812-1    TASCIOVANUS THIRD COINAGE          ER
15–10 B.C.
Æ Unit 1.9 gms. 15 mm

OBV: Geometric pattern
Identifying points:
    1) box with X in centre
    2) geometric pattern of loops and triangles
    3) pellet-in-ring motifs in field

REV: Celticized horse left
Identifying points:
    1) pellet-in-ring motif above horse
    2) TASCI below horse
    3) wind flower missing some petals above horse

CLASSIFICATION: Trinovantian O

1814-1    TASCIOVANUS THIRD COINAGE          ER
15–10 B.C.
Æ Unit 2.3 gms. 15 mm

OBV: Romanized head right
Identifying points:
    1) head completely Romanized
    2) TASCIO in front of face

REV: Lion right
Identifying points:
    1) TASCIO above lion
    2) exergual line below lion

CLASSIFICATION: Trinovantian O

NOTES: Head is that of Augustus, copied from a
    Roman denarius.
    Reverse possibly adapted from a gemstone,
    similar images appear on a fifth century
    B.C. Greek gem, a seal from Cyrene and a
    paste Roman Republican gem in Munich.

1816-1    TASCIOVANUS THIRD COINAGE    ER
    15-10 B.C.
    Æ Unit 1.8 gms. 15 mm

OBV: Romanized head right
Identifying points:
    1) head somewhat more Celticized than
    1814-1

REV: Seated figure left
Identifying points:
    1) VER below chair
    2) figure wears hat
    3) standard in front of and behind figure

CLASSIFICATION: Trinovantian O

NOTES: Some in museums.
    Head probably adapted from a Roman
    denarius of Augustus.
    Verulamium mint.

1818-1    TASCIOVANUS THIRD COINAGE    ER
    15-10 B.C.
    Æ Unit 4.5 gms. 17 mm

OBV: Romanized head right
Identifying points:
    1) TASCIAVA in front of face

REV: Pegasus left
Identifying points:
    1) Pegasus raises right foreleg
    2) TAS around pegasus

CLASSIFICATION: Trinovantian O

NOTES: Many in museums.
Obverse probably adapted from a Roman denarius of Augustus.
Reverse adapted from an Augustan denarius of P. Petronius Turpilianus.

1820-1    TASCIOVANUS THIRD COINAGE          ER
15-10 B.C.
Æ Unit 2.5 gms. 13 mm

OBV: Romanized head right
Identifying points:
    1) head more Celticized than 1816-1
    2) laurel wreath on head

REV: Celticized horse left
Identifying points:
    1) pellet-in-ring motif above horse
    2) VIR below horse

CLASSIFICATION: Trinovantian O

NOTES: Some in museums.
Verulamium mint.

1822-1    TASCIOVANUS THIRD COINAGE          ER
15-10 B.C.
Æ Unit 12 mm

OBV: Romanized head left
Identifying points:
    1) head has laurel wreath
    2) ring behind head

REV: Animal left
Identifying points:
    1) ring with pellets around it in front of animal
    2) curved tail

CLASSIFICATION: Trinovantian O

1824-1    TASCIOVANUS THIRD COINAGE          ER
15-10 B.C.
Æ Unit 12 mm

OBV: Animal right
Identifying points:
    1) head turned back to left
    2) pellet border

REV: Standing sphinx left
Identifying points:
    1) S-shaped tail
    2) pellet border

CLASSIFICATION: Trinovantian O

NOTES: Some in museums.
      Sphinx possibly a griffin as on 1895-1.
      Reverse also may be adapted from gems—
      an intaglio from Aquilia and a Chichester
      sard intaglio have similar devices.
      Animal on obverse possibly a lion, or may
      be adapted from panther gems—examples
      from Ham Hill and Aquilia have similar
      devices.

1826-1    TASCIOVANUS THIRD COINAGE      ER
              15-10 B.C.
              Æ Unit 1.2 gms. 12 mm

OBV: Romanized head right
Identifying points:
    1) band of pellets above face for hair

REV: Boar right
Identifying points:
    1) pellets and ring above boar

CLASSIFICATION: Trinovantian O

NOTES: Most in museums.
      Head possibly that of Mercury.
      Mack described the obverse as having three
      rings around the head, but these are not in
      evidence on the plate coin.

## THE INTERREGNUM

The Interregnum is a period of great confusion, and superficially the coins appear difficult to place into order. However, the task is not all that complicated for the major rulers. Apparently two issued coins, and there are two other coin types, either of local authorities or contestants for the leadership. The two rulers who issued complete coinages, Sego and Andoco, may be placed in reasonable order. The staters of Sego and Andoco are struck lighter than those of Tasciovanus—to the standard of the Interregnum. Thus, Sego and Andoco follow Tasciovanus.

    The relative chronology of Sego and Andoco is unfortunately problematical. Sego copies Tasciovanus' later issues trying to instill a sense of continuity; but

CLASSIFICATION: Trinovantian Q

NOTES: Some in museums.
Head on obverse is similar to that on Tasciovanus bronzes.
Pegasus adapted from a Roman denarius of Q. Titius.

1871-1    ANDOCO 10 B.C.–10 A.D.        ER
Æ Unit 1.4 gms. 15 mm

OBV: Romanized head right
Identifying points:
    1) ANDOCO to right of face

REV: Celticized horse right
Identifying points:
    1) ANDOCO around horse
    2) anemone above horse
    3) pellet-in-ring motif above horse

CLASSIFICATION: Trinovantian Q

NOTES: Some in museums.
End of the ANDOCO inscription may be rings and a crescent.

1873-1    ANDOCO 10 B.C.–10 A.D.        ER
Æ Unit 1.6 gms.

OBV: Celticized head right
Identifying points:
    1) TAS ANDO around head

REV: Celticized horse right
Identifying points:
    1) double pellet-ring border

CLASSIFICATION: Trinovantian Q

NOTES: Most in museums.
Mack listed this coin twice, once as 170a and again as 175a.

## COINS INSCRIBED *DIAS*

DIAS issued a small number of silver and bronze coins. He was probably a minor contestant for the Trinovantian/Catuvellaunian leadership, but this is not completely certain.

1877-1    DIAS 10 B.C.-10 A.D.                              ER
          Æ Unit 1.3 gms. 13 mm
          OBV: Inscription in tablet
          Identifying points:
             1) two interlaced squares
             2) tablet with DIAS in centre
             3) letter 'C' above tablet
             4) letter 'O' below tablet
          REV: Celticized horse left
          Identifying points:
             1) curve above horse
             2) VIR below horse
          CLASSIFICATION: Trinovantian R
          NOTES: Some in museums.
                 Verulamium mint.

1882-1    DIAS 10 B.C.-10 A.D.                              VR
          Æ Unit 1.3-1.6 gms. 13 mm
          OBV: Head of Hercules right
          Identifying points:
             1) beard and short hair
             2) TASC DIAS around head
          REV: Centaur right
          Identifying points:
             1) Centaur plays double pipes
             2) ring in front of Centaur
             3) curve above Centaur
             4) VER in field
          CLASSIFICATION: Trinovantian R
          NOTES: Some in museums.
                 Head of Hercules copied from Roman
                 denarius of Cn. Domitius M.f. M.n. Calvi-
                 nus, or is adapted from an intaglio such as
                 the Vetera I intaglio.
                 Verulamium mint.

1882-3    DIAS 10 B.C.-10 A.D.                              ER
          Æ Unit 1.6 gms.
          OBV: Head of Hercules right
          Identifying points:
             1) as 1882-1

REV: Horse
Identifying points:
    1) as 1882–1 but animal is a horse

CLASSIFICATION: Trinovantian R
NOTES: Not illustrated.

## COINS INSCRIBED *RUES*

RUES issued only bronze coins, and like DIAS may have been a minor contestant for the Trinovantian/Catuvellaunian leadership.

1890–1    RUES 10 B.C.–10 A.D.        ER
           Æ Unit 2.4 gms. 15 mm

OBV: Lion right
Identifying points:
    1) lion in bezel
    2) RVII above lion

REV: Eagle
Identifying points:
    1) eagle stands with spread wings

CLASSIFICATION: Trinovantian S

NOTES: Obverse adapted from a Roman denarius of
       Mark Anthony.
       Reverse adapted from a Roman denarius of
       Augustus.

1890–3    RUES 10 B.C.– 10 A.D.        ER
           Æ Unit

OBV: Lion right
Identifying points:
    1) as 1890–1

REV: Eagle
Identifying points:
    1) as 1890–1
    2) RVE in field

CLASSIFICATION: Trinovantian S

NOTES: Obverse adapted from a Roman denarius of
       Mark Anthony.
       Reverse adapted from a Roman denarius of
       Augustus.

1892–1     RUES 10 B.C.–10 A.D.                                    VR
Æ Unit 1.9 gms. 15 mm

OBV: Celticized head right
Identifying points:
    1) similiar to 1707–1
    2) RVIIS infront of face

REV: Celtic warrior on horse right
Identifying points:
    1) VIR to right
    2) warrior brandishes spear or carnyx

CLASSIFICATION: Trinovantian S

NOTES: Verulamium mint.

1895–1     RUES 10 B.C.–10 A.D.                                    ER
Æ Unit 1.9 gms. 14 mm

OBV: Inscription in tablet
Identifying points:
    1) RVIIS in tablet
    2) ring above and below
    3) bezel around edge

REV: Griffin left
Identifying points:
    1) exergue line below griffin
    2) three pellets below griffin

CLASSIFICATION: Trinovantian S

NOTES: Some in museums.
        Mack was uncertain what the animal was,
        better centred examples now show it to be
        a griffin.

1903–1     RUES 10 B.C.–10 A.D.                                    ER
Æ Fraction 0.6–0.9 gms. 12 mm

OBV: Geometric pattern
Identifying points:
    1) two curved-side squares, one inside the other
    2) ring in centre

REV: Eagle right
Identifying points:
    1) RVII to right of eagle
    2) eagle has wings partly folded

CLASSIFICATION: Trinovantian S

1925–2    CUNOBELINE LINEAR TYPE      ER
10–20 A.D.
Ν/Æ Plated Stater 4.8 gms. 19 mm

OBV: Corn ear
Identifying points:
     1) as 1925–1

REV: Celticized horse right
Identifying points:
     1) as 1925–1

CLASSIFICATION: Trinovantian U

NOTES: Many in museums.
          Ancient forgery from forger's dies.

1925–3    CUNOBELINE LINEAR TYPE      ER
10–20 B.C.
Ν Stater 5.6 gms. 20 mm

OBV: Corn ear
Identifying points:
     1) as 1925–1
     2) Letter 'X' above V in CAMV

REV: Celticized horse right
Identifying points:
     1) as 1925–1

CLASSIFICATION: Trinovantian U

NOTES: Letter 'X' is probably a moneyer's privy
          mark.
          Standard weight given

1925–5    CUNOBELINE LINEAR TYPE      ER
10–20 B.C.
Ν Stater 5.6 gms. 18 mm

OBV: Corn ear
Identifying points:
     1) as 1925–1
     2) small letter 'X' below A in CAMV

REV: Celticized horse right
Identifying points:
     1) as 1925–1

CLASSIFICATION: Trinovantian U

NOTES: Letter 'X' is probably a moneyer's privy
          mark.
          Standard weight given

1927-1    CUNOBELINE LINEAR TYPE                ER
10-20 A.D.
N Quarter Stater 1.35 gms. 11 mm

OBV: Corn ear
Identifying points:
    1) as 1925-1

REV: Celticized horse right
Identifying points:
    1) as 1925-1
    2) no pellets above and below wreath

CLASSIFICATION: Trinovantian U

NOTES: Some in museums.
        Standard weight given.

1927-3    CUNOBELINE LINEAR TYPE                ER
10-20 A.D.
N/Æ Plated Quarter Stater
1.0 gm. 13 mm

OBV: Corn ear
Identifying points:
    1) as 1927-1

REV: Celticized horse right
Identifying points:
    1) as 1927-1

CLASSIFICATION: Trinovantian U

NOTES: Ancient forgery, probably from forger's
        dies.

1931-1    CUNOBELINE WILD TYPE 10-20 A.D.      VR
N Stater 5.6 gms. 18 mm

OBV: Corn ear
Identifying points:
    1) CAMV about corn ear
    2) central stalk

REV: Celticized horse right
Identifying points:
    1) branch above horse
    2) CVNO below horse

CLASSIFICATION: Trinovantian V

NOTES: Standard weight given.
        Star is probably a privy mark.
        Some in museums.

1931–3   CUNOBELINE WILD TYPE 10–20 A.D.        ER
AV Stater 5.6 gms. 18 mm

OBV: Corn ear
Identifying points:
    1) as 1931–1
    2) no central stalk
    3) heart between front legs

REV: Celticized horse right
Identifying points:
    1) as 1931–1
    2) star above horse

CLASSIFICATION: Trinovantian V

NOTES: Standard weight given.
        Pellets are probably privy marks.

1931–5   CUNOBELINE WILD TYPE 10–20 A.D.        ER
AV Stater 5.6 gms. 20 mm

OBV: Corn ear
Identifying points:
    1) as 1931–1
    2) pellet below A in CAMV
    3) pellet above M in CAMV
    4) no central stalk

REV: Celticized horse right
Identifying points:
    1) as 1931–1
    2) no pellet-in-ring motif in front of horse

CLASSIFICATION: Trinovantian V

NOTES: Standard weight given.
        Pellets are probably privy marks.

1931–7   CUNOBELINE WILD TYPE 10–20 A.D.        ER
AV Stater 5.6 gms. 18 mm

OBV: Corn ear
Identifying points:
    1) as 1931–5

REV: Celticized horse right
Identifying points:
    1) as 1931–1
    2) pellet-in-ring motif in front of horse

CLASSIFICATION: Trinovantian V

NOTES: Standard weight given.

**1931-9**    CUNOBELINE WILD TYPE 10-20 A.D.    ER

Æ Stater 5.6 gms. 19 mm

OBV: Corn ear
Identifying points:
    1) as 1931-1
    2) pellet above A in CAMV
    3) three pellets above M in CAMV

REV: Celticized horse right
Identifying points:
    1) as 1931-1

CLASSIFICATION: Trinovantian V

NOTES: Standard weight given.

**1933-1**    CUNOBELINE WILD TYPE 10-20 A.D.    VR

Æ Stater 5.6 gms. 17 mm

OBV: Corn ear
Identifying points:
    1) as 1931-1
    2) no central stalk

REV: Celticized horse right
Identifying points:
    1) as 1931-1
    2) pellet-in-ring motif below horse
    3) large star above horse

CLASSIFICATION: Trinovantian V

NOTES: Some in museums.
       Standard weight given.

**1933-3**    CUNOBELINE WILD TYPE 10-20 A.D.    ER

Æ Stater 5.6 gms. 18 mm

OBV: Corn ear
Identifying points:
    1) as 1933-1
    2) no central stalk

REV: Celticized horse right
Identifying points:
    1) as 1933-1
    2) small star above horse

CLASSIFICATION: Trinovantian V

NOTES: Standard weight given.
       Star is probably a privy mark.

1935-1  CUNOBELINE WILD TYPE 10–20 A.D.  ER
Æ' Quarter Stater 1.35 gms. 12 mm

OBV: Corn ear
Identifying points:
    1) CAMV about corn ear
    2) corn ear has central stalk

REV: Celticized horse right
Identifying points:
    1) branch above horse
    2) CVN below horse

CLASSIFICATION: Trinovantian V

NOTES: Many in museums.
      Standard weight given.

## EARLY SILVER UNITS

1947-1  CUNOBELINE 10–20 A.D.  ER
Æ Unit 0.8 gms. 13 mm

OBV: Two serpents intertwined
Identifying points:
    1) serpents have heads of bulls
    2) border of intertwined line

REV: Celticized horse left
Identifying points:
    1) horse has necklace
    2) anemone above horse
    3) pellet-in-ring motif below horse
    4) exergual line with CVNO below horse

CLASSIFICATION: Trinovantian T

NOTES: Most in museums.

1948-1  CUNOBELINE 10–20 A.D.  ER
Æ Unit ca. 1.2 gms. 12 mm

OBV: Fantastic creature left
Identifying points:
    1) creature is part boar
    2) duck-bill on animal

3) pellet-in-ring below animal
4) corded exergual line

REV: Coiled serpent
Identifying points:
    1) tassled tail
    2) short zigzag line below

CLASSIFICATION: Trinovantian T

NOTES: Most in museums.

1949-1    CUNOBELINE 10-20 A.D.           ER
            Æ Unit 1.3 gms. 13 mm

OBV: Inscribed tablet
Identifying points:
    1) CVNO in tablet
    2) plain field

REV: Celticized horse left
Identifying points:
    1) daisy above horse
    2) possible inscription below horse—may be a
       CVN monogram

CLASSIFICATION: Trinovantian T

NOTES: Most in museums.

## MIDDLE SILVER UNITS

1951-1    CUNOBELINE 10-20 A.D.           ER
            Æ Unit 1.0 gm 14 mm

OBV: Inscribed tablet
Identifying points:
    1) CVNO BELI in tablet in two lines
    2) star above and below tablet

REV: Celtic warrior on horse right
Identifying points:
    1) CVN below horseman
    2) exergual line

CLASSIFICATION: Trinovantian U

NOTES: Most in museums.

1953–1     **CUNOBELINE** 10–20 A.D.        ER
Æ Unit 0.9 gms. 12 mm

OBV: Inscribed tablet
Identifying points:
    1) **CVNO BELI** retrograde in two lines in
       tablet
    2) star above and below tablet

REV: Celtic warrior on horse right
Identifying points:
    1) probably **CVN** retrograde below horseman

CLASSIFICATION: Trinovantian U

## EARLY BRONZE UNITS

1963–1     **CUNOBELINE** 10–20 A.D.        ER
Æ Unit 2.1 gms. 14 mm

OBV: Celticized head facing
Identifying points:
    1) beard and moustache

REV: boar left
Identifying points:
    1) branch above boar
    2) **CVN** below boar
    3) boar has curled tail, indicated by a pellet-
       in-ring motif

CLASSIFICATION: Trinovantian T

1965–1     **CUNOBELINE** 10–20 A.D.        ER
Æ Unit 1.9 gms. 16 mm

OBV: coiled animal
Identifying points:
    1) ram's head
    2) bezel border

REV: animal left
Identifying points:
    1) head turned back to right
    2) **CAM** monogram below animal

CLASSIFICATION: Trinovantian T

NOTES: Most in museums.

1967-1    CUNOBELINE 10-20 A.D.           ER
Æ Unit 0.9 gms. 13 mm

OBV: Animal left
Identifying points:
     1) animal looks back to right
     2) CAM below animal

REV: Celticized horse left
Identifying points:
     1) CVN below horse

CLASSIFICATION: Trinovantian T

## MIDDLE BRONZE UNITS

1969-1    CUNOBELINE 10-20 A.D.           ER
Æ Unit 1.2 gms. 13 mm

OBV: Celticized head left
Identifying points:
     1) CVNO in front of face
     2) head bare, beardless

REV: Boar left
Identifying points:
     1) pellet-in-ring motif below boar
     2) two stars below boar
     3) branch above boar

CLASSIFICATION: Trinovantian U

1971-1    CUNOBELINE 10-20 A.D.           S
Æ Unit 2.3 gms. 14 mm

OBV: Inscribed tablet
Identifying points:
     1) CVNOB ELINI in two line in tablet
     2) pellet-in-ring motif above and below tablet

REV: Seated victory left
Identifying points:
     1) hand extended and holding a wreath

CLASSIFICATION: Trinovantian U

NOTES: Some in museums.
     Reverse adapted from a Roman denarius of M. Porcius Cato or M. Porcius Cato Uticensis.
     Victory may commemorate Cunobeline's elevation, or a victory over Eppillus in Kent.

2020-1    CUNOBELINE PLASTIC TYPE    ER
20–43 A.D.
N Stater 5.40 gms. 19 mm

OBV: Corn ear
Identifying points:
    1) CA MV beside corn ear
    2) corn ear has no central stalk

REV: Celticized horse right
Identifying points:
    1) no branch above horse
    2) pellet above and in front of horse
    3) CVNO below horse

CLASSIFICATION: Trinovantian W

NOTES: Standard weight given.
    Some in museums.

2025-1    CUNOBELINE CLASSIC TYPE    ER
20–43 A.D.
N Stater 5.40 gms. 16 mm

OBV: Corn ear
Identifying points:
    1) CA MV beside corn ear
    2) no central stalk on corn ear

REV: Romanized horse right
Identifying points:
    1) branch above horse
    2) CVNO and exergual line below horse

CLASSIFICATION: Trinovantian X

NOTES: Standard weight given.
    Some in museums.

2025-3    CUNOBELINE CLASSIC TYPE    ER
20–43 A.D.
N/Æ Plated Stater 3.1–4.4 gms. 18 mm

OBV: Corn ear
Identifying points:
    1) as 2025–1

REV: Celticized horse right
Identifying points:
    1) as 2025–1

CLASSIFICATION: Trinovantian X

NOTES: Ancient forgery from forger's dies.

2027-1    CUNOBELINE CLASSIC TYPE                    ER
20-43 A.D.
Ṋ Stater 5.40 gms. 15 mm
OBV: Corn ear
Identifying points:
    1) CA MV beside corn ear
    2) corn ear has central stalk
REV: Romanized horse right
Identifying points:
    1) as 2025-1

CLASSIFICATION: Trinovantian X

NOTES: Standard weight given.
        Some in museums.

2029-1    CUNOBELINE CLASSIC TYPE                    ER
20-43 A.D.
Ṋ Stater 5.40 gms. 17 mm
OBV: Corn ear
Identifying points:
    .1) as 2027-1
REV: Romanized horse left
Identifying points:
    1) as 2027-1, but horse faces opposite direction

CLASSIFICATION: Trinovantian X

NOTES: Standard weight given.

2029-3    CUNOBELINE PLASTIC TYPE                    ER
20-43 A.D.
Ṋ/Æ Plated Stater 4.5-5.0 gms. 20 mm
OBV: Corn ear
Identifying points:
    1) as 2029-1
REV: Celticized horse left
Identifying points:
    1) as 2029-1

CLASSIFICATION: Trinovantian X

NOTES: Ancient forgery from forger's dies.

Allen listed it as a Linear Type, but the horse is reversed without the retrograde lettering of coins from blundered dies. Thus either there is a horse left Linear Type, for which no example exists today, or the coin is simply a poorly-engraved Classic Type.

2038-1    CUNOBELINE CLASSIC TYPE                ER
20-43 A.D.

A̸ Quarter Stater 1.30 gms. 12 mm

OBV: Corn ear
Identifying points:
 1) CA MV beside corn ear
 2) corn ear has no central stalk

REV: Romanized horse right
Identifying points:
 1) branch above horse
 2) CVNO below horse

CLASSIFICATION: Trinovantian X

NOTES: Standard weight given.
 Most in museums.
 Modern forgery exists—see 2038-1F.

2038-3    CUNOBELINE CLASSIC TYPE                ER
20-43 A.D.

A̸/Æ Plated Quarter Stater 0.9 gms. 11 mm

OBV: Corn ear
Identifying points:
 1) as 2038-1

REV: Celticized horse right
Identifying points:
 1) as 2038-1

CLASSIFICATION: Trinovantian X

NOTES: Ancient forgery from forger's dies.

# SILVER COINAGE OF THE EXPANSION PERIOD

2045-1     CUNOBELINE 20-43 A.D.                    ER
ÆR Unit 1.2 gms. 15 mm

OBV: Romanized head left
Identifying points:
    1) CAMVL in front of face
    2) pellet border

REV: Seated victory right
Identifying points:
    1) pellet-in-ring motif in front of victory
    2) CVNO below chair

CLASSIFICATION: Trinovantian W

NOTES: Some in museums.
    Reverse adapted from a Roman denarius of M. Porcius Cato or M. Porcius Cato Uticensis.

2047-1     CUNOBELINE 20-43 A.D.                    ER
ÆR Unit 1.1 gms. 12 mm

OBV: Floral pattern
Identifying points:
    1) CV NO beside pattern

REV: Celtic warrior on horse right
Identifying points:
    1) CAM and exergual line below rider
    2) warrior holds sword

CLASSIFICATION: Trinovantian W

NOTES: Some in museums.

2049-1     CUNOBELINE 20-43 A.D.                    ER
ÆR Unit 13 mm

OBV: Flower
Identifying points:
    1) CA MV beside flower

REV: Celtic warrior on horse right
Identifying points:
    1) similar to 2047-1, but the horse stands on the exergual line and CVNO is below the line

CLASSIFICATION: Trinovantian W

NOTES: Obverse adapted from a Roman denarius of Mark Anthony—caduceus on globe has been transformed into a flower.

2051-1    CUNOBELINE 20-43 A.D.                    ER
Æ Unit 1.1 gms. 13 mm

OBV: Inscribed tablet in wreath
Identifying points:
    1) CVNO in tablet
    2) pellet border

REV: Griffin right on inscribed tablet
Identifying points:
    1) CAMV in tablet

CLASSIFICATION: Trinovantian W

NOTES: Most in museums.
    Griffin copied from coin of Dubnovellaunus (Cantii), see number 165-1, however the ultimate source of the griffin may be an intaglio or seal—an intaglio from Rome and a seal from Cyrene have similar designs.

2053-1    CUNOBELINE 20-43 A.D.                    ER
Æ Unit 1.2 gms. 13 mm

OBV: Inscribed tablet in wreath
Identifying points:
    1) as 2051-1

REV: Pegasus right
Identifying points:
    1) Pegasus and TASC F on exergual line

CLASSIFICATION: Trinovantian W

NOTES: Many in museums.
    The reverse is adapted from a Roman denarius of Q. Titius.

2055-1    CUNOBELINE 20-43 A.D.                    ER
Æ Unit 12 mm

OBV: Romanized head right
Identifying points:
    1) CVNOBELINI around head

REV: Romanized horse right
Identifying points:
    1) TASCIO below horse
    2) horse stands on exergual line

CLASSIFICATION: Trinovantian W

NOTES: Many in museums.

2057-1    CUNOBELINE 20-43 A.D.    ER
    Æ Unit 1.2 gms. 13 mm

OBV: Winged bust right
Identifying points:
    1) CVNO in front of face

REV: Sphinx left
Identifying points:
    1) sphinx sits on exergual line
    2) TASCIO in front of sphinx

CLASSIFICATION: Trinovantian W

NOTES: Some in museums.
    Reverse adapted from a Roman denarius of
    T. Carisius, or less likely, one of Augustus.

2059-1    CUNOBELINE 20-43 A.D.    ER
    Æ Unit 1.3 gms. 13 mm

OBV: Romanized bust right
Identifying points:
    1) TASCIIOVAN around bust
    2) hair in bun at rear

REV: Seated figure right
Identifying points:
    1) female figure with hair in bun at back
    2) figure playing lyre
    3) tree behind figure
    4) exergual line

CLASSIFICATION: Trinovantian W

NOTES: Most in museums.
    Obverse is adapted from and unidentified
    Roman denarius.
    Reverse is adapted from a Roman denarius
    of Augustus.

2061–1 CUNOBELINE 20–43 A.D. ER
Æ Unit 1.2 gms. 13 mm

OBV: Hercules standing right
Identifying points:
1) Hercules holds club
2) Hercules hold uncertain object, probably lion skin
3) CV NO beside Hercules

REV: Celtic woman on horse right
Identifying points:
1) Woman rides side-saddle
2) TASCIOVA below horse

CLASSIFICATION: Trinovantian W

NOTES: Hercules adapted from a Roman denarius of C. Vibius Varus.

2063–1 CUNOBELINE 20–43 A.D. ER
Æ Unit 1.1 gms. 11 mm

OBV: Walking hunter right
Identifying points:
1) holds staff or sword and a dead animal
2) CVNOBELINVS around figure

REV: Standing hunter
Identifying points:
1) holds bow
2) animal at side, probably his hunting dog

CLASSIFICATION: Trinovantian W

NOTES: Most in museums.
Obverse posssibly adapted from an intaglio, a Vetera I fortress intaglio has a similar design.
Reverse adapted from a Roman denarius of Augustus.

2065–1 CUNOBELINE 20–43 A.D. ER
Æ Unit 1.1 gms. 13 mm

OBV: Inscribed tablet
Identifying points:
1) CVNO in tablet
2) horn above tablet
3) two birds below tablet

REV: Standing figure right
Identifying points:
1) altar behind figure
2) altar possibly in front of figure

CLASSIFICATION: Trinovantian W

NOTES: Many in museums.
Obverse possibly adapted from a gem, an engraved gem in Berlin has a similar design.

2067-1    CUNOBELINE 20-43 A.D.            ER
Æ Unit 1.0 gm 12 mm

OBV: Inscribed tablet
Identifying points:
1) CVN in tablet
2) pellet-in-ring motif above and below tablet

REV: Walking figure right
Identifying points:
1) figure carries staff or club
2) CV N beside (possibly CV NO)
3) pellet above CV

CLASSIFICATION: Trinovantian W

NOTES: Most in museums.
Figure possibly adapted from an intaglio, one from Verulamium has a similar design.

2069-1    CUNOBELINE 20-43 A.D.            ER
Æ Unit 1.2 gms. 14 mm

OBV: Inscription in wreath
Identifying points:
1) CVN in wreath

REV: Dog or she-wolf right
Identifying points:
1) animal tramples serpent
2) exergual line below
3) CAM below exergual line

CLASSIFICATION: Trinovantian W

NOTES: Reverse possibly adapted from a paste gem, one from Launceston, Cornwall has a similar design, but another coin may be an intermediate.

2071–1 CUNOBELINE 20–43 A.D. ER
Æ Unit 1.2 gms. 13 mm

OBV: Pegasus left
Identifying points:
    1) Pegasus stands on exergual line
    2) CVN in field

REV: Seated figure right
Identifying points:
    1) figure hold caduceus in right hand
    2) left hand on knee

CLASSIFICATION: Trinovantian W

NOTES: Obverse possibly adapted from an engraved
        gem, one from Aquilia has a similar design.

2073–1 CUNOBELINE 20–43 A.D. ER
Æ Unit 1.1 gms. 13 mm

OBV: Inscription in chain ring
Identifying points:
    1) SOLIDV in centre
    2) chain ring has pellet in each loop

REV: Standing figure
Identifying points:
    1) mantle over shoulder
    2) holding lance in left hand

CLASSIFICATION: Trinovantian W

NOTES: Reverse adapted from a Roman denarius of
        L. Papius, Caligula or Tiberius.
        The meaning of SOLIDV is still a mystery.

# BRONZE COINAGE OF THE EXPANSION PERIOD

2081–1 CUNOBELINE 20–43 A.D. R
Æ Unit 2.5 gms. 15 mm

OBV: Griffin right
Identifying points:
    1) griffin raises left front leg
    2) CAMV in front of griffin
    3) pellet border

REV: Celticized horse right
Identifying points:
1) horse rearing
2) CVN below horse

CLASSIFICATION: Trinovantian W

NOTES: Many in museums.
        Allen dated this one early, but the designs
        appear to be later.
        Obverse possibly adapted from a paste gem,
        one from Launceston, Cornwall is similar.

2083-1    CUNOBELINE 20-43 A.D.                    ER
          Æ Unit 2.2 gms. 15 mm

OBV: Head of Augustus right
Identifying points:
1) CVNO in front of face

REV: Bull butting left
Identifying points:
1) bull stands on exergual line
2) CVN below exergual line

CLASSIFICATION: Trinovantian W

NOTES: Most in museums.
        Obverse and reverse copied from a Roman
        denarius of Augustus.

2085-1    CUNOBELINE 20-43 A.D.                    ER
          Æ Unit 2.2 gms. 18 mm

OBV: Romanized head left
Identifying points:
1) head is bearded
2) CAMV in front of face

REV: Celticized horse left
Identifying points:
1) wavy line below horse
2) CVNO below horse

CLASSIFICATION: Trinovantian W

NOTES: Many in museums.
Reverse possibly adapted from a paste gem, one from Launceston, Cornwall is similar, with another coin possibly as an intermediate.
Dating uncertain, possibly an early type.

2087–1    CUNOBELINE 20–43 A.D.                        ER
Æ Unit 3.2 gms. 16 mm

OBV: Head left
Identifying points:
    1) CAM in front of face
    2) pellet border

REV: Eagle
Identifying points:
    1) eagle has spread wings
    2) head turned left
    3) CVNO and five-pointed star below

CLASSIFICATION: Trinovantian W

NOTES: Many in museums.
Dating uncertain, possibly an early type.
Mack described eagle as a 'Lugdunum' type of eagle.

2089–1    CUNOBELINE 20–43 A.D.                         S
Æ Unit 2.3 gms. 18 mm

OBV: Head of Tiberius left
Identifying points:
    1) CVNOBELINI around head
    2) pellet border

REV: Centaur right
Identifying points:
    1) centaur blows horn
    2) TASCIOVANI F around centaur
    3) pellet border

CLASSIFICATION: Trinovantian W

NOTES: Some in museums.
Obverse copied from a Roman denarius of Tiberius.
Centaur possibly adapted from an intaglio, one from Wall is similar.

2091-1    CUNOBELINE 20–43 A.D.                    S
Æ Unit 2.3 gms. 15 mm

OBV: Romanized head right
Identifying points:
1) head laureate and beardless
2) CVNOBELINUS around head

REV: Sow right
Identifying points:
1) sow stands on exergual line
2) TASCIOVANI F around boar, the F below the exergual line

CLASSIFICATION: Trinovantian W

2093-1    CUNOBELINE WARRIOR TYPE              S
20–43 A.D.
Æ Unit 2.5 gms. 16 mm

OBV: Celtic warrior on horse right
Identifying points:
1) CVNOB around scene
2) rider holds large shield in left hand and brandishes a spear in his right

REV: Standing warrior
Identifying points:
1) warrior wears helmet
2) warrior holds spear and shield
3) TASCIIOVANTIS around figure

CLASSIFICATION: Trinovantian W

2095-1    CUNOBELINE 20–43 A.D.                    S
Æ Unit 2.3 gms. 17 mm

OBV: Romanized bust right
Identifying points:
1) CVNOBELINUS REX around bust
2) pellet border

REV: Bull butting right
Identifying points:
1) bull stands on exergual line
2) TASC below exergual line

CLASSIFICATION: Trinovantian W

NOTES: Some in museums.
Obverse and reverse copied from a Roman denarius of Augustus.

2097-1    CUNOBELINE METAL-WORKER TYPE    C
20-43 A.D.
Æ Unit 1.9-2.6 gms. 16 mm

OBV: Romanized head left
Identifying points:
1) CVNOBELIN around head
2) pellet border

REV: Seated metal-worker right
Identifying points:
1) metal-worker hammers vase
2) hair in bun at back
3) hat with brim
4) pellet border

CLASSIFICATION: Trinovantian W

NOTES: Some in museums.
Reverse copies coin of Dubnovellaunus (Cantii), see number 178-1, ultimate source of image may be a gem–a late Roman one in the Ashmolean is similar.

2099-1    CUNOBELINE 20-43 A.D.    S
Æ Unit 2.2 gms. 14 mm

OBV: Pegasus right
Identifying points:

1) CVNO below Pegasus
2) pellet border

REV: Victory sacrificing a bull right
Identifying points:
1) victory holds knife about to kill bull
2) pellet border
3) TASCI below bull

CLASSIFICATION: Trinovantian W

NOTES: Reverse copied from a Roman denarius of Augustus.

2101-1    CUNOBELINE FACING HORSE TYPE    R
20-43 A.D.
Æ Unit 1.3 gms. 13 mm

OBV: Inscribed tablet in wreath
Identifying points:
1) CVNO in tablet

REV: Romanized horse right
Identifying points:
    1) horse faces viewer
    2) horse and CAMV on exergual line
    3) horse raises left front leg

CLASSIFICATION: Trinovantian W

NOTES: Many in museums.
        The horse was copied by the Icnei for their
        silver units of ECEN, see number 760-1.

2103-1    CUNOBELINE 20-43 A.D.                    R
          Æ Unit 2.3 gms. 14 mm

OBV: Romanized head of Jupiter Ammon right
Identifying points:
    1) CVNOBELIN around head

REV: Celtic warrior on horse right
Identifying points:
    1) pellet below horse
    2) horse and CAM on exergual line
    3) warrior hold sword in right hand and shield
       in left

CLASSIFICATION: Trinovantian W

NOTES: Many in museums.
        Obverse copied from a Roman denarius of
        Q. Cornuficius.
        Reverse copied from a Roman denarius of
        Augustus.

2105-1    CUNOBELINE 20-43 A.D.                    R
          Æ Unit 2.6 gms. 13 mm

OBV: Janus head
Identifying points:
    1) CVNO in tablet below head

REV: Sow right
Identifying points:
    1) CAMV in tablet below
    2) tree behind sow

CLASSIFICATION: Trinovantian W

| 80 | 75 | 70 | 65 | 60 | 55 | 50 | 45 | 40 | 35 |
|---|---|---|---|---|---|---|---|---|---|
| IAGE | | EARLY BRITISH COINAGES | | | | EARLIEST DYNASTIC COINAGES | | | |
| 6.65 | 6.45 | 6.35 | 6.20 | 6.00 | | 5.80 | | 5.60 | |

| 80 | 75 | 70 | 65 | 60 | 55 | 50 | 45 | 40 | 35 |
|---|---|---|---|---|---|---|---|---|---|
| GALLO-BELGIC C | G-B C TRIN B | G-B E TRIN C | G-B E | G-B E TRIN D | TRIN D | TR E F G H | TRIN I | TRIN J | TRIN K |
|  | TRIN B |  | GALLO-BELGIC D | G-B D TRIN D | TRIN D | TRIN E | TRIN I | TRIN J | TRIN K |
|  |  |  |  | TRIN D | TRIN D | TRIN F | TRIN I | TRIN J | TRIN K |
|  |  |  |  |  |  |  | TRIN I | TRIN J | TRIN K |
|  |  |  | ICENIAN A | | | ICENIAN B | TRIN I | TRIN J | TRIN K |
|  |  |  |  |  |  | ICENIAN B | TRIN I | TRIN J | TRIN K |
|  |  |  |  |  |  | TRIN F | TRIN I | TR.J | IC C |
|  |  |  |  |  |  |  |  |  | IC C |
|  |  |  |  |  |  |  | TRIN I |  |  |
| GALLO-BELGIC C | | | GALLO-BELGIC E | | | CANTIAN F | CANTIAN G | CANTIAN H | CANTIAN I |
|  |  |  | GALLO-BELGIC D | | | CANTIAN F | CANTIAN G | CANTIAN H | CANTIAN I |
|  |  | CANTIAN D | | | | CANTIAN E | | | |
| ALLO-BELGIC C | G-B C ATRE A | | G-B E ATRE A | G-B E&F | G-B E & F ATRE B | ATRE B | ATREBATIC C | | |
|  |  |  | GALLO-BELGIC D | | G-B D ATRE B | ATRE B | ATREBATIC C | | |
|  |  |  |  |  |  | ATRE B | ATREBATIC C | | |
|  |  |  |  |  |  | ATREBATIC B | | | DOBUN A |
|  |  |  |  |  |  | ATREBATIC B | | | DOBUN A |
|  |  |  |  |  |  |  |  |  | DOBUN A |
|  |  | CORIELTAUVIAN A | | | CORIELTAUVIAN B | | CORIELTAUVIAN C-D-E-F-G-H | | |
|  |  |  |  |  | CORIELTAUVIAN B | | CORIELTAUVIAN D | | |
|  |  |  |  |  | CORIELTAUVIAN B | | CORIELTAUVIAN D | | |
|  |  |  | DURO A & B | | DU C / DU D | | | | |
|  |  |  | DUROTRIG A | | | | | | |
|  |  |  |  | DUROTRIGAN E & F | | DURO G | DURO H | | |
|  |  |  |  | DUROTRIGAN E | | DURO G | DURO H | DURO I | |
|  |  |  |  |  |  |  |  | DURO I | |

| DATE BC | 30 | 25 | 20 | 15 | 10 | 5 | 1 | 5 (AD) |
|---|---|---|---|---|---|---|---|---|
| PERIOD | EARLY | DYNASTIC | COINAGES | | | THE | INTERREGNUM | |
| STD WT of a STATER (gms) | | | | | 5.40 | | | |

**No. of the THAMES**

**TRINOVANTES/CATUVELLAUNI**

| Denomination | 30 | 25 | 20 | 15 | 10 | 5 | 1 | 5 (AD) |
|---|---|---|---|---|---|---|---|---|
| AV Staters | TRINOV L | TRINOV M | TRINOV N | TRINOV O | TRINOV P | TRINOV Q | | |
| AV Fractions | TRINOV L | TRINOV M | TRINOV N | TRINOV O | TRINOV P | TRINOV Q | | |
| AR Units | | TRINOV M | TRINOV N | TRINOV O | TRINOV P | TRINOV Q | TRINOV R | |
| AE Units | TRINOV L | TRINOV M | TRINOV N | TRINOV O | TRINOV P | TRINOV Q | TRINOV R | TRIN |
| AE Cast Bronzes | | | | TRINOVANTIAN A | | | | |

**ICENI**

| Denomination | 30 | 25 | 20 | 15 | 10 | 5 | 1 | 5 (AD) |
|---|---|---|---|---|---|---|---|---|
| AV Staters | TRINOV L | TRINOV M | TRINOV N | TRINOV O | | | | ICENIAN G |
| AV Fractions | TRINOV L | TRINOV M | TRINOV N | TRINOV O | | | | |
| AR Units | ICENIAN C | ICENIAN D | ICENIAN E | | ICENIAN F | | ICENIAN G | |
| AR Fractions | ICENIAN C | | | | ICENIAN F | | ICENIAN G | |
| AE Units | | | | | | | | |

**So. of the THAMES**

**CANTII**

| Denomination | 30 | 25 | 20 | 15 | 10 | 5 | 1 | 5 (AD) |
|---|---|---|---|---|---|---|---|---|
| AV Staters | CANTIAN J | | CANTIAN K | CANTIAN L | CANTIAN M | ATREBATIC H | | |
| AV Fractions | CANTIAN J | | CANTIAN K | | CANTIAN M | ATREBATIC H | | |
| AR Units | CANTIAN J | | CANTIAN K | CANTIAN L | CANTIAN M | ATREBATIC H | | |
| AE Cast Bronzes | | | | | | | | |
| AE Struck Bronzes | CANTIAN J | | CANTIAN K | CANTIAN L | CANTIAN M | ATREBATIC H | | |

**ATREBATES/REGNI**

| Denomination | 30 | 25 | 20 | 15 | 10 | 5 | 1 | 5 (AD) |
|---|---|---|---|---|---|---|---|---|
| AV Staters | ATRE D | ATRE E | | ATREBATIC F | | ATREBATIC G | | |
| AV Fractions | ATRE D | ATRE E | | ATREBATIC F | | ATREBATIC G | | |
| AR Units | ATRE D | ATRE E | | ATREBATIC F | | ATREBATIC G | | |
| AR Fractions | | | | | | ATREBATIC G | | |

**PERIPHERAL TRIBES**

**DOBUNNI**

| Denomination | 30 | 25 | 20 | 15 | 10 | 5 | 1 | 5 (AD) |
|---|---|---|---|---|---|---|---|---|
| AV Staters | | | DOBUNNIC B | DOBUN C | | DOBUNNIC D | | |
| AV Fractions | | | DOBUNNIC B | | | | | |
| AR Units | | | DOBUNNIC B | DOBUN C | | DOBUNNIC D | | |

**CORIELTAUVI**

| Denomination | 30 | 25 | 20 | 15 | 10 | 5 | 1 | 5 (AD) |
|---|---|---|---|---|---|---|---|---|
| AV Staters | | CORIELTAUVIAN D-E-F-G-H | | | CORIEL I | CORIEL J | CORIEL K | CO L |
| AR Units | | CORIELTAUVIAN D-G | | | | CORIEL J | CORIEL K | CO L |
| AR Fractions | | CORIELTAUVIAN D | | | | CORIEL J | | CO L |

**DUROTRIGES**

| Denomination | 30 | 25 | 20 | 15 | 10 | 5 | 1 | 5 (AD) |
|---|---|---|---|---|---|---|---|---|
| AV Staters | | | | | | | | |
| AV Fractions | | | | | | | | |
| AR Staters | | | | | | | | |
| AR Units | | | | | | | | |
| AR Fractions | | | | | | | | |
| AR Struck Bronzes | | DUROTRIGAN J | | | | | | |
| AE Cast Bronzes | | | | | | | | |

| 15 | 20 | 25 | 30 | 35 | 40 | 45 | 50 | 55 | 60 |
|---|---|---|---|---|---|---|---|---|---|
| RESTORATION | | EXPANSION PERIOD | | | | LAST BRITISH COINAGES | | | |

| 15 | 20 | 25 | 30 | 35 | 40 | 45 | 50 | 55 | 60 |
|---|---|---|---|---|---|---|---|---|---|
| TRINOVANTIAN T-U-V | | TRINOVANTIAN W-X | | | | | | | |
| TRINOVANTIAN T-U-V | | TRINOVANTIAN W-X | | | | | | | |
| TRINOVANTIAN T-V | | | TRINOVANTIAN W | | | | | | |
| TRINOVANTIAN T-V | | | TRINOVANTIAN W | | | | | | |
| | ICENIAN G | | | | | | | | |
| | ICENIAN G | | ICENIAN H | | IC I | ICENIAN J | ICENIAN K | IC L-M · IC M-N · IC O | |
| | ICENIAN G | | ICENIAN H | | IC I | | | | |
| | | TRINOVANTIAN T-U-V-W-X | | | | | | | |
| | | TRINOVANTIAN T-U-V-W-X | | | | | | | |
| | | TRINOVANTIAN T-U-V-W-X | | | TR W CA N · TR W CA O · TR W | | | | |
| | | TRINOVANTIAN T-V-W | | | TR W CA N · TR W CA O · TR W | | | | |
| ATREBATIC I | ATRE J | | ATREBATIC K | | ATREBATIC L | | | | |
| ATREBATIC I | ATRE J | | ATREBATIC K | | | | | | |
| ATREBATIC I | ATRE J | | ATREBATIC K | | ATREBATIC L | ATREBATIC M | | | |
| ATREBATIC I | ATRE J | | ATREBATIC K | | ATREBATIC L | ATREBATIC M | | | |
| DOBUNNIC E | DOBUNNIC F | | | DOBUNNIC G | DO H | | | | |
| DOBUNNIC E | DOBUNNIC F | | | DOBUNNIC G | | | | | |
| CO N | CORIEL O | | CORIELTAUVIAN P | | CORIELTAUVIAN Q | | | | |
| CO N | CORIEL O | | CORIELTAUVIAN P | | CORIELTAUVIAN Q | | CORIELTAUVIAN R | | |
| CO N | | | CORIELTAUVIAN P | | | | | | |
| | | DUROTRIGAN K | | | | | | | |

| DATE BC | 125 | 120 | 115 | 110 | 105 | 100 | 95 | 90 |
|---|---|---|---|---|---|---|---|---|
| PERIOD | | IMPORTED COINAGE | | | | | EARLIEST BRIT | |
| STD WT of a STATER (gms) | 7.80 | | | | | 7.25 | | 7.00 |

| | TRINOVANTES/CATUVELLAUNI | | | | | | | | |
|---|---|---|---|---|---|---|---|---|---|
| No. | AV Staters | LARGE FLAN-DEFACED DIE | | | LARGE FLAN | | ABSTRACT TYPE | | |
| of | AV Fractions | LARGE FLAN-DEFACED DIE | | | LARGE FLAN | | | | |
| the | AR Units | | | | | | | | |
| T | AE Units | | | | | | | | |
| H | AE Cast Bronzes | | | | | | THURROCK TYPE | | |
| A | ICENI | | | | | | | | |
| M | AV Staters | | | | | | | | |
| E | AV Fractions | | | | | | | | |
| S | AR Units | | | | | | | | |
| | AR Fractions | | | | | | | | |
| | AE Units | | | | | | | | |
| So. | CANTII | | | | | | | | |
| So. | AV Staters | LARGE FLAN-DEFACED DIE | | | LARGE FLAN | | ABSTRACT TYPE | | |
| of | AV Fractions | LARGE FLAN-DEFACED DIE | | | LARGE FLAN | | | | |
| the | AR Units | | | | | | | | |
| T | AE Cast Bronzes | | | | | | PROTOTYPE, EXPERI-MENTAL, INNOVATIVE | OP | |
| H | AE Struck Bronzes | | | | | | | | |
| A | ATREBATES/REGNI | | | | | | | | |
| M | AV Staters | LARGE FLAN-DEFACED DIE | | | LARGE FLAN | | ABSTRACT TYPE | | |
| E | AV Fractions | LARGE FLAN-DEFACED DIE | | | LARGE FLAN | | | | |
| S | AR Units | | | | | | | | |
| | AR Fractions | | | | | | | | |
| P | DOBUNNI | | | | | | | | |
| E | AV Staters | | | | | | | | |
| R | AV Fractions | | | | | | | | |
| I | AR Units | | | | | | | | |
| P | CORIELTAUVI | | | | | | | | |
| H | AV Staters | | | | | | | | |
| E | AR Units | | | | | | | | |
| R | AR Fractions | | | | | | | | |
| A | DUROTRIGES | | | | | | | | |
| L | AV Staters | | | | | | | | |
| T | AV Fractions | | | | | | | | |
| R | AR Staters | | | | | | | | |
| I | AR Units | | | | | | | | |
| B | AR Fractions | | | | | | | | |
| E | AR Struck Bronzes | | | | | | | | |
| S | AE Cast Bronzes | | | | | | | | |

| 80 | 75 | 70 | 65 | 60 | 55 | 50 | 45 | 40 | 35 |
|---|---|---|---|---|---|---|---|---|---|
| INAGE | | | EARLY BRITISH COINAGES | | | | EARLIEST DYNASTIC COINAGES | | |
| 6.65 | 6.45 | 6.35 | 6.20 | 6.00 | | 5.80 | 5.60 | | |

| 80 | 75 | 70 | 65 | 60 | 55 | 50 | 45 | 40 | 35 |
|---|---|---|---|---|---|---|---|---|---|
| ABSTRACT TYPE | | ABSTRACT CLACTON | GALLIC WAR WALDINGFIELD | GALLIC WAR | GALLIC WAR WHADDON-CH. | WHADDON CHASE | M/L WHAD WON-SAV | ADD 1 | ADD 2 | ADD 3 |
| | | CLACTON | GEOMETRIC TYPE | | GEOMETRIC WHADDON CH. | WHADDON CH. | M WHADDON | ADD 1 | ADD 2 | ADD 3 |
| | | | | | WHADDON CHASE | WHADDON CHASE | LATE WHADDON | ADD 1 | ADD 2 | ADD 3 |
| | | | | | | | | ADD 1 | ADD 2 | ADD 3 |
| | | | NORFOLK WOLF TYPE | | | | FRECKENHAM | ADD 1 | ADD 2 | ADD 3 |
| | | | | | | | FRECKENHAM | ADD 1 | ADD 2 | ADD 3 |
| | | | | | | | LATE WHADDON CH. | ADD 1 | A 2 | BOAR TYPE |
| | | | | | | | | | | BOAR TYPE |
| | | | | | | | | ADD 1 | | |
| ABSTRACT TYPE | | | GALLIC WAR TYPE | | | ORNAMENTED | EARLY WEALD | LATE WEALD | "IVII" |
| | | | GEOMETRIC TYPE | | | KENTISH GEOMETRIC | TROPHY | LATE WEALD | S. THAMES BANDED |
| OPTIMIZATION PERIOD | | | | | | ADJUSTMENT PERIOD | | | |
| STRACT TYPE | | ABSTRACT WESTERHAM | GALLIC WAR WESTERHAM | GALLIC WAR TT HORSE | G-W TTH ATRE ABST | ATREBATIC ABSTRACT | COMMIUS | | |
| | | | GEOMETRIC TYPE | | GEOMETRIC ATRE ABST | ATREBATIC ABSTRACT | COMMIUS | | |
| | | | | | | EARLY ATREBATIC | COMMIUS | | |
| | | | | | | ATREBATIC ABSTRACT TYPE | | | EMBLEM |
| | | | | | | ATREBATIC ABSTRACT TYPE | | | ABSTRACT |
| | | | | | | | | | HEAD CLASS A |
| | | NORTH EAST COAST TYPE | | | REDUCED WEIGHT TYPE | | SUNFLOWER SO. FERRIBY-WHEEL-TREFOIL-KITE-DOMINO | | |
| | | | | | HOSTIDIUS TYPE | | SOUTH FERRIBY TYPE | | |
| | | | | | HOSTIDIUS TYPE | | SOUTH FERRIBY TYPE | | |
| | | | CHUTE-YARMOUTH | CCT | CHER | | | | |
| | | | EARLY GEOMETRIC | | | | | | |
| | | | | | ABSTRACT TYPE-SPREAD TAIL TYPE | | PELLET AND RING | 1-2-3-4 BRANCH | |
| | | | | | LATER GEOMETRIC TYPE | | SECOND GEOMETRIC | THIRD GEOMETRIC | STARFISH |
| | | | | | | | | | STARFISH |

| DATE BC | 30 | 25 | 20 | 15 | 10 | 5 | 1 | 5 |
|---|---|---|---|---|---|---|---|---|
| PERIOD | | EARLY DYNASTIC COINAGES | | | | THE INTERREGNUM | | |
| STD WT of a STATER (gms) | | | | | 5.40 | | | |

**No. of the THAMES**

### TRINOVANTES/CATUVELLAUNI

| | 30 | 25 | 20 | 15 | 10 | 5 | 1 | 5 |
|---|---|---|---|---|---|---|---|---|
| AV Staters | DUBNO ESSEX | TASCIO 1 | TASCIO 2 | TASCIO 3 | SEGO | ANDOCO | | |
| AV Fractions | DUBNO ESSEX | TASCIO 1 | TASCIO 2 | TASCIO 3 | SEGO | ANDOCO | | |
| AR Units | | TASCIO 1 | TASCIO 2 | TASCIO 3 | SEGO | ANDOCO | DIAS | |
| AE Units | DUBNO ESSEX | TASCIO 1 | TASCIO 2 | TASCIO 3 | SEGO | ANDOCO | DIAS | RU |
| AE Cast Bronzes | | | | | | | | |

### ICENI

| | 30 | 25 | 20 | 15 | 10 | 5 | 1 | 5 |
|---|---|---|---|---|---|---|---|---|
| AV Staters | DUBNO ESSEX | TASCIO 1 | TASCIO 2 | TASCIO 3 | | | ANTED | |
| AV Fractions | DUBNO ESSEX | TASCIO 1 | TASCIO 2 | TASCIO 3 | | | | |
| AR Units | BOAR TYPE | CAN DURO | CELTIC HEAD | CRESCENT TYPE | | | ANTED | |
| AR Fractions | BOAR TYPE | | | CRESCENT TYPE | | | ANTED | |
| AE Units | | | | | | | | |

**So. of the THAMES**

### CANTII

| | 30 | 25 | 20 | 15 | 10 | 5 | 1 | 5 |
|---|---|---|---|---|---|---|---|---|
| AV Staters | DUBNO K 1 | | DUBNO K 2 | DUBNO K 3 | VOSENOS | EPPILLUS KENTISH TYPE | | |
| AV Fractions | DUBNO K 1 | | DUBNO K 2 | | VOSENOS | EPPILLUS KENTISH TYPE | | |
| AR Units | DUBNO K 1 | | DUBNO K 2 | DUBNO K 3 | VOSENOS | EPPILLUS KENTISH TYPE | | |
| AE Cast Bronzes | | | | | | | | |
| AE Struck Bronzes | DUBNO K 1 | | DUBNO K 2 | DUBNO K 3 | VOSENOS | EPPILLUS KENTISH TYPE | | |

### ATREBATES/REGNI

| | 30 | 25 | 20 | 15 | 10 | 5 | 1 | 5 |
|---|---|---|---|---|---|---|---|---|
| AV Staters | TINCOM 1 | TINCOM 2 | TINCOMMIUS 3 | | EPPILLUS CALLEVA TYPES | | | |
| AV Fractions | TINCOM 1 | TINCOM 2 | TINCOMMIUS 3 | | EPPILLUS CALLEVA TYPES | | | |
| AR Units | TINCOM 1 | TINCOM 2 | TINCOMMIUS 3 | | EPPILLUS CALLEVA TYPES | | | |
| AR Fractions | | | | | EPPILLUS CALLEVA TYPES | | | |

**PERIPHERAL TRIBES**

### DOBUNNI

| | 30 | 25 | 20 | 15 | 10 | 5 | 1 | 5 |
|---|---|---|---|---|---|---|---|---|
| AV Staters | | CORIO | | | BODVOC | ANTED MONOGRAM-ANTEDRIG | | |
| AV Fractions | | CORIO | | | | | | |
| AR Units | | HEAD CLASS B-C-D | | | BODVOC-HD CLASS LMNO | HEAD CLASS EF-ANTED-HEAD CLASS LM | | |

### CORIELTAUVI

| | 30 | 25 | 20 | 15 | 10 | 5 | 1 | 5 |
|---|---|---|---|---|---|---|---|---|
| AV Staters | SUNFLOWER SO. FERRIBY-WHEEL-TREFOIL-KITE-DOMINO | | | | VEP | AVN AST | ESVP ASV | VC 1 |
| AR Units | SO. FERRIBY TYPE-KITE | | | | | AVN AST | ESVP ASV | VC 1 |
| AR Fractions | SO. FERRIBY TYPE | | | | | AVN AST | | VC 1 |

### DUROTRIGES

| | 30 | 25 | 20 | 15 | 10 | 5 | 1 | 5 |
|---|---|---|---|---|---|---|---|---|
| AV Staters | | | | | | | | |
| AV Fractions | | | | | | | | |
| AR Staters | | | | | | | | |
| AR Units | | | | | | | | |
| AR Fractions | | | | | | | | |
| AR Struck Bronzes | STRUCK BRONZE COINAGE | | | | | | | |
| AE Cast Bronzes | | | | | | | | |

| 15 | 20 | 25 | 30 | 35 | 40 | 45 | 50 | 55 | 60 |
|---|---|---|---|---|---|---|---|---|---|
| RESTORATION | | | EXPANSION PERIOD | | | LAST | BRITISH | COINAGES | |

| | | | | | | | | | | |
|---|---|---|---|---|---|---|---|---|---|---|
| NO-BIGA-LINEAR-WILD | CUNOBELINE-PLASTIC-CLASSICAL TYPES | | | | | | | | | |
| CUNO-BIGA-ENTAUR-LIN-WILD | CUNOBELINE-PLASTIC-CLASSICAL TYPES | | | | | | | | | |
| -EARLY-MIDDLE-SILVER | CUNOBELINE LATE SILVER COINAGE | | | | | | | | | |
| CUNO EARLY MIDDLE BRONZE | CUNOBELINE LATE BRONZE COINAGE | | | | | | | | | |
| | | | | | | | | | | |
| ANTED | | | | | | | | | | |
| | | | | | | | | | | |
| ANTED | ECEN (ECEN-E-EDN) | | | ECEN (ED) | ECEN (SYMBOL) | ECEN (ECE) | SUB EISICO SAENV | SUB EISICO AESV | BOU | |
| ANTED | ECEN (ECE-ECN) | | | ECEN (ED) | | | | | | |
| | | | | | | | | | | |
| | CUNOBELINE TYPES | | | | | | | | | |
| | CUNOBELINE TYPES | | | | | | | | | |
| | CUNOBELINE TYPES | | | CUNO AM 1 | CUNO AM 2 | CUNO | | | | |
| | CUNOBELINE TYPES | | | CUNO AMI 1 | CUNO AM 2 | CUNO | | | | |
| RICA 1st COINAGE | VER 2nd COINAGE | VERICA 3rd COINAGE | | EPATICCUS | | | | | | |
| RICA 1st COINAGE | VER 2nd COINAGE | VERICA 3rd COINAGE | | | | | | | | |
| RICA 1st COINAGE | VER 2nd COINAGE | VERICA 3rd COINAGE | | EPATICCUS | | CARATACUS | | | | |
| RICA 1st COINAGE | VER 2nd COINAGE | VERICA 3rd COINAGE | | EPATICCUS | | CARATACUS | | | | |
| MUX | EISV | | | CATTI | | INAM | | | | |
| CL MX-LMNO | EISV-HEAD CLASS LMNO | | | HEAD CLASS I-J | | | | | | |
| VC 3 | DUMNO TIGIR SENO | VOLISIOS DUMNOCOVEROS | | V DUMNOVELLAUNUS | | | | | | |
| VC 3 | DUMNO TIGIR SENO | VOLISIOS DUMNOCOVEROS | | V DUMNOVELLAUNUS | | VOLISIOS CARTIVEL | | | | |
| VC 3 | | VOLISIOS DUMNOCOVEROS | | | | | | | | |
| | | CAST BRONZE COINAGE | | | | | | | | |

# GLOSSARY

Anemone

Bezel Border

Box

Box with Cross-Hatching

Coffee Bean

Cog Wheel

Curve

Dahlia

Daisy

Five-Spoked Wheel

Five-Spoked Wheel with Axle

In Double Box

Large Pellet-In-Ring

Meandering Wreath

Opposed Crescents

Outline Crescent

Pellet

Pellet-In-Ring

Pointed Star

Ring

Single Strand Tail

Six-Armed Spiral

Solid Crescent

Spike-With-Crescent

Spike-With-Curve

Sunburst

Sunflower

Tablet

Triple-Tail with Pellet Terminal

Wavy-Armed Star

Wind Flower

Wreath: Leaves Downwards

Wreath: Leaves Inwards

Wreath: Leaves Outwards

Wreath: Leaves Upwards

| MACK'75 NUMBER | ALLEN CLASS | CATALOGUE NUMBER | CATALOGUE CLASSIFICATION |
|---|---|---|---|
| 120a (120c) | — | 484-1 | Atrebatic I |
| 120b | — | 510-1 | Atrebatic J |
| 120c (120a) | — | 484-1 | Atrebatic I |
| 120d | — | 511-1 | Atrebatic J |
| 120e | — | 552-1 | Atrebatic K |
| 121 | — | 500-1 | Atrebatic J |
| 122 | — | 501-1 | Atrebatic J |
| 123 | — | 505-1 | Atrebatic J |
| 124 | — | 525-1 | Atrebatic K |
| 125 | — | 520-1 | Atrebatic K |
| 126 | — | 526-1 | Atrebatic K |
| 127 | — | 527-1 | Atrebatic K |
| 128 | — | 530-1 | Atrebatic K |
| 129 | — | 531-1 | Atrebatic K |
| 130 | — | 532-1 | Atrebatic K |
| 131 | — | 533-1 | Atrebatic K |
| 131a | — | 534-1 | Atrebatic K |
| 131b | — | 473-1 | Atrebatic I |
| 132 | — | 551-1 | Atrebatic K |
| 133 | Brit LA | 1470-1 | Trinovantian D |
| 134 | Brit LA | 1472-1 | Trinovantian D |
| 134a | Brit LA | 1474-1 | Trinovantian D |
| 135 | Brit LA | 1476-3 | Trinovantian D |
| 135a | Brit LA | —(deleted) | —(deleted) |
| 136 | Brit LB | 1485-1 | Trinovantian E |
| 137 | Brit LB | 1487-1 | Trinovantian E |
| 138 | Brit LB | 1493-1 | Trinovantian E |
| 138a | Brit LB | —(deleted) | —(deleted) |
| 138b | Brit LB | —(deleted) | —(deleted) |
| 139 (now 62) | Brit MB | 1526-1 | Trinovantian H |
| 139a | Brit LC | 1491-1 | Trinovantian E |
| 140 | Brit LB | 1498-1 | Trinovantian F |
| 141 | Brit LB | 1500-1 | Trinovantian F |
| 142 | Brit LB | 1502-1 | Trinovantian F |
| 143 | Brit LB | 1505-1 | Trinovantian F |
| 144 (145) | LZ3 | 1507-1 | Trinovantian F |
| 145 (144) | LZ3 | 1507-1 | Trinovantian F |
| 146 | LX5 | 1509-1 | Trinovantian F |
| 147 | Brit MA | 1522-1 | Trinovantian G |
| 148 | Brit MA | 1520-1 | Trinovantian G |
| 149 | — | 1680-1 | Trinovantian M |
| 150 | — | 1682-1 | Trinovantian M |

| MACK'75 NUMBER | ALLEN CLASS | CATALOGUE NUMBER | CATALOGUE CLASSIFICATION |
|---|---|---|---|
| 151 | — | 1688-1 | Trinovantian M |
| 152 | — | 1690-1 | Trinovantian M |
| 153 | — | 1692-1 | Trinovantian M |
| 154 | — | 1730-1 | Trinovantian N |
| 155 | — | 1732-1 | Trinovantian N |
| 156 | — | 1734-1 | Trinovantian N |
| 157 | — | 1736-1 | Trinovantian N |
| 158 | — | 1745-1 | Trinovantian N |
| 159 | — | 1790-1 | Trinovantian O |
| 160 | — | 1792-1 | Trinovantian O |
| 161 | — | 1699-1 | Trinovantian M |
| 162 | — | 1747-1 | Trinovantian N |
| 163 | — | 1794-1 | Trinovantian O |
| 164 | — | 1796-1 | Trinovantian O |
| 165 | — | 1798-1 | Trinovantian O |
| 166 | — | 1800-1 | Trinovantian O |
| 167 | — | 1705-1 | Trinovantian M |
| 168 | — | 1707-1 | Trinovantian M |
| 169 | — | 1709-1 | Trinovantian M |
| 170 | — | 1711-1 | Trinovantian M |
| 170a (175a) | — | 1873-1 | Trinovantian Q |
| 171 | — | 1750-1 | Trinovantian N |
| 172 | — | 1808-1 | Trinovantian O |
| 173 | — | 1855-1 | Trinovantian P |
| 174 | — | 1810-1 | Trinovantian O |
| 175 | — | 1812-1 | Trinovantian O |
| 175a (170a) | — | 1873-1 | Trinovantian Q |
| 176 | — | 1814-1 | Trinovantian O |
| 177 | — | 1816-1 | Trinovantian O |
| 178 | — | 1818-1 | Trinovantian O |
| 179 | — | 1713-1 | Trinovantian M |
| 180 | — | 1820-1 | Trinovantian O |
| 181 | — | 1824-1 | Trinovantian O |
| 182 | — | 1715-1 | Trinovantian M |
| 183 | — | 1826-1 | Trinovantian O |
| 183a | — | 1717-1 | Trinovantian M |
| 183b (183c) | — | 1822-1 | Trinovantian O |
| 183c (183b) | — | 1822-1 | Trinovantian O |
| 184 | — | 1780-1 | Trinovantian O |
| 185 | — | 1786-1 | Trinovantian O |
| 186 (186a) | — | 1684-1 | Trinovantian M |
| 186a (186) | — | 1684-1 | Trinovantian M |

| MACK'75 NUMBER | ALLEN CLASS | CATALOGUE NUMBER | CATALOGUE CLASSIFICATION |
|---|---|---|---|
| 187 | — | 1694-1 | Trinovantian M |
| 188 | — | 1877-1 | Trinovantian R |
| 189 | — | 1890-1 | Trinovantian S |
| 190 | — | 1892-1 | Trinovantian S |
| 191 | — | 1895-1 | Trinovantian S |
| 192 | — | 1882-1 | Trinovantian R |
| 193 | — | 1903-1 | Trinovantian S |
| 194 | — | 1845-1 | Trinovantian P |
| 195 | — | 1848-1 | Trinovantian P |
| 196 | — | 1851-1 | Trinovantian P |
| 197 | — | 1860-1 | Trinovantian Q |
| 198 | — | 1863-1 | Trinovantian Q |
| 199 | — | 1868-1 | Trinovantian Q |
| 200 | — | 1871-1 | Trinovantian Q |
| 201 | — | 1910-1 | Trinovantian T |
| 202 | — | 1913-1 | Trinovantian T |
| 203 | — | 2010-1 | Trinovantian W |
| 204 | — | 2015-1 | Trinovantian W |
| 205 | — | 2017-1 | Trinovantian W |
| 206 | — | 2025-1 | Trinovantian X |
| 207 | — | 2027-1 | Trinovantian X |
| 208 | — | 2029-1 | Trinovantian X |
| 209 | — | 1927-1 | Trinovantian U |
| 210 | — | 1925-1 | Trinovantian U |
| 210a | — | 1925-3 | Trinovantian U |
| 211 | — | 1931-1 | Trinovantian V |
| 212 | — | 1933-1 | Trinovantian V |
| 213 | — | 2020-1 | Trinovantian W |
| 214 | — | 1947-1 | Trinovantian T |
| 215 | — | 2045-1 | Trinovantian W |
| 216 | — | 1951-1 | Trinovantian U |
| 217 | — | 1953-1 | Trinovantian U |
| 218 | — | 2047-1 | Trinovantian W |
| 219 | — | 2049-1 | Trinovantian W |
| 220 | — | 1969-1 | Trinovantian U |
| 221 | — | 1971-1 | Trinovantian U |
| 222 | — | 1973-1 | Trinovantian U |
| 222a | — | 1973-3 | Trinovantian U |
| 223 | — | 1963-1 | Trinovantian T |
| 224 | — | 1965-1 | Trinovantian T |
| 225 | — | 2081-1 | Trinovantian W |
| 226 | — | 2131-1 | Trinovantian - |

| MACK'75 NUMBER | ALLEN CLASS | CATALOGUE NUMBER | CATALOGUE CLASSIFICATION |
|---|---|---|---|
| 227 | — | 2083-1 | Trinovantian W |
| 228 | — | 2135-1 | Trinovantian - |
| 229 | — | 2085-1 | Trinovantian W |
| 230 | — | 1977-1 | Trinovantian U |
| 231 | — | 1979-1 | Trinovantian U |
| 232 | — | 1981-1 | Trinovantian U |
| 233 | — | 2087-1 | Trinovantian W |
| 233a | — | 1967-1 | Trinovantian T |
| 234 | — | 2051-1 | Trinovantian W |
| 234a | — | 1918-1 | Trinovantian T |
| 235 | — | 2053-1 | Trinovantian W |
| 236 | — | 2055-1 | Trinovantian W |
| 237 | — | 2057-1 | Trinovantian W |
| 238 | — | 2059-1 | Trinovantian W |
| 239 | — | 2061-1 | Trinovantian W |
| 240 | — | 2063-1 | Trinovantian W |
| 241 | — | 2065-1 | Trinovantian W |
| 241a (was 257) | — | 2065-1 | Trinovantian W |
| 242 | — | 2089-1 | Trinovantian W |
| 243 | — | 2091-1 | Trinovantian W |
| 244 | — | 2093-1 | Trinovantian W |
| 245 | — | 1983-1 | Trinovantian U |
| 246 | — | 2095-1 | Trinovantian W |
| 247 | — | 1985-1 | Trinovantian U |
| 248 | — | 2097-1 | Trinovantian W |
| 249 | — | 2099-1 | Trinovantian W |
| 250 | — | 2101-1 | Trinovantian W |
| 251 | — | 2103-1 | Trinovantian W |
| 252 | — | 2105-1 | Trinovantian W |
| 253 | — | 2107-1 | Trinovantian W |
| 254 | — | 2067-1 | Trinovantian W |
| 255 | — | 1949-1 | Trinovantian T |
| 256 | — | 2069-1 | Trinovantian W |
| 257 (now 241a) | — | 2065-1 | Trinovantian W |
| 257a | — | 2137-1 | Trinovantian - |
| 258 | — | 2071-1 | Trinovantian W |
| 259 | — | 2073-1 | Trinovantian W |
| 260 | — | 2109-1 | Trinovantian W |
| 260a | — | 2109-1 | Trinovantian W |
| 261 | — | 1987-1 | Trinovantian U |
| 262 | — | 575-1 | Atrebatic L |
| 263 | — | 580-1 | Atrebatic L |

| MACK'75 NUMBER | ALLEN CLASS | CATALOGUE NUMBER | CATALOGUE CLASSIFICATION |
|---|---|---|---|
| 263a | — | 581-1 | Atrebatic L |
| 264 | — | 585-1 | Atrebatic L |
| 265 | — | 593-1 | Atrebatic M |
| 266 | — | 1605-1 | Trinovantian I |
| 267 | — | 1620-1 | Trinovantian J |
| 268 | — | 1635-1 | Trinovantian K |
| 269 | — | 1638-1 | Trinovantian K |
| 270 | LX2 | 1623-1 | Trinovantian J |
| 271 | LX3 | 1608-1 | Trinovantian I |
| 272 (was 444) | LX15 | 1643-1 | Trinovantian K |
| 272a | LX17 | 164-1 | Cantian J |
| 273 | LX21 | 1646-1 | Trinovantian K |
| 274 | LX22 | 1615-1 | Trinovantian I |
| 274a | — | 1613-1 | Trinovantian I |
| 275 | — | 1650-1 | Trinovantian L |
| 275a | — | 1655-1 | Trinovantian L |
| 276 | — | 1660-1 | Trinovantian L |
| 277 | LX24 | 1665-1 | Trinovantian L |
| 278 | — | 1667-1 | Trinovantian L |
| 279 | — | 162-1 | Cantian J |
| 280 | LX9 | —(deleted) | —(deleted) |
| 280a | LX27 | —(deleted) | —(deleted) |
| 280b | LX25 | —(deleted) | —(deleted) |
| 280c | — | —(deleted) | —(deleted) |
| 280d | — | —(deleted) | —(deleted) |
| 281 | LX23 | 1669-1 | Trinovantian L |
| 282 | — | 169-1 | Cantian K |
| 283 | — | 176-1 | Cantian L |
| 284 | LY4 | 170-1 | Cantian K |
| 285 | LY5 | 163-1 | Cantian J |
| 286 | — | 171-1 | Cantian K |
| 287 | — | 178-1 | Cantian L |
| 288 | — | 165-1 | Cantian J |
| 289 | — | 180-1 | Cantian L |
| 290 | — | 166-1 | Cantian J |
| 291 | — | 181-1 | Cantian L |
| 291a | — | 173-1 | Cantian K |
| 292 | LZ1 | 144-1 | Cantian G |
| 293 | LY1 | 142-1 | Cantian F |
| 294 | LY2 | 157-1 | Cantian I |
| 295 | LY6 | 154-1 | Cantian - |
| 296 | LY7 | 154-3 | Cantian - |

| MACK'75 NUMBER | ALLEN CLASS | CATALOGUE NUMBER | CATALOGUE CLASSIFICATION |
|---|---|---|---|
| 297 | — | 184-1 | Cantian M |
| 298 | — | 185-1 | Cantian M |
| 299 | — | 187-1 | Cantian M |
| 299a | — | 186-1 | Cantian M |
| 300 | — | 430-1 | Atrebatic H |
| 301 | — | 431-1 | Atrebatic H |
| 302 | — | 435-1 | Atrebatic H |
| 303 | — | 436-1 | Atrebatic H |
| 304 | — | 437-1 | Atrebatic H |
| 305 | — | 417-1 | Atrebatic G |
| 306 | — | 441-1 | Atrebatic H |
| 307 | — | 442-1 | Atrebatic H |
| 308 | — | 443-1 | Atrebatic H |
| 308a | — | 443-1 | Atrebatic H |
| 309 | — | 450-1 | Atrebatic H |
| 310 | — | 451-1 | Atrebatic H |
| 311 | — | 452-1 | Atrebatic H |
| 312 | — | 453-1 | Atrebatic H |
| 313 | — | 192-1 | Cantian N |
| 314 | — | 194-1 | Cantian O |
| 315 | — | 195-1 | Cantian O |
| 316 | — | 561-1 | Atrebatic K |
| 316a | LY8 | 154-5 | Cantian - |
| 316b | — | —(deleted) | —(deleted) |
| 316c | LY10 | 154-9 | Cantian - |
| 316d | — | 154-11 | Cantian - |
| 316e | — | 153-1 | Cantian - |
| 316f | — | 154-13 | Cantian - |
| 317 | A | 1235-1 | Durotrigan E |
| 318 | C | 1290-1 | Durotrigan J |
| 319 (pl 20) | B | 1249-1 | Durotrigan G |
| 319 (pl.30) | — | 1242-1 | Durotrigan E |
| 320 | — | 1270-1 | Durotrigan I |
| 321 | — | 1280-1 | Durotrigan - |
| 321a | — | —(deleted) | —(deleted) |
| 322 | D | 1322-1 | Durotrigan K |
| 323 | D | 1323-1 | Durotrigan K |
| 324 | D | 1324-1 | Durotrigan K |
| 325 | D | 1325-1 | Durotrigan K |
| 326 | D | 1326-1 | Durotrigan K |
| 327 | D | 1327-1 | Durotrigan K |
| 328 | D | 1328-1 | Durotrigan K |

| MACK'75 NUMBER | ALLEN CLASS | CATALOGUE NUMBER | CATALOGUE CLASSIFICATION |
|---|---|---|---|
| 329 | D | 1329-1 | Durotrigan K |
| 330 | D | 1330-1 | Durotrigan K |
| 331 | D | 1331-1 | Durotrigan K |
| 332 | D | 1332-1 | Durotrigan K |
| 333 | D | 1333-1 | Durotrigan K |
| 334 | D | 1334-1 | Durotrigan K |
| 335 | D | 1335-1 | Durotrigan K |
| 336 | D | 1336-1 | Durotrigan K |
| 337 | D | 1337-1 | Durotrigan K |
| 338 | D | 1338-1 | Durotrigan K |
| 339 | D | 1339-1 | Durotrigan K |
| 340 | D | 1340-1 | Durotrigan K |
| 341 | D | 1341-1 | Durotrigan K |
| 342 | D | 1342-1 | Durotrigan K |
| 343 | D | 1343-1 | Durotrigan K |
| 344 | D | 1344-1 | Durotrigan K |
| 345 | D | 1345-1 | Durotrigan K |
| 346 | D | 1346-1 | Durotrigan K |
| 347 | D | 1347-1 | Durotrigan K |
| 348 | D | 1348-1 | Durotrigan K |
| 349 | D | 1349-1 | Durotrigan K |
| 350 | D | 1350-1 | Durotrigan K |
| 351 | D | 1351-1 | Durotrigan K |
| 352 | D | 1352-1 | Durotrigan K |
| 353 | D | 1353-1 | Durotrigan K |
| 354 | D | 1354-1 | Durotrigan K |
| 355 | D | 1355-1 | Durotrigan K |
| 356 | D | 1356-1 | Durotrigan K |
| 357 | D | 1357-1 | Durotrigan K |
| 358 | D | 1358-1 | Durotrigan K |
| 359 | D | 1359-1 | Durotrigan K |
| 360 | D | 1360-1 | Durotrigan K |
| 361 | D | 1361-1 | Durotrigan K |
| 362 | D | 1362-1 | Durotrigan K |
| 363 | D | 1363-1 | Durotrigan K |
| 364 | D | 1364-1 | Durotrigan K |
| 365 | D | 1365-1 | Durotrigan K |
| 366 | D | 1366-1 | Durotrigan K |
| 367 | D | 1367-1 | Durotrigan K |
| 368 | D | 1368-1 | Durotrigan K |
| 369 | D | 1369-1 | Durotrigan K |
| 370 | D | 1370-1 | Durotrigan K |

| MACK'75 NUMBER | ALLEN CLASS | CATALOGUE NUMBER | CATALOGUE CLASSIFICATION |
|---|---|---|---|
| 371 | — | 1285-1 | Durotrigan - |
| 372 | — | 1286-1 | Durotrigan - |
| 373 | — | —(deleted) | —(deleted) |
| 374 | Brit RA | 1005-1 | Dobunnic A |
| 374a | — | —(deleted) | —(deleted) |
| 374b | — | —(deleted) | —(deleted) |
| 375 | — | 1558-1 | Trinovantian F |
| 376 | A | 1020-1 | Dobunnic A |
| 377 | L | 1170-1 | Dobunnic - |
| 378 | B | 1042-1 | Dobunnic B |
| 378a | C | 1045-1 | Dobunnic B |
| 379 | D | 1049-1 | Dobunnic B |
| 380 (381) | E | 1074-1 | Dobunnic D |
| 381 (380) | E | 1074-1 | Dobunnic D |
| 382 | F | 1078-1 | Dobunnic D |
| 383 | I | 1135-1 | Dobunnic G |
| 384 | J | 1137-1 | Dobunnic G |
| 384a | M | 1175-1 | Dobunnic - |
| 384b | MX | 1095-1 | Dobunnic E |
| 384c | N | 1180-1 | Dobunnic - |
| 384d | O | 1185-1 | Dobunnic - |
| 385 | — | 1062-1 | Dobunnic D |
| 386 | — | 1066-1 | Dobunnic D |
| 387 | G | 1082-1 | Dobunnic D |
| 388 | — | 1105-1 | Dobunnic F |
| 389 | H | 1110-1 | Dobunnic F |
| 390 | — | 1140-3 | Dobunnic H |
| 391 | — | 1130-1 | Dobunnic G |
| 392 | — | 1092-1 | Dobunnic E |
| 393 | — | 1035-1 | Dobunnic B |
| 394 | — | 1039-1 | Dobunnic B |
| 395 | — | 1052-1 | Dobunnic C |
| 396 | K | 1057-1 | Dobunnic C |
| 396a | — | —(deleted) | —(deleted) |
| 396b | — | 1231-1 | Durotrigan - |
| 397 | I(a) (Brit NA) | 620-4 | Icenian B |
| 398 | I(a) (Brit NA) | 620-9 | Icenian B |
| 399 | I(a) (Brit NA) | 620-1 | Icenian B |
| 400 | I(b) (Brit NC) | 624-1 | Icenian B |
| 400a | I(b) (Brit NC) | 624-4 | Icenian B |
| 401 | I(b) (Brit NB) | 626-1 | Icenian B |
| 402 | I(c) (Brit NB) | 626-9 | Icenian B |

| MACK'75 NUMBER | ALLEN CLASS | CATALOGUE NUMBER | CATALOGUE CLASSIFICATION |
|---|---|---|---|
| 403 | I(c) (Brit NB) | 626-4 | Icenian B |
| 403a | I(c) (Brit NB) | 626-7 | Icenian B |
| 403b | (Brit NB) | 620-7 | Icenian B |
| 403c | (Brit NB) | 626-12 | Icenian B |
| 404 | I(d) (Brit ND) | 628-1 | Icenian B |
| 405 | G | 857-1 | Corieltauvian B |
| 405a | F | 855-3 | Corieltauvian B |
| 405b | F | 855-5 | Corieltauvian B |
| 406 | H | 860-1 | Corieltauvian B |
| 406a | J | 862-1 | Corieltauvian B |
| 407 | II(a) | 655-1 | Icenian C |
| 408 | II(c) | 657-1 | Icenian C |
| 409 | II(e) | 659-1 | Icenian C |
| 410 | U | 875-2 | Corieltauvian D |
| 410a | U | 875-1 | Corieltauvian D |
| 410b | U | 877-1 | Corieltauvian D |
| 411 | II(b) | 661-1 | Icenian C |
| 412 | III(a) | 665-1 | Icenian E |
| 413 | III(b) | 790-1 | Icenian O |
| 413a | III(a) | 665-9 | Icenian E |
| 413b | III(a) | 665-3 | Icenian E |
| 413c | III(a) | 665-5 | Icenian E |
| 413d | III(c) | 792-1 | Icenian O |
| 413d | III(c) | 794-1 | Icenian O |
| 413e | III(a) | 665-7 | Icenian E |
| 414 | LX20 | 679-1 | Icenian F |
| 415 | IV(c) | 675-1 | Icenian F |
| 416 | — | 998-1 | Corieltauvian - |
| 417 | IV(d) | 681-1 | Icenian F |
| 417a | IV(d) | 683-1 | Icenian F |
| 418 | V(a) | 705-1 | Icenian G |
| 419 | V(b) | 710-1 | Icenian G |
| 420 | V(b) | 711-1 | Icenian G |
| 421 | V(c) | 715-1 | Icenian G |
| 422 | V(d) | 720-1 | Icenian G |
| 423 | VI(b) | 740-1 | Icenian I |
| 424 | VI(a) | 730-1 | Icenian H |
| 425 | VII | 760-1 | Icenian K |
| 425a | VI(e) | 761-1 | Icenian K |
| 425b | VI(b) | 734-1 | Icenian H |
| 426 | VIII | 764-1 | Icenian K |
| 427 | VIII | 762-1 | Icenian K |

| MACK'75 NUMBER | ALLEN CLASS | CATALOGUE NUMBER | CATALOGUE CLASSIFICATION |
|---|---|---|---|
| 428 | VIII | 766-1 | Icenian K |
| 429 | VI(c) | 752-1 | Icenian J |
| 430 | VI(c) | 758-1 | Icenian J |
| 431 | VI(d) | 736-1 | Icenian H |
| 432 | IX(b) | 775-1 | Icenian N |
| 433 | IX(a) | 770-1 | Icenian L |
| 434 | II(f) | 663-1 | Icenian D |
| 434a | X | 780-1 | Icenian M |
| 435 | LX6 | 1546-1 | Trinovantian E |
| 436 | LX7 | 1549-1 | Trinovantian E |
| 437 | LX8 | 1552-1 | Trinovantian E |
| 438 | LX10 | 80-1 | Gallo-Belgic XD |
| 439 | LX18 | 1543-1 | Trinovantian D |
| 440 | LX19 | 1611-1 | Trinovantian I |
| 441 | LX11 | 1555-1 | Trinovantian F |
| 442 | LX14 | 1626-1 | Trinovantian J |
| 443 | LX14 | 474-1 | Atrebatic I |
| 444 (now 272) | LX15 | 1643-1 | Trinovantian K |
| 444a | — | 1540-1 | Trinovantian D |
| 445 | LX16 | 1948-1 | Trinovantian T |
| 445a | — | —(deleted) | —(deleted) |
| 445b | — | —(deleted) | —(deleted) |
| 445c | — | —(deleted) | —(deleted) |
| 446 | LX26 | 1629-1 | Trinovantian J |
| 446a (not used) | — | —(deleted) | —(deleted) |
| 446b | LZ8 | 355-1 | Atrebatic C |
| 446c | LZ9 | 1644-1 | Trinovantian K |
| 446d | LZ10 | 1662-1 | Trinovantian L |
| 447 | M (Brit KA) | 825 | Corieltauvian G |
| 448 | L (Brit KA) | 829 | Corieltauvian H |
| 449 | O (Brit KB) | 811 | Corieltauvian D |
| 449a | N (BRIT KB) | 809-1 | Corieltauvian C |
| 449b | Brit KB | 815-1 | Corieltauvian D |
| 449c | Brit KB | 817-1 | Corieltauvian E |
| 450 | P (Brit KB) | 811 | Corieltauvian D |
| 450a | T (Brit KB) | 821-1 | Corieltauvian F |
| 451 | I | 864-1 | Corieltauvian B |
| 451a | — | 866-1 | Corieltauvian B |
| 452 | V | 877-7 | Corieltauvian D |
| 452a | — | 877-5 | Corieltauvian D |
| 453 | W | 877-3 | Corieltauvian D |
| 453a | — | 887-1 | Corieltauvian D |

| MACK'75 NUMBER | ALLEN CLASS | CATALOGUE NUMBER | CATALOGUE CLASSIFICATION |
|---|---|---|---|
| 454 | X | 884-1 | Corieltauvian D |
| 455 | ZA | 879-1 | Corieltauvian D |
| 456 | — | 889-7 | Corieltauvian D |
| 456a | — | 881-1 | Corieltauvian D |
| 456b | — | 920-1 | Corieltauvian K |
| 456c | — | 924-1 | Corieltauvian K |
| 457 | — | 910-1 | Corieltauvian J |
| 458 | — | 914-1 | Corieltauvian J |
| 459 | — | 940-1 | Corieltauvian M |
| 460 | — | 930-1 | Corieltauvian L |
| 460a | — | 905-2 | Corieltauvian I |
| 460b | — | 934-1 | Corieltauvian L |
| 461 | — | 972-1 | Corieltauvian O |
| 462 | — | 974-1 | Corieltauvian O |
| 463 | — | 978-1 | Corieltauvian P |
| 463a (pl.32) | — | 978-1 | Corieltauvian P |
| 463a (pl.33) | — | 980-1 | Corieltauvian P |
| 464 | — | 950-1 | Corieltauvian M |
| 464a | — | 938-1 | Corieltauvian L |
| 464b | — | 967-1 | Corieltauvian N |
| 465 | — | 984-1 | Corieltauvian P |
| 466 | — | 988-1 | Corieltauvian Q |
| 467 | — | 992-1 | Corieltauvian Q |
| 468 | — | 994-1 | Corieltauvian R |
| 469 | — | 996-1 | Corieltauvian - |

# TREND-SURFACE MAPS

Eighty maps show where the various coin-types have been found. Forty different coin-types are plotted, two maps for each type.

The first map plots all the coins and answers the question 'is this type ever found here?' The second map plots only more frequent (ie: intense) finds and answers the question 'where are the coins usually found?'

The maps are not the normal 'dot' maps, that is, individual finds are not plotted as points. Instead, the finds have been analyzed statistically, and plotted as contours—the plots are similiar to those on weather or topographic maps.

The maps help illustrate some themes from the historical section of the book. A discussion of these themes and the interpretation of the maps is given below.

A discussion of the methods used to construct the maps appears at the end of this section. There is also a discussion of the problems associated with distribution maps. The interpretations offered below should be viewed with an understanding of these problems.

## THEME 1—THE 'THAMES MOUTH' DISTRIBUTION

The early imported coins and the Kentish Cast Bronzes are found around the mouth of the Thames. Tribal territories are not well-defined by the distribution of these coins.

The finds of Gallo-Belgic A, B and C (maps 1 to 6) fall mostly in the territories of the Trinovantes/Catuvellauni, Cantii and Atrebates/Regni (115). Most Gallo-Belgic A coins are found east of London, and on the Essex coast. Gallo-Belgic B occur near London and in east Kent, and Gallo-Belgic C east of London. A few coins are found near Hengistbury and Dorchester, in the territory of the Durotriges. Gallo-Belgic B and C are generally too rare to say their distributions are different from each other or from Gallo-Belgic A.

Cantian A to D (maps 9 and 10), the Cast Bronzes of the Prototype, Experimental, Innovative and Optimization Periods are also found around the mouth of the Thames. Most are found near London, Eastbourne, the Hengistbury area and in east Kent. The distribution is about the same as for Gallo-Belgic A, B and C. The stronger south Thames focus, however, suggests a Cantian origin for these pieces. The distribution of Cantian E (maps 11 and 12) are similar to all these types, suggesting a date not much later than the Gallic War.

Cantian cast bronzes are also found well inside Durotrigan territory, often in hillforts. They may have been imported as scrap metal after the coins went out of use some time after 50 B.C. (116).

## THEME 2 — DUROTRIGAN INTERACTION

Before the Gallic War, the Durotriges had trading contacts with their neighbouring tribes (117).

Gallo-Belgic A and C coins are found in Durotrigan territory (maps 1 and 5), possibly arriving via Atrebatic/Regnan intermediaries. Cantian A to D coins also appear (map 9), but these may not have arrived as circulating coins, but instead as scrap metal.

Most importantly, Durotrigan A and E coins, Chute staters and Abstract Type silver staters appear in Atrebatic/Regnan territory (maps 55 to 58), and Atrebatic A coins, the Westerham type, appear in Durotrigan territory (maps 17 and 18). The finds suggest a trading link existed between the Hengistbury and Chichester/Hayling Island regions prior to the war—there may have been coastal traders plying the British coast. However, some evidence for an exchange zone north of the New Forest has recently been discovered (118). The coins may have been carried by traders using a northerly route between the two tribes.

Durotrigan A and E types also appear in Dobunnic territory in small numbers, suggesting trading contacts, but there were no Dobunnic coins at this time to show the reciprocal relationship. Significantly, Durotrigan A shows two 'arms'—one aiming at Camerton, the other towards Bagendon (map 55)— suggesting a pre-war importance for these places. More finds are needed, however, to prove the importance of these places in Durotrigan trade.

## THEME 3 — DUROTRIGAN ISOLATION

At some time during the Gallic War, the Durotriges became isolated from the other tribes. Durotrigan and Atrebatic coins, for example, no longer cross the frontier between the two tribes. This isolation became complete after the war, and interaction was never reestablished—coin-exchange between the Durotriges and the other tribes ceased.

Gallo-Belgic E coins, the Gallic War Type, completely shun Durotrigan territory (map 7). Later Cantian coins do not appear (maps 11 to 16), and Atrebatic B coins appear only in small numbers in the east (maps 19 and 20). The way the very late Atrebatic L coins skirt Durotrigan territory (maps 31 and 32) is possibly significant—it may delineate the path of Caratacus as he fled before the Romans.

Similarly, Durotrigan coins no longer appear outside Durotrigan territory. Post-war types Durotrigan I and K, the Silver Starfish and cast bronzes only appear in Durotrigan territory (maps 59, 60, 63 and 64).

Durotrigan J, the struck bronzes, do appear in Dobunnic and Atrebatic/ Regnan territory (maps 61 and 62), but, as Allen noted, it is difficult to distinguish a struck bronze from a core of a forged silver stater. Thus the distribution of Durotrigan J is possibly contaminated with earlier Durotrigan E intruders—some forgeries of silver staters are likely included in the struck bronze map. Alternatively, an earlier date for Durotrigan J is possible, but not enough information exists at this time to fix it with more accuracy.

The great outpouring of gold types Gallo-Belgic E and Atrebatic B may have been caused by an influx of gold provided by the Romans. By financing the Atrebatic/Regnan competition for war materiel in Britain, the Romans could have prevented the Durotriges from obtaining goods for the Venetii (119).

## THEME 4—TRADE NETWORKS DURING THE GALLIC WAR

The great quantity of gold staters imported during the Gallic War spurred trade within Britain. The results of this show clearly in the coin distributions (120). Coins are found in areas that did not have them before, and several places now stand out because of the large numbers of coins found.

The distributions of Gallo-Belgic E (maps 7 and 8), Atrebatic B (maps 19 and 20) and Trinovantian D,E and F (maps 65 and 66) show the wartime trade networks. There are important similarities in the distributions.

Imported coins now appear in Icenian, Dobunnic and Corieltauvian territory in quantity for the first time. The imported coins still appear around the Thames mouth—Gallo-Belgic E show a similar distribution in this region as Gallo-Belgic A. Thus the Trinovantes/Catuvellauni, Atrebates/Regni and Cantii still shared in the trade.

Atrebatic B, the Atrebatic Abstract Types show the Chichester/Hayling Island, Eastbourne, North Kent, Verulamium/Harlow, Camulodunum, and Oxford/Dorchester-on-Thames regions as important nodes in the trading networks. One 'arm' extends to Bagendon—suggesting the Atrebates were vying with the Durotriges for the Dobunnic trade. Camerton, however, does not show up on the Atrebatic B Maps.

Atrebatic B shows the most widespread influence of the Atrebates/Regni, later Atrebatic/Regnan coin types show a much more limited distribution—as the Trinovantes/Catuvellauni became more influential at their expense.

Trinovantian D, E and F, the Whaddon Chase Types show the Chichester/ Hayling Island, Verulamium/Harlow and Camulodunum nodes, and 'arms' extending to Bagendon, again, and also to the Thetford/Norwich area (maps 65 and 66). The Bagendon and Thetford/Norwich links show the early influence of the Trinovantes/Catuvellauni in Dobunnic and Icenian territory.

Interestingly, small numbers of Trinovantian/Catuvellaunian coins appear in the Chichester/Hayling Island region from this time on, but Atrebatic/Regnan ones do not appear at Verulamium/Harlow. This suggests the Trinovantes/ Catuvellauni became the key trading tribe, and their coins eventually became the trading currency of Britain.

## THEME 5—TRACKWAYS IN BRITAIN

Two ancient trackways, attested in the archaeological record also appear on the coin maps.

Segments of a trackway along the 'Jurassic ridge', from Corieltauvian territory to Dobunnic territory show in the distribution of Corieltauvan B, C to H and I to R, the Reduced Weight, South Ferriby and Dynastic Types (maps 41 to 45). The trackway is also suggested by the distribution of Dobunnic D and F (maps 51 and 53).

The Stour Valley trade route between Durotrigan and Dobunnic territory shows in the distribution of Dobunnic B, D and F, the dynastic coins of Corio, Antedrig and Eisu (maps 47, 48, 51 and 53), and Durotrigan A and E (maps 55, 57 and 58).

## THEME 6—RESTRICTED COIN DISTRIBUTIONS AFTER THE GALLIC WAR

After the Gallic War there was less coin exchange between the tribes, and the maps show the tribal territories with greater clarity. The exception is the Trinovantian/Catuvellaunian coinage, which becomes widely used throughout Britain (121).

Except for a few coins in the Chichester/Hayling Island region, Cantian F, G and H, the Weald Types, appear only in Kent—thus defining Cantian territry (maps 13 and 14). The later dynastic types, Cantian I to N appear in quantity primarily in Kent (maps 15 and 16).

Atrebatic C, D, E, and F, the dynastic coins of Commius and Tincommius appear primarily in the Chichester/Hayling Island region and in the area to the north (maps 21 to 24). Only a few of Commius' coins appear in Kent, and none of those struck by Tincommius. Verica's coins, Atrebatic I, J and K show a similar distribution, but with a few coins found in the Eastbourne region (maps 29 and 30).

Durotrigan I, the Silver Starfish types, appear only in the Hengistbury area, and the cast bronzes, Durotrigan K, have a similar distribution (maps 59, 60, 63 and 64).

Trinovantian I, J and K, the dynastic issues of Addedomaros, show a wider distribution than the coins of the other tribes. They spread into Dobunnic and Icenian territory (maps 67 and 68). However, they no longer appear in quantity in the Chichester/Hayling Island region, as the earlier Trinovantian D, E and F types had (maps 65 and 66).

Overall, inter-tribal contact, as shown by coin-exchange, decreased immediately after the Gallic War. The widespread use of Atrebatic/Regnan coins, as seen in the distribution of Atrebatic B stopped immediately. Trinovantian/Catuvellaunian issues eventually replaced them and finally became the trade coins of Britain.

# THEME 7—TRINOVANTIAN/CATUVELLAUNIAN EX-
## PANSION

The expansion of Trinovantian/Catuvellaunian influence, if not actual political control, gradually increased after the Gallic War (122).

Addedomaros begins the process. During his rule, quantities of Trinovantian/Catuvellaunian coins appear in Cantian and Icenian territory for the first time. Trinovantian I, J and K show a much wider distribution than the earlier types (maps 67 and 68). The Camulodunum, Verulamium/Harlow and Oxford/Dorchester-on-Thames regions show plainly on the maps.

Dubnovellaunus-in-Essex continues the influence in Cantian and Icenian territory (maps 69 and 70). Although the Oxford/Dorchester-on-Thames region does not appear because of the scarcity of the coins, the Thetford/Norwich region and north Kent show plainly.

During the reign of Tasciovanus, the coin distributions show even wider spread (maps 71 and 72). Trinovantian M, N and O now start to appear south of the Thames in Atrebatic/Regnan territory, and north towards Corieltauvian territory.

The coins of the Interregnum (maps 73 to 78) are very rare and not too much significance should be read into their distributions. The maps merely indicate the coins are Trinovantian/Catuvellaunian ones. However, the distributions are based on too few finds to prove, statistically, the types favour one area of the tribal territory over another.

Cunobeline completes the expansion, showing the widest distribution of all (maps 79 and 80). Trinovantian T, U, V, W and X appear throughout the southeast of Britain, even in the Chichester/Hayling Island region. They overrun Kent, and Cantian coinage disappears entirely. Cunobeline's coins also appear in Dobunnic territory, in both the Bagendon and Camerton areas, though the distributions there are not so well-defined. A few of his coins even appear in Corieltauvian territory.

The expansion of Trinovantian/Catuvellaunian influence, traditionally credited to Cunobeline, may be seen instead to have its roots in the reign of Addedomaros. During the reigns of Addedomaros, Dubnovellaunus-in-Essex, Tasciovanus and Cunobeline, there was an increasing spread of the coins throughout Britain.

The growth of Trinovantian/Catuvellaunian influence, and the decline of Atrebatic/Regnan is likely to be the result of Roman manipulation. After Commius fled Gaul to join the British portion of his tribe, the Atrebates/Regni would have fallen into disfavour amongst the Romans. The Trinovantes would have been the natural recipients of Roman support, since they had cooperated with Caesar's incursions into Britain during the Gallic War. It is likely they received special favour (possibly the trading rights for Roman goods) and Addedomaros and his successors used this to their advantage.

# THEME 8—ATREBATIC/REGNAN DISFAVOUR AFTER THE GALLIC WAR

The position of the Atrebates/Regni changed drastically after the war, and this shows clearly in the coin distributions. The coins of Commius, Atrebatic C (maps 21 and 22), are much rarer and circulate in a much reduced area compared to Atrebatic B (maps 19 and 20). It should be kept in mind, however, that rarer types normally show a more restricted distribution. This is partly because the outer contour-lines 'disappear' as the total number of coins becomes smaller.

# THEME 9—ATREBATIC/REGNAN INCURSION INTO KENT

During the Trinovantian/Catuvellaunian Interregnum, an Atrebatic/Regnan ruler, Eppillus, invaded Kent. Some of Eppillus' coins appear only in the traditional Atrebatic/Regnan territory, notably the Atrebatic G 'Calleva' Types (maps 25 and 26).

However, others appear primarily in Kent—the Atrebatic H Types (maps 27 and 28). These were the coins used to finance the incursion. A few of these appear in the Camulodunum and Verulamium/Harlow regions, perhaps brought back from Kent by Trinovantian/Catuvellaunian troops after the incursion was suppressed by Cunobeline.

# THEME 10—DOBUNNIC RULERS

Allen suggested the Dobunnic rulers were paired, one ruling in the northern part of Dobunnic territory, the other in the south (123). The best evidence was the coin distributions of Corio and Bodvoc—the coins seemed to be found in different areas. Corio's were primarily found to the south and west, Bodvoc's to the east.

The distributions for Dobunnic B and C (maps 47 to 50) show this can no longer be accepted (124). Corio's coins completely encompass the territory of Bodvoc's, and the distribution for Corio shows both the Bagendon and Camerton centres. In the past, Bodvoc's coins seemed to occur only around the Bagendon centre, but an example is now known from Bath, so the distribution of 'all coins' is now wider than before.

Although Corio's uninscribed silver types (1042-1, 1045-1 and 1049-1) are plotted with the inscribed gold, there is no significant difference for the two metals. When the gold is plotted alone, for example, it shows about the same contours, reveals the Camerton and Bagendon centres, and overlaps all but the most easterly of Bodvoc's coins.

Bodvoc's coins are generally rarer than Corio's, and would naturally show a more restricted distribution. If more finds were known, the distribution for Bodvoc could be wider, still.

Thus, the idea of mutual exclusivity, the proof for Allen's argument, is no longer tenable. At best, it could be asserted Bodvoc's coins shun the south and west of Dobunnic territory, but there is little proof. Certainly the distribution of Corio's coins overlaps that of Bodvoc's.

# CONSTRUCTING THE TREND SURFACE MAPS

The methods of constructing trend surface maps are discussed in detail elsewhere (125) and will not be elaborated here. Findspots were taken from Allen 1960, Haselgrove 1978 and Haselgrove 1984a.

The coin findspots were first plotted on a map. Hoards were treated in two ways. Those with a narrow range of types—many of these would have been 'concealment hoards'—were treated as a single find. Hoards with a wide range of types, often individual coins collected over a long period of time, were treated as if each coin were a single find. Many of these hoards represent 'temple offerings' or 'temple savings'. The hoards were treated differently because the first type would emphasize certain locations unfairly, but the second kind would be more representative of coin use in a region over time.

Modern forgeries which had crept into the records have been deleted, and the many inaccuracies in the reported National Grid Coordinates for the findspots were corrected.

The attribution of coins follows the catalogue listings, not the attributions of previous workers. For this reason Gallo-Belgic D and Allen's 'British O and P' are not plotted—the records confuse the types and they cannot be disentangled. However, Allen's British Lx, Ly and Lz have been reattributed and are included.

The maps for Durotrigan J, the struck bronzes, are probably compromised by the inclusion of cores of forged silver staters, and for this reason maps 61 and 62 are suspect, though it was decided to include them despite the problems.

Maps were not prepared if the types were too rare to reveal distributions adequately.

The maps were then gridded off in 32 km. (20 mile) squares. This grid size was chosen because each square encompasses enough coins to give useful averaging, but the grid is still fine enough to resolve (ie. distinguish) major regions, like Camulodunum and Verulamium/Harlow. It does not resolve local sites; for example, Oxford, Dorchester-on-Thames and other sites in that vicinity are all shown as a single, blurred area.

Thirty-two km. squares do not produce extreme 'edge-effect' distortions. Edge-effects mostly occur near coastlines, where averages are calculated using the 'zero finds' in the water areas. On the maps, edge-effects are generally small and show up primarily in the Icenian and Cantian territories.

One other attempt was made to eliminate edge-effects—the placing of the grid corner. The grid corner was placed at National Grid Coordinate SX (20) 500 500 for all the maps, except the Dobunnic ones. This placement helps minimize edge-effects for a 32 km. square grid, especially in Icenian territory.

Dubunnic B, C, D and F, however, were constructed with the grid corner shifted slightly—to ST (31) 000 000. This shift resolves Camerton and Bagendon as two sites—instead of a single, elongated area. For these maps, the edge-effects in Icenian territory are acceptable because that region is not important for Dobunnic coins.

The number of coin-finds in each square was then counted.

The process known as 'grid generalization', a smoothing technique, was done in the simplest manner. The average value of four adjacent squares was placed at the intersection of each group of four. The contours were then drawn in without resorting to regression analysis. Each contour line connects equal frequency of coin finds (per 32 km. square) averaged over a 4096 square km. (1600 square mile) area.

The upper map in each pair shows the 0.25 coins per 4096 square km. contour, it encompasses all the known finds. The lower map has an outermost contour of 0.50 coins per 4096 square km., encompassing areas with two coin-finds. Higher frequency contours were selected based on the individual requirements of the types—a general scheme was not helpful. Voids are areas in which no coins have been found, these are indicated where ambiguity might occur.

Coins found north of York are generally off the map, and are not included. The important site at Mount Batten is similarly off the map, as is the Carn Brae hoard of Cornwall. Finds in the Isle of Wight are included, but Wight only appears on those maps partly shaded with 'voids'. That is, the Isle of Wight does not appear totally inside any contour, but is partly included in a few.

## PROBLEMS OF TREND SURFACE MAPS

It is wrong to assume trend surface maps are objective representations just because they appear 'scientific'. They are actually very subjective, and must be used with care.

First, findspots are often recorded without precision, and the reporting of finds is haphazard at best. The activities of local collectors and archaeological groups in the nineteenth century distorted the reporting even further. The importance of some sites on the maps could merely reflect the activities of interested individuals—the old joke about findspot maps showing where people have gone looking for coins should be kept in mind. These problems are probably discussed best in Rodwell 1981.

The methods of constructing the maps can shift the contours and even create 'statistical artifacts'—areas of seeming importance where none existed. The depiction of Bagendon and Camerton as one big region or two separate sites is an example of this problem. Usually the problem is solved by creating different maps, using different techniques, and comparing them. In the case of the Dobunnic coins, the best representation of the data showed two sites, not one.

The inaccuracy of findspot reports, and the placement of the grid corner can shift a contour—and even a site—several miles in any direction. Thus the maps do not have the precision they suggest.

Despite all these problems, it must be said the maps do have validity. Far too many coins have been found and recorded properly, over a long period of time, for the distortions to have a serious impact. The maps based on a small number of finds can be expected to suffer the most, but those for the commonest, and usually the most important types hardly suffer at all.

The maps could have been constructed to answer many different questions— for example gold coins could have been plotted on different maps from the bronzes. The resulting map-pairs might show areas within a tribe's influence where small change was used.

The maps in this book were constructed, first, to average as many coins as possible. Secondly, they were plotted with an eye to identifying the early use of coinage in Britain, the growth of trading networks, the extent of tribal territories and the influence of individual rulers.

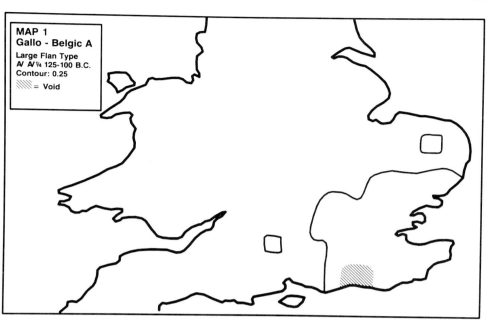

MAP 1
Gallo - Belgic A

Large Flan Type
N/ N/¼ 125-100 B.C.
Contour: 0.25

▨ = Void

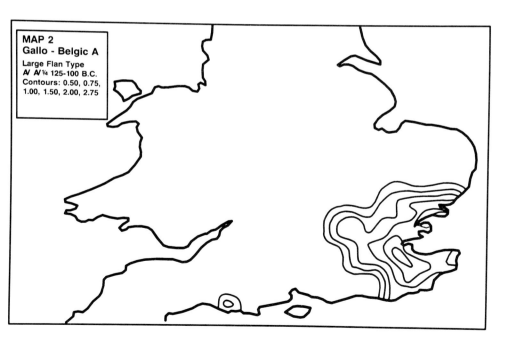

MAP 2
Gallo - Belgic A

Large Flan Type
N/ N/¼ 125-100 B.C.
Contours: 0.50, 0.75,
1.00, 1.50, 2.00, 2.75

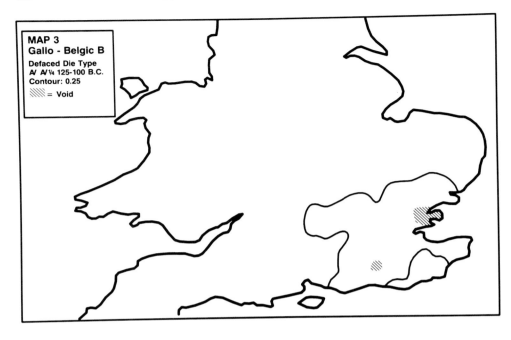

MAP 3
Gallo - Belgic B

Defaced Die Type
A/ A/¼ 125-100 B.C.
Contour: 0.25

= Void

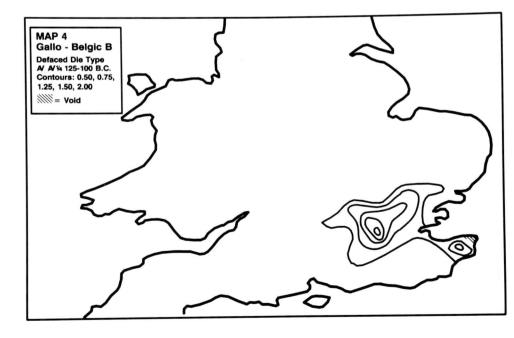

MAP 4
Gallo - Belgic B

Defaced Die Type
A/ A/¼ 125-100 B.C.
Contours: 0.50, 0.75,
1.25, 1.50, 2.00

= Void

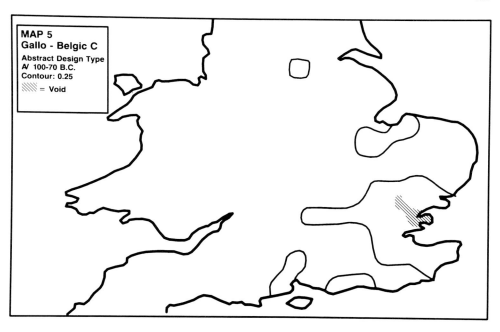

MAP 5
Gallo - Belgic C

Abstract Design Type
A/ 100-70 B.C.
Contour: 0.25

= Void

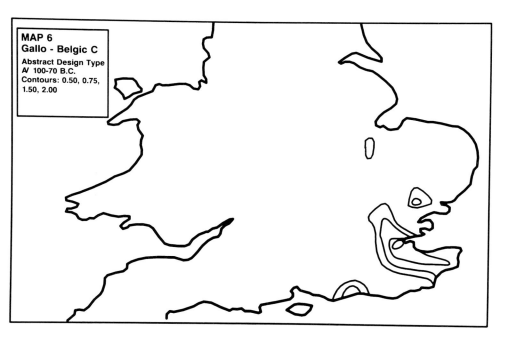

MAP 6
Gallo - Belgic C

Abstract Design Type
A/ 100-70 B.C.
Contours: 0.50, 0.75,
1.50, 2.00

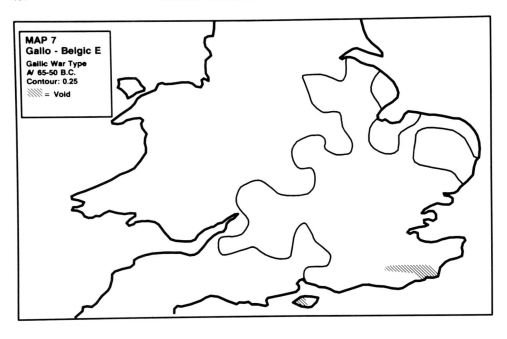

MAP 7
Gallo - Belgic E

Gallic War Type
AV 65-50 B.C.
Contour: 0.25

= Void

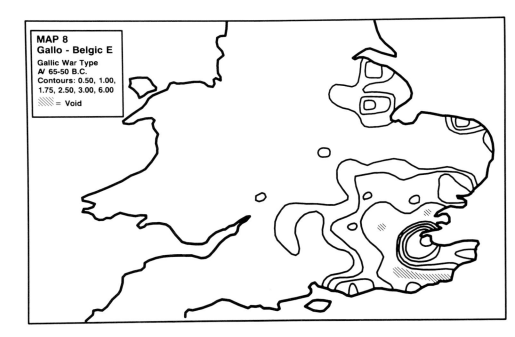

MAP 8
Gallo - Belgic E

Gallic War Type
AV 65-50 B.C.
Contours: 0.50, 1.00,
1.75, 2.50, 3.00, 6.00

= Void

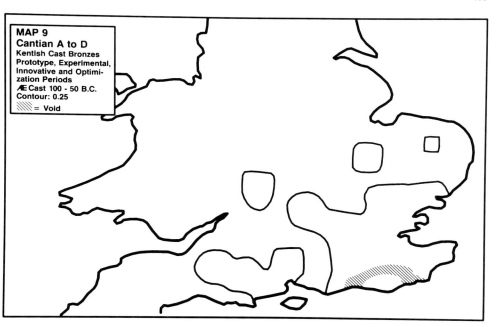

**MAP 9**
**Cantian A to D**
Kentish Cast Bronzes
Prototype, Experimental,
Innovative and Optimi-
zation Periods
Æ Cast 100 - 50 B.C.
Contour: 0.25
= Void

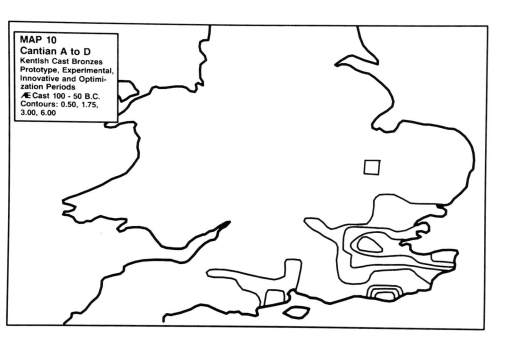

**MAP 10**
**Cantian A to D**
Kentish Cast Bronzes
Prototype, Experimental,
Innovative and Optimi-
zation Periods
Æ Cast 100 - 50 B.C.
Contours: 0.50, 1.75,
3.00, 6.00

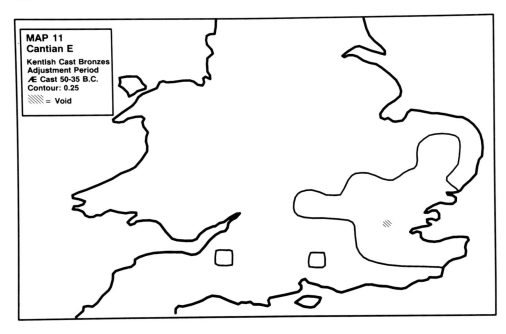

**MAP 11**
**Cantian E**

Kentish Cast Bronzes
Adjustment Period
Æ Cast 50-35 B.C.
Contour: 0.25

= Void

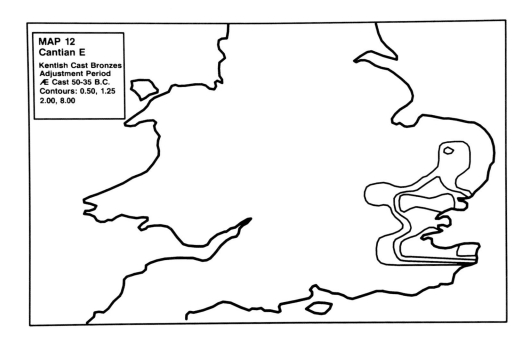

**MAP 12**
**Cantian E**

Kentish Cast Bronzes
Adjustment Period
Æ Cast 50-35 B.C.
Contours: 0.50, 1.25
2.00, 8.00

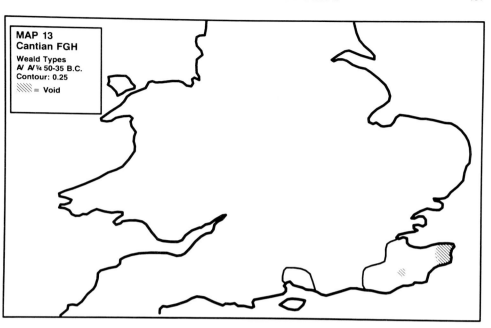

MAP 13
Cantian FGH

Weald Types
A/ A/ ¼ 50-35 B.C.
Contour: 0.25

▨ = Void

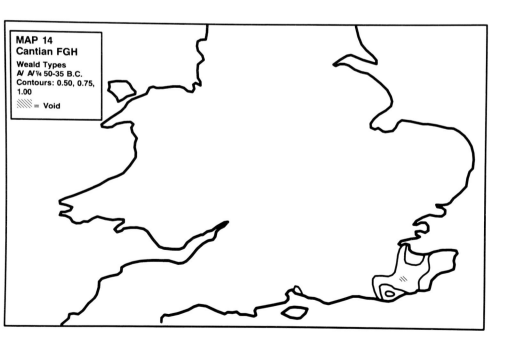

MAP 14
Cantian FGH

Weald Types
A/ A/ ¼ 50-35 B.C.
Contours: 0.50, 0.75,
1.00

▨ = Void

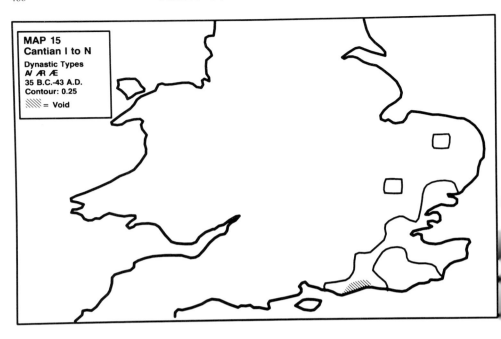

**MAP 15**
**Cantian I to N**

Dynastic Types
Ƃ ÆR Æ
35 B.C.-43 A.D.
Contour: 0.25

▨ = Void

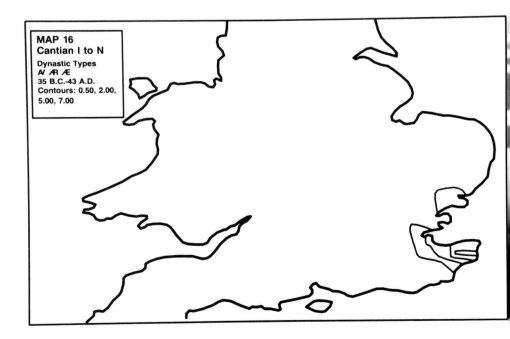

**MAP 16**
**Cantian I to N**

Dynastic Types
Ƃ ÆR Æ
35 B.C.-43 A.D.
Contours: 0.50, 2.00,
5.00, 7.00

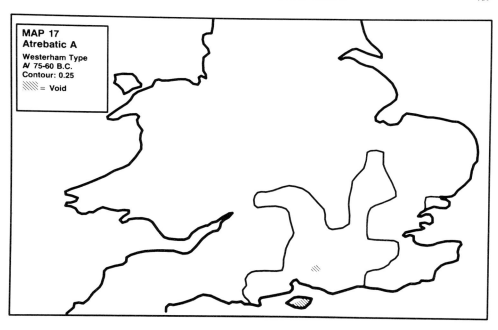

MAP 17
Atrebatic A

Westerham Type
A/ 75-60 B.C.
Contour: 0.25

= Void

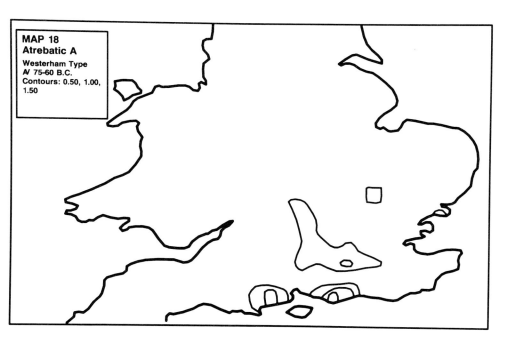

MAP 18
Atrebatic A

Westerham Type
A/ 75-60 B.C.
Contours: 0.50, 1.00,
1.50

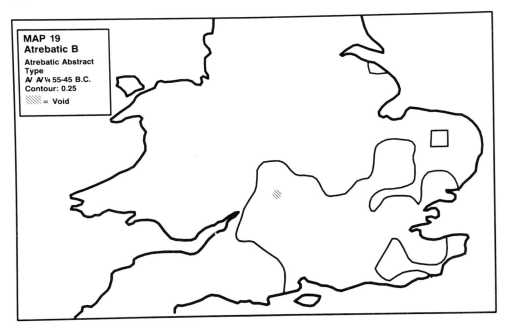

MAP 19
Atrebatic B

Atrebatic Abstract
Type
A/ A/ ¼ 55–45 B.C.
Contour: 0.25

= Void

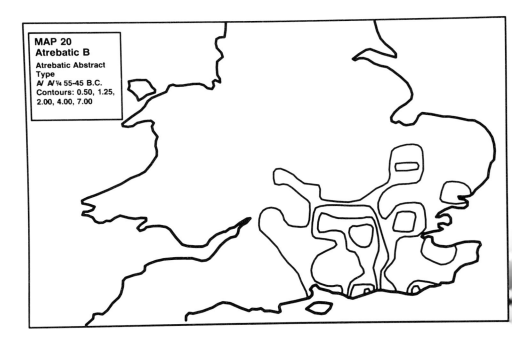

MAP 20
Atrebatic B

Atrebatic Abstract
Type
A/ A/ ¼ 55–45 B.C.
Contours: 0.50, 1.25,
2.00, 4.00, 7.00

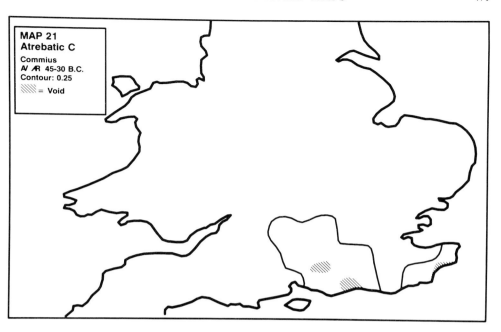

MAP 21
Atrebatic C

Commius
N Æ 45-30 B.C.
Contour: 0.25

= Void

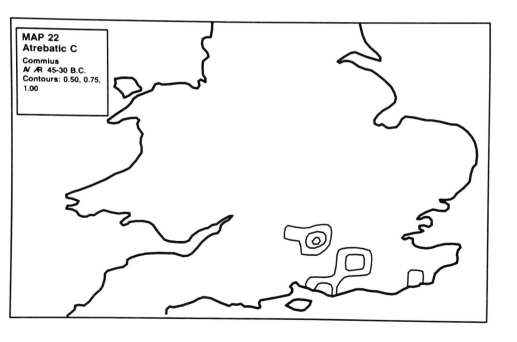

MAP 22
Atrebatic C

Commius
N Æ 45-30 B.C.
Contours: 0.50, 0.75, 1.00

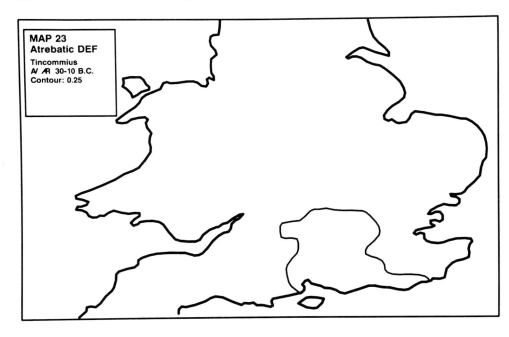

**MAP 23**
**Atrebatic DEF**
Tincommius
A/ Æ 30-10 B.C.
Contour: 0.25

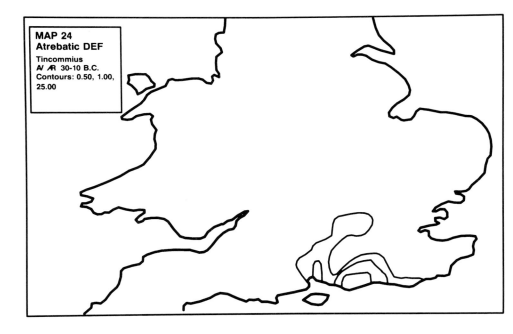

**MAP 24**
**Atrebatic DEF**
Tincommius
A/ Æ 30-10 B.C.
Contours: 0.50, 1.00,
25.00

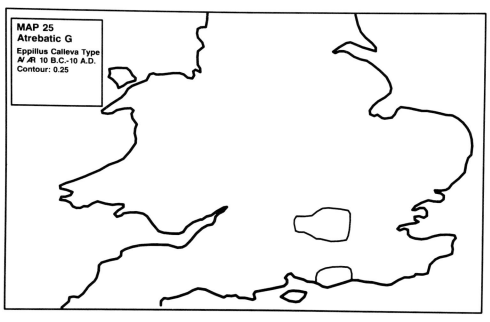

MAP 25
Atrebatic G

Eppillus Calleva Type
AV AR 10 B.C.-10 A.D.
Contour: 0.25

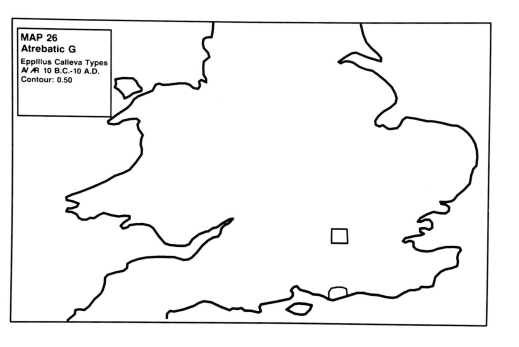

MAP 26
Atrebatic G

Eppillus Calleva Types
AV AR 10 B.C.-10 A.D.
Contour: 0.50

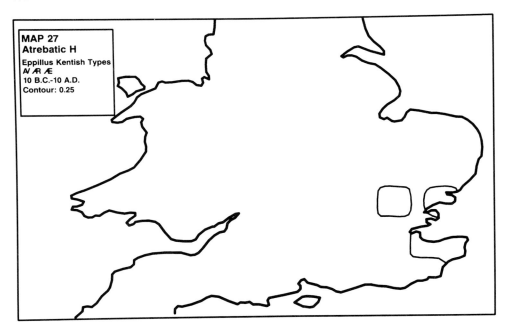

MAP 27
Atrebatic H
Eppillus Kentish Types
Ǝ /Ʀ Æ
10 B.C.-10 A.D.
Contour: 0.25

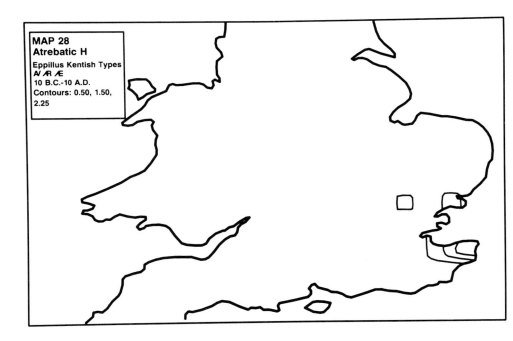

MAP 28
Atrebatic H
Eppillus Kentish Types
Ǝ /Ʀ Æ
10 B.C.-10 A.D.
Contours: 0.50, 1.50,
2.25

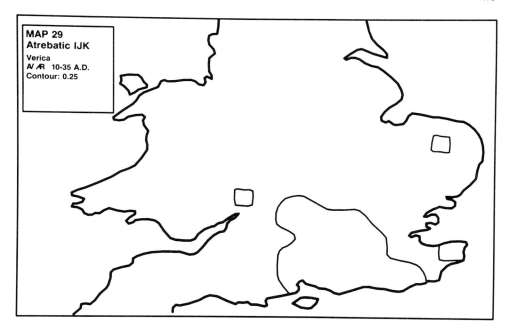

MAP 29
Atrebatic IJK

Verica
A/ Æ 10-35 A.D.
Contour: 0.25

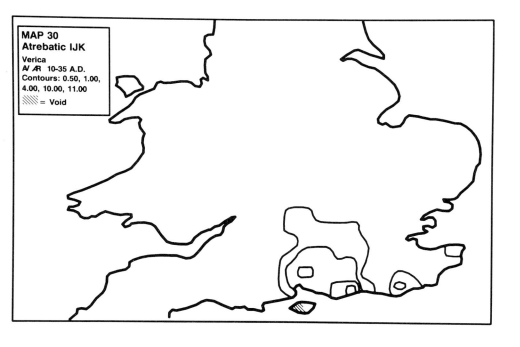

MAP 30
Atrebatic IJK

Verica
A/ Æ 10-35 A.D.
Contours: 0.50, 1.00,
4.00, 10.00, 11.00
= Void

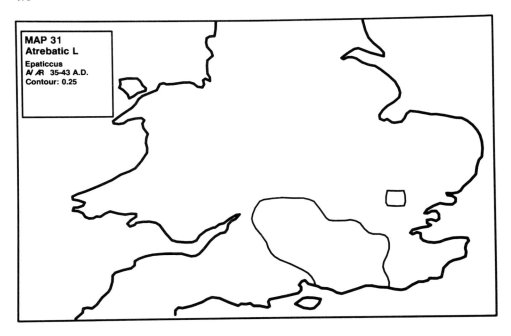

MAP 31
**Atrebatic L**

Epaticcus
Æ/ÆR 35-43 A.D.
Contour: 0.25

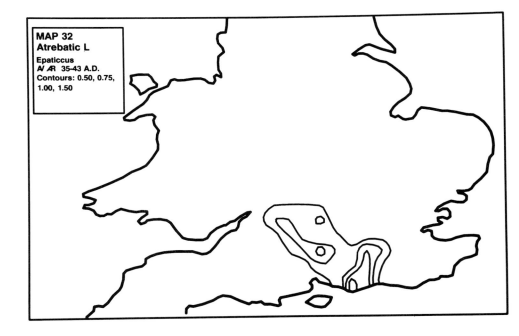

MAP 32
**Atrebatic L**

Epaticcus
Æ/ÆR 35-43 A.D.
Contours: 0.50, 0.75,
1.00, 1.50

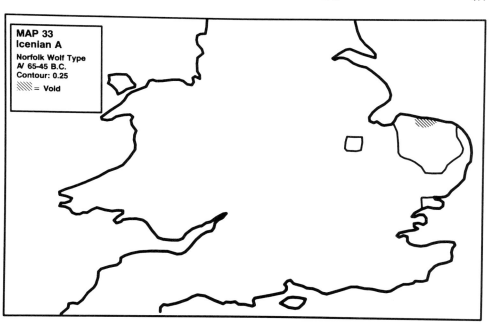

MAP 33
Icenian A

Norfolk Wolf Type
A/ 65–45 B.C.
Contour: 0.25

///// = Void

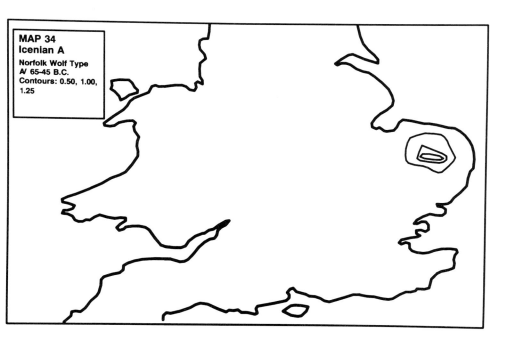

MAP 34
Icenian A

Norfolk Wolf Type
A/ 65–45 B.C.
Contours: 0.50, 1.00,
1.25

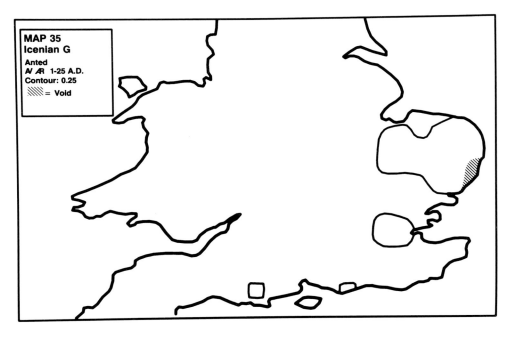

MAP 35
Icenian G
Anted
A/ÆR 1-25 A.D.
Contour: 0.25
▨ = Void

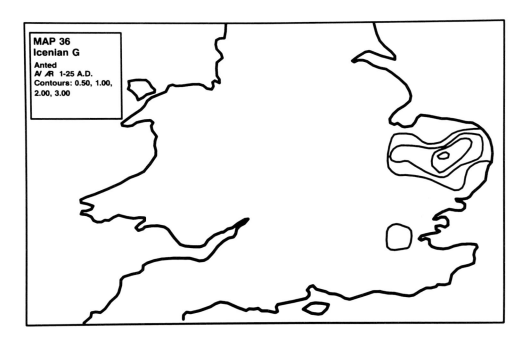

MAP 36
Icenian G
Anted
A/ÆR 1-25 A.D.
Contours: 0.50, 1.00,
2.00, 3.00

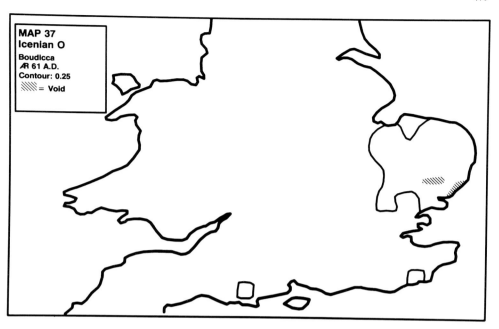

MAP 37
Icenian O

Boudicca
Æ 61 A.D.
Contour: 0.25
▨ = Void

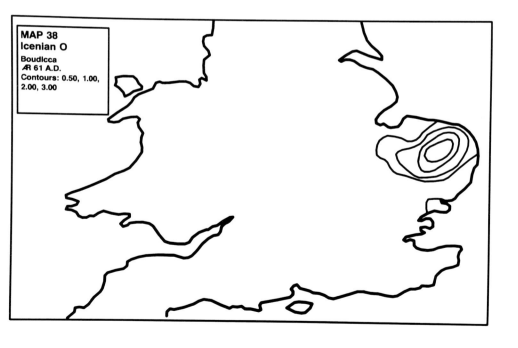

MAP 38
Icenian O

Boudicca
Æ 61 A.D.
Contours: 0.50, 1.00,
2.00, 3.00

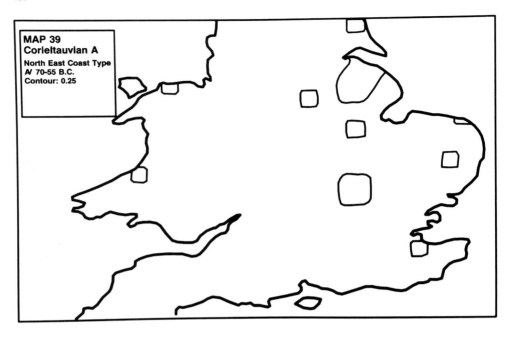

MAP 39
Corieltauvian A

North East Coast Type
A/ 70-55 B.C.
Contour: 0.25

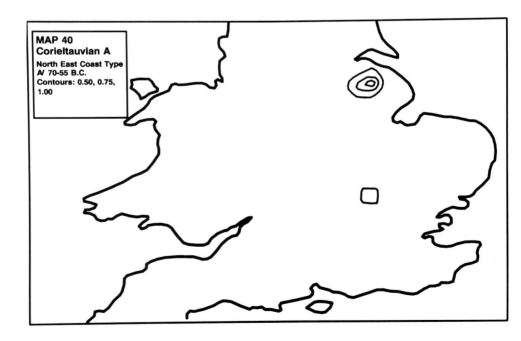

MAP 40
Corieltauvian A

North East Coast Type
A/ 70-55 B.C.
Contours: 0.50, 0.75,
1.00

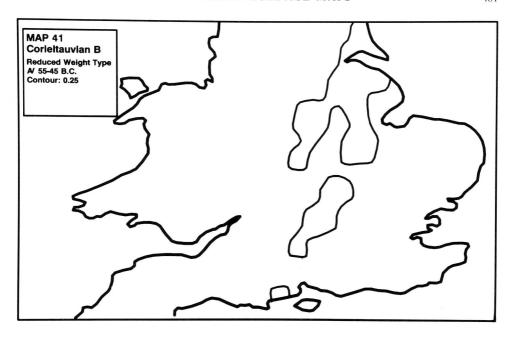

MAP 41
Corieltauvian B
Reduced Weight Type
A/ 55–45 B.C.
Contour: 0.25

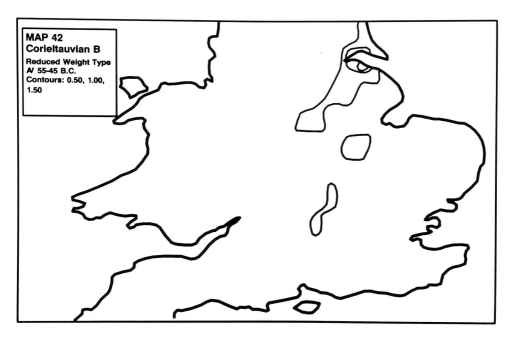

MAP 42
Corieltauvian B
Reduced Weight Type
A/ 55–45 B.C.
Contours: 0.50, 1.00,
1.50

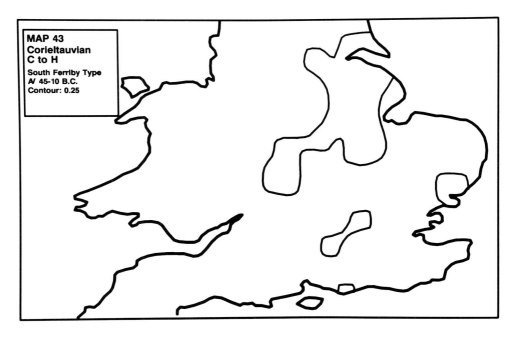

MAP 43
Corieltauvian
C to H

South Ferriby Type
A/ 45-10 B.C.
Contour: 0.25

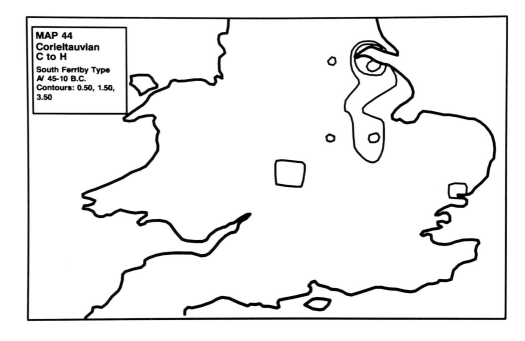

MAP 44
Corieltauvian
C to H

South Ferriby Type
A/ 45-10 B.C.
Contours: 0.50, 1.50,
3.50

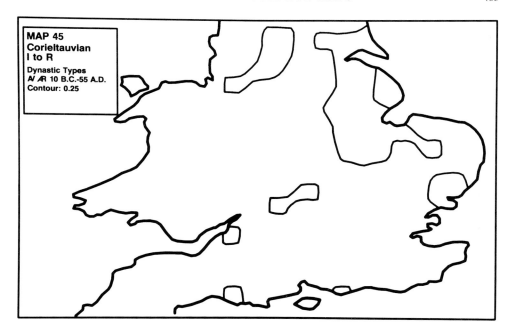

MAP 45
Corieltauvian
I to R

Dynastic Types
A/ R 10 B.C.-55 A.D.
Contour: 0.25

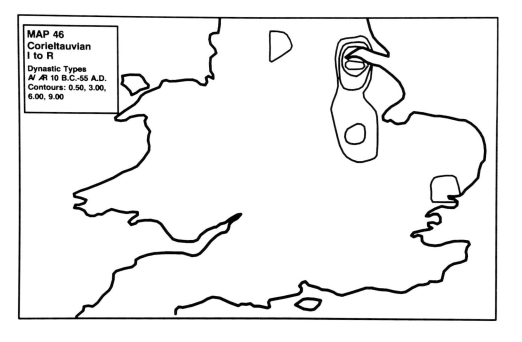

MAP 46
Corieltauvian
I to R

Dynastic Types
A/ R 10 B.C.-55 A.D.
Contours: 0.50, 3.00,
6.00, 9.00

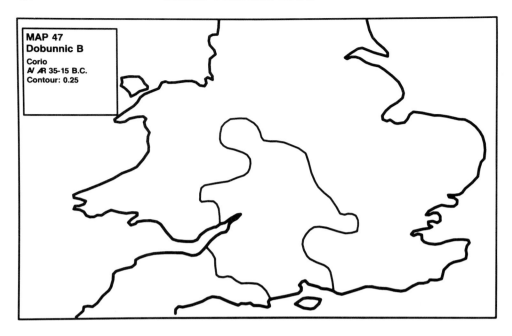

MAP 47
Dobunnic B

Corio
A/ ÆR 35–15 B.C.
Contour: 0.25

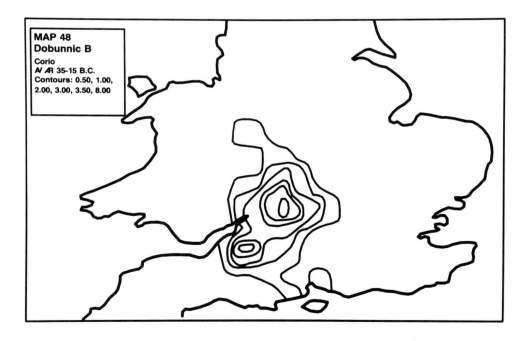

MAP 48
Dobunnic B

Corio
A/ ÆR 35–15 B.C.
Contours: 0.50, 1.00,
2.00, 3.00, 3.50, 8.00

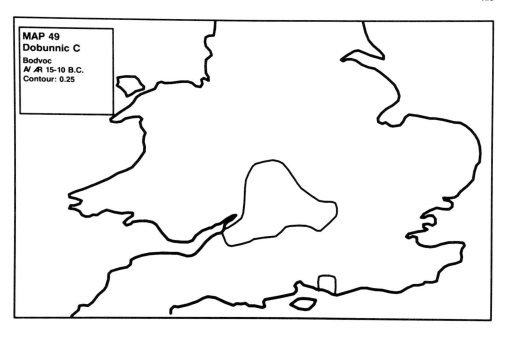

MAP 49
Dobunnic C

Bodvoc
A/ Æ 15-10 B.C.
Contour: 0.25

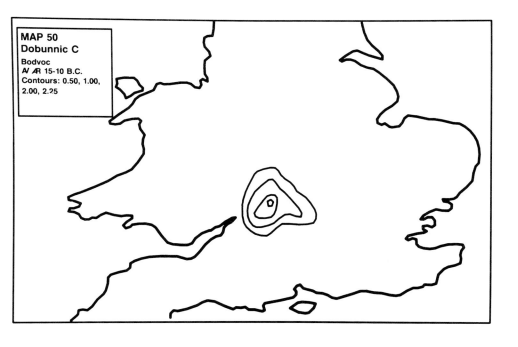

MAP 50
Dobunnic C

Bodvoc
A/ Æ 15-10 B.C.
Contours: 0.50, 1.00,
2.00, 2.25

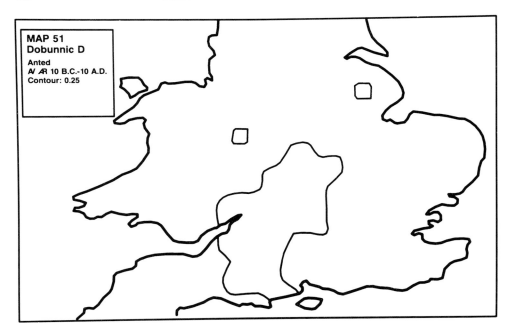

MAP 51
Dobunnic D
Anted
N/ÆR 10 B.C.-10 A.D.
Contour: 0.25

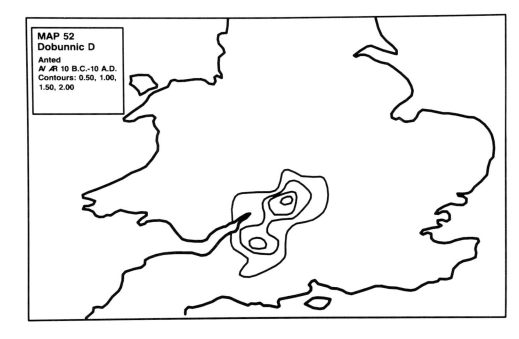

MAP 52
Dobunnic D
Anted
N/ÆR 10 B.C.-10 A.D.
Contours: 0.50, 1.00,
1.50, 2.00

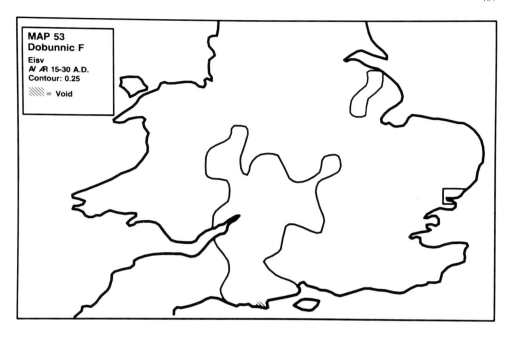

MAP 53
Dobunnic F

Eisv
A/ Æ 15-30 A.D.
Contour: 0.25

▨ = Void

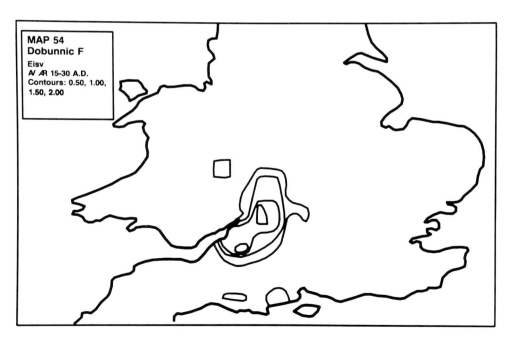

MAP 54
Dobunnic F

Eisv
A/ Æ 15-30 A.D.
Contours: 0.50, 1.00,
1.50, 2.00

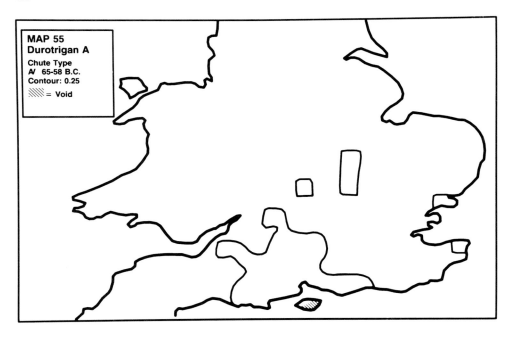

**MAP 55**
**Durotrigan A**

Chute Type
A/  65-58 B.C.
Contour: 0.25

▨ = Void

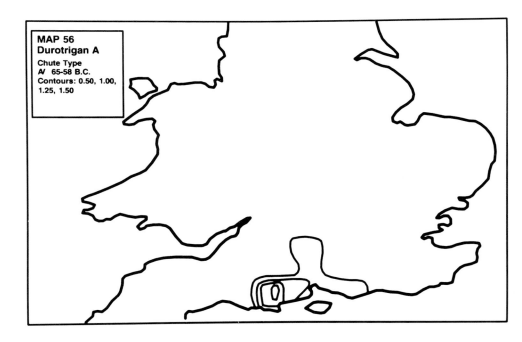

**MAP 56**
**Durotrigan A**

Chute Type
A/  65-58 B.C.
Contours: 0.50, 1.00,
1.25, 1.50

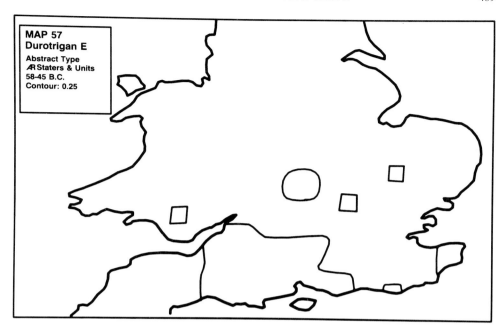

MAP 57
Durotrigan E

Abstract Type
Æ Staters & Units
58–45 B.C.
Contour: 0.25

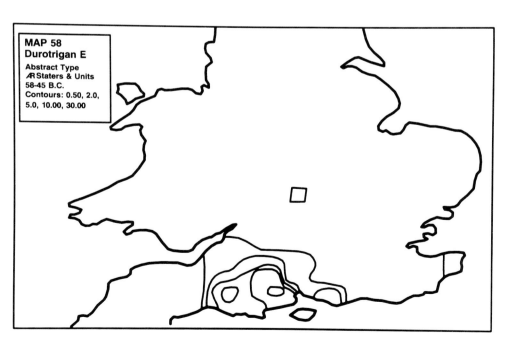

MAP 58
Durotrigan E

Abstract Type
Æ Staters & Units
58–45 B.C.
Contours: 0.50, 2.0,
5.0, 10.00, 30.00

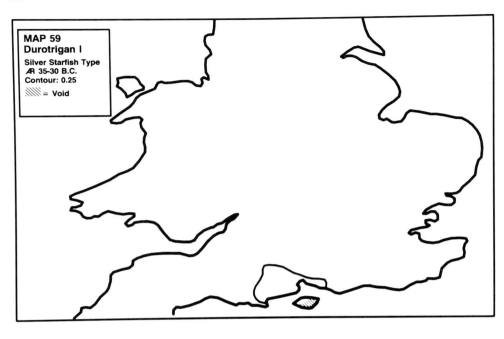

MAP 59
Durotrigan I
Silver Starfish Type
Æ 35–30 B.C.
Contour: 0.25
////// = Void

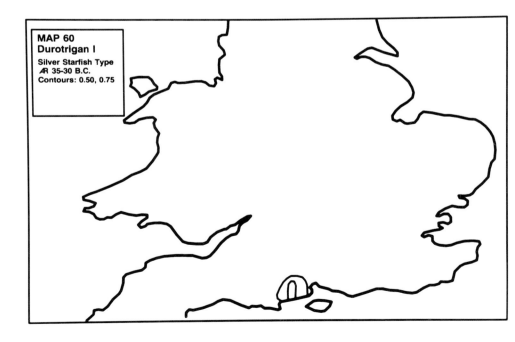

MAP 60
Durotrigan I
Silver Starfish Type
Æ 35–30 B.C.
Contours: 0.50, 0.75

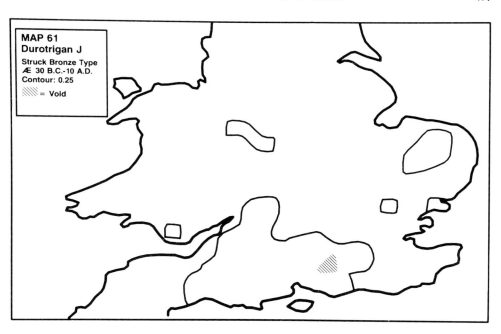

**MAP 61**
**Durotrigan J**

Struck Bronze Type
Æ 30 B.C.-10 A.D.
Contour: 0.25

▨ = Void

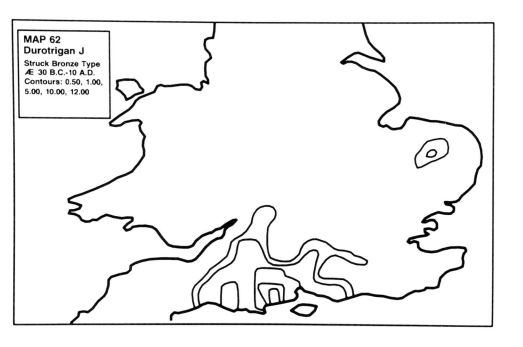

**MAP 62**
**Durotrigan J**

Struck Bronze Type
Æ 30 B.C.-10 A.D.
Contours: 0.50, 1.00,
5.00, 10.00, 12.00

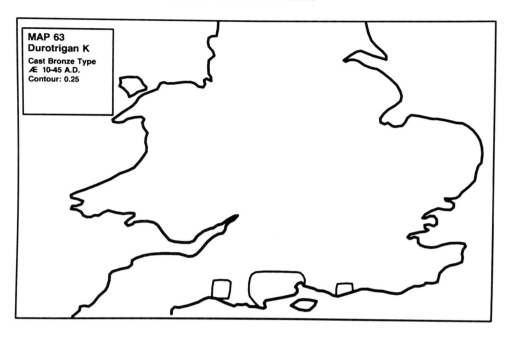

MAP 63
Durotrigan K

Cast Bronze Type
Æ 10–45 A.D.
Contour: 0.25

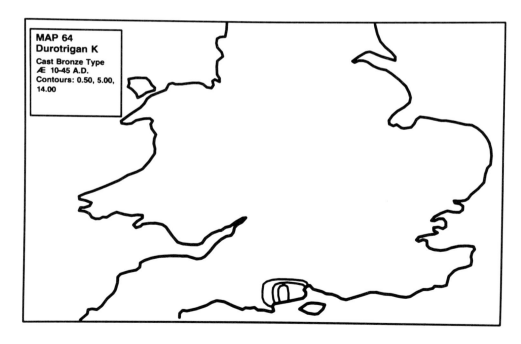

MAP 64
Durotrigan K

Cast Bronze Type
Æ 10–45 A.D.
Contours: 0.50, 5.00,
14.00

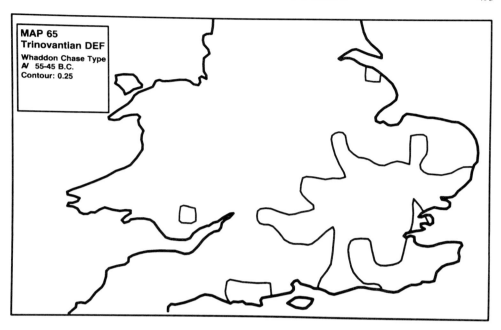

MAP 65
Trinovantian DEF

Whaddon Chase Type
A/ 55–45 B.C.
Contour: 0.25

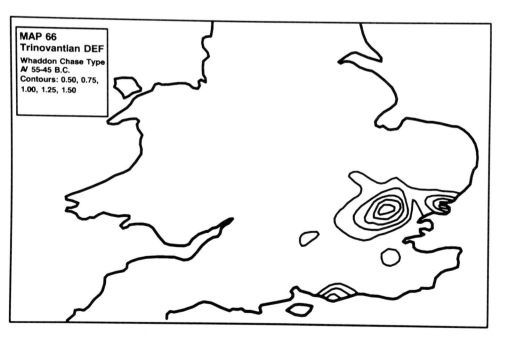

MAP 66
Trinovantian DEF

Whaddon Chase Type
A/ 55–45 B.C.
Contours: 0.50, 0.75,
1.00, 1.25, 1.50

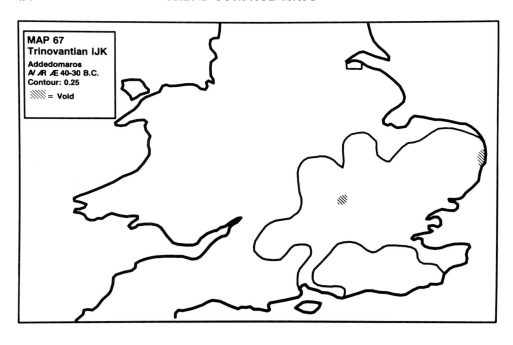

MAP 67
Trinovantian IJK
Addedomaros
N ÆR Æ 40-30 B.C.
Contour: 0.25
= Void

MAP 68
Trinovantian IJK
Addedomaros
N ÆR Æ 40-30 B.C.
Contours: 0.50, 0.75,
1.50, 2.00, 5.00

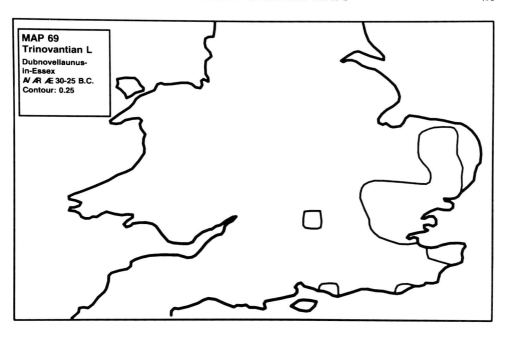

MAP 69
Trinovantian L
Dubnovellaunus-
in-Essex
AV AR AE 30-25 B.C.
Contour: 0.25

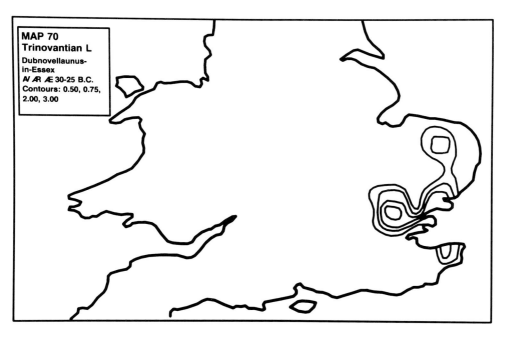

MAP 70
Trinovantian L
Dubnovellaunus-
in-Essex
AV AR AE 30-25 B.C.
Contours: 0.50, 0.75,
2.00, 3.00

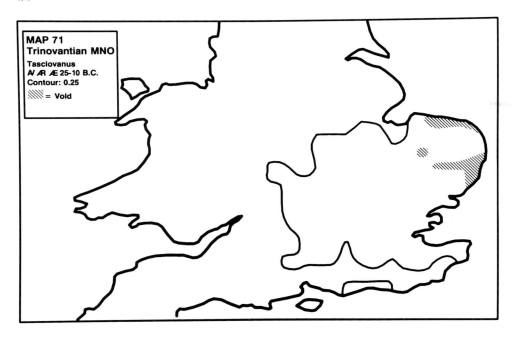

MAP 71
**Trinovantian MNO**
Tasciovanus
Ν ÆR Æ 25-10 B.C.
Contour: 0.25

 = Void

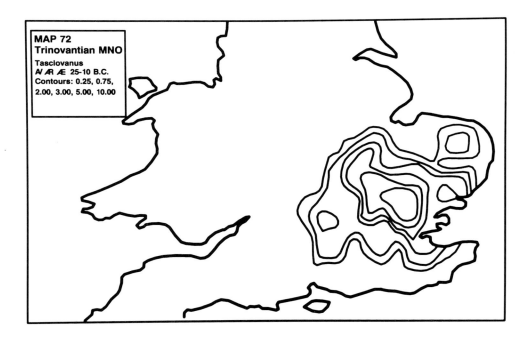

MAP 72
**Trinovantian MNO**
Tasciovanus
Ν ÆR Æ 25-10 B.C.
Contours: 0.25, 0.75,
2.00, 3.00, 5.00, 10.00

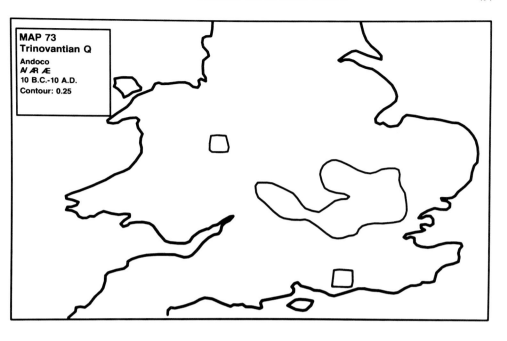

MAP 73
**Trinovantian Q**

Andoco
*N AR AE*
10 B.C.-10 A.D.
**Contour: 0.25**

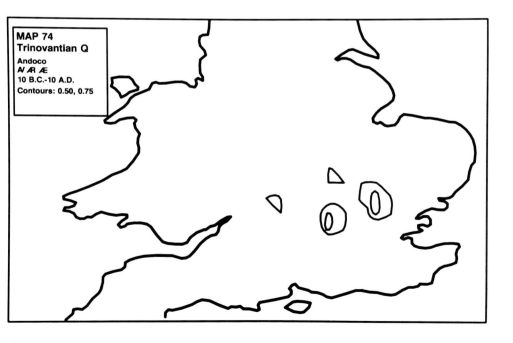

MAP 74
**Trinovantian Q**

Andoco
*N AR AE*
10 B.C.-10 A.D.
**Contours: 0.50, 0.75**

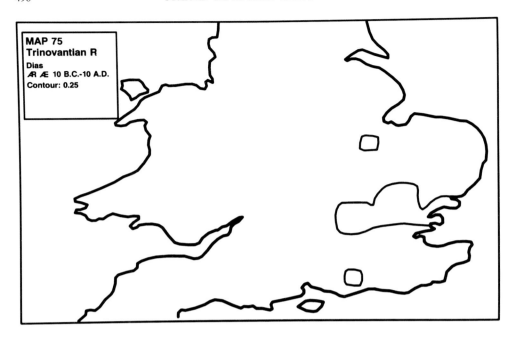

MAP 75
Trinovantian R
Dias
Æ Æ 10 B.C.-10 A.D.
Contour: 0.25

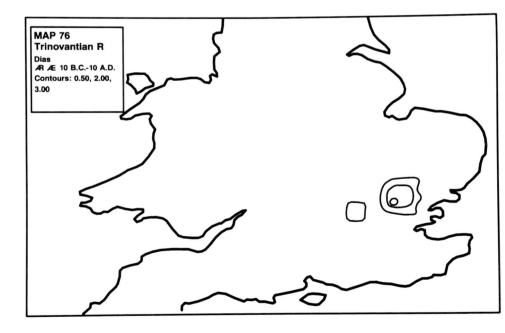

MAP 76
Trinovantian R
Dias
Æ Æ 10 B.C.-10 A.D.
Contours: 0.50, 2.00,
3.00

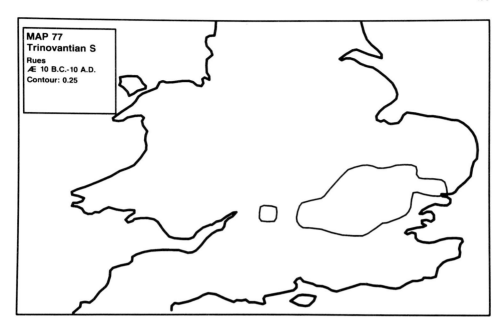

MAP 77
**Trinovantian S**
Rues
Æ 10 B.C.-10 A.D.
Contour: 0.25

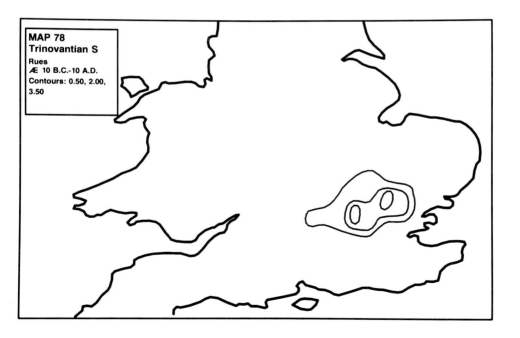

MAP 78
**Trinovantian S**
Rues
Æ 10 B.C.-10 A.D.
Contours: 0.50, 2.00,
3.50

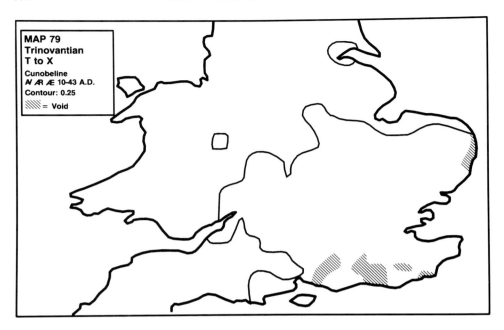

MAP 79
Trinovantian
T to X

Cunobeline
N AR AE 10–43 A.D.
Contour: 0.25

░░░ = Void

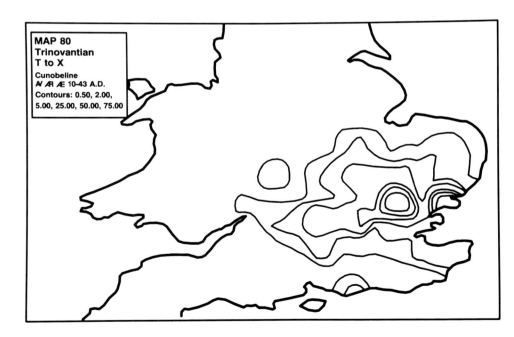

MAP 80
Trinovantian
T to X

Cunobeline
N AR AE 10–43 A.D.
Contours: 0.50, 2.00,
5.00, 25.00, 50.00, 75.00

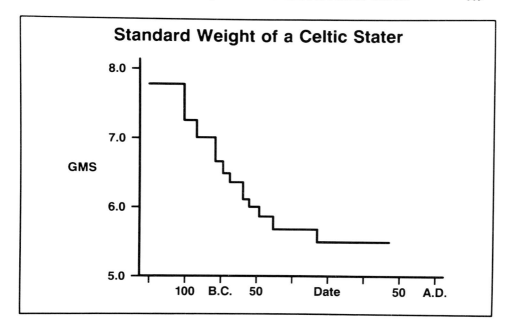

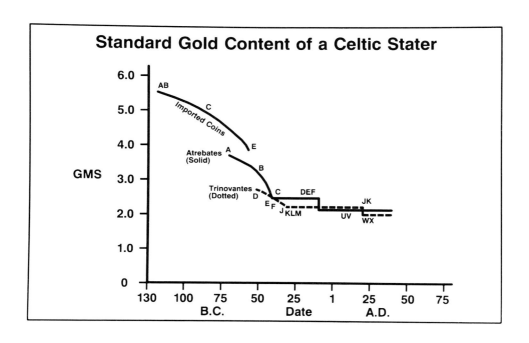

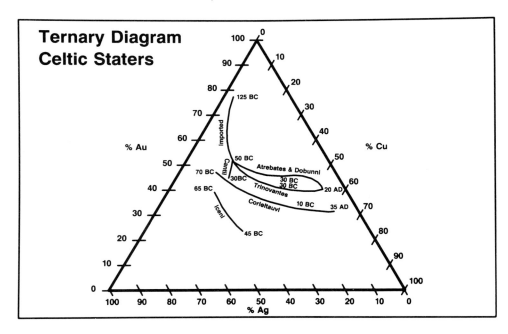

**Ternary Diagram Celtic Staters**

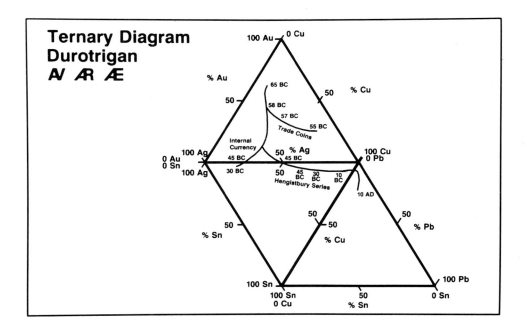

**Ternary Diagram Durotrigan**
**Aʹ ÆR Æ**

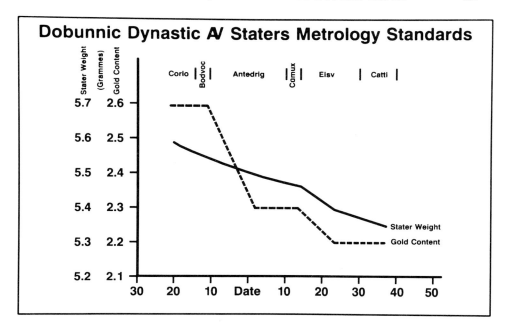

One Æ Unit of DIAS (1882–1), analyzed just before this book went to press, has proven to be made of brass. This coin was likely made from a melted-down Roman coin.

# SELECTED METALLURGICAL/METROLOGICAL DATA

*Imported Coins—Gallo-Belgic*

| Class | A Quarter | A Stater | B Stater | C Stater | E Stater | E Stater |
|---|---|---|---|---|---|---|
| Number | 15–1 | 12–1 | 30–1 | 48–1 | 52–1 | 54–1 |
| Std. Wt. | 1.95 | 7.8 | 7.85 | 6.45 | 6.25 | 6.2 |
| Typical Wt. | 1.4–2.1 | 7.0–7.7 | 7.5–7.9 | 6.2–6.4 | 6.0–6.25 | 6.0–6.2 |
| Wt. this coin | 1.81 | 6.03 | 7.76 | 6.48 | 6.01 | 6.12 |
| Au | 71.54 | 68.96 | 74.52 | 73.46 | 62.50 | 62.76 |
| Ag | 24.25 | 24.10 | 21.57 | 21.65 | 27.99 | 28.01 |
| Cu | 4.00 | 5.79 | 3.04 | 4.76 | 9.36 | 9.12 |
| As | — | — | — | — | — | — |
| Zn | — | 0.06 | 0.23 | Tr | 0.02 | — |
| Pb | 0.14 | 0.05 | 0.02 | 0.07 | 0.02 | 0.03 |
| Sn | — | 0.01 | — | — | 0.03 | — |
| Sb | 0.01 | Tr | 0.01 | — | — | 0.01 |
| Fe | 0.04 | 0.01 | 0.05 | 0.05 | 0.07 | 0.06 |
| Ni | Tr | 0.02 | 0.01 | Tr | Tr | — |
| Co | 0.01 | — | — | — | — | Tr |
| Bi | — | — | — | — | — | — |
| Location | Norwich | Norwich | RDV | Norwich | Norwich | |

*Cantian Coins*

| Class | B Cast Æ | C Cast Æ | D Cast Æ | G Quarter | I Stater |
|---|---|---|---|---|---|
| Number | 110–1 | 112–1 | 129–1 | 147–1 | 157–1 |
| Std. Wt. | — | — | — | — | 5.6 |
| Typical Wt. | c.1.9 | c.1.7 | c.1.6 | 1.3–1.6 | — |
| Wt. this coin | — | — | — | 1.24 | 5.59 |
| Au | — | 0.02 | — | 50.53 | 43.04 |
| Ag | 0.01 | 0.07 | 0.29 | 33.72 | 15.82 |
| Cu | 76.62 | 70.03 | 61.52 | 15.32 | 39.99 |
| As | — | 5.00 | 6.48 | — | — |
| Zn | Tr | 0.06 | — | 0.09 | — |
| Pb | 1.34 | 0.97 | 7.95 | 0.29 | 0.53 |
| Sn | 21.71 | 21.92 | 19.16 | — | 0.61 |
| Sb | 0.01 | 1.68 | 3.99 | 0.02 | 0.08 |
| Fe | 0.11 | 0.09 | 0.31 | 0.02 | — |
| Ni | 0.04 | 0.08 | 0.05 | 0.01 | 0.05 |
| Co | 0.16 | 0.06 | 0.04 | — | Tr |
| Bi | — | 0.02 | 0.21 | — | — |
| Location | Norwich | Norwich | Norwich | Ashm.25 | RDV |

*Atrebatic Coins*

| Class | A | B | C | D | E | F | G | J | K |
|---|---|---|---|---|---|---|---|---|---|
| Number | Stater 200-1 | Stater 210-1 | Stater 350-1 | Stater 363-1 | Quarter 379-1 | Quarter 390-1 | Stater 405-1 | Stater 500-1 | Stater 520-1 |
| Std. Wt. | 6.5 | 5.9 | 5.45 | 5.45 | 1.35 | 1.35 | — | 5.4 | 5.4 |
| Typical Wt. | 6.0-6.5 | 5.2-5.8 | 5.3-5.45 | 5.3-5.45 | c.1.1 | c.1.1 | — | 5.1-5.4 | 5.1-5.4 |
| Wt. this coin | | | | | | | | | |
| Au | 6.36 | 5.95 | 5.46 | 5.41 | 1.13 | 1.15 | 5.21 | 5.30 | 5.28 |
| Ag | 58.28 | 55.89 | 46.78 | 45.31 | 46.06 | 50.10 | 48.17 | 40.77 | 41.47 |
| Cu | 30.71 | 29.54 | 21.97 | 18.72 | 15.07 | 13.61 | 14.23 | 8.54 | 11.50 |
| As | 10.91 | 13.83 | 33.76 | 35.31 | 38.17 | 36.05 | 37.35 | 50.38 | 46.58 |
| Zn | — | — | — | — | — | — | — | — | — |
| Pb | 0.06 | 0.06 | 0.05 | 0.06 | 0.13 | Tr | 0.02 | 0.04 | 0.04 |
| Sn | | 0.05 | 0.06 | 0.14 | 0.05 | 0.09 | 0.11 | 0.02 | 0.03 |
| Sb | Tr | 0.22 | 0.27 | 0.39 | 0.02 | 0.04 | | 0.01 | 0.15 |
| Fe | 0.01 | Tr | 0.02 | 0.04 | 0.47 | 0.06 | 0.07 | 0.02 | 0.07 |
| Ni | 0.01 | 0.06 | 0.02 | 0.02 | Tr | Tr | Tr | 0.06 | 0.14 |
| Co | Tr | | 0.02 | 0.02 | 0.01 | 0.01 | 0.02 | 0.12 | 0.02 |
| Bi | — | — | 0.02 | — | — | 0.01 | 0.02 | Tr | Tr |
| Location | Ashm.3 | RDV | RDV | Ashm.44 | Ashm.49 | Ashm.46 | NMW.C238 | Ashm.54 | Ashm.51 |

*Icenian Coins*          *Corieltauvian Coins*

| Class | A Stater | A Stater | A Stater | B Stater | D Stater | P Stater |
|---|---|---|---|---|---|---|
| Number | 610–1 | 610–2 | 800 | 804–3 | 815–1 | 978–1 |
| Std. Wt. | — | — | 6.4 | 6.1 | 5.7 | 5.4 |
| Typical Wt. | 5.7–6.2 | 5.7–6.2 | 5.7–6.4 | 5.6–6.1 | 5.2–5.7 | 5.0–5.4 |
| Wt. this coin | — | 5.41 | — | 6.12 | 5.57 | 5.34 |
| Au | 39.44 | 22.93 | 41.22 | 46.89 | 32.53 | 31.46 |
| Ag | 45.52 | 44.72 | 39.02 | 40.71 | 19.68 | 9.39 |
| Cu | 14.91 | 32.08 | 19.60 | 11.76 | 47.36 | 59.09 |
| As | — | — | — | — | — | — |
| Zn | — | Tr | — | 0.02 | Tr | 0.04 |
| Pb | 0.12 | 0.05 | 0.09 | 0.23 | 0.07 | — |
| Sn | — | — | — | — | — | — |
| Sb | Tr | 0.02 | 0.01 | — | 0.03 | 0.01 |
| Fe | 0.01 | Tr | 0.01 | 0.01 | — | 0.01 |
| Ni | 0.02 | 0.01 | 0.03 | — | 0.01 | 0.01 |
| Co | 0.01 | 0.02 | Tr | 0.01 | — | 0.01 |
| Bi | — | — | — | — | — | — |
| Location | NMW.C058 | RDV | NMW.C076 | RDV | Ashm.74 | Ashm.72 |

*Dobunnic Coins*

| Class | A Stater | B Stater | C Stater | D Stater | G Stater |
|---|---|---|---|---|---|
| Number | 1000–1 | 1035–1 | 1052–1 | 1069–1 | 1130–1 |
| Std. Wt. | 5.55 | 5.6 | 5.55 | 5.5 | 5.35 |
| Typical Wt. | 5.4–5.55 | 5.2–5.6 | 5.3–5.5 | 5.0–5.4 | 5.1–5.3 |
| Wt. this coin | 5.57 | 5.37 | 5.48 | 5.37 | 5.35 |
| Au | 45.93 | 48.12 | 45.53 | 40.51 | 40.95 |
| Ag | 26.89 | 13.31 | 4.92 | 7.23 | 11.00 |
| Cu | 27.28 | 38.39 | 47.90 | 52.54 | 47.87 |
| As | — | — | — | — | — |
| Zn | Tr | Tr | — | Tr | Tr |
| Pb | 0.08 | 0.05 | — | 0.03 | 0.05 |
| Sn | 0.03 | — | 0.05 | 0.03 | 0.02 |
| Sb | 0.06 | 0.05 | 0.03 | 0.03 | 0.06 |
| Fe | 0.03 | 0.02 | 0.50 | 0.01 | 0.01 |
| Ni | 0.02 | 0.04 | 0.03 | 0.02 | 0.03 |
| Co | 0.01 | — | — | 0.01 | 0.01 |
| Bi | — | — | — | — | — |
| Location | Ashm.37 | Ashm.39 | RDV | Ashm.41 | Ashm.38 |

## Durotrigan Coins

| Class | Number | Std. Wt. | Typical Wt. | Wt. this coin | Au | Ag | Cu | Sn | As | Zn | Pb | Sb | Fe | Ni | Co | Bi | Location |
|---|---|---|---|---|---|---|---|---|---|---|---|---|---|---|---|---|---|
| A | Stater 1205 | 6.2 | 5.9–6.2 | 5.13 | 55.16 | 35.76 | 9.01 | — | Tr | 0.03 | — | 0.01 | — | — | Tr | — | Ashm.2 |
| A | Quarter 1229-1 | — | — | 1.31 | 55.72 | 30.31 | 13.48 | — | 0.06 | 0.27 | — | 0.02 | 0.11 | 0.01 | — | — | Ashm.30 |
| A | Stater 1205-1 | 6.2 | 5.9–6.2 | 6.15 | 35.93 | 49.81 | 14.11 | — | — | 0.08 | — | 0.02 | 0.02 | Tr | 0.01 | — | RDV |
| A | Quarter 1225-1 | — | — | — | 36.38 | 39.86 | 23.70 | — | — | 0.01 | — | Tr | Tr | 0.01 | 0.01 | — | NMW. C539 |
| A | Stater 1205-5 | 6.2 | 5.9–6.2 | 6.03 | 30.61 | 46.35 | 22.94 | — | — | 0.08 | — | Tr | — | Tr | 0.01 | — | RDV |
| C | Stater 1210-1 | 6.2 | — | 5.98 | 36.19 | 31.83 | 31.62 | — | — | Tr | — | — | — | 0.01 | 0.01 | — | RDV |
| D | Stater 1215-1 | — | c.5.1 | 5.08 | 26.98 | 14.77 | 54.98 | 2.99 | 0.03 | 0.13 | — | 0.06 | 0.03 | 0.03 | 0.02 | — | RDV |
| E | Stater 1235-1 | — | 4.9–5.8 | — | 9.46 | 54.48 | 35.60 | — | 0.33 | 0.09 | — | 0.04 | — | — | — | Tr | NMW. C563 |
| E | Quarter 1242-1 | — | c.1.1 | — | 9.50 | 69.77 | 19.77 | — | Tr | 0.02 | 0.34 | 0.45 | 0.06 | — | Tr | 0.08 | NMW. C551 |
| E | Stater 1235-1 | — | 4.9–5.8 | — | 1.10 | 69.38 | 28.72 | — | 0.09 | — | 0.66 | — | 0.02 | 0.02 | — | Tr | NMW. C531 |
| E | Stater 1235-1 | — | 4.9–5.8 | 5.35 | — | 0.66 | 78.13 | 20.18 | 0.03 | 0.06 | 0.64 | 0.28 | Tr | — | Tr | 0.02 | Ashm. D6 |
| E | Quarter 1242-1 | — | c.1.1 | — | — | 0.22 | 80.64 | 14.71 | 0.01 | 0.18 | 1.15 | 2.49 | 0.47 | 0.07 | 0.02 | 0.04 | NMW. C545 |
| E | Unit 1270-1 | — | c.1.2 | — | — | 0.38 | 80.16 | 15.19 | 0.05 | 0.68 | 3.42 | 0.04 | 0.03 | 0.04 | — | 0.01 | NMW. C549 |
| E | Stater 1235-1 | — | 4.9–5.8 | 4.17 | — | 0.16 | 41.07 | 55.96 | 0.08 | 0.09 | 0.50 | 2.05 | 0.21 | Tr | — | 0.02 | Ashm. D12 |
| E | Quarter 1242-1 | — | c.1.1 | — | — | 0.44 | 45.56 | 52.32 | 0.09 | 0.03 | 1.17 | — | 0.30 | 0.01 | — | 0.07 | NMW. C530 |
| E | Stater 1235-1 | — | 4.9–5.8 | 4.25 | — | 0.19 | 24.07 | 69.89 | 0.01 | 0.07 | 0.24 | 4.99 | 0.48 | 0.01 | — | 0.04 | Ashm. D16 |
| J | Stater 1290-1 | — | c.3.4 | — | — | 0.07 | 13.02 | 83.89 | 0.05 | 0.18 | 0.23 | 2.28 | 0.25 | 0.01 | 0.01 | 0.02 | NMW. C534 |
| J | Stater 1345-1 | — | c.3.4 | — | — | Tr | 2.39 | 93.78 | — | 0.05 | 0.08 | 3.45 | 0.08 | 0.03 | 0.02 | 0.03 | NMW. C535 |
| K | Stater | — | 2.2–2.5 | — | — | 0.05 | 0.08 | 80.48 | — | 0.44 | 6.52 | 12.11 | 0.14 | 0.13 | 0.03 | 0.01 | NMW. C537 |

*Trinovantian Coins*

| Class | B | D | E | E | F | J | K | L | M | U | V | W | X |
|---|---|---|---|---|---|---|---|---|---|---|---|---|---|
| Number | Stater 1458-1 | Stater 1472-1 | Stater 1487-1 | Stater 1491-1 | Stater 1507-1 | Stater 1620-1 | Stater 1635-1 | Stater 1650-1 | Stater 1680-1 | Stater 1925-1 | Stater 1933-1 | Stater 2010-1 | Stater 2029-1 |
| Std. Wt. | — | 5.9 | — | — | — | 5.6 | 5.6 | 5.6 | 5.55 | 5.6 | 5.6 | 5.4 | 5.4 |
| Typical Wt. | c.6.4 | 5.7-5.9 | 5.4-5.9 | 5.4-5.9 | 5.4-5.9 | 5.2-56 | 5.2-5.6 | 5.2-5.6 | 5.3-5.55 | 5.2-5.5 | 5.1-5.5 | 5.2-5.4 | 5.2-5.4 |
| Wt. this coin | 6.39 | 5.73 | 5.25 | 5.52 | 5.47 | 5.57 | 5.49 | 5.44 | 5.47 | 5.27 | 5.42 | 5.37 | 5.30 |
| Au | 36.24 | 47.05 | 42.21 | 38.70 | 39.65 | 40.19 | 48.97 | 39.29 | 40.06 | 40.29 | 41.60 | 39.93 | 39.44 |
| Ag | 43.66 | 36.89 | 32.73 | 27.86 | 7.67 | 11.69 | 9.99 | 20.00 | 20.93 | 11.12 | 11.86 | 16.84 | 22.49 |
| Cu | 20.22 | 15.87 | 24.95 | 32.49 | 52.50 | 47.86 | 40.76 | 39.91 | 38.48 | 48.19 | 46.21 | 42.91 | 37.88 |
| As | — | — | — | — | — | — | — | — | — | — | — | — | — |
| Zn | Tr | 0.04 | — | 0.04 | 0.05 | 0.09 | 0.07 | 0.08 | 0.01 | 0.06 | — | 0.05 | — |
| Pb | 0.14 | 0.11 | 0.05 | 0.31 | 0.01 | 0.07 | 0.09 | 0.24 | 0.11 | 0.09 | 0.07 | 0.13 | 0.14 |
| Sn | — | — | — | 0.21 | Tr | — | 0.04 | 0.34 | 0.07 | 0.04 | 0.16 | — | — |
| Sb | 0.01 | Tr | 0.04 | 0.33 | 0.03 | 0.05 | 0.02 | 0.08 | 0.14 | 0.08 | 0.07 | 0.14 | 0.05 |
| Fe | 0.02 | 0.02 | — | — | 0.02 | 0.01 | 0.03 | 0.01 | 0.01 | 0.04 | 0.03 | 0.01 | — |
| Ni | Tr | 0.02 | 0.02 | 0.02 | 0.06 | 0.08 | 0.03 | 0.03 | 0.02 | 0.02 | 0.02 | 0.02 | 0.02 |
| Co | Tr | — | — | 0.01 | 0.01 | — | — | 0.01 | 0.01 | — | — | — | — |
| Bi | — | — | — | — | — | — | — | — | — | — | — | — | — |
| Location | Ashm.1 | Ashm.18 | Ashm.20 | Ashm.15 | Ashm.16 | Ashm.71 | Ashm.69 | Ashm.56 | RDV | Ashm.67 | Ashm.64 | Ashm.65 | Ashm.62 |

# ANCIENT BRITISH HOARDS

There are 104 recorded 'hoards' of Ancient British coins, though not all of them were intentionally concealed treasures, or casual losses. Some are temple offerings, collected over a long period of time—similar to 'wishing-well' deposits—and others are merely coins found during archaeological excavations.

The hoards are presented in two ways. First, they are summarized in tables, so their contents can be compared. Second, each hoard is listed in a master list and its contents given in detail.

The hoards are summarized in ten tables as follows:

Table 1 (Early Hoards)—These are deposits of imported coins, sometimes with early British types. The latest coins in these hoards are from the Gallic War period.

Table 2 (Cast Bronze Hoards)—These include cast bronze coins from Kent and Essex. They generally do not include other types. Some could have been votive offerings—several were found along the Thames—others represent scrap metal collected for re-use. The Snettisham I Hoard (no. 64) is included for comparison as a probable scrap metal collection.

Table 3 (Coastal Mixed Hoards)—These include coins from several tribes, and are usually found near coastal sites. They may indicate trading patterns along the coast.

Table 4 (Interior Mixed Hoards)—These have coins from several tribes, but are found inland. They are sometimes found in suspected border areas and may indicate trading patterns. The Snettisham II Hoard (no. 102) is included for comparison, it could have been placed on the Coastal Mixed Hoard table, instead.

The last six tables are 'tribal hoards'—ones containing coins from a single tribe for the most part:

Table 5 (Atrebatic Hoards)

Table 6 (Icenian Hoards)—The silver hoards were mostly deposited during the Boudiccan Revolt of A.D. 61.

Table 7 (Corieltauvian Hoards)

Table 8 (Dobunnic Hoards)

Table 9 (Durotrigan Hoards)—Most of these were deposited sometime after the Gallic War. One small group, containing only gold coins, was deposited in the early War years.

Table 10 (Trinovantian Hoards)—One temple-offering assemblage is given for comparison here, the Harlow Temple finds (no. 98).

Not every hoard is included in the tables; however, all are listed in the master list. This was constructed using the list in Mack's Coinage of Ancient Britain, third edition, as a starting point. However, several hoards were re-appraised, and many were added using information given in Haslegrove's 1978 and 1982 Gazetteers, a paper presented at the Royal Numismatic Society, and numerous reports from archaeologists.

Several more were reconstructed by the author from statistical analyses of coin dealer price-lists, auction catalogues and bourse activity, notably the Wanborough (no. 95) and Badbury-Shapwick (no. 93) finds (130). The Cast Bronzes in the Snettisham I Hoard (no. 64) were also re-evaluated by the author. The catalogue numbers and classifications given are the ones used in this book—reports of earlier hoards have been converted to the new system using the Concordance.

The hoards provide insight into the 'ten themes', as do the Trend Surface Maps and the Metallurgical/Metrological Data.


## THEME 1—THE 'THAMES MOUTH' DISTRIBUTION

The Early Hoards contain most of the deposits with Gallo-Belgic A, B, and C—the coins which display the 'Thames Mouth Distribution' (see maps 1 to 6). These hoards also include the earliest British-made staters.

The Cast Bronze Hoards contain only bronzes, and do not include gold types. The cast bronzes also display the Thames Mouth Distribution (see maps 9 to 12). It is somewhat surprising the hoards lack Gallo-Belgic A, B, and C types, but this may have something to do with the way the hoards were put together. The Early Hoards may have shunned the bronzes because they were worth little, and the Cast Bronze Hoards may have shunned the gold coins as too valuable for votive or scrap-metal deposits.

The Snettisham I and II Hoards (nos. 64 and 102) are unique—difficult to fit in with the general pattern—though Snettisham I can be explained as a collection of different kinds of scrap metal.

Later deposits, those containing British types struck during or after the Gallic War (see the Coastal Mixed and Interior Mixed Hoards) do not include the earliest imported coins. The Harpsden Hoard (no. 80), an Early Hoard, is the only one with both Gallo-Belgic A and E together, and the Clacton II Hoard (no. 49) is the only one with Gallo-Belgic A and later British types—hardly proof of a late date for Gallo-Belgic A imports. Consequently, when the Thames Mouth Distribution was replaced by the restricted distributions after the Gallic War, the earlier imports were no longer in circulation.


## THEME 2—DUROTRIGAN INTERACTION

There is some hoard evidence to demonstrate the inter-tribal ties of the Durotriges before and during the Gallic War.

Two mixed hoards suggest Durotrigan trading ties. Two Durotrigan E staters were found at Mt. Batten (no. 13), and a Durotrigan A stater appeared in the Whaddon Chase Hoard (no. 21).

Several Durotrigan hoards, particularly the ones containing the early gold and silver staters, were found in Hampshire. These findspots would be on the border of, or just inside, Atrebatic territory. Although several of these hoards also contained struck bronzes, the identification of these is always problematical—they may have been forgeries of the earlier silver staters instead.

A trade zone has been identified between the Atrebates/Regni and the Durotriges, based on trend surface evidence. This is discussed under Theme 4, below.


## THEME 3—DUROTRIGAN ISOLATION

The later Durotrigan silver coins (Durotrigan F, G, H and I) have not appeared in hoards outside Durotrigan territory. The Durotrigan J types do occur, but are always difficult to distinguish from forged silver staters, and so dating them is problematical. One was found at Bagendon (no. 69), and another at Harlow Temple (no. 98). The Holdenhurst Hoard (no. 50), containing late Durotrigan cast bronzes (and Roman coins), was found to the northwest of Hengistbury head—well within Durotrigan territory.

Generally, hoards found in Durotrigan territory do not contain the coins of other tribes. Dobunnic coins were found at Hengistbury (no. 52)—probably attesting to the Stour River trade-route. Significantly, virtually no inscribed gold coins of any tribe have been found in hoards from Durotrigan territory.


## THEME 4—TRADE NETWORKS DURING THE GALLIC WAR

The Trend surface maps identified the Trinovantes/Catuvellauni, Cantii, and Atrebates/Regni as the major trading tribes in Britain during the Gallic War. First they imported Gallo-Belgic E staters—these appear around the Thames mouth just at the outset of the War. Later, they struck their own staters. Atrebatic B and Trinovantian D, E and F soon appear in quantity. These staters were the wartime coins of Celtic Britain. They occur together in the Scartho Hoard (no. 31—Coastal Mixed), and the Whaddon Chase Hoard (no. 21—Interior Mixed).

Snettisham II (no. 102—Interior Mixed) contained both Trinovantian F and Atrebatic B, along with the wartime Icenian A staters. The Icenian E silver units—dated after the war—may actually date earlier than the Icenian C types, because the style is quite abstract. However, reappraising the date of these is not warranted on the basis of a single hoard.

The Wonersh Hoard (no. 20—Interior Mixed) contained Atrebatic B and Trinovantian G. It also contained Cantian H and I, struck during the thirties B.C.—thus the hoard was deposited a bit late to offer evidence of Gallic War trade. However, Trinovantian G is a light weight contemporary of Trinovantian F, and is believed to be a trade coin (it usually occurs outside Trinovantian territory). The hoard may just show the last flickering embers of the trading networks before coin circulation became more restricted.

The Scartho Hoard (no. 31) suggests just how far the trading networks extended: in this case, nearly to Yorkshire. Atrebatic coins were finding their way to Colchester—witness the Marks Tey Hoard (no. 6) and Harlow Temple offerings (no. 98), both containing Gallo-Belgic E and Atrebatic B. Atrebatic B staters appeared as far west as Cornwall in the Penzance Hoard (no. 76).

In general, the evidence of the maps—linking the circulation of Gallo-Belgic E, Atrebatic B and Trinovantian D, E, and F—is supported by the hoards. These coins are found together, or with other coins of the Gallic War period for the most part.

The concept of an Exchange Zone or Gateway—a place where goods passed between two tribes—is suggested by the hoards and single finds found around the River Test. A number of hoards, found on either side of the river, suggest a trade zone existed between the Durotriges and the Atrebates into the early years of the Gallic War.

The Durotrigan coins found in Hampshire (the ones around the River Test) map out the trade zone between the two tribes with great clarity. All the coins are prewar or wartime types. A single Atrebatic A stater was found in the Ringwood II Hoard (no. 82), showing the Atrebatic link in this area.

It is tempting to think the hoards represent coins 'trapped' in the exchange zone just as it was closed down (131). The hoards contain Durotrigan coins for the most part, suggesting it was the Atrebates who closed the frontier. Few Atrebatic coins are represented—holders of Atrebatic coins had no reason to conceal them. It would have been Durotrigan traders seeking goods who would have been affected.

The Romans would have wanted to prevent the Durotriges from supplying the Venetii prior to Caesar's Venetic campaign. Durotrigan D type staters found in the Cheriton Hoard suggest the Durotriges had been obtaining goods in Atrebatic territory. The great outpouring of Atrebatic B staters occurred just after this—perhaps the Atrebates received payment for closing the frontier.

The later Atrebatic hoards from the region—Alresford (no. 41), Andover (no. 94) and Finkley Down (no. 87), seem to add to the evidence. These contained mostly dynastic coins and would have been deposited after the trade had been severed for many years. They may be evidence for unsettled relations on the border, rather than trade. The territory around the border, previously an Exchange Zone, had by this time become impermeable—coins no longer flowed through it in either direction.

There are only hints the events occurred in this way. It is important to keep in mind other interpretations are possible—for example, the Alresford Hoard (no. 41) could have been deposited during the Claudian Invasion. The 'Border Closing' interpretation must be considered a hypothesis.

## THEME 5—TRACKWAYS IN BRITAIN

Two trackways were identified by the trend surface maps: the ones along the Jurassic ridge and the River Stour. Neither is shown with any clarity in the hoard evidence, but there are some hints for the Stour.

Four hoards point to the Stour trackway. Dobunnic coins appeared in the Hengistbury I Hoard (no. 52), at the southern end of the trade route between the Durotriges and the Dobunni. A Dobunnic hoard was found at Sherbourne (no. 47), about 10 kilometres from the river—this would have been in Durotrigan territory, or on the border between the two tribes. A hoard of Durotrigan coins was found at Okeford Fitzpaine (no. 3), about 2 kilometres from the river. The Badbury-Shapwick Hoard (no. 93) would also have been found 2 kilometres from the river—if the findspot is reliable.

There is virtually no hint of the trackway along the Jurassic ridge in the hoard evidence. Corieltauvian coins do not occur in Dobunnic or Durotrigan hoards. Neither Durotrigan nor Dobunnic coins occur in Corieltauvian hoards—and none of the Corieltauvian hoards was found near the Jurassic ridge. The Whaddon Chase Hoard (no. 21) contained two Corieltauvian coins and one Durotrigan, but this really offers no evidence. One Durotrigan coin was found in the Bagendon excavations (no. 69), this would have been near the trackway along the Jurassic ridge, but the find offers little evidence.

## THEME 6—RESTRICTED DISTRIBUTIONS AFTER THE GALLIC WAR

The trend surface maps indicate the post Gallic War types tend to stay within tribal territories, by, say 40 B.C. The hoards begin to show limited distributions about the same time.

Ignoring the problematic struck bronzes, the postwar Durotrigan coins do not appear in hoards outside Durotrigan territory. The restriction had begun to set in well before 40 B.C.

After 40 B.C., Atrebatic and Trinovantian types no longer appear in hoards together (see Tables 5 and 10). The Savernake Hoard (no. 39), the only exception, is felt to be two hoards mixed together. Even Harlow Temple (no. 98) lacks Atrebatic types after B.

The Atrebatic hoards are restricted to Sussex and Hampshire and they do not stray over to Durotrigan territory. Trinovantian hoards are refined to Trinovantian territory, as well.

Dobunnic hoards similarly stay within the territory of the Dobunni. The Icenian and Corieltauvian hoards appear to be from the period of the Roman invasion, and do not offer insight into the period from 40 B.C. to the close of the millennium. The hoards in general show ample evidence of the restricted coin distributions after the Gallic War. By 40 B.C., the trading networks of the War years had broken down to the extent coins no longer flowed between tribes at the rates they previously had.

## THEME 7—TRINOVANTIAN/CATUVELLAUNIAN EXPANSION

Because Trinovantian hoards generally appear well inside Trinovantian territory after 40 B.C., they offer little insight into the expansion of the tribe's influence. The expansion was first seen in Cantian and Icenian territory, with finds of single coins, but the hoards offer little supporting evidence. Only the Tunstall Hoard (no. 37), found in Kent, and the Lakenheath Hoard (no. 72), found in Norfolk, contain late coins of Cunobeline.

## THEME 8—ATREBATIC/REGNAN DISFAVOUR AFTER THE GALLIC WAR

There is no insight offered by the hoards.

## THEME 9—ATREBATIC/REGNAN INCURSION INTO KENT

There is no evidence in the hoards for an Atrebatic incursion in Kent. Atrebatic H (Eppillus in Kent) coins are not found in hoards, and there are no hoards from Kent in the period of interest. Atrebatic H coins are generally extremely rare, so the lack of evidence is not too surprising.

## THEME 10—DOBUNNIC RULERS

The small number of Dobunnic hoards offers little evidence for the order of Dobunnic rulers. The very large hoard of Corio staters found at Farnborough, Avon (no. 88) suggests these were the only types in circulation when the hoard was assembled—thus the first inscribed type could have been Corio. However, Corio staters could have been selected specifically from a wider range of types, or the coins may have been new from the mint, so the hoard offers little real proof.

## TABLE 1 *Early Hoards*

| Class | 2 Carnbrae | 5 Haverhill | 7 Cainmuir | 27 Ryarsh | 40 Folkestone I | 45 Clacton I | 53 Higham |
|---|---|---|---|---|---|---|---|
| Gallo-Belgic | | | | | | | |
| A | 5 | | | | | | |
| B | 5 | | | | | | |
| C | | c.50 | | 1 | | 4 | 11 |
| D | 2 | | | | | | |
| E | | | | 6–8 | 6 | 32 | |
| Atrebatic | | | | | | | |
| A | 4 | | | | | 5 | |
| B | | | | | | | |
| Trinovantian | | | | | | | |
| B | | | | | | 83 | |
| Other | 1 N Quarter Uncertain | | 40+ G–B XB | | | | |

| Class | 56 Westerham | 61 Weybourne | 68 Grimsby | 75 Gunnersby | 80 Harpsden | 81 Southend-on-Sea | 82 Ringwood II |
|---|---|---|---|---|---|---|---|
| Gallo-Belgic | | | | | | | |
| A | 1 | | | | 1 | | |
| B | | | | | | | |
| C | 1 | | | | | | |
| D | | | | | | | 1 |
| E | | 12+ | 4 | | 16 | 33 | |
| Atrebatic | | | | | | | |
| A | 12 | | | | | | 1 |
| B | | | | 5 | | | |
| Trinovantian | | | | | | | |
| B | | | | | | | |
| Other | | | | | | 43 N Baiocasses | |

## TABLE 2 *Cast Bronze Hoards*

| Class | 4 Lenham Heath | 24 Birchington | 29 Brentwood | 30 St James's Park | 32 Braughing | 54 Hammersmith | 63 Canterbury |
|---|---|---|---|---|---|---|---|
| Gallo-Belgic | | | | | | | |
| A | | | | | | | |
| C | | | | | | | |
| D | | | | | | | |
| Cantian | | | | | | | |
| A to D | Many | 600+ | 266+ | Many | 4 | 4 | |
| E | | | | | | | 13+ |
| Trinovantian | | | | | | | |
| A | | | | | | | |

| Class | 64 Snettisham I | 65 Sunbury-on-Thames | 74 Bardwell | 91 Folkestone II | 92 West Thurrock | 103 Hengistbury II |
|---|---|---|---|---|---|---|
| Gallo-Belgic | | | | | | |
| A | 7 | | | | | |
| C | 4 | | | | | |
| D | 1 | | | | | |
| Cantian | | | | | | |
| A to D | 116+ | c.360 | | | | 8 |
| E | | | Some | | | |
| Trinovantian | | | | | | |
| A | | | | 100–300 | c.2,000 | |

TABLE 3 *Coastal Mixed Hoards*

| Class | 12 Portsmouth | 13 Mt. Batten | 18 Bognor | 31 Scartho | 52 Hengistbury I | 59 Birling |
|---|---|---|---|---|---|---|
| Gallo-Belgic | | | | | | |
| D | | | 7 | | | |
| E | | | | 3 | | 1 |
| Cantian | | | | | | |
| F | | | 1 | | 1 | |
| H | | | | | | 1 |
| J | | | | | | 1 |
| Atrebatic | | | | | | |
| B | | | 7+ | 1 | | 1 |
| C | | | 1 | | | |
| E | | | 1 | | | |
| I | | | 2 | | | |
| Icenian | | | | | | |
| H | 1 | | | | | |
| I | 1 | | | | | |
| Dobunnic | | | | | | |
| A | | 5 | | | | |
| BDG | | 1 | | | 11+ | |
| F | | | | | 1 | |
| Durotrigan | | | | | | |
| A | | | | | 1 | |
| E | | 2 | | | Many | |
| I | | | | | 1 | |
| J | | | | | c.1308 | |
| K | | | | | c.1660 | |
| THIN | 1 | | | | | |
| Trinovantian | | | | | | |
| DEF | | | | 3 | 1 | |
| G | | | | | | 1 |

TABLE 4 *Interior Mixed Hoards*

| Class | 20 Wonersh | 21 Whaddon Chase | 39 Savernake | 43 Wallingford | 102 Snettisham II |
|---|---|---|---|---|---|
| Gallo-Belgic | | | | | |
| E | | 1 | | | |
| F | | 1 | | | |
| Cantian | | | | | |
| G | 6 | | | | |
| I | 3 | | | | |
| Atrebatic | | | | | |
| B | 1 | 72+ | | Some | 9 |
| L | | | 5 | | |
| Icenian | | | | | |
| A | | | | | 42 |
| E | | | | | 3 |
| Dobunnic | | | | | |
| A | | | | Some | |
| DEFHJV | | | | Some | |
| Corieltauvian | | | | | |
| B | | 2 | | | |
| Durotrigan | | | | | |
| A | | 1 | | | |
| Trinovantian | | | | | |
| D | | 226+ | | | |
| F | | | | | 21 |
| G | 19 | | | | |
| H | | | Many | | |
| Other | | | Roman: Tiberius (clearly two finds) | | 7 Æ New types (Trinovantian) |

TABLE 5 *Atrebatic/Regnan Hoards*

| Class | 6 Markstey | 9 Ashdown Forest | 14 Lancing | 17 Alfriston | 41 Alresford | 76 Penzance |
|---|---|---|---|---|---|---|
| Gallo-Belgic | | | | | | |
|   E | 3 | | | 1 | | |
| Cantian | | | | | | |
|   H | | 2+ | | | | |
| Atrebatic | | | | | | |
|   A | 1+ | | | | | |
|   B | 1+ | 8 | | | | 5 |
|   DEF | | | Some | 3 | | |
|   IJK | | | Some | | 76+ | |
|   L | | | | | 4+ | |
| Other | 33 A' Uncertain | | | | | |

| Class | 79 Camberly | 83 Possible Hoard | 86 Farnham | 87 Finkley Down | 94 Andover | 101 Unknown Site |
|---|---|---|---|---|---|---|
| Gallo-Belgic | | | | | | |
|   E | | | 5 | | | |
| Cantian | | | | | | |
|   H | | | | | | |
| Atrebatic | | | | | | |
|   A | | | | | | |
|   B | 4–5 | | 4 | 1 | Some | |
|   DEF | | | | 5 | Some | 3 |
|   IJK | | | | 1 | Some | |
|   L | | 9+ | | | Some | |
| Other | | | | | 2 Cantian F | |

TABLE 6 *Icenian Hoards*

| Class | 1 Thorpe-next-Norwich | 15 Battle | 22 Weston | 25 Wimblington | 26 March |
|---|---|---|---|---|---|
| Icenian | | | | | |
| A | | | | | |
| B | | | | | |
| C | | | 5+ | 7 | 1 |
| D | Some | | 1 | | |
| E | | | | 3 | 1 |
| F | | | 2 | | |
| G | Many | | 9+ | 13 | 1 |
| HIJK | Many | Many | 11 | 15 | 4 |
| L | | | | 1 | |
| M | | | | | |
| N | | | 2 | 1 | |
| O | | Many | 14+ | 6 | 1 |
| Atrebatic | | | | | |
| B | | | | | |
| Trinovantian | | | | | |
| F | | | | | |
| 'New Type' | | | | | |
| X | | | | | |
| Total Icenian | | | 150–300 | *c*.300 | 40–50 |
| Other | | | Some Roman | | |

| Class | 35 Santon Downham | 42 Freckenham | 46 Burnham Thorpe | 67 Honingham | 72 Lakenheath |
|---|---|---|---|---|---|
| Icenian | | | | | |
| A | | | | | |
| B | | 92+ | | | |
| C | 3 | | | 19 | 21 |
| D | | | Some | 1 | 3 |
| E | | | | 1 | |
| F | | | Some | 4 | 2 |
| G | 11 | | | 69 | 84 |
| HIJK | 33 | | | 142 | 180 |
| L | | | | 2 | 2 |
| M | | | | | |
| N | 4 | | | 5 | 7 |
| O | 26+ | | | 84 | 88 |
| Atrebatic | | | | | |
| B | | | | | |
| Trinovantian | | | | | |
| F | | | | | |
| 'New Type' | | | | | |
| X | | | | | 2 |
| Total Icenian | 107 | 92+ | | 341 | 479 |
| Other | Roman to Claudius AD 41 | | | | Roman to Caligula AD 34 |

### TABLE 6 *Icenian Hoards* (*cont.*)

| Class | 73 Joist Fen | 77 Brettenham | 89 Stonea | 102 Snettisham II[1] |
|---|---|---|---|---|
| Icenian | | | | |
| A | | | | 42 |
| B | | | | |
| C | | | | |
| D | Some | | | |
| E | | | | 3 |
| F | | | | |
| G | 3 | 2 | Many | |
| HIJK | 8 | 1 | Many | |
| L | | | | |
| M | 4 | | | |
| N | | | | |
| O | | 2 | | |
| Atrebatic | | | | |
| B | | | | 9 |
| Trinovantian | | | | |
| F | | | | 21 |
| 'New Type' | | | | 7 |
| X | | | | |
| Total Icenian | | 5+ | | |
| Other | | | One Roman | |

[1] This Interior Mixed Hoard included for comparison.

### TABLE 7 *Corieltauvian Hoards*

| Class | 11 Lightcliff | 44 Honley | 48 South Ferriby | 66 Dewsbury | 100 Grimsby II |
|---|---|---|---|---|---|
| Corieltauvian | | | | | |
| A | | | | 30–40 | |
| B | | | | | 3–4 |
| C to H | | | 135 | | |
| K | 1 | | | | |
| LMN | 5 | | | | |
| O | 1 | | | | |
| P | 8+ | 1 | | | |
| Q | | 3 | | | |
| R | | 1 | | | |
| Other | Roman | 18 Roman to Vespasian | | | |

TABLE 8 *Dobunnic Hoards*

| Class | 28 Nunney | 47 Sherbourne | 60 Near Wanborough | 69 Bagendon | 88 Farnborough |
|---|---|---|---|---|---|
| Dobunnic | | | | | |
| B | Many | | | Some | 61 |
| D | Many | 7 | 6 | Some | |
| E | | | | Some | |
| F | 27 | 1 | | 1 | |
| G | 2 | 1 | | Some | |
| Atrebatic | | | | | |
| L | | | | 1 | |
| Durotrigan | | | | | |
| J | | | | 1 | |
| Other | | | 1 D or F | | |

TABLE 9 *Durotrigan Hoards*

| Class | 3 Okeford-Fitzpaine | 16 Cranbourne Chase | 23 Farley Heath | 33 Cotley Farm | 34 Yarmouth | 50 Holdenhurst |
|---|---|---|---|---|---|---|
| Gallo-Belgic | | | | | | |
| D | | | | | | |
| Durotrigan | | | | | | |
| A | | | | | | |
| B | | | | | 7–8 | |
| D | | | | | | |
| E | 70–80 | 27 | | c.66 | | 83 |
| F | | | | | | |
| G | | | | | | |
| H | | | | | | |
| I | | | | | | |
| J | | | 11 + | 4 + | | 206 |
| K | | | | | | 306 |
| Thin | | | | | | |
| Other | | | | | | 43 Roman Agrippa to Domitian AD 86 |

## TABLE 9 *Durotrigan Hoards* (cont.)

| Class | 51<br>*Romsey* | 57<br>*Chute* | 70<br>*Le Catillon* | 71<br>*Armsley* | 78<br>*Tollard<br>Royal* |
|---|---|---|---|---|---|
| Gallo-Belgic | | | | | |
|   D | | | 1 | | |
| Durotrigan | | | | | |
|   A | | 65 | 2 | | |
| B | | | | | |
|   D | | | | | |
|   E | | | 6 | 1 | *c.*20 |
|   F | | | | | |
|   G | | | | | |
|   H | | | | | |
|   I | | | | | |
|   J | 18 | | | 3 | |
|   K | | | | | |
|   Thin | | | 4 | | |
| Other | | | 1 Æ Gaulish,<br>1 Æ<br>Uncertain | | |

| Class | 83<br>*Cheriton* | 85<br>*Corfe<br>Common* | 90<br>*Ringwood I* | 93<br>*Badbury-<br>Shapwick* | 99<br>*New<br>Forest:<br>Ashurst* |
|---|---|---|---|---|---|
| Gallo-Belgic | | | | | |
|   D | | | | | |
| Durotrigan | | | | | |
|   A | 3 | 1 | 119 | *c.* 32 | 19 |
|   B | | | | | |
|   D | 27 | | | | |
|   E | | 34 | | *c.*642 | |
|   F | | | | *c.* 5 | |
|   G | | | | *c.* 55 | |
|   H | | | | *c.* 23 | |
|   I | | | | *c.* 93 | |
|   J | | | | | |
|   K | | | | | |
|   Thin | | | | | |
| Other | | | | | |

TABLE 10 *Trinovantian Hoards*

| Class | 8 Colchester | 10 High Wycombe | 19 Markstey | 37 Tunstall | 49 Clacton II | 58 Colchester | 98 Harlow Temple |
|---|---|---|---|---|---|---|---|
| Gallo-Belgic | | | | | | | |
| A | | | | | | | |
| E | | | | | 3 | | 2 |
| Trinovantian | | | | | | | |
| DEF | | | | | 2 | | 3 |
| IJK | 1 | | Many | | 1 | | 7 |
| L | | | 1 | | | 4 | 9 |
| M | | 8 | | | | Some | 18 |
| N | | 3 | | | | | 1 |
| O | | | | | | Some | 29 |
| P | | | | | | Some | |
| Q | | | | | | | 1 |
| R | | | | | | | 7 |
| S | | | | | | | 8 |
| TUV | | | | 2 | | Many | 32 |
| WXYZ | | | | | | | 204 |
| Atrebatic | | | | | | | |
| B | | | | | | | 6 |
| Icenian | | | | | | | |
| O | | | | | | | 1 |
| Corieltauvian | | | | | | | |
| D | | | | | | | |
| G | | | | | | 1 | 1 |
| Durotrigan | | | | | | | |
| J | | | | | | | 1 |
| Other | Parcel of base coins | | | 1 N Roman Claudius | | | 1 Æ Gaulish |

# ANCIENT BRITISH HOARDS AND THEIR CONTENTS

1) Thorpe-Next-Norwich, Norfolk, 17th Century (Icenian)

| | | | |
|---|---|---|---|
| Some | Icenian A | (663-1) | Æ |
| Many | Icenian G | (710-1ff) | Æ |
| Many | Icenian H-K | (730-1ff, 760-1ff) | Æ |
| Some | Unidentified Æ | | Æ |

2) Carn Brae, Cornwall, 1749 (Early)

| | | | |
|---|---|---|---|
| 5 | Gallo-Belgic A | (10-1ff) | Æ |
| 5 | Gallo-Belgic B | (30-1ff) | Æ |
| 2 | Gallo-Belgic D | (69-1) | Æ |
| 4 | Atrebatic A | (200-2, 202-1) | Æ |
| 1 | Unidentified Æ | Quarter Stater (143-1?) | Æ |

3) Okeford Fitzpaine, Dorset, 1753 (Durotrigan)

| | | | |
|---|---|---|---|
| 70-80 | Durotrigan E | (1235-1) | Æ |

4) Lenham Heath, Kent, 1781 (Cast Bronze)

| | | | |
|---|---|---|---|
| Many | Cantian D | (122-1ff) | Æ |

5) Haverhill, Suffolk, 1788 (Early)

| | | | |
|---|---|---|---|
| Ca. 50 | Gallo-Belgic C | (44-1, 46-1) | Æ |

6) Marks Tey I, Essex, 1803 (Atrebatic)

| | | | |
|---|---|---|---|
| 3+ | Gallo-Belgic E | (50-1ff) | Æ |
| 1+ | Atrebatic A | (200-1, 202-1) | Æ |
| 1+ | Atrebatic B | (210-1, 216-1) | Æ |
| 33 | Unidentified Æ Staters | | Æ |
| 38 | Total gold coins | | Æ |

7) Cairnmuir (Netherurd, Kirkurd.), Peebleshire, 1806 (Early)

| | | |
|---|---|---|
| 40+ | Gallo-Belgic XB 'bullets' | Æ |

8) Near Colchester, Essex, 1807 (Trinovantian)

| | | | |
|---|---|---|---|
| At least 1 | Trinovantian K | (1635-1) | Æ |

Parcel of base coins included

9) Ashdown Forest, Sussex, 1825 (Atrebatic)

| 2+ | Cantian H   | (151-1)                | Ν |
|----|-------------|------------------------|---|
| 1  | Atrebatic B | (250-1)                | Ν |
| 7  | Atrebatic B | (264-1, 268-1, 270-1)  | Ρ |

10) High Wycombe, Bucks., 1827 (Trinovantian)

| 7 | Trinovantian M | (1680-1, 1682-1) | Ν |
|---|----------------|------------------|---|
| 3 | Trinovantian N | (1730-1ff)       | Ν |
| 1 | Trinovantian M | (1684-1)         | Ν |

Concealed in a hollow flint

11) Lightcliffe, Yorks., 1829 (Corieltauvian)

| 8+ | Corieltauvian P   | (978-1)         | Ν |
|----|-------------------|-----------------|---|
| 1  | Corieltauvian K   | (920-1)         | Ν |
| 5  | Corieltauvian L-M | (930-1, 940-1)  | Ν |
| 1  | Corieltauvian O   | (972-1)         | Ν |

This hoard is confused with another hoard, supposedly found at Almondbury, but probably a part of this hoard.

12) Portsmouth, Hants., 1830 (Coastal Mixed)

| 1       | Icenian I    | (740-1)  | Ρ |
|---------|--------------|----------|---|
| 1       | Icenian H    | (730-1)  | Ρ |
| Several | Durotrigan E | (1235-1) | Ρ |
| 1       | Durotrigan E | (1242-1) | Ρ |
| 1       | Durotrigan—  | (1280-1) | Ρ |

13) Mount Batten, Devon, 1832 (Coastal Mixed)

| 5  | Dobunnic A   | (1005-1) | Ν |
|----|--------------|----------|---|
| 1+ | Dobunnic D   | (1078-1) | Ρ |
| 2  | Durotrigan E | (1235-1) | Ρ |

14) Lancing, Sussex, 1838 (Atrebatic)

| 11—12 | total coins: | | |
|-------|--------------|-----------------|---|
|       | Atrebatic I  | (480-1 to 483-1) | Ρ |
|       | Atrebatic E  | (383-1)          | Ρ |
|       | Atrebatic K  | (530-1, 532-1)   | Ρ |

15) Battle, Sussex, Before 1839 (Icenian)

| Many | Icenian O | (790-1) | Ρ |
|------|-----------|---------|---|
| Many | Icenian H | (730-1) | Ρ |

16) Cranbourne Chase, Farnham, Dorset, 1838 (Durotrigan)

| 27 | Durotrigan E | (1235-1) | Æ |

17) Alfriston, Sussex, Ca. 1840 (Atrebatic)

| 1 | Gallo-Belgic E | (50-1ff) | Aʹ |
| 1 | Atrebatic D | (363-1) | Aʹ |
| 2 | Atrebatic F | (385-1) | Aʹ |

18) Bognor, Sussex, 1842 (Coastal Mixed)

| 3 | Gallo-Belgic DB | (69-3) | Aʹ |
| 4 | Gallo-Belgic DC | (69-1) | Aʹ |
| 1 | Atrebatic C | (353-1 ff) | Aʹ |
| 5+ | Atrebatic B | (226-1, 228-1, 250-1) | Aʹ |
| 1 | Atrebatic B | (230-1) | Aʹ |
| 1 | Cantian F | (143-1) | Aʹ |
| 1 | Atrebatic B | (250-1) | Aʹ |
| 1 | Atrebatic E | (378-1) | Aʹ |
| 1+ | Atrebatic I | (466-1) | Aʹ |
| 1 | Atrebatic I | (467-1 | Aʹ |

19) Marks Tey II, Essex, 1843 (Trinovantian)

| 1 | Trinovantian L | (1650-1) | Aʳ |
| Many | Trinovantian I, J | (1605-1, 1620-1) | Aʹ |

The total is uncertain.

20) Wonersh, Surrey, 1848 (Interior Mixed)

| 3 | Cantian I | (158-1) | Aʹ |
| 19 | Trinovantian G | (1520-1, 1522-1) | Aʹ |
| 6 | Cantian G | (147-1) | Aʹ |
| 1 | Atrebatic B | (210-1) | Aʹ |

21) Whaddon Chase, Bucks., 1849 (Interior Mixed)

| 1 | Gallo-Belgic E | (50-1ff) | Aʹ |
| 1 | Gallo-Belgic F | (85-1) | Aʹ |
| 1 | Durotrigan A | (1205-1) | Aʹ |
| 2 | Corieltauvian B | (804-1ff) | Aʹ |
| 226+ | Trinovantian D | (1470-1ff) | Aʹ |
| 72+ | Atrebatic B | (210-1, 216-1) | Aʹ |

May have included other types.

22) Weston, Norfolk, 1852 (Icenian)

| Many | Icenian C | (655-1ff) | Æ |

| 1+ | Icenian D | (663-1) | Æ |
| Many | Icenian G | (710-1ff) | Æ |
| Many | Icenian F,H,K | (730-1ff) | Æ |
| Several | Icenian N | (775-1) | Æ |

Likely more than 300 coins in the hoard.

23) Farley Heath, Surrey, before 1853 (Durotrigan)

| 11+ | Durotrigan J | (1290-1) | Æ |

24) Birchington, Kent, 1853 (Cast Bronze)

| 600+ | Cantian D | (122-1ff) | Æ |

25) Wimblington, Cambs., 19th Century (Icenian)

13 Coins:

| | Icenian C | (659-1) | Æ |
| | Icenian O | (790-1) | Æ |
| | Icenian E | (665-3, 665-9) | Æ |
| | Icenian F | (681-1) | Æ |
| 13+ | Icenian G | (710-1ff) | Æ |
| 4 | Icenian I | (740-1) | Æ |
| 11+ | Icenian H,K | (730-1ff, 760-1ff) | Æ |
| 1+ | Icenian N | (775-1) | Æ |
| 1 | Icenian L | (770-1) | Æ |
| 7 | Icenian— | Uncertain | Æ |

26) March, Cambs., 19th Century (Icenian)

| Ca.20 | Icenian C,E,O | (655-1, 665-1, 790-1) | Æ |
| Many | Icenian G | (710-1ff) | Æ |
| Some | Icenian H,K | (730-1ff, 760-1ff) | Æ |
| Ca. 20 | Icenian— | Uncertain | Æ |

27) Ryarsh, Cambs., 19th Century (Early)

| 1+ | Gallo-Belgic C | (44-1, 46-1) | Ν |
| 6-8 | Gallo-Belgic E | (50-1ff) | Ν |

28) Nunney, Somerset, 1860 (Dobunnic)

| Ca. 195 | Dobunnic B,D | (1042-1ff, 1074-1ff) | Æ |
| 7-8 | Dobunnic D | (1066-1) | Ν |
| 16+ | Dobunnic D | (1082-1) | Æ |
| 27 | Dobunnic F | (11101-) | Æ |
| 2 | Dobunnic G | (1130-1) | Ν |

Found at West Down Farm.

29) Brentford, Middlesex, 1860 (Cast Bronze)

| | | | |
|---|---|---|---|
| 266+ | Cantian D | (122-1ff) | Æ |

Likely more than one parcel found.


30) St. James's Park, London, 1864 (Cast Bronze)

| | | | |
|---|---|---|---|
| Many | Cantian D | (122-1ff) | Æ |


31) Scartho, Lincs., Ca. 1865 (Coastal Mixed)

| | | | |
|---|---|---|---|
| 2 | Gallo-Belgic E | (50-1ff) | Aʹ |
| 3 | Trinovantian D | (1470-1ff) | Aʹ |
| 1 | Atrebatic B | (210-1) | Aʹ |


32) Braughing, Herts., 1865-9, (Cast Bronze)

| | | | |
|---|---|---|---|
| 4 | Cantian E | (138-1ff) | Æ |


33) Cotley Farm, East Devon, Feb. 1865, (Durotrigan)

| | | | |
|---|---|---|---|
| Ca. 66 | Durotrigan E | (1235-1) | ǼR |
| 4+ | Durotrigan J | (1290-1) | Æ |

Found two miles southwest of Chard, in a mound of broken flints. The Durotrigan J coins may actually have been plated forgeries of Durotrigan E.


34) Yarmouth, Isle of Wight, 1867 (Durotrigan)

| | | | |
|---|---|---|---|
| 7 or 8 | Durotrigan B | (1220-1) | Aʹ |


35) Santon Downham, Suffolk, 1869 (Icenian)

| | | | |
|---|---|---|---|
| 14 | Icenian G | (710-1ff) | ǼR |
| 1+ | Icenian I | (740-1) | ǼR |
| 31 | Icenian F,H,K | (730-1ff, 760-1ff) | ǼR |
| 4 | Icenian N | (775-1) | ǼR |
| 29 | Icenian— | 'Uninscribed' | ǼR |
| — | Icenian— | Uncertain | ǼR |

The 'uninscribed' coins are likely Icenian C and O. The hoard included Roman coins down to Claudius, 41 A.D.


36) Pitstone Common, Herts., 1870 (Not a Celtic hoard)

| | | | |
|---|---|---|---|
| 1 | Trinovantian W | (2097-1) | Æ |

One Ancient British coin was found in a hoard of 116 Roman bronzes down to Tetricus II. The Trinovantian coin was likely a curiosity at the time of deposit.

37) Tunstall, Kent, 1873 (Trinovantian)

| 1 | Trinovantian W | (2010-1) | Æ |
| 1 | Trinovantian U,V or W | | Æ |

The hoard included one Aureus of Claudius.

38) Selsey, Sussex, 1873 to the present (Coastal Mixed)

| 1 | Gallo-Belgic B | (30-1ff) | Æ |
| 1 | Gallo-Belgic C | (44-1 or 46-1) | Æ |
| Ca. 16 coins: | | | |
| | Gallo-Belgic D | (67-1, 69-1) | Æ |
| | Cantian C | (146-1) | Æ |
| 4 | Gallo-Belgic E | (50-1ff) | Æ |
| 26 | Atrebatic C | (353-1 ff) | Æ |
| 2 | Atrebatic A | (200-1, 202-1) | Æ |
| 1 | Trinovantian G | (1520-1, 1522-1) | Æ |
| Ca. 15 coins: | | | |
| | Cantian F | (143-1) | Æ |
| | Durotrigan A | (1225-1, 1227-1, 1229-1) | Æ |
| 47 | Atrebatic B | (210-1ff, 220-1ff) | Æ |
| 1 | Cantian I | (158-1) | Æ |
| 2 | Atrebatic B | (250-1, 254-1) | Æ |
| 1 | Atrebatic C | (350-1) | Æ |
| 1 | Atrebatic D | (366-1) | Æ |
| 22 | Atrebatic E | (378-1) | Æ |
| 10+ | Atrebatic E | (379-1) | Æ |
| 1 | Atrebatic F | (385-1) | Æ |
| 40+ | Atrebatic F | (389-1 to 390-1) | Æ |
| 2 | Atrebatic F | (397-1) | Æ |
| 1 | Atrebatic F | (396-1) | Ær |
| 2+ | Atrebatic I | (465-1) | Æ |
| 9+ | Atrebatic I | (466-1) | Æ |
| 2 | Atrebatic I | (468-1) | Æ |
| 1 | Atrebatic I | (470-1) | Ær |
| 1 | Atrebatic J | (500-1) | Æ |
| 9+ | Atrebatic J | (501-1) | Æ |
| 2 | Atrebatic K | (525-1) | Æ |
| 1 | Atrebatic K | (526-1) | Æ |
| 1 | Atrebatic K | (527-1) | Æ |
| 1 | Atrebatic K | (530-1) | Ær |
| 1 | Atrebatic K | (531-1) | Ær |

The 'hoard' has appeared as multiple finds over the last hundred years. The coins are known to wash up on Selsey Beach after storms. Judging by the long run of types, the coins may be from a temple or market site that is today beneath the sea. The deposit, if it is a single deposit, is unlikely to be a concealment-type hoard. It is more likely to be a group collected piecemeal over a long period of time.

There is a possibility the 47 Atrebatic B Quarter Staters included Dobunnic varieties, because the exact coin-types are not distinguished, however, this is unlikely.

39) Savernake, Wilts., 1875 (Interior Mixed)

| Many | Trinovantian H | (1526-1) | N |
| 5+ | Atrebatic L | (580-1) | R |

This 'hoard' also included silver coins of Tiberius, and there is some confusion over whether it may have been two hoards. The most likely explanation for the contents is that this is indeed two deposits, and not a single hoard. One hoard would have contained the Trinovantian Staters, and the other the Atrebatic and Roman silver coins.

40) Folkestone I, Kent, ca. 1877 (Early)

| 6 | Gallo-Belgic E | (50-1ff) | N |

Found on the beach.

41) Alresford, Hants., ca. 1880 (Atrebatic)

| 36+ | Atrebatic J | (500-1) | N |
| 40+ | Atrebatic K | (520-1) | N |
| 4+ | Atrebatic L | (575-1) | N |

The circumstances of the find were surrounded with mystery, and the exact findspot is doubtful. Another spot, Bentley, near Alton, has been suggested as more likely.

42) Freckenham, Suffolk, 1885 (Icenian)

| 1 | Icenian B | (620-1ff) | N |
| 69 | Icenian B | (626-1ff, 628-1ff) | N |
| 8 | Icenian B | (624-1ff) | N |

The coins were found in a pot in a garden. At least 90, possible a few more, were discovered. All were Icenian B types.

43) Wallingford, Berks., or Watlington, Oxon., ca. 1890 (Interior Mixed)

5 coins:

|   | Atrebatic | B (228-1) | N |
|   | Dobunnic A | (1015-1) | N |
|   | Atrebatic D | (366-1) | N |
| 1 | Atrebatic D | (365-1) | N |
| 1 | Atrebatic F | (390-1) | N |

| 1 | Atrebatic F | (388-1) | N |
| 1 | Atrebatic F | (385-1) | N |
| 1 | Atrebatic E | (378-1) | N |
| 1 | Atrebatic J | (501-1) | N |
| 1 | Atrebatic H | (431-1) | N |
| 1 | Trinovantian U | (1927-1) | N |

There is some confusion over the findspot. The Trinovantian U Stater is only 'possibly' a part of the hoard, and the exact contents are in doubt.

44) Honley, Yorks., 1897 (Corieltauvian)

| 1 | Corieltauvian P | (984-1) | Æ |
| 3 | Corieltauvian Q | (992-1) | Æ |
| 1 | Corieltauvian R | (994-1) | Æ |

Hoard contained 18 Roman coins down to Vespasian 72-3 AD.

45) Clacton I, Essex, 1899 (Early)

| 4 | Gallo-Belgic C | (44-1, 46-1) | N |
| 32 | Gallo-Belgic E | (50-1ff) | N |
| 5 | Atrebatic A | (200-1, 202-1) | N |
| 15 | Trinovantian B | (1458-1ff) | N |
| 63 | Trinovantian B | (1455-1, 1458-1) | N |
| 5 | Trinovantian B | (1460-1) | N |

The hoard was reconstructed from a group of coins belonging to Sir John Evans, given to the British Museum after his death. There were no tickets under the coins, and evidently Evans had not taken the time to describe the find. The hoard was reconstructed by G.F. Hill in 1919.

Hill indicated that two Gallo-Belgic A Staters were included on the coin-trays, but he did not consider these coins to be a part of the 'hoard'. Unfortunately, D.F. Allen included these in his table of hoards in 'Origins'— thus concocting the second Ancient British hoard with Gallo-Belgic A and E types together (see hoard 80, Harpsden, Oxon, 1981). There is no proof Allen was correct when he reinterpreted Hill's reconstruction of the hoard, and the find has been recorded here following Hill's original work.

46) Burnham Thorpe, Norfolk, ca. 1900 (Icenian)

| Quantity? | Icenian— | 'Uninscribed' | Æ |

This has been described as a 'lost hoard'.

47) Sherborne, Dorset, ca. 1903 (Dobunnic)

| 7 | Dobunnic D | (1066-1) | N |
| 1 | Dobunnic F | (1105-1) | N |
| 1 | Dobunnic G | (1130-1) | N |

48) South Ferriby, Lincs., 1904-8 (Corieltauvian)

| 69+ | Corieltauvian C,D,E,G,H | (809-1ff) | N |
| 1 | Corieltauvian F | (821-1) | N |
| 45 | Corieltauvian D | (875-1ff) | R |
| 20 | Corieltauvian D | (875-1ff) | R |

The hoard was discovered in several groups over time, as the coins washed out of a stream bank. The 20 Corieltauvian D silver coins were found after 1905.

49) Clacton II, Essex, 1905 (Trinovantian)

| 1 | Gallo-Belgic A | (12-1) | N |
| 1 | Trinovantian D | (1476-1) | N |
| 1 | Trinovantian F | (1500-1) | N |
| 1 | Trinovantian J | (1620-1) | N |

Found on the beach—at least four coins were recovered.

50) Holdenhurst, Hants., 1905 (Durotrigan)

| 83 | Durotrigan E | (1235-1, 1242-1) | R |
| 206 | Durotrigan J | (1290-1) | Æ |
| 306 | Durotrigan K | (1322-1ff) | Æ |

51) Romsey, Hants., 1907 (Durotrigan)

| 18 | Durotrigan J | (1290-1) | Æ |

Hoard included 43 Roman bronzes from Agrippa to Domitian, 86 AD.

52) Hengistbury I, Hants., 1911-2 (Coastal Mixed)

| Some | Durotrigan E | (1235-1, 1242-1) | R |
| 1 | Cantian F | (143-1) | N |
| Ca. 1308 | Durotrigan J | (1290-1) | Æ |
| Ca. 1660 | Durotrigan K | (1322-1ff) | Æ |
| 1 | Durotrigan A | (1205-1) | N |
| 1 | Durotrigan I | (1270-1) | R |
| 10+ | Dobunnic B,D,G | (1049-1, 1074-1ff, 1135-1) | R |
| 1 | Dobunnic D | (1082-1) | R |
| 1 | Dobunnic F | (1110-1) R | |

Found during the Bushe-Fox excavations, not necessarily a hoard.

53) Higham, Kent, 1912 (Early)

| 11 | Gallo-Belgic C | (44-1, 46-1) | N |

81) Southend-on-Sea, Essex, 1985 (Early)

|    |               |              |    |
|----|---------------|--------------|----|
| 33 | Gallo-Belgic E | (50-1ff)    | A⃓ |

82) Ringwood II, Hants., 1979 (Early)

|    |               |                  |    |
|----|---------------|------------------|----|
| 43 | Baiocasses    | —                | A⃓ |
| 1  | Gallo-Belgic D | —               | A⃓ |
| 1  | Atrebatic A   | (200-1 or 202-1) | A⃓ |

83) Possible Hoard, ca. 1969 (Atrebatic)

|    |             |          |    |
|----|-------------|----------|----|
| 9+ | Atrebatic L | (580-1)  | Æ  |

Between 1969 and 1974 a small number of silver units of Epaticcus were offered for sale by coin dealers. The type had previously been extremely rare. Though the coins may have been found individually, it is possible a small parcel was discovered and sold piecemeal. No hoard has ever been reported, but an unsuspected one may have been dispersed.

84) Cheriton, Hants., 1983 (Durotrigan)

|    |              |             |    |
|----|--------------|-------------|----|
| 27 | Durotrigan D | (1215-1)    | A⃓ |
| 3  | Durotrigan A | (1225-1ff)  | A⃓ |

85) Corfe Common, Bournemouth, Hants., 1980 (Durotrigan)

|    |              |            |    |
|----|--------------|------------|----|
| 1  | Durotrigan A | (1205-1)   | A⃓ |
| 30 | Durotrigan E | (1235-1)   | Æ  |
| 4  | Durotrigan E | (1242-1)   | Æ  |

86) Farnham, Surrey, 1980 (Atrebatic)

|   |               |            |    |
|---|---------------|------------|----|
| 5 | Gallo-Belgic E | (50-1ff)  | A⃓ |
| 4 | Atrebatic B   | (210-1ff)  | A⃓ |

87) Finkley Down, near Andover, Hants., 1980-2 (Atrebatic)

|   |             |          |    |
|---|-------------|----------|----|
| 1 | Atrebatic B | (210-1)  | A⃓ |
| 2 | Atrebatic E | (375-1)  | A⃓ |
| 3 | Atrebatic F | (385-1)  | A⃓ |
| 1 | Atrebatic I | (461-1)  | A⃓ |

Two staters were found in a field near Andover, and then five more. The coins may be part of a scattered hoard, or several hoards. All are now in the Museum of the Iron Age, Andover. The hoard contents, listed above, conflict with those reported in a paper to the Royal Numismatic Society, but are based on the actual holdings of the Museum. Possible strays appeared in the Unknown Site Hoard, (no. 101).

88) Farnborough, Avon, 1982 (Dobunnic)

|    |            |           |    |
|----|------------|-----------|----|
| 61 | Dobunnic B | (1035-1)  | A⃓ |

89) Stonea, Cambs., 1982 (Icenian)

| | | | |
|---|---|---|---|
| 860 | Icenian G,F,H,L— | | Æ |
| 35 | Icenian— | Uncertain | Æ |

The 35 Icenian silver coins were found with one Roman coin.

90) Ringwood I, Hants., 1976 (Durotrigan)

| | | | |
|---|---|---|---|
| 119 | Durotrigan A | (1205-1) | N |

Found in two parcels, in the same area. The hoard was called the 'Ringwood Hoard' to protect the site—the actual findspot was reportedly to the east in the New Forest.

91) Folkestone II, Kent, 1983 (Cast Bronze)

| | | | |
|---|---|---|---|
| 100-300 | Trinovantian A | (1402-1ff) | Æ |

92) West Thurrock, Essex, 1987 (Cast Bronze)

| | | | |
|---|---|---|---|
| Ca. 2000 | Trinovantian A | (1402-1 to 1422-1) | Æ |

Found together in a pit.

93) Badbury-Shapwick, Dorset, 1983 (Durotrigan)

| | | | |
|---|---|---|---|
| Ca. 32 | Durotrigan A | (1205-1) | N |
| Ca. 300 | Durotrigan E | (1235-1) | Æ |
| Ca. 342 | Durotrigan E | (1242-1) | Æ |
| Ca. 5 | Durotrigan F | (1238-1) | Æ |
| Ca. 32 | Durotrigan G | (1246-1) | Æ |
| Ca. 23 | Durotrigan G | (1249-1) | Æ |
| Ca. 23 | Durotrigan H | (1260-1) | Æ |
| Ca. 65 | Durotrigan I | (1270-1) | Æ |
| Ca. 23 | Durotrigan I | (1273-1) | Æ |
| Ca. 5 | Durotrigan I | (1276-1) | Æ |

A dispersed hoard, reportedly found one-half mile from Badbury Rings hillfort in the direction of Shapwick. About 850 coins were found.

94) Andover, Hants., 1984 (Atrebatic)

| | | | |
|---|---|---|---|
| 2 | Cantian F | (143-1) | N |
| 1 | Atrebatic B | (242-1) | N/Æ |
| 1 | Atrebatic B | (280-1) | Æ |
| 1 | Atrebatic F | (397-1) | Æ |
| 1 | Atrebatic K | (564-1) | Æ |
| Many? | Atrebatic B | — | Æ |
| Some? | Atrebatic C | (355-1) | Æ |
| Many? | Atrebatic D,E,F | — | Æ |
| Many? | Atrebatic L | (580-1, 581-1) | Æ |

| Some? | Atrebatic M | (593-1) | Æ |
| Many? | Atrebatic I,J,K | — | Æ |

A dispersed hoard, about 85 coins were found throughout a plough-disturbed field. Roughly half found their way to the British Museum, another seven were placed in the Museum of the Iron Age, Andover. The coins appear to come from a temple or market site because of the extremely long time span represented.

95) Wanborough, Surrey, 1984 (Atrebatic)

All the following counts are estimates:

| 99 | Atrebatic D | (366-1) | Aʋ |
| 58 | Atrebatic D | (370-1) | Æ |
| 189 | Atrebatic D | (371-1) | Æ |
| 13 | Atrebatic E | (379-1) | Aʋ |
| 40 | Atrebatic E | (378-1) | Aʋ |
| 73 | Atrebatic E | (382-1) | Æ |
| 15 | Atrebatic E | (383-1) | Æ |
| 7 | Atrebatic F | (381-1) | Aʋ |
| 73 | Atrebatic F | (388-1) | Aʋ |
| 7 | Atrebatic F | (390-1) | Aʋ |
| 87 | Atrebatic F | (397-1) | Æ |
| 44 | Atrebatic F | (396-1) | Æ |
| 15 | Atrebatic F | (395-1) | Æ |
| 30 | Atrebatic F | (398-1) | Æ |
| 99 | Atrebatic G | (407-1) | Aʋ |
| 40 | Atrebatic G | (408-1) | Aʋ |
| 33 | Atrebatic G | (415-1) | Æ |
| 319 | Atrebatic G | (417-1) | Æ |
| 26 | Atrebatic H | (409-1) | Aʋ |
| 119 | Atrebatic H | (435-1) | Aʋ |
| 15 | Atrebatic H | (420-1) | Æ |
| 29 | Atrebatic H | (421-1) | Æ |
| 145 | Atrebatic H | (416-1) | Æ |
| 132 | Atrebatic I | (466-1) | Aʋ |
| 73 | Atrebatic I | (467-1) | Aʋ |
| 73 | Atrebatic I | (468-1) | Aʋ |
| 508 | Atrebatic I | (470-1) | Æ |
| 29 | Atrebatic I | (482-1) | Æ |
| 319 | Atrebatic I | (471-1) | Æ |
| 15 | Atrebatic I | (472-1) | Æ |
| 15 | Atrebatic I | (485-1) | Æ |
| 7 | Atrebatic J | (501-1) | Aʋ |
| 203 | Atrebatic J | (505-1) | Æ |

| 232 | Atrebatic J | (506-1) | Æ |
| 30 | Atrebatic J | (512-1) | Æ |
| 145 | Atrebatic K | (530-1) | Æ |
| 276 | Atrebatic K | (531-1) | Æ |
| 44 | Atrebatic K | (532-1) | Æ |
| 218 | Atrebatic K | (533-1) | Æ |
| 44 | Atrebatic K | (551-1) | Æ |
| 44 | Atrebatic K | (554-1) | Æ |
| 29 | Atrebatic K | (553-1) | Æ |
| 58 | Atrebatic K | (555-1) | Æ |
| 15 | Atrebatic K | (556-1) | Æ |
| 15 | Atrebatic K | (560-1) | Æ |
| 15 | Atrebatic K | (550-1) | Æ |
| 29 | Atrebatic K | (558-1) | Æ |
| 29 | Atrebatic K | (557-1) | Æ |
| 15 | Atrebatic K | (562-1) | Æ |
| 15 | Atrebatic K | (563-1) | Æ |
| 29 | Atrebatic K | (561-1) | Æ |
| 5000 | Atrebatic L | (580-1) | Æ |
| 261 | Atrebatic L | (581-1) | Æ |
| 15 | Atrebatic L | (586-1) | Æ |
| 15 | Atrebatic L | (585-1) | Æ |
| 149 | Atrebatic M | (593-1) | Æ |
| 15 | Cantian O | (194-1) | Æ |

The following types may be Wanborough finds:

| Some | Atrebatic H | (422-1) | Æ |
| 1 | Atrebatic M | (595-1) | Æ |
| 1 | Atrebatic G | (405-1) | AV |
| 3 | Atrebatic J | (500-1) | AV |
| 1 | Atrebatic L | (575-1) | AV |

The 595-1 is likely an Andover or Waltham St. Lawrence (number 94 or 96) stray, rather than a Wanborough find. The 405-1 is now in the National Museum of Wales. A large number of Caratacus silver minims, a few quarter staters of Tasciovanus and Cunobeline, a few silver units of Cunobeline and about a hundred Icenian silver coins have been reported from the hoard, but it is not possible to confirm the reports.

A major Romano-Celtic temple site was badly damaged during the discovery, removal and dispersal of the hoard. Partial excavations in 1985 recorded the remains of a temple (Britannia, 1986, p. 424).

The estimates of the number of coins found run as high as 30,000 total pieces, but a figure closer to 20,000 (5000 of which were 580-1 types) is probably correct.

96) Waltham St. Lawrence, Berks., 1977 (Atrebatic)

| | | | |
|---|---|---|---|
| 1 | Gallo-Belgic E | (50-1ff) | A̸ |
| 1 | Atrebatic C | (353-1 ff) | A̸ |
| 3 | Atrebatic B | Uncertain | Æ |
| 5 | Atrebatic B | (210-1ff) | A̸/Æ |
| 1 | Atrebatic D | (365-1) | A̸ |
| 2 | Atrebatic E | (385-1) | A̸ |
| 1 | Atrebatic E | (375-1) | A̸ |
| 1 | Atrebatic E | (390-1) | A̸ |
| 1 | Atrebatic E | (383-1) | Æ |
| 12 | Atrebatic G | (407-1) | A̸ |
| 4 | Atrebatic G | (415-1) | Æ |
| 1 | Atrebatic G | Uncertain | Æ |
| 5 | Atrebatic H | (435-1) | A̸ |
| 9 | Atrebatic I | (466-1) | A̸ |
| 6 | Atrebatic I | (467-1) | A̸ |
| 2 | Atrebatic I | (468-1) | A̸ |
| 5 | Atrebatic I | (470-1) | Æ |
| 1 | Atrebatic I | (473-1) | Æ |
| 6 | Atrebatic J | (505-1) | Æ |
| 3 | Atrebatic K | (531-1) | Æ |
| 12 | Atrebatic K | (530-1) | Æ |
| 14 | Atrebatic K | (533-1) | Æ |
| 1 | Atrebatic K | (551-1) | Æ |
| 45 | Atrebatic L | (580-1) | Æ |
| 15 | Atrebatic L | (581-1) | Æ |
| 1 | Atrebatic L | (585-1, but uncertain) | Æ |
| 4 | Atrebatic M | (595-1) | Æ |
| 7 | Atrebatic M | (593-1) | Æ |
| 2 | Atrebatic D,E,F | Uncertain | Æ |
| 15 | Atrebatic I,J,K | Uncertain | Æ |
| 1 | Trinovantian F | (1558-1) | Æ |
| 2 | Trinovantian W | (2057-1) | Æ |
| 1 | Dobunnic— | (1170-1) | Æ |

Two Gaulish Quarter Staters, one Gaulish silver coin and one unidentified bronze were also recovered.

The coins were found at the Weycock Hill Temple site, and were dispersed after discovery. Some were reported as from the 'Thames Gravels', but all are believed to have come from Weycock Hill.

97) Hayling Island, Hants., 1977-80 (Coastal Mixed)

| | | | |
|---|---|---|---|
| 2 | Gallo-Belgic E | (50-1ff) | A̸ |
| 1 | Gallo-Belgic XD | (80-1) | A̸ |

| 1 | Atrebatic A | (200-1 or 202-1) | AV/Æ |
|---|---|---|---|
| 2 | Atrebatic B | (210-1ff) | AV/Æ |
| 2 | Atrebatic E | (385-1) | AV/Æ |
| 1 | Atrebatic E | (390-1) | AV |
| 1 | Atrebatic E | (378-1) | AV |
| 1 | Atrebatic E | (383-1) | AV |
| 1 | Atrebatic F | (396-1 variety?) | Æ |
| 1 | Atrebatic D,E,F | Uncertain | Æ/Æ |
| 2 | Atrebatic I | (473-1) | Æ |
| 1 | Atrebatic I | (481-1) | Æ |
| 1 | Atrebatic J | (500-1) | AV |
| 1 | Atrebatic K | (520-1) | AV |
| 3 | Atrebatic K | (533-1) | Æ |
| 1 | Atrebatic K | (530-1) | Æ |
| 1 | Atrebatic K | (531-1) | Æ |
| 1 | Atrebatic K | (561-) | Æ |
| 1 | Atrebatic I,J,K | Uncertain | Æ |
| 1 | Atrebatic I,J,K | Uncertain | Æ/Æ |
| 1 | Atrebatic L | (580-1) | Æ/Æ |
| 1 | Durotrigan A | (1205-1) | AV |
| 6 | Durotrigan A | (1225-1) | AV |
| 7 | Durotrigan A | (1225-1) | AV/Æ |
| 9 | Durotrigan E | (1235-1) | Æ |
| 3 | Durotrigan E | (1235-3) | Æ/Æ |
| 1 | Durotrigan I | (1270-1) | Æ |
| 10 | Durotrigan— | (1280-1) | Æ |
| 1 | Durotrigan— | (1285-1) | Æ |
| 1 | Durotrigan J | (1290-1) | Æ |
| 1 | Cantian G | (144-1) | AV |
| 2 | Cantian— | Uncertain | AV/Æ |
| 1 | Trinovantian E | (1485-1ff) | AV/Æ |
| 1 | Trinovantian K | (1643-1) | Æ |
| 1 | Dobunnic A | (1020-1) | Æ |
| 2 | Dobunnic B | (1042-1) | Æ |
| 2 | Dobunnic D | (1078-1) | Æ |
| 3 | Dobunnic— Uncertain | Æ/Ae | |
| 2 | Dobunnic— | Uncertain | Æ |
| 1 | Corieltauvian M | (940-1) | AV/Æ |

Seven Gaulish potin coins, three Gaulish bronzes, two Gaulish silver pieces (M87 and M87a), one Gaulish Æ/Æ (Togirix) and one Gaulish Æ/Æ (Cricirv) were also found. One Armorican coin of the Coriosolites was also found.

The coins were found during archaeological excavation of a temple. However, the wide range of tribes represented is typical of a Coastal Mixed hoard.

98) Harlow Temple, Essex, 1962-83 (Trinovantian)

| 2 | Gallo-Belgic E | (50-1ff) | Æ |
|---|---|---|---|
| 3 | Trinovantian D | (1472-1ff) | Æ |
| 4 | Trinovantian D | (1474-1ff) | Æ |
| 3 | Trinovantian I | (1615-1) | Æ |
| 2 | Trinovantian J | (1626-1) | R |
| 2 | Trinovantian J | Uncertain | R |
| 2 | Trinovantian K | (1646-1) | Æ |
| 1 | Trinovantian L | (1669-1) | Æ |
| 7 | Trinovantian L | (1667-1) | Æ |
| 1 | Trinovantian L | Uncertain | Æ |
| 6 | Trinovantian M | (1713-1) | Æ |
| 2 | Trinovantian M | (1717-1) | Æ |
| 3 | Trinovantian M | (1711-1) | Æ |
| 1 | Trinovantian M | (1705-1) | Æ |
| 3 | Trinovantian M | (1707-1, 1709-1) | Æ |
| 1 | Trinovantian N | (1750-1) | Æ |
| 1 | Trinovantian O | (1818-1) | Æ |
| 4 | Trinovantian O | (1814-1) | Æ |
| 5 | Trinovantian O | (1812-1) | Æ |
| 1 | Trinovantian O | Uncertain | Æ |
| 5 | Trinovantian O | (1816-1) | Æ |
| 2 | Trinovantian O | (1820-1) | Æ |
| 7 | Trinovantian O | (1808-1) | Æ |
| 3 | Trinovantian O | (1810-1) | Æ |
| 1 | Trinovantian O | (1824-1) | Æ |
| 1 | Trinovantian R | (1877-1) | R |
| 6 | Trinovantian R | (1882-1) | Æ |
| 3 | Trinovantian S | (1892-1) | Æ |
| 3 | Trinovantian S | (1890-1) | Æ |
| 1 | Trinovantian S | (1895-1) | Æ |
| 1 | Trinovantian S | (1903-1) | Æ |
| 1 | Trinovantian Q | (1868-1) | R |
| 1 | Trinovantian U | (1973-3) | Æ |
| 1 | Trinovantian U | (1973-1) | Æ |
| 7 | Trinovantian U | (1983-1) | Æ |
| 3 | Trinovantian U | (1979-1) | Æ |
| 3 | Trinovantian U | (1977-1) | Æ |
| 17 | Trinovantian U | (1971-1) | Æ |
| 1 | Trinovantian W | (2015-1) | Æ |
| 1 | Trinovantian W | (2057-1) | R |
| 2 | Trinovantian W | (2085-1) | Æ |
| 1 | Trinovantian W | (2087-1) | Æ |
| 4 | Trinovantian W | (2081-1) | Æ |

| | | | |
|---|---|---|---|
| 7 | Trinovantian W | (2101-1) | Æ |
| 1 | Trinovantian W | (2103-1) | Æ |
| 15 | Trinovantian W | (2107-1) | Æ |
| 7 | Trinovantian W | (2105-1) | Æ |
| 5 | Trinovantian W | (2109-1) | Æ |
| 13 | Trinovantian W | (2095-1) | Æ |
| 23 | Trinovantian W | (2091-1) | Æ |
| 21 | Trinovantian W | (2089-1) | Æ |
| 38 | Trinovantian W | (2097-1) | Æ |
| 27 | Trinovantian W | (2093-1) | Æ |
| 39 | Trinovantian W | (2099-1) | Æ |
| 5 | Atrebatic B | (220-1ff) | N |
| 1 | Atrebatic H | (452-1) | Æ |
| 1 | Durotrigan J | (1290-1) | Æ |
| 1 | Corieltauvian D | (877-3) | R |
| 1 | Icenian O | (790-1) | R |

One uncertain Gaulish bronze coin was also found. The coins were recovered during archaeological excavations at a Celtic Temple site.

99) New Forest/Ashurst, Hants., 1987 (Durotrigan)

| | | | |
|---|---|---|---|
| 19 | Durotrigan A | (1205-1) | N |

100) Grimsby II, South Humberside, Ca. 1984 (Corieltauvian)

| | | | |
|---|---|---|---|
| 3-4 | Corieltauvian B | (804-1ff) | N |

The appearance of several Corieltauvian Staters during a 2-3 month period suggests a small hoard was dispersed.

101) Unknown Site, Ca. 1988 (Atrebatic)

| | | | |
|---|---|---|---|
| 1 | Atrebatic E | (375-1) | N |
| 3 | Atrebatic F | (385-1) | N |

Three coins, all similarly toned, appeared at the same time, possibly a small hoard, or Finkley Down (number 86) strays.

102) Snettisham II, Norfolk, 1987-8 (Interior Mixed)

Parcel one, 1987:

| | | | |
|---|---|---|---|
| 26 | Icenian A | (610-1) | N |
| 3 | Atrebatic B | (210-1ff) | N |
| 5 | Uncertain | Uncertain | N |
| 8 | Trinovantian F | (1505-1) | N |
| 1 | Icenian E | (665-9) | R |

Parcel two, 1988:

| 16 | Icenian A       | (610-1)              | N       |
|----|-----------------|----------------------|---------|
| 6  | Atrebatic B     | (210-1ff)            | N       |
| 2  | Uncertain       | Uncertain            | N       |
| 13 | Trinovantian F  | (1505-1)             | N       |
| 2  | Icenian E       | (665-9)              | R       |

Two parcels from the same hoard were found scattered over a 10 by 20 metre area.

103) Hengistbury II, Hants., 1970-1 (Cast Bronze)

| 8 | Cantian D | (122-1ff) | Æ |
|---|-----------|-----------|---|

Found during the Peacock excavations, not necessarily a hoard. The coins may represent scrap metal imported into Hengistbury for reworking, perhaps after they had been demonetized in Kent.

104) Hengistbury III, Hants., 1979-84 (Durotrigan)

| 1 | Durotrigan E | (1235-1)              | R       |
|---|--------------|-----------------------|---------|
| 1 | Durotrigan E | (1242-1)              | R       |
| 1 | Durotrigan I | (1270-1)              | R       |
| 1 | Durotrigan J | (1290-1)              | Æ       |
| 1 | Durotrigan K | Uncertain             | Æ       |
| 1 | Uncertain    | Uncertain             | Æ       |
| 4 | Uncertain    | Uncertain (fragments) | R or Æ  |

Nineteen Roman coins, Claudius to Constantine II, were also found. The coins were recovered during Barry Cunliffe's excavations, not necessarily a hoard.

# MODERN FORGERIES

Prior to 1960, modern forgeries—ones intended to deceive collectors—had not been a problem. One false stater made from a bronze alloy, carrying a reverse of 50-1 and an obverse of 1736-1, appeared in 1929. It is difficult to explain such a piece, but a modern origin is as likely as an ancient one. The coin now resides in the Museum of the American Numismatic Society.

Early in 1961, however, the picture changed. A 'hoard', supposedly found by a farmer between Guildford and Haslemere in 1944, appeared on the market. The farmer had hidden the coins but now wanted to sell them and the lot was quickly dispersed. Over the next few years, about 150 gold staters of the Gallo-Belgic E, Gallo-Belgic X and Whaddon Chase types were sold.

The coins all had a strange appearance, but an ingenious theory explained this. The coins must have been the work of an ancient forger who never managed to place his forgeries into circulation.

During the next twenty years, additional coins were offered—and all had the same unusual appearance. A hoard of Chute staters appeared in the early 1970's. By the late 1970's, however, suspicions were raised about the Haslemere hoard, and opinion was divided as to its authenticity. Haselgrove mentioned the controversy in his 1978 Gazetteer.

By 1984, the forgery was exposed, and evidence was offered in the form of die-cutting and metallurgical analyses (132). The forgeries were unlike ancient coins and must have been the work of a modern forger.

The forger, an inept die-cutter, was an incompetent metal worker as well. The coins, supposedly struck over a hundred-year period, all contained the same die-cutting error. Furthermore many different types were made from the same alloy—too many to be restrikes.

The full die-cutting and metallurgical evidence cannot be published until the forger is apprehended. At the time of writing, his identity is not known.

The Haslemere forgeries may be detected easily—once you know the identifying points. The primary means of detection lies in the die-cutting on the curves of the design. The forger was unable to cut smooth curves with a single stroke, as a Celtic craftsman did. Instead, he cut the curves with a series of hammer-blows to the graver, and these produced 'steps' on their sides. The steps can be seen with a 14x magnifying glass: one with good optical properties, such as the Bauch and Lomb Hastings Triplet, catalogue number 81-61-75.

The forger often recut his dies to create new types. Thus, much of his output is die-linked, and coins linked to those published here may be assumed to be false.

A few silver forgeries are known, and these are all illustrated. There are a few false gold staters which are not illustrated—all have pronounced steps and are easily detected. The coins lacking illustrations are:

—An example of 10-1F same obverse die, but a new reverse.

—Two examples of 33-1F, with the reverse die recut. One adds a pellet below the lyre, the second has the pellet changed to a line.

—Several examples of 87-1F, same reverse die, but new obverses.

—210-1F, 236-1F, 610-1F, 626-9F, a variety of 626-9F, 829-1F and 1635-1F.

In 1985, another forger produced copies of Durotrigan silver staters (1235-1), apparently cast. The coins are easily recognized by the unsharp images and the rough fields.

In 1988, a few struck forgeries have appeared. The coins display a poor style, and the numismatic trade quickly condemned the pieces. The types included a fantasy Dobunnic quarter stater, and forgeries of 353-5, 407-1, 467-1 and 2027-1.

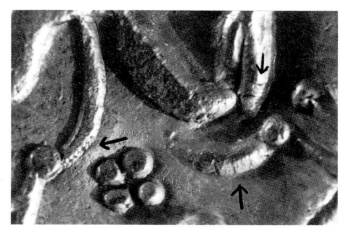

Arrows: three kinds of 'steps'
on a Haslemere forgery

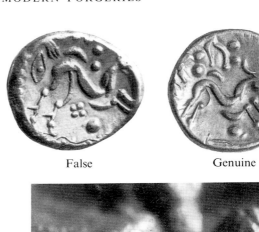

False                                    Genuine

False

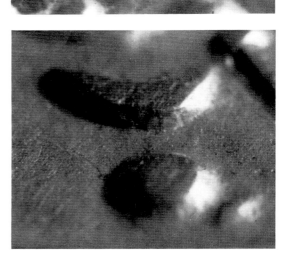

Genuine

# MODERN FORGERIES 1

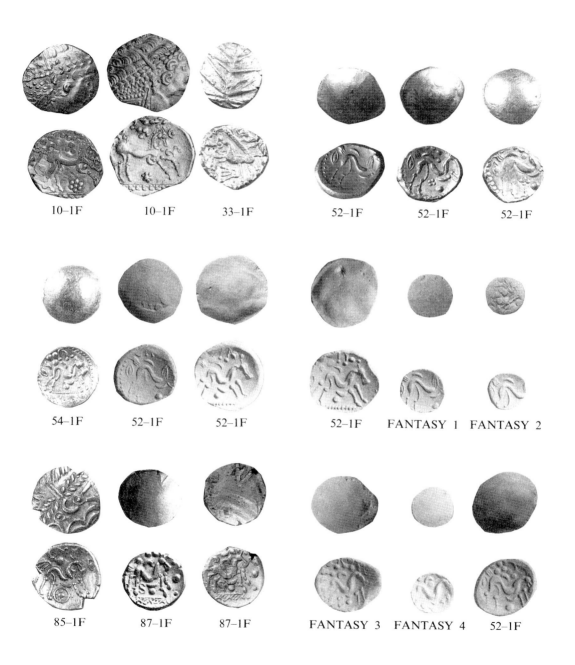

10–1F     10–1F     33–1F       52–1F     52–1F     52–1F

54–1F     52–1F     52–1F       52–1F     FANTASY 1     FANTASY 2

85–1F     87–1F     87–1F       FANTASY 3     FANTASY 4     52–1F

# MODERN FORGERIES 2

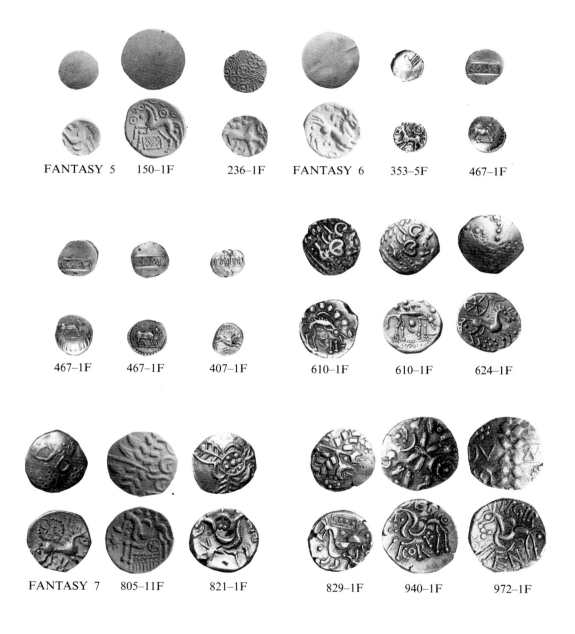

FANTASY 5    150–1F      236–1F      FANTASY 6    353–5F      467–1F

467–1F      467–1F      407–1F       610–1F      610–1F      624–1F

FANTASY 7    805–11F      821–1F       829–1F      940–1F      972–1F

# MODERN FORGERIES 3

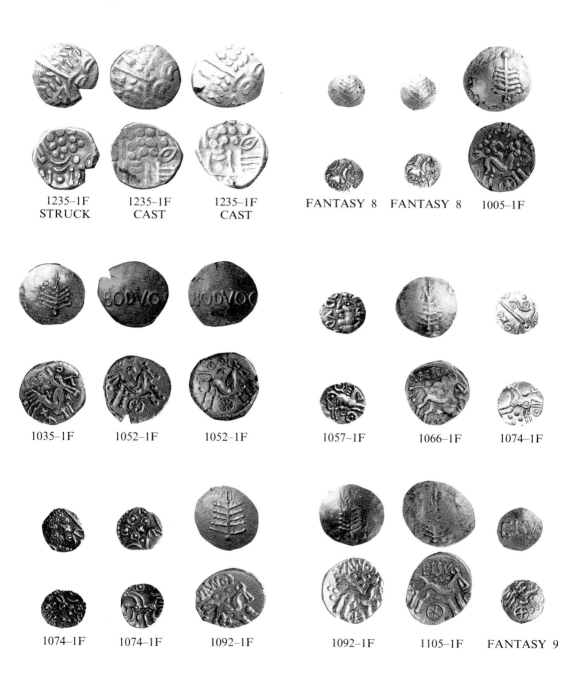

1235–1F
STRUCK

1235–1F
CAST

1235–1F
CAST

FANTASY 8

FANTASY 8

1005–1F

1035–1F

1052–1F

1052–1F

1057–1F

1066–1F

1074–1F

1074–1F

1074–1F

1092–1F

1092–1F

1105–1F

FANTASY 9

# MODERN FORGERIES 4

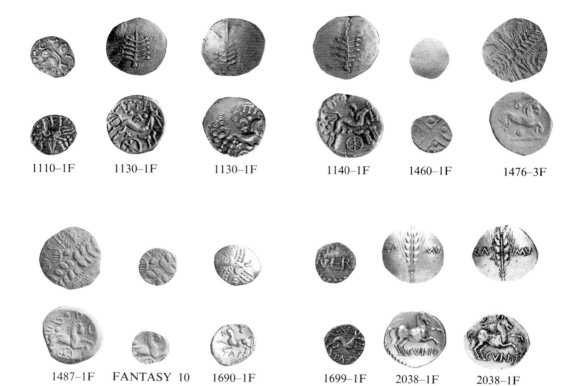

1110–1F     1130–1F     1130–1F     1140–1F     1460–1F     1476–3F

1487–1F     FANTASY 10     1690–1F     1699–1F     2038–1F     2038–1F

# FURTHER READING

It ought to be easy to learn about the Celts—but it isn't. Although there are scores of books about Celtic Society, most miss the point.

Celtic society provided a good standard of living for large numbers of people, but no Celt wrote about that success. Instead, we have only the written accounts of their enemies, the Greeks and Romans—and enemies seldom have good things to say.

If you look for tales of Druid sacrifices, incessant warfare, drunken brawls and superstition, these you will find. But if you want to find out why Celtic society was so successful at providing a good life for so many people, you run into a dead end—almost, except for the work of two men.

Peter J. Reynolds and Barry Cunliffe, using vastly different approaches, have arrived at a similiar conclusion—Celtic society functioned to control the environment for the benefit of the people. Peter J. Reynolds is an experimental archaeologist. He heads the Butser Iron Age Farm experiment, which tries to recreate the way a Celtic farm operated. Barry Cunliffe's work stays closer to the Celtic remains, using excavation as the means to obtain raw data.

Peter J. Reynolds' book, Iron Age Farm is a landmark study in experimental archaeology. Written for the general reader, it gives a remarkable account of Celtic agriculture and animal husbandry. Iron Age Farm is out of print, so locating a copy may be difficult—but the quest is worth it. Shire Archaeology has published a booklet (No. 50) entitled Ancient Farming which serves as a substitute.

Barry Cunliffe's Danebury: Anatomy of an Iron Age Hillfort gives the other side of the story—again written for the general reader. Based on fifteen years' excavations at Danebury, it shows how a hillfort worked: how the people lived, and how they organized their food supply, clothing and shelter. The degree of social organization attained, and the prosperity the people enjoyed as a result, are shown with great clarity.

The excellent Museum of the Iron Age at Andover is the place to start if you want to experience Celtic Society firsthand. The same clarity expressed in Danebury: Anatomy of an Iron Age Hillfort is shown in the displays—and the Hillfort is only a short distance away. Butser Iron Age Farm, only 40 miles from Andover, just south of Petersfield, is open to the public, and it completes a fascinating one-day tour. The farm has live displays and re-enactments—and complements the Andover material perfectly.

Scholarly books abound. The standard work on Celtic Britain is Barry Cunliffe's Iron Age Communities in Britain.

Trade in the Celtic world is discussed in Macready and Thompson's Cross-Channel Trade Between Gaul and Britain in the Pre-Roman Iron Age, and Cunfliffe's Greeks, Romans and Barbarians—Spheres of Interaction. The latter starts with a model of ancient trade, described with unusual clarity. It then discusses the ancient evidence, especially the Roman wine trade with Gaul, and finishes with a re-appraisal of the model.

Cunliffe and Miles' Aspects of the Iron Age in Central Southern Britain contains papers on a number of topics, including metallurgy and findspot analysis.

Tylecote's The Early History of Metallurgy in Europe, provides an overview of ancient metal-working, though its scope is much wider than the Iron Age.

Miranda Green's remarkable The Gods of the Celts seemingly draws blood from a stone. Evidence dating to the Pre-Roman Iron Age is rare, so most works on Celtic religion rely on artifacts from the Roman period or written accounts from the Anglo-Saxon. They sometimes fail to separate the later material out when they discuss the earlier period. But Dr. Green has separated the material carefully, drawn Iron Age inferences from Iron Age artifacts— and given us a work of great insight.

Barry Cunliffe's general work, The Celtic World provides an overview of Celtic Society throughout Europe.

Numismatic works abound, as well, but most are in the form of articles, rather than books.

Camden and Speed both used illustrations of Ancient British coins in their works. Paul Petavius published plates of Gallo-Belgic A, B and F types in 1610. But it was not until the eighteenth century that the first serious attempts to explain the Ancient coins were made.

Cunobeline's coinage received attention in Pegge (1766a). Pettingal (1763) argued the inscription TASCIA referred to the tax levied by Caesar on the British tribes. The tax idea was not new because others, including Horsely (Britannia Romana, 1732), had mentioned it before.

Borlase (1769) published an account of the Carn Brae hoard, a very early example of accurate recording, showing the way for future workers.

Stukeley attempted to create a general work on the British coinage, but this was never printed. However, the plates he prepared were published separately in 1776. It would be almost ninety years before the first general work on the coinage appeared.

The nineteenth century saw an incease in publishing activity. Ruding illustrated many new types in his Annals of the Coinage (1840). Coloured illustrations, using the chromolithographic process, appeared in Humphrey's The Coinage of the British Empire (1855). Scholars soon began to unravel the complexities of the coinage, using new analytical techniques.

By 1849, Akerman placed the study on a sounder footing by publishing the first distribution map of coin findspots. He demonstrated some types must be British, because they were found in Britain. This study was to be the forerunner of modern trend surface analysis.

1849 also saw a paper by Evans, arguing chronology and typology. Evans was to go on to become the leading man in the field of Ancient British coins by the 1860's. His book The Coins of the Ancient Britons (1864, Supplement

1890), the first general work on the coinage, was to stand for ninety years. In many ways, it has never been replaced, and is still an essential reference for anyone studying the coinage.

The brilliance of Evans' work was in the integrated approach he took to analyze the coins. He demonstrated the proper way to study Celtic coins was to analyze them from different viewpoints and synthesize the results. Evans argued using typology, metrology, findspot distribution analysis and the accounts of the ancient authors—in unison. He even made an attempt to bring metallurgical studies into the picture, but the technology of the day did not provide the means to do this with precision.

A contemporary of Evans', Beale Poste, wrote a series of books about the coinage, but these have been largely forgotten. Poste and Evans disagreed on their interpretations, and the disagreements often spilled into print. Poste's views eventually lost out—but his books contain a wealth of information about findspots and new discoveries.

After Evans' death, the study of the Ancient British coins languished for a time. Hill published an important paper on the Clacton hoard in 1919, and Brooke published two papers in 1933, analyzing the imported coins. But no major work was done until Derek Allen appeared on the scene.

Brooke had died before he had a chance to analyze the dynastic coins, and this work was left for Allen to complete. Allen's landmark 'The Belgic Dynasties of Britain and their Coins', appeared in 1944, establishing him as the expert in the field. Allen, using typological studies and findspot distributions, was able to revise Evans' work and reorganize the coinage. His work enabled Mack to produce the first catalogue of the coins in 1953.

By 1958, Allen had gathered and organized the findspot data from all the diverse sources, and reinterpreted the introduction of coinage in Britain. The work was published in 1960 as 'The Origins of Coinage in Britain: A Reappraisal', his second landmark paper. One of his most significant studies appeared in Proceedings of the Prehistoric Society, 1958. It was concerned with the artistic inspiration of the coins, and its reflection of the daily life of the Celts. Scheers, 1969, and Henig, 1972 continued the work on the artistic inspiration—most of the comments about type-derivations come from these two important articles.

Allen went on to study the coinage of the different tribes, one by one. He wrote on the Dobunni (1961), the Corieltauvi (1963), the Durotriges (1968) and the Iceni (1970). He then studied several inscribed coinages in detail, publishing a major article on Cunobeline's gold in 1975. An article on Verica's gold appeared posthumously in 1979, completed by Colin Haselgrove. Haselgrove continued Allen's publication of coin findspots, publishing Gazetteers in 1978 and 1984, and a collation of finds from archaeological excavations in 1988.

Allen also wrote on the cast bronzes of Kent in 1971, using typology as a major approach to interpretation. J. P. Wild had suggested papyrus was used to make the moulds for some of these coins, and Allen's article published experiments which seemed to support the idea. This was to excite the imagination of many who saw contacts between Britain and Egypt in the evidence.

Mack, however, had been assembling a series of cast bronzes starting in the late 1950's. By 1970 he knew most of the major varieties, and could have written a reinterpretation of these coins. Although the way he assembled his collection shows he had new insights, he never published anything to question the papyrus idea.

Even before 1970, some of Allen's work began to be questioned, because the archaeological record no longer provided support. A series of invasions could not be the mechanism by which coins were introduced in Britain because evidence for invasions (at the time the coins were imported) could not be found. Even the existence of tribes with groups on both sides of the Channel was not proof of invasion—these could be the result of treaties, marriages or peaceful immigration.

Rodwell published his iconoclastic 'Coinage, Oppida and the Rise of Belgic Power in Southeast Britain' in 1976. He raised many important objections to the traditional interpretation, and offered some alternatives. Other workers, Collis in 1971 and 1974, and Kent in 1976, suggested new approaches to analyzing the coins.

Initially, it appeared models could be constructed and tested to offer a new explanation of the coinage. Although this approach suggested some interesting new directions, the scientific data were not available for the tests. It was not until metallurgical, metrological and trend-surface analyses were completed in the mid-1980's that a new synthesis could be offered.

# NOTES

[1] Caesar, The Gallic War, V, 12.
[2] Cunliffe 1978a, p. 292ff.
[3] Northover 1982.
[4] Macready and Thompson 1982, Cunliffe 1987b, and Cunliffe and Miles 1984, for a general discussion.
[5] Cunliffe 1988, for a general discussion.
[6] Van Arsdell forthcoming, numbers 25 and 29.
[7] Cunliffe 1988, for a general discussion, Haselgrove 1988, p.7ff.
[8] Van Arsdell forthcoming, numbers 25 and 29.
[9] Van Arsdell 1986e.
[10] Van Arsdell forthcoming, number 29.
[11] Van Arsdell forthcoming, number 8.
[12] Van Arsdell forthcoming, number 29.
[13] Laing 1969, p.177.
[14] Scheers 1983, p. 268ff.
[15] Scheers 1983, p. 274ff.
[16] Van Arsdell forthcoming, number 29.
[17] Scheers 1972.
[18] Van Arsdell 1984c, 1985a and 1986c.
[19] Van Arsdell 1984a.
[20] Allen 1960, Haselgrove 1978, 1984a.
[21] Allen 1960, p.105, Van Arsdell forthcoming, number 30.
[22] Van Arsdell 1983a, 1984d, forthcoming, numbers 4, 10, 25.
[23] Van Arsdell forthcoming, number 7.
[24] Van Arsdell 1983a, 1986b.
[25] Van Arsdell 1986b, for a general discussion.
[26] Van Arsdell forthcoming, numbers 18, 19, 20, 25, for a general discussion.
[27] Van Arsdell forthcoming, numbers 5, 25.
[28] Van Arsdell forthcoming, number 30, for a general discussion.
[29] Van Arsdell 1984a, forthcoming, numbers 16, 17, 32.
[30] Van Arsdell forthcoming, number 15.
[31] Van Arsdell forthcoming, number 30.
[32] Van Arsdell forthcoming, number 29.
[33] Van Arsdell forthcoming, number 29.
[34] Van Arsdell forthcoming, number 3.
[35] Van Arsdell forthcoming, numbers 21, 25, 26.
[36] Van Arsdell forthcoming, number 24.
[37] Van Arsdell forthcoming, number 26.
[38] Van Arsdell forthcoming, numbers 25, 26.
[39] Van Arsdell forthcoming, number 3, for a general discussion.
[40] Cunliffe 1978b, for a general discussion.
[41] Van Arsdell forthcoming, number 24.
[42] Van Arsdell forthcoming, number 29.
[43] Van Arsdell forthcoming, numbers 3, 4.
[44] Van Arsdell forthcoming, number 29.
[45] Haselgrove 1988, p. 317ff, Van Arsdell forthcoming, number 2.
[46] Allen 1944.
[47] Van Arsdell forthcoming, number 33.
[48] Van Arsdell forthcoming, number 29.
[49] Van Arsdell 1984a.
[50] Van Arsdell 1985b.
[51] Van Arsdell forthcoming, number 24, for a general discussion.
[52] Van Arsdell forthcoming, numbers 4, 18.
[53] Van Arsdell forthcoming, number 17.

[54]  Van Arsdell forthcoming, number 17.
[55]  Van Arsdell forthcoming, number 19.
[56]  Van Arsdell forthcoming, number 20.
[57]  Van Arsdell forthcoming, numbers 19, 20.
[58]  Van Arsdell 1986h, 1987a.
[59]  Van Arsdell forthcoming, numbers 3, 24.
[60]  Van Arsdell forthcoming, number 2.
[61]  Van Arsdell forthcoming, number 15.
[62]  Van Arsdell 1985b.
[63]  Van Arsdell forthcoming, number 24.
[64]  Henig 1972, Scheers 1969, 1982a.
[65]  Van Arsdell forthcoming, number 17.
[66]  Van Arsdell forthcoming, number 17.
[67]  Van Arsdell 1985a, 1985c.
[68]  Van Arsdell forthcoming, number 6.
[69]  Van Arsdell forthcoming, number 11.
[70]  Van Arsdell forthcoming, numbers 11, 20.
[71]  Van Arsdell forthcoming, number 24.
[72]  Van Arsdell forthcoming, number 24.
[73]  Van Arsdell forthcoming, numbers 16, 31, for a general discussion.
[74]  Van Arsdell forthcoming, numbers 17, 24, for a general discussion.
[75]  Van Arsdell forthcoming, number 32.
[76]  Mossop 1979.
[77]  Van Arsdell 1987b.
[78]  Van Arsdell forthcoming, numbers 17, 24, for a general discussion.
[79]  Van Arsdell forthcoming, number 15.
[80]  Van Arsdell 1986a, Forthcoming number 4, for a general discussion.
[81]  Van Arsdell 1986c, forthcoming number 29, for a general discussion.
[82]  Van Arsdell 1985a, 1985c.
[83]  Van Arsdell 1987b.
[84]  Collis 1971a, p. 79, 1974a, p. 5, Rodwell 1976, pp. 212, 314.
[85]  Van Arsdell 1986a.
[86]  Clifford 1961, pp. 98—99.
[87]  Van Arsdell forthcoming, number 4.
[88]  Allen 1975.
[89]  Van Arsdell forthcoming, numbers 4, 18.
[90]  Van Arsdell 1984a.
[91]  Van Arsdell 1985b.
[92]  Henig 1972, Scheers 1969, 1982a.
[93]  Van Arsdell 1984a.
[94]  Henig 1972, for a general discussion.
[95]  Allen 1958a.
[96]  Hawkes and Hull 1947, p. 129, Frere 1983, p. 30.
[97]  Sellwood, D. 1963, 1976, for a general discussion.
[98]  Sellwood, D. 1976.
[99]  Sellwood. D. 1976.
[100]  Debord 1982b, Clifford 1961, p. 147.
[101]  Frere 1983, p. 32.
[102]  Hawkes and Hull 1947, p. 129, Frere 1983, p. 32.
[103]  Frere 1983, p. 32.
[104]  Van Arsdell forthcoming, numbers 22, 29, for a general discussion.
[105]  Van Arsdell forthcoming, number 27.
[106]  Van Arsdell forthcoming, numbers 22, 28.
[107]  Clifford 1961, p. 97.
[108]  Van Arsdell 1987b.
[109]  Van Arsdell 1986b, for a general discussion.
[110]  Clifford 1961, p. 98.
[111]  Van Arsdell forthcoming, numbers 27, 29, 30.

[112] Kellner 1970, for a general discussion.
[113] Van Arsdell forthcoming, numbers 2, 5, 6, 7.
[114] Allen 1970.
[115] Van Arsdell forthcoming, number 25.
[116] Van Arsdell forthcoming, number 1.
[117] Van Arsdell forthcoming, number 3.
[118] Van Arsdell forthcoming, number 3.
[119] Van Arsdell forthcoming, number 3.
[120] Van Arsdell forthcoming, number 26.
[121] Van Arsdell forthcoming, number 17.
[122] Van Arsdell forthcoming, number 17.
[123] Allen 1961a.
[124] Van Arsdell forthcoming, number 15.
[125] Hodder and Orton 1976, p. 155ff, Orton 1980, p. 124ff.
[126] Van Arsdell forthcoming, number 29.
[127] Van Arsdell forthcoming, number 27.
[128] Van Arsdell forthcoming, number 3.
[129] Van Arsdell forthcoming, number 15.
[130] Van Arsdell forthcoming, numbers 2 and 6.
[131] Van Arsdell forthcoming, number 3.
[132] Van Arsdell 1984c and 1986i.

# SELECT BIBLIOGRAPHY

Abbreviations: BAR    —British Archaeological Reports
              BARS  —British Archaeological Reports Supplementary
                         Series
              BNJ     —British Numismatic Journal
              CBA     —Council for British Archaeology
              JNG     —Jahrbuch fuer Numismatik und Geldgeschichte
              NC      —Numismatic Chronicle
              NCIRC —Spink Numismatic Circular
              OJA     —Oxford Journal of Archaeology
              PPS     —Proceedings of the Prehistoric Society
              RN      —Revue Numismatique
              SCBI    —Sylloge of Coins of the British Isles

Akerman, J. Y., 1846, Ancient Coins of Cities and Princes, London.

Akerman, J. Y., 1849, 'On the Condition of Britain from the Descent of Caesar to the Coming of Claudius', Archaeologia, Vol. 33, p.177.

Allen, D. F., 1944, 'The Belgic Dynasties and their Coins', Archaeologia, Vol. XC, p. 1.

Allen, D. F., 1958a, 'Belgic Coins as Illustrations of Life in the Pre-Roman Iron Age of Britain', PPS, Vol. 24, p. 43.

Allen, D. F., 1958b, 'A New Celtic Coin from Worcester', Trans. Worcs. Arch. Soc., Vol. XXXV, p. 71.

Allen, D. F., 1960, 'The Origins of Coinage in Britain: a Reappraisal', in: Frere, S. S. (ed.) 1960.

Allen, D. F., 1961a, 'A Study of the Dobunnic Coinage', in: Clifford, E. M. 1961, p. 75.

Allen, D. F., 1962, 'Celtic Coins', in: Ordnance Survey, Map of Southern Britain in the Iron Age, Chessington.

Allen, D. F., 1963, The Coinage of the Coritani, SCBI, No.3, 1963.

Allen, D. F., 1964, 'Celtic Coins from the Romano-British Temple at Harlow', Essex, BNJ, Vol. 33, p. 1.

Allen, D. F., 1967a, 'Celtic Coins from the Romano-British Temple at Harlow', Essex, BNJ, Vol. 36, p. 1.

Allen, D. F., 1967b, 'Iron Currency Bars in Britain', PPS, Vol. 33, p. 307.

Allen, D. F., 1968a, 'Celtic Coins from the Romano-British Temple at Harlow, Essex', BNJ, Vol. 37, p. 1.

Allen, D. F., 1968b, 'The Celtic Coins', in Richmond, I. 1968, p. 43.

Allen, D. F., 1970a, 'The Coins of the Iceni', Britannia I, 1970, p. 1.

Allen, D. F., 1971, 'British Potin Coins: a Review', in: Jesson, D. and Hill, D. 1970, p. 127.

Allen, D. F., 1973, 'Temples or Shrines on Gaulish Coins', Antiquaries Journal, Vol. LIII, Part I, p. 71.

Allen, D. F., 1975, 'Cunobeline's Gold', Britannia VI, 1975, p. 1.

Allen, D. F., 1976a, 'Wealth, Money and Coinage in a Celtic Society', in: Megaw, J. V. S., To Illustrate the Monuments, 1976, p. 200.

Allen, D. F., 1976b, 'Some Contrasts in Gaulish and British Coins', in: Duval, P. and Hawkes, C. 1976, p. 265.

Allen, D. F., 1978, An Introduction to Celtic Coins, British Museum Publications, London.

Allen, D. F., and Haselgrove, C. C., 1979, 'The Gold Coinage of Verica', Britannia X, 1979, p. 1.

Allen, D. F., and Nash, D., 1980, The Coins of the Ancient Celts.

Barral, M., Gruel, K., Barralis, J. and Widemann, F., 1983, 'Quelques éléments de métallurgie monétaire Gauloise', Journées de Paléometallurgie, p. 129.

Bierbrier, M. L., (ed.), 1986, Papyrus: Structure and Usage, British Museum Occasional Paper No. 60.

Blunt, C. E., Elmore Jones, F. and Mack, R. P., 1971, Collection of Ancient British, Romano-British and English Coins formed by Mrs. Emery May Norweb, SCBI No. 16.

Boon, G. C., 1985, 'Ancient British and Gaulish Coins from Silchester', in: Fulford, M. 1985, p. 13.

Borlase, W. 1769, Antiquities, Historical and Monumental, of the County of Cornwall, Second Edition, p. 258.

Brady, J., 1982, American Collections, SCBI Vol. 30.

Brooke, G. C., 1933a, 'The Philippus in the West and the Belgic Invasions of Britain', NC, Series 5, Vol. 13, p. 88.

Brooke, G. C., 1933b, 'The Distribution of Gaulish and British Coins in Britain', Antiquity, Vol. 7, p. 268.

Capers, R. M. and Maddox, J., 1965, Images and Imagination—An Introduction to Art, New York.

Casey, P. J., and Reece, R., 1974 (eds.), Coins and the Archaeologist, BAR Vol. 4, Oxford.

Clarke, R. R., 1954, 'The Early Iron Age Treasure from Snettisham, Norfolk', PPS, Vol. 20, p. 27.

Clifford, E. M., 1961, Bagendon: a Belgic Oppidum, Cambridge.

Colbert de Beaulieu, J.-B., 1958, 'Armorican Coin Hoards in the Channel Islands', PPS, Vol. 24, p. 201.

Colbert de Beaulieu, J.-B., 1973, Traité de Numismatique Celtique—I: Methodologie des ensembles, Paris.

Collis, J. R., 1971a, 'Functional and Theoretical Interpretations of British Coinage', World Archaeology, Vol. 3, p. 71.

Collis, J. R., 1971b, 'Markets and Money', in: Jesson, M. and Hill, D. 1971, p. 97.

Collis, J. R., 1974a, 'A Functionalist Approach to Pre-Roman Coinage', in: Casey and Reece 1974, p. 1.

Collis, J. R., 1984, The European Iron Age, London.

Cunliffe, B. W., 1978a, Iron Age Communities in Britain, Second Edition, London.

Cunliffe, B. W., 1978b, Hengistbury Head, London.

Cunliffe, B. W., 1979, The Celtic World, Maidenhead.

Cunliffe, B. W., (ed.), 1981a, Coinage and Society in Britain and Gaul: Some Current Problems, CBA Research Report No. 38, London.

Cunliffe, B. W., 1981b, 'Money and Society in Pre-Roman Britain', in: Cunliffe, B. W. (ed.) 1981c, p. 29.

Cunliffe, B. W., (ed.), 1981c, Coinage and Society in Britain and Gaul: Some Current Problems, in: Cunliffe, B. W. 1981a.

Cunliffe, B. W., 1983, Danebury—Anatomy of an Iron Age Hillfort, London.

Cunliffe, B. W., 1984, Danebury: An Iron Age Hillfort in Hampshire, CBA Publication no. 52.

Cunliffe, B. W., 1987a, Danebury—The Story of an Iron Age Hillfort, Hampshire County Council—Museum of the Iron Age, Andover.

Cunliffe, B. W., 1987b, Hengistbury Head Dorset, Oxford University Committee for Archaeology, Monograph No 13.

Cunliffe, B. W., 1988, Greeks, Romans and Barbarians—Spheres of Interaction, London.

Cunliffe, B. W. and Miles, D., 1984, Aspects of the Iron Age in Central Southern Britain, University of Oxford: Committee for Archaeology Monograph No. 2.

Cunliffe B. W., and Rowley, T., 1976, Oppida in Barbarian Europe, BARS No. 11, Oxford.

Debord, J., 1981, 'Découverte d'un nouveau statère du type: 'British Q' à Villeneuve-Saint-Germain (Aisne)', Cahiers Numismatiques, No. 69 and 70, p. 71.

Debord, J., 1982a, 'Nouvelles découvertes de monnaies gauloises à Villeneuve-Saint-Germain (Aisne)', RN, Vol. 24, p. 27.

Debord, J., 1982b, 'Premier bilan de huit années de fouilles à Villeneuve-Saint-Germain (Aisne)', Rev. Num. de Picardie, p. 213.

Debord, J., 1983a, 'Attribution de la monnaie gauloise en potin du type BN 7602—7605', Cahiers Numismatiques, No. 76, p. 252.

Debord, J., 1983b, 'Découverte à Villeneuve-Saint-Germain (Aisne) d'un 'Bronze d'Ambleny'', Cahiers Numismatiques, No. 78, p. 283.

Debord, J., 1984, 'Nouvel additif aux découvertes monétaires à l'oppidum de Pommiers (Aisne)', Bull. de la Soc. Arch., Hist. et Sci. de Soissons, Vol. 14, p. 159.

Debord, J, Giroussens, C., Gruel, K, Romero, P. and Tarrats-Saugnac, A., 1985, 'Étude métallographique et analyse de materiél monétaire de l'atelier de Villenueve-Saint-Germain (Aisne)', in: Les Âges du Fer dans la Vallée de la Sâone (6e Supplement RAE, Eds. du CNRS), Paris, p. 271.

Debord, J. and Huysecom, E., 1981, 'Une contrefaçon en laiton de statère Ambien uniface', Cahiers Numismatiques, No. 68, p. 54.

Debord, J. and Scheers, S., 1984, 'Les monnaies Gauloises tardives en argent attribuables aux Suessiones trouvées à Villeneuve-Saint-Germain (Aisne)', Revue du Nord, p. 69.

Dolley, R. H. M., 1954, 'The Speculum ('Tin') Coins in Hoards C', in: Clarke, R. R. 1954, p. 72.

(Doubleday, J.), 1848, 'Remarks on the Ancient British Coins', and 'A Descriptive Catalogue of the Coins', in: Monumenta Historica Britannica or Materials for the History of Britain, London, p. cli.

Duval, P. and Hawkes, C., (eds.), 1976, Celtic Art in Europe, London.

Duval, P., 1978, Die Kelten, Universum der Kunst Band 25, Muenchen.

Evans, J., 1849, 'On the Date of British Coins', NC, Vol. 12, 127.

Evans, J., 1864, The Coins of the Ancient Britons, London.

Evans, J., 1890, The Coins of the Ancient Britons: Supplement, London.

Fischer, B., 1985, 'Les monnaies gauloises de Mailain (Côte-d'Or)', Revue Archéologique de l'Est, p. 229.

Fitzpatrick, A. P., 1985, 'The Celtic Coins', in: France, N. E. and Gobel, B. M. 1985.

Foster, J., 1986, The Lexden Tumulus: a Reappraisal of an Iron Age Burial from Colchester, Essex, BAR 156, Oxford.

France, N. E., and Gobel, B. M., 1985, The Romano-British Temple at Harlow, Gloucester.

Frere, S. S., (ed.) 1960, Problems of the Iron Age in Southern Britain, Institute of Archaeology London Occasional Paper number 11, London.

Frere, S. S., 1983, 'The Belgic Mint', in: Verulamium Excavations, Vol. II, London, p. 30.

Fulford, M., (nd) Guide to the Silchester Excavations: the Forum Basilica 1982—84, Reading.

Furger-Gunti, A,. 1982, 'Zur Chronologie Keltischer Gold- und Potinmuenzen', Actes du 9e Congrès International de Numismatique, Berne, 1979, Vol. I, p. 587, Louvain-la-Neuve, Luxembourg.

Glendining, 1917, Watters Sale Part 1, 21 May.

Glendining, 1939, Drabble Sale Part 1, 4 July.

Glendining, 1944, Lord Grantley Sale Part 2, 27 June.

Glendining, 1956, Taffs Sale, 21 November.

Glendining, 1955, Lockett Sale Part 1, 6 June.

Glendining, 1975, Mack Collection Sale, Part 1, 18 November.

Goebl, R., 1972, 'Neue technische Forschungsmethoden in der keltischen Numismatik', Oesterreichische Akademie der Wissenschaft, Wien.

Grasmann, G., Janssen, W. and Brandt, M., 1984, Keltische Numismatik und Archaeologie, BAR. Vol 200, Oxford.

Green, M., 1986, The Gods of the Celts, Gloucester.

Grierson, P., 1958, Fitzwilliam Museum Cambridge, SCBI Vol 1.

Grinsell, L. V., Blunt, C. E. and Dolley, M., Bristol and Gloucester Museums, SCBI Vol. 19.

Gruel, K., 1981a, Le Trèsor de Trebry (Côtes du Nord), ler siècle avant notre ère, Paris.

Gruel, K., 1981b, 'Étude des liasons de coins dans le trèsor de monnaies Coriosolites de Trebry', PACT Vol. 5, Statistics and Numismatics, p. 214.

Gruel, K., 1986, 'Propositions for a Relative Chronology of the Coriosolitea Coinage (First Century BC)', in: Johnson, (ed.), The Archaeology of the Channel Islands, p. 98, Chichester.

Gruel, K. and Clement, M., 1985, Les Monnaies Gauloises du fanum de Trogouzel (29), Essai d'Interpretation.

Gunstone, A. J. H., 1971, Ancient British, Anglo-Saxon and Norman Coins in Midlands Museums, SCBI Vol. 17.

Gunstone, A. J. H., 1977, Ancient British, Anglo-Saxon and Norman Coins in West Country Museums, SCBI Vol. 24.

Gunstone, A.J. H., 1981, Coins in Lincolnshire Collections, SCBI Vol. 27, pl. LV.

Hall, E. T., and Metcalf, D. M., (eds.), 1972, Methods of Chemical and Metallurgical Investigation of Ancient Coinage, London.

Harding, D. W., 1972, The Iron Age in the Upper Thames Basin, Oxford.

Harding, D. W., 1974, The Iron Age in Lowland Britain, London.

Haselgrove, C. C., 1976, 'External Trade as a Stimulus to Urbanization', in: Cunliffe, B. W. and Rowley, T. 1976.

Haselgrove, C. C., 1978, Supplementary Gazetteer of Findspots of Celtic Coins in Britain, 1977, Institute of Archaeology, London, Occasional Paper, No. 11a, London.

Haselgrove, C. C., 1984a, 'Celtic Coins found in Britain 1977— 82', Bulletin No. 20, of the Institute of Archaeology of London, London, p. 107.

Haselgrove, C. C., 1987, Iron Age Coinage in South-East England: The Archaeological Context, BAR British Series, No. 174, Oxford.

Hawkes, C. F. C., and Hull, M. R., 1947, Camulodunum, Research Report of the Society of Antiquaries of London, No. 15, Oxford.

Henig, M., 1972, 'The Origin of Some Ancient British Coin Types', Britannia III, p. 209.

Hill, G. F., 'A Find of Ancient British Gold Coins', NC, 1919, p. 172.

Holmes, T. R., 1907, Ancient Britain and the Invasions of Julius Caesar, Oxford.

Hodder, I. and Orton, C., 1976, Spatial Analysis in Archaeology, Cambridge.

Humphreys, N., 1855, The Coinage of the British Empire, London.

Jacobstal, P., 1944, Early Celtic Art, Oxford.

Jesson, M., and Hill, D., (eds.), 1971 The Iron Age and Its Hillforts, Southampton.

Kellner, H., 1970, 'Der Fund von Tayac, ein Zeugnis des Cimbernzuges?', JNG, Band XX, p. 13.

Kent, J. P. C., 1978a, 'The Origin and Development of Celtic Gold Coinage in Britain', Actes du Colloque International D'archéologie, Rouen, p. 313.

Kent, J. P. C., 1978b, 'The London Area in the Late Iron Age: An Interpretation of the Earliest Coins', in: Collectanea Londiniensia: Studies Presented to Ralph Merrifield, p. 53.

Kent, J. P. C., 1981, 'The Origins of Coinage in Britain', in: Cunliffe, B. W. 1981c.

Koenig, M., 1977, Das Fenster in der Halle der Kreissparkasse Koeln—die Muenzen der Kelten.

Kruta, V. and Foreman, W., 1985, The Celts of the West, London.

Laing, L., 1969, Coins and Archaeology, New York.

Lengyel, L., 1954, L'Art Gaulois dans les Médailles, Paris.

Lengyel, L., 1969, Le Secret des Celtes.

Mack, R. P., 1953, The Coinage of Ancient Britain, London.

Mack, R. P., 1964, The Coinage of Ancient Britain, London.

Mack, R. P., 1973, R. P. Mack Collection—Ancient British, Anglo-Saxon and Norman Coins, SCBI Vol 20.

Mack, R. P., 1975, The Coinage of Ancient Britain, London.

Mackensen, M., 1974, 'Die Aelteste Keltische Geld- und Silberpraegung in England', JNG, Band XXIV, p. 7.

Macready, S. and Thompson, F. H., 1984, (eds.), Cross-Channel Trade Between Gaul and Britain in the Pre-Roman Iron Age, London.

Mays, M., 1987, 'Durotrigan Coins', in: Cunliffe, B. W. 1987b.

Megaw, J. V. S., 1970, Art of the European Iron Age, Bath and New York.

Megaw, R. and Megaw, V., 1986, Early Celtic Art in Britain and Ireland, Shire Archaeology, Aylesbury.

Montagu, H., 1886, 'Find of Ancient British Gold Coins in Suffolk', NC ser. 3 vi, p. 23.

Mossop, H. R., 1979, 'An Elusive Icenian Legend', Britannia X, 1979, p. 258.

Muckelroy, K., Haselgrove, C. C., and Nash, D., 1979, 'A Pre-Roman Coin from Canterbury and the Ship Represented on it, PPS, Vol. 44, p. 439.

Nash, D., 1978, Settlement and Coinage in Central Gaul C. 200 - 50 B.C., BARS 39, Oxford.

Nash, D., 1982, 'Adminius Did Strike Coins', OJA, Vol. 1, p. 111.

Nash, D., 1987, Coinage in the Celtic World, London.

Niblett, R., 1985, Sheepen: An Early Roman Industrial Site at Camulodunum, CBA Research Report No 47, London.

Northover, P., 1982, 'The Metallurgy of the Wilburton Hoards', OJA, Mar., p. 69.

Ordnance Survey, 1962, Map of Southern Britain in the Iron Age, Chessington.

Orton, C., 1980, Mathematics in Archaeology, London.

Partridge, C., 1981, Skeleton Green, CBA Research Report No. 2, London.

Peacock, D. P. S., 1971, 'Roman Amphorae in Pre-Roman Britain', in: Jesson, M. and Hill, D. 1971.

Peacock, D. P. S., 1984, 'Amphorae in Iron Age Britain': A Reassessment, in: Macready, S. and Thompson, F. H. 1984.

Pegge, S., 1766a, An Essay on the Coins of Cunobelin, London.

Pegge, S., 1766b, A Dissertation on the Seat of the Coritani, London.

Petavius, P., 1610, Veterum Nummorum Gnorisma, Paris.

Pettingal, J., 1763, A Dissertation upon the Tascia or Legend on the British Coins of Cunobelin and Others, London.

Pirie, J. E., 1975, Coins in Yorkshire Collections, Part II, SCBI Vol 21.

Pitt-Rivers, A. H., 1881, 'Excavations at Mount Caburn Camp, Near Lewes, Conducted in September and October, 1877, and July, 1878', Archaeologia Vol. 46, p. 423.

Poste, B., 1853, The Coins of Cunobeline and of the Ancient Britons, London.

Poste, B., 1861, Celtic Inscriptions on Gaulish and British Coins, London.

Reding, L., 1972, Les Monnaies Gauloises du Tetelbierg, Luxembourg.

Reece, R., 1984, 'The Coins', in: Frere, S. S. 1983.

Reynolds, P. J., 1976, Farming in the Iron Age, Cambridge University Press, Cambridge.

Reynolds, P. J., 1979, Iron-Age Farm—The Butser Experiment, British Museum Publications, London.

Reynolds, P. J. 1987, Ancient Farming, Shire Archaeology, Aylesbury.

Roach Smith, C., 1863, 'Coins Found in Kent', in: Collectanea Antiqua No. 1, p. 5.

Roach Smith, C., 1863, 'Gold British, or Gaulish Coins Found at Bognor and Alfriston in Sussex', in: Collectanea Antiqua Vol. 1, p. 9.

Robinson, P. H., 1977 'A Local Iron Age Coinage in Silver and Perhaps Gold in Wiltshire', BNJ Vol. 47, p. 5.

Rodwell, W. J., 1976, 'Coinage, Oppida and the Rise of Belgic Power in Southeast Britain', in: Cunliffe, B. W. and Rowley, T. 1976.

Rodwell, W. R., (1981), 'Lost and Found: the Archaeology of Find-Spots of Celtic Coins', in: Cunliffe, B. W. 1981c, p. 43.

Ross, A., 1968, Pagan Celtic Britain, London.

Rowlands, M., Larsen, M., and Kristiansen, K. (eds.), 1987, Centre and Periphery in the Ancient World, New Directions in Archaeology Series, Cambridge University Press.

Ruding, R., 1840, Annals of the Coinage of Britain, 3rd edition, London.

Salway, P., 1981, Roman Britain, Oxford.

Scheers, S., 1969, Les monnaies de la Gaule inspirées de celles de la République romaine, Leuven.

Scheers, S., 1970, 'L'histoire monétaire des Suessiones avant l'arrivée de César', Ancient Society, Vol. 1, p. 135.

Scheers, S., 1972 'Coinage and Currency of the Belgic Tribes during the Gallic War', BNJ Vol 41, p. 1.

Scheers, S., 1975, Les monnaies gauloises de la collection A. Danicourt à Peronne (France, Somme), Bruxelles.

Scheers, S., 1978, Monnaies gauloises de Seine-Maritime, Rouen.

Scheers, S., 1980, 'Les monnaies gauloises trouvées à Vermand', Cahiers Numismatiques No 7, p. 105.

Scheers, S., 1981a, 'The Origins and Evolution of Coinage in Belgic Gaul', in: Cunliffe, B. W. 1981c, p. 18.

Scheers, S., 1981b, Les monnaies gauloises du musée d'Evreux, Rouen.

Scheers, S., 1982a, 'Les imitations celtiques des monnaies romaines en Angleterre et leur signification historique, Actes du 9e Congrès International de Numismatique, Berne, Vol. I, p. 619, Louvain-la-Neuve, Luxembourg.

Scheers, S., 1982b, 'Les monnaies trouvées au fanum de Chilly (Somme) de 1978 à 1980', Rev. Arch. de Picardie, Vol. 4, p. 92.

Scheers, S. 1983, La Gaule Belgique, second edition, Leuven.

Scheers, S., 1984a, 'La datation des monnaies d'or au cavalier arme, in: Grasmann, G., Janssen, W. and Brandt, M. 1984, p. 360.

Scheers, S., 1984b, 'Les Potins au Rameau B', Revue du Nord, P. 99.

Seaby, B. A. Ltd. 1988, Standard Catalogue of British Coins, Coins of England and the United Kingdom, vol. 1, 23rd Edition, London.

Sealey, P., 1985, Amphoras from the 1970 Excavations at Colchester Sheepen, BAR no. 142.

Sellwood, D. G., 1963, 'Experiments in Greek Minting Technique', NC, Series 7, Vol, 3, p. 226.

Sellwood, D. G., 1976, 'Minting', in: Strong, D. and Brown, D. Roman Crafts, London and New York, p. 63.

Sellwood, L. C., 1983a, 'A Numismatic Note on the Dobunnic Branched Emblem', OJA, Mar. 1983, p. 113.

Sellwood, L. C., 1983b, 'The Mount Battan Celtic Coins', OJA, Jul. 1983, p. 199.

Sellwood, L. C., 1984a, 'Gallo-Belgic C Stater', in: Cunliffe, B. W. 1984, p. 332.

Sellwood, L. C., 1984b, 'Verica Stater, Mack no 121', in: Cunliffe, B. W. 1984, p. 334.

Sellwood, L. C., 1984c, 'Tribal Boundaries Viewed from the Perspective of Numismatic Evidence', in: Cunliffe, B. W. and Miles, D. 1984, p. 191.

Sellwood, L. C., 1984d, 'Peripheral Celtic Coinages in Britain: New Research', in: Grasmann, G., Janssen W. and Brandt, M. 1984, p. 406.

Sellwood, L. C., 1987, 'Non-Durotrigan Celtic Coins', in: Cunliffe 1987b, p. 138.

Sotheby, Wilkinson and Hodge, 1895, Montagu Sale Part 1, 18 November.

Sotheby, Wilkinson and Hodge, 1909, Rashleigh Sale, 21 June.

Sotheby, Wilkinson and Hodge, 1912, Burstal Sale, 6 November.

Sotheby, Wilkinson and Hodge, 1913, Carlyon-Britton Sale Part 1, 17 November.

Sotheby, Wilkinson and Hodge, 1916, Bliss Sale, 22 March.

Sotheby, Wilkinson and Hodge, 1917, Roth Sale Part 1, 19 July.

Sotheby, Wilkinson and Hodge, 1917, Mann Sale, 29 October.

Sotheby, Wilkinson and Hodge, 1918, Roth Sale Part 2, 14 October.

Sotheby, Wilkinson and Hodge, 1920, W. Talbot Ready Sale, 15 November.

Spink and Son, 1985, Norweb Sale Part 1, 13 June.

Storck, I., 1984, 'Ueberlegungen zuer Chronologie Spaetlatene- zeitlicher Potinmuenzen am Suedlichen Oberrhein', in: Grasmann, Janssen and Brandt 1984, p. 420.

Strong, D. and Brown, D., (eds.), 1976, Roman Crafts, London and New York.

Stukeley, W., 1776a, Itinerarium Curiosum, 2nd edition, London.

Stukeley, W., 1776b, Twenty-Three Plates of the Coins of the Ancient British Kings, London.

Thirion, M., 1967, Les trésors monetaires gaulois et romaines trouvés en Belgique, Brussel.

Tylecote, R. R., 1986, The Prehistory of Metallurgy in the British Isles, Institute of Metals, London.

Tylecote, R. R., 1987, The Early History of Metallurgy in Europe, London.

Van Arsdell, R. D., 1983a, 'A Note on the Earliest Types of British Potin Coins', NCIRC, Feb. 1983, p. 8.

Van Arsdell, R. D., 1983b, 'Dumnoc Tigir Seno', NCIRC, June. 1983, p. 154.

Van Arsdell, R. D., 1984a, 'The Origin of the British L Stater and the Problem of the Catuvellauni', NCIRC, Feb. 1984, p. 9.

Van Arsdell, R. D., 1984b, 'The Missing Coins from the Collection of Sir John Evans', NCIRC, Mar. 1984, p. 44.

Van Arsdell, R. D., 1984c, 'Yet Another Surprise from the Haslemere Hoard', NCIRC, Sep. 1984, p. 216.

Van Arsdell, R. D., 1984d, 'A Note on the Date of the British Potin Coinage', NCIRC, Oct. 1984, p. 257.

Van Arsdell, R. D., 1985a, 'The Hallmark of the Haslemere Forger', NCIRC, April 1985, p. 79.

Van Arsdell, R. D., 1985b, 'The Origin and Date of the Silver Coritanian Coinage', NCIRC, May 1985, p. 119.

Van Arsdell, R. D., 1985c, 'False Coritanian Staters from the Hand of the Haslemere Forger', NCIRC, Oct. 1985, p. 259.

Van Arsdell, R. D., 1986a, 'Ancient Forgeries Demonstrate Celts Used Coins as Money', NCIRC, May 1986, p. 111.

Van Arsdell, R. D., 1986b, 'An Industrial Engineer (but no Papyrus) in Celtic Britain', OJA, Jul. 1986, p. 205.

Van Arsdell, R. D., 1986c, 'A Metallurgical Condemnation of the Haslemere Hoard', in: Van Arsdell, R. D. 1986i.

Van Arsdell, R. D., 1986d, 'False Dobunnic Coins from the Hand of the Haslemere Forger', in: Van Arsdell, R. D. 1986i.

Van Arsdell, R. D., 1986e, 'The Second Haslemere Hoard and some Haslemere Stragglers', in: Van Arsdell, R. D. 1986i.

Van Arsdell, R. D., 1986f, 'Rescuing a North East Coast Stater', in: Van Arsdell, R. D. 1986i.

Van Arsdell, R. D., 1986g, 'Rescuing a Catti Stater', in: Van Arsdell, R. D. 1986i.

Van Arsdell, R. D., 1986h, 'The Silver Coinage of Commius', NCIRC, Dec. 1986, p. 330.

Van Arsdell, R. D., 1986i, The Forgery of the Haslemere Hoard, BNTA Special Publication Number 1, London.

Van Arsdell, R. D., 1987a, 'The Silver Coins of Commius—A New Variety', NCIRC, Mar. 1987, p. 42.

Van Arsdell, R. D., 1987b, 'The Coinage of Queen Boudicca', NCIRC, June 1987, p. 150.

Van Arsdell, R. D., 1988a, 'Celtic Chicanery', NCIRC, April 1988, p. 78.

Van Arsdell, R. D., forthcoming 1, 'Thurrock Type Coin', in: Maiden Castle Excavation Report, forthcoming.

Van Arsdell, R. D., forthcoming 2, 'The Badbury-Shapwick Hoard and the Date of the Maiden Castle Coins from Sir Mortimer Wheeler's 1934—1937 Excavations'.

Van Arsdell, R. D., forthcoming 3, 'From Chute to Cheriton—The Collapse of Durotrigan/Atrebatic Trade During the Gallic War'.

Van Arsdell, R. D., forthcoming 4, 'Model for Money Supply and Credit in Late Iron Age Britain'.

Van Arsdell, R. D., forthcoming 5, 'The Snettisham Cast Bronze Coins: A Reappraisal'.

Van Arsdell, R. D., forthcoming 6, 'The Wanborough Hoard: A Reconstruction'.

Van Arsdell, R. D., forthcoming 7, 'The Thurrock Hoard: The Cast Bronzes of Essex'.

Van Arsdell, R. D., forthcoming 8, 'The Face on the Defaced Die Staters'.

Van Arsdell, R. D., forthcoming 9, 'Celtic Chicanery II—The Hidden Face on an Atrebatic Stater'.

Van Arsdell, R. D., forthcoming 10, 'The Date of the Kentish Cast Bronze Coinage—Evidence from Hengistbury and the Caburn'.

Van Arsdell, R. D., forthcoming 11, 'The Dismantling of British Lx'.

Van Arsdell, R. D., forthcoming 12, 'Kentish Cast Bronze Coins Found at Stanstead Airport'.

Van Arsdell, R. D., forthcoming 13, 'Camerton—An Important Dobunnic Centre'.

Van Arsdell, R. D., forthcoming 14, 'The Flight of Caratacus'.

Van Arsdell, R. D., forthcoming 15, 'The Dobunnic Dynastic Coinage'.

Van Arsdell, R. D., forthcoming 16, 'The Trinovantian/Catuvellaunian Dynastic Coinage'.

Van Arsdell, R. D., forthcoming 17, 'Trinovantian Ascendency after the Gallic War'.

Van Arsdell, R. D., forthcoming 18, 'Addedomaros and the Introduction of Small Change in Iron Age Essex'.

Van Arsdell, R. D., forthcoming 19, 'A New (but Illegible) Inscription on a Cantian Stater'.

Van Arsdell, R. D., forthcoming 20, 'Reconstructing the Coinage of Dubnovell-aunus-in-Kent'.

Van Arsdell, R. D., forthcoming 21, 'Trade Routes in Celtic Britain Via Trend Surface Analysis'.

Van Arsdell, R. D., forthcoming 22, 'Take Out the Gold but keep the Colour'.

Van Arsdell, R. D., forthcoming 23, 'The Danebury Celtic Coins', in: Danebury Excavations, Vol. 5, forthcoming.

Van Arsdell, R. D., forthcoming 24, 'Post Gallic War Coinage in Britain: a Trend Surface Analysis'.

Van Arsdell, R. D., forthcoming 25, 'Gold Staters and Cast Bronzes: a Trend Surface Analysis'.

Van Arsdell, R. D., forthcoming 26, 'Trade Networks During the Gallic War in Britain'.

Van Arsdell, R. D., forthcoming 27, 'Standard Weight and Gold Content of the Trinovantian/Catuvellaunian and Atrebatic/Regnan Staters'.

Van Arsdell, R. D., forthcoming 28, 'Coordination of Monetary Policy in Iron Age Britain'.

Van Arsdell, R. D., forthcoming 29 , 'Metallurgical and Metrological Analysis of Pre-Dynastic Celtic Staters in Britain'.

Van Arsdell, R. D., forthcoming 30, 'The Date of the Earliest Gold Staters Struck in Britain'.

Van Arsdell, R. D., forthcoming 31, 'The Trinovantian/Catuvellaunian Interregnum'.

Van Arsdell, R. D., forthcoming 32, 'Cunobeline's aborted Coinage Reform—Evidence for Monetary Manipulation in Iron Age Britain'.

Van Arsdell, R. D., forthcoming 33, 'The Trinovantes and the Catuvellauni—Two Tribes Indistinguishable'.

Van Arsdell, R. D., forthcoming 34, 'The Quarter Staters of Commius'.

Varagnac, A., 1964, L'Art Gaulois, Second Edition, Zodiaque,

Wedlake, W. J., 1958, Excavations at Camerton, Somerset, Camerton Excavation Club, Bath.

Wheeler, R. E. M. and Wheeler, T. V., 1936, Verulamium—A Belgic and Two Roman Cities, Oxford.

Whitwell, J. B., 1982, The Coritani, BAR No. 99, Oxford.

Wild, J. P., 1966, 'Papyrus in Pre-Roman Britain?', Antiquity, Vol. 40, p. 139.

Willett, E. H. 1879 and 1880, 'The Ancient British Coins of Sussex', Sussex Archaeological Collections XXIX and XXX, p. 1.

# GENERAL INDEX

# HOARD INDEX

PLATES

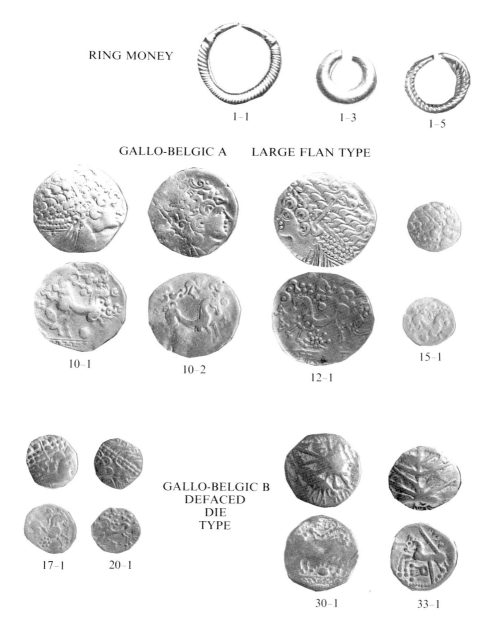

RING MONEY

1–1

1–3

1–5

GALLO-BELGIC A    LARGE FLAN TYPE

10–1

10–2

12–1

15–1

GALLO-BELGIC B
DEFACED
DIE
TYPE

17–1

20–1

30–1

33–1

GALLO-BELGIC B
DEFACED DIE TYPE

GALLO-BELGIC C
ABSTRACT DESIGN TYPE

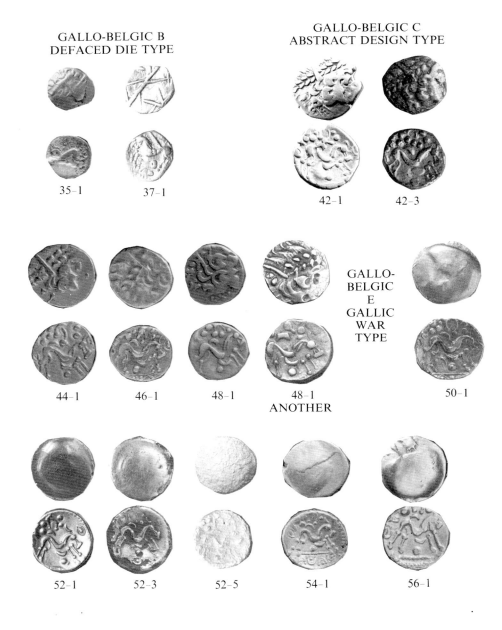

35–1

37–1

42–1

42–3

GALLO-
BELGIC
E
GALLIC
WAR
TYPE

44–1

46–1

48–1

48–1
ANOTHER

50–1

52–1

52–3

52–5

54–1

56–1

GALLO-
BELGIC
D
GEOMETRIC
TYPE

65–1 67–1 67–3 69–1 69–3

GALLO-
BELGIC
XD
DIADEM
TYPE

78–1

GALLO-
BELGIC
F
TRIPLE-TAILED
HORSE TYPE

80–1 81–1

85–1

GALLO-
BELGIC
XC
VE
MONOGRAM
TYPE

87–1

CANTIAN
A
PROTOTYPE
PERIOD

102–1 104–1 105–1

CANTIAN
B
EXPERIMENTAL
PERIOD

106–1

CANTIAN B

CANTIAN
C
INNOVATIVE
PERIOD

108–1        108–3        110–1        110–3                    112–1

112–1
ANOTHER      114–1        115–1        117–1        119–1        119–3

CANTIAN
D
OPTIMIZATION
PERIOD

119–5                     122–1        123–1        125–1        125–3

CANTIAN D

CANTIAN
E
ADJUSTMENT
PERIOD

127–1    129–1    131–1    133–1         135–1    136–1

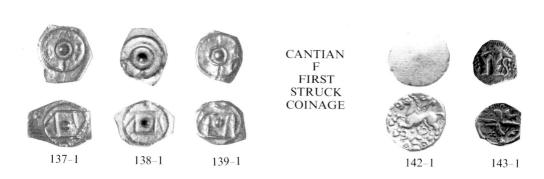

CANTIAN
F
FIRST
STRUCK
COINAGE

137–1    138–1    139–1              142–1    143–1

CANTIAN
G
SECOND
STRUCK
COINAGE

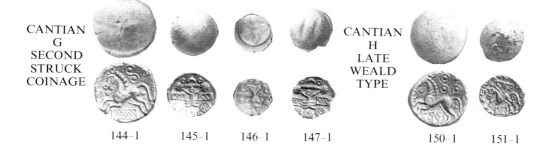

CANTIAN
H
LATE
WEALD
TYPE

144–1    145–1    146–1    147–1         150–1    151–1

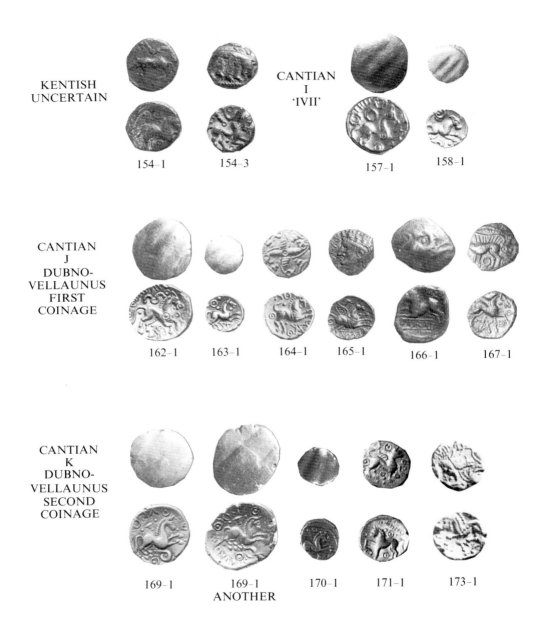

KENTISH
UNCERTAIN

CANTIAN
I
'IVII'

154-1    154-3    157-1    158-1

CANTIAN
J
DUBNO-
VELLAUNUS
FIRST
COINAGE

162-1    163-1    164-1    165-1    166-1    167-1

CANTIAN
K
DUBNO-
VELLAUNUS
SECOND
COINAGE

169-1    169-1
ANOTHER    170-1    171-1    173-1

CANTIAN
L
DUBNOVELLAUNUS
THIRD COINAGE

176–1          178–1          180–1          181–1

CANTIAN
M
VOSENOS

184–1          185–1          186–1          187–1

CANTIAN
N
AMMINIUS
FIRST
COINAGE

CANTIAN
O
AMMINIUS
SECOND
COINAGE

192–1          193–1                   194–1          195–1

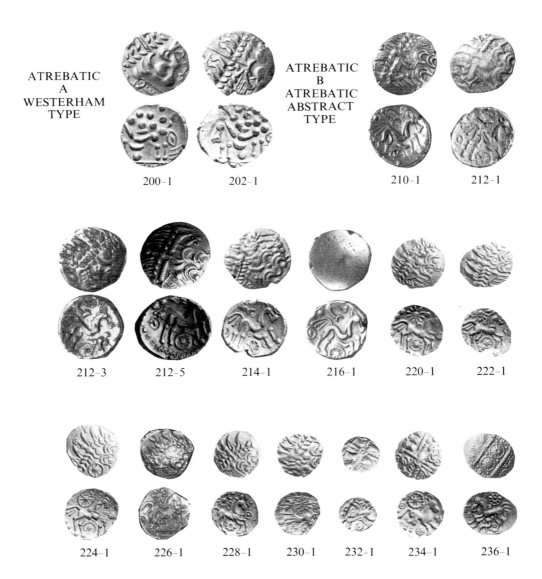

ATREBATIC
A
WESTERHAM
TYPE

ATREBATIC
B
ATREBATIC
ABSTRACT
TYPE

200–1    202–1    210–1    212–1

212–3    212–5    214–1    216–1    220–1    222–1

224–1    226–1    228–1    230–1    232–1    234–1    236–1

ATREBATIC
B
ATREBATIC
ABSTRACT
TYPE

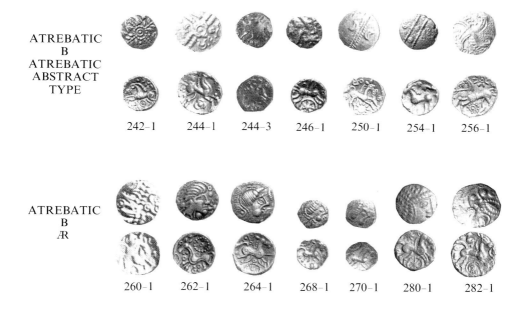

242–1      244–1      244–3      246–1      250–1      254–1      256–1

ATREBATIC
B
Æ

260–1      262–1      264–1      268–1      270–1      280–1      282–1

284–1      286–1      288–1      290–1      292–1

## ATREBATIC  C  COMMIUS

350–1  352–1  353–1  353–1  353–1  353–5  355–1  355–3  355–5

OTHERS

## ATREBATIC  D  TINCOMMIUS FIRST COINAGE

362–1  363–1  365–1  366–1  370–1  371–1  371–1  372–1

ANOTHER

## ATREBATIC E  TINCOMMIUS SECOND COINAGE

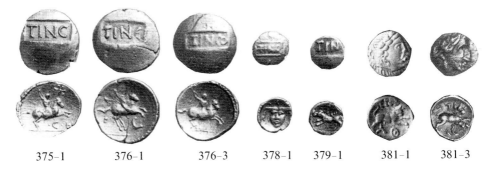

375–1  376–1  376–3  378–1  379–1  381–1  381–3

PLATE 11

ATREBATIC
E
TINCOMMIUS
SECOND
COINAGE

382–1    383–1    383–5    383–7    384–1

ATREBATIC
F
TINCOMMIUS
THIRD
COINAGE

385–1    387–1    388–1    389–1    390–1    396–1    397–1

ATREBATIC
G
EPPILLUS
CALLEVA

405–1    407–1    408–1    409–1    415–1    416–1

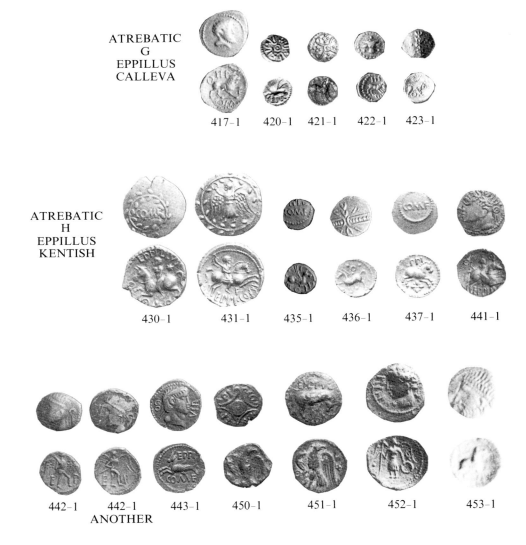

ATREBATIC
G
EPPILLUS
CALLEVA

417–1     420–1     421–1     422–1     423–1

ATREBATIC
H
EPPILLUS
KENTISH

430–1          431–1          435–1          436–1          437–1          441–1

442–1     442–1     443–1     450–1     451–1     452–1     453–1
          ANOTHER

**ATREBATIC**
**I**
**VERICA**
**FIRST**
**COINAGE**

460–1        461–1        465–1        466–1        467–1        468–1

470–1        470–3        470–5        470–7        471–1        472–1

473–1        474–1        482–1        483–1        484–1        485–1        486–1   487–1

## ATREBATIC  J   VERICA SECOND COINAGE

500–1        500–3        501–1     505–1      506–1      510–1    510–5    511–1   512–1

## ATREBATIC K   VERICA THIRD COINAGE

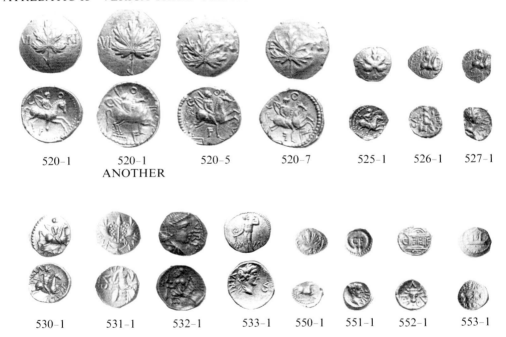

520–1              520–1              520–5             520–7             525–1      526–1      527–1
           ANOTHER

530–1          531–1          532–1          533–1        550–1     551–1     552–1      553–1

## ATREBATIC K   VERICA THIRD COINAGE

| 554–1 | 555–1 | 556–1 | 557–1 | 558–1 | 559–1 | 560–1 | 561–1 |

| 563–1 | 564–1 |

## ATREBATIC L   EPATTICCUS

| 575–1 | 575–3 | 580–1 | 580–3 | 581–1 | 582–1 | 583–1 | 585–1 |

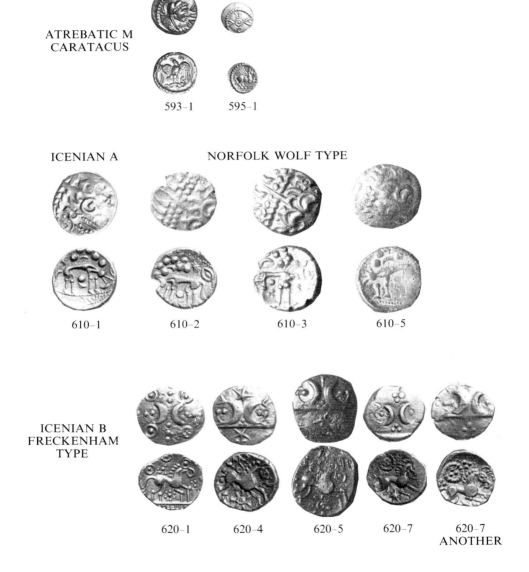

ATREBATIC M
CARATACUS

593-1    595-1

ICENIAN A    NORFOLK WOLF TYPE

610-1    610-2    610-3    610-5

ICENIAN B
FRECKENHAM
TYPE

620-1    620-4    620-5    620-7    620-7
ANOTHER

## ICENIAN B    FRECKENHAM TYPE

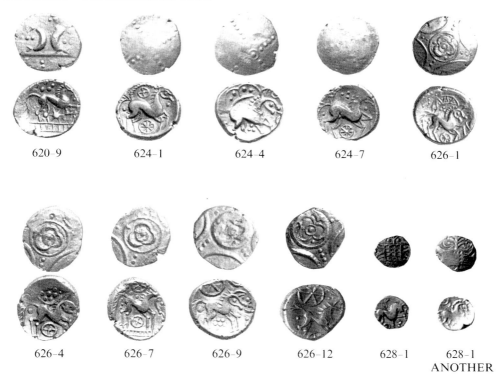

| 620–9 | 624–1 | 624–4 | 624–7 | 626–1 |

| 626–4 | 626–7 | 626–9 | 626–12 | 628–1 | 628–1 ANOTHER |

## ICENIAN C    BOAR TYPE

| 655–1 | 657–1 | 657–3 | 657–3 ANOTHER | 659–1 | 659–1 ANOTHER | 659–2 |

ICENIAN C
BOAR TYPE

ICENIAN D
CAN DURO

659–3        661–1

663–1        663–1
             ANOTHER

ICENIAN E
CELTIC
HEAD
TYPE

665–1        665–3        665–5        665–7        665–9

ICENIAN F
CRESCENT
TYPE

675–1        679–1        681–1        683–1

## ICENIAN G   ANTED

705–1          710–1          710–1          711–1          715–1          720–1
                              ANOTHER

## ICENIAN H   ECEN

730–1          732–1          734–1          736–1          738–1

## ICENIAN I   ECEN

740–1          740–1          742–1          744–1
               ANOTHER

ICENIAN J   ECEN SYMBOL TYPE

| 750–1 | 752–1 | 752–1 ANOTHER | 754–1 | 754–1 ANOTHER | 756–1 | 758–1 |

ICENIAN K   ECEN

| 760–1 | 760–1 ANOTHER | 761–1 | 762–1 | 764–1 | 766–1 |

ICENIAN L SAENU

770–1

ICENIAN N AESU

775–1

ICENIAN M PRATSUTAGUS

| 780–1 | 780–1 ANOTHER |

ICENIAN O
BOUDICCA

CORIELTAUVIAN A
NORTH EAST
COAST TYPE

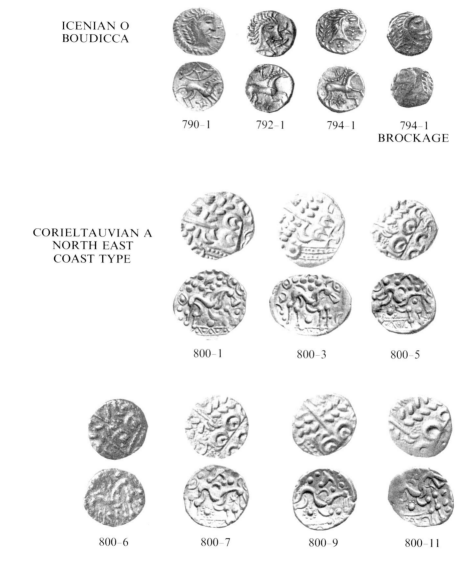

790–1      792–1      794–1      794–1
BROCKAGE

800–1      800–3      800–5

800–6      800–7      800–9      800–11

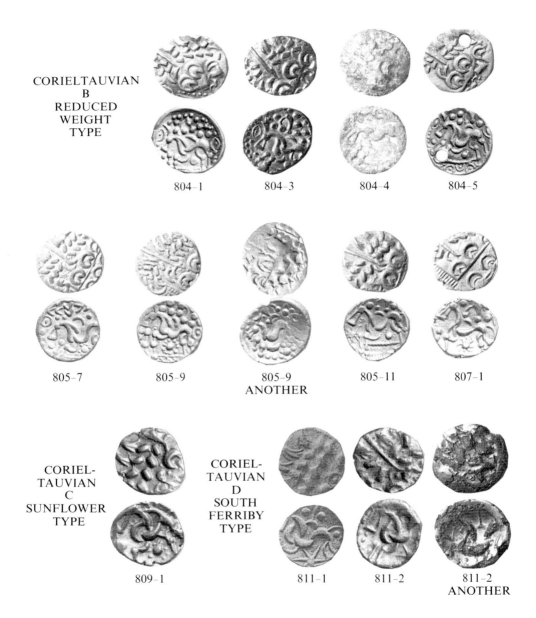

CORIELTAUVIAN
B
REDUCED
WEIGHT
TYPE

804–1        804–3        804–4        804–5

805–7        805–9        805–9        805–11       807–1
                          ANOTHER

CORIEL-
TAUVIAN
C
SUNFLOWER
TYPE

CORIEL-
TAUVIAN
D
SOUTH
FERRIBY
TYPE

809–1                     811–1        811–2        811–2
                                                    ANOTHER

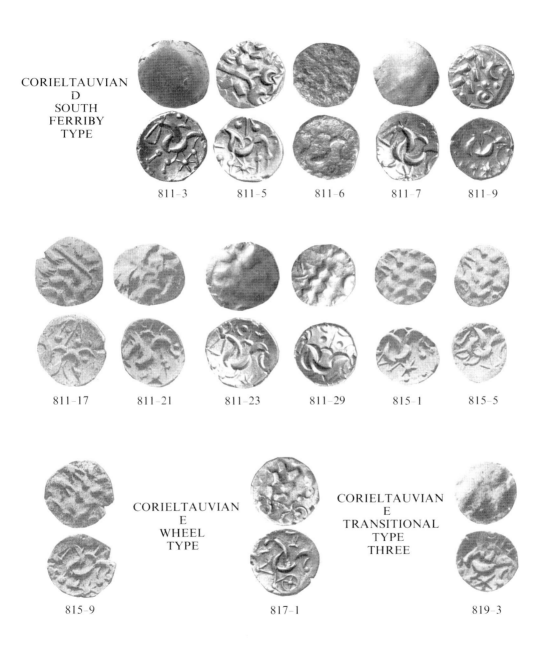

**CORIELTAUVIAN D SOUTH FERRIBY TYPE**

811–3    811–5    811–6    811–7    811–9

811–17    811–21    811–23    811–29    815–1    815–5

815–9

**CORIELTAUVIAN E WHEEL TYPE**

817–1

**CORIELTAUVIAN E TRANSITIONAL TYPE THREE**

819–3

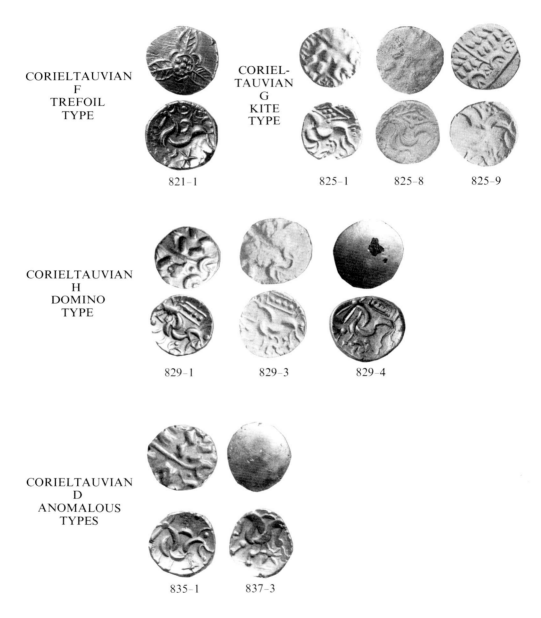

CORIELTAUVIAN
F
TREFOIL
TYPE

CORIEL-
TAUVIAN
G
KITE
TYPE

821-1

825-1

825-8

825-9

CORIELTAUVIAN
H
DOMINO
TYPE

829-1

829-3

829-4

CORIELTAUVIAN
D
ANOMALOUS
TYPES

835-1

837-3

## CORIELTAUVIAN B HOSTIDIUS TYPE

855–3    855–5    855–7    855–8    857–1    857–3    857–5

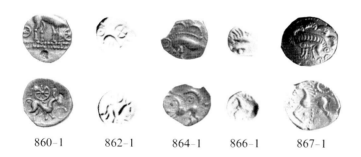

860–1    862–1    864–1    866–1    867–1

875–1    875–2    877–1    877–3    877–3    877–5    877–7
ANOTHER

## CORIELTAUVIAN D   SOUTH FERRIBY TYPE

879–1          881–1          884–1          887–1

## CORIELTAUVIAN I   VEP

## CORIELTAUVIAN G   KITE TYPE

889–1          889–3          889–5          889–7          905–1          905–2

## CORIELTAUVIAN J   AVN AST OR AVN COST

910–1          910–2          910–2          914–1          914–3          918–1          918–3
                              ANOTHER

CORIELTAUVIAN
K
ESVP ASV

920-1        920-3

CORIELTAUVIAN
L
VEP CORF
FIRST
COINAGE

930-1        934-1        938-1

CORIELTAUVIAN
M
VEP CORF
SECOND
COINAGE

940-1        950-1        955-1

## CORIELTAUVIAN N VEP CORF THIRD COINAGE

| 960-1 | 960-2 | 965-1 | 965-1 ANOTHER | 967-1 | 969-1 |

### CORIELTAUVIAN O
### DVMNOC TIGIR SENO

| 972-1 | 974-1 |

### CORIELTAUVIAN P
### VOLISIOS DUMNOCOVEROS

| 978-1 | 978-2 | 984-1 |

### CORIELTAUVIAN Q
### VOLISIOS DUMNOVELLAUNUS

| 988-1 | 988-2 | 992-1 |

### CORIELTAUVIAN R
### VOLISIOS CARTIVEL

994-1

CORIELTAUVIAN
UNCERTAIN
ALE SCA

996–1

CORIELTAUVIAN
UNCERTAIN
'IAT ISO'

998–1

DOBUNNIC
A
PRE-DYNASTIC
COINS

1005–1        1010–2        1010–3        1015–1        1020–1

DOBUNNIC
B
CORIO

1035–1      1039–1      1042–1      1045–1      1045–1      1049–1
                                                ANOTHER

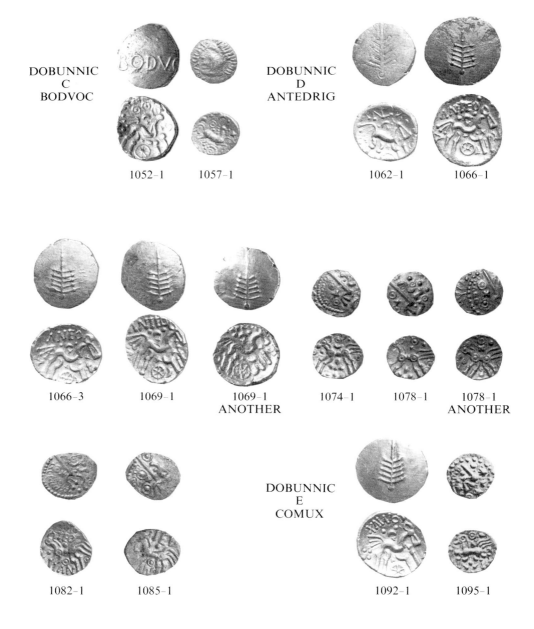

DOBUNNIC
C
BODVOC

1052–1    1057–1

DOBUNNIC
D
ANTEDRIG

1062–1    1066–1

1066–3    1069–1    1069–1
ANOTHER

1074–1    1078–1    1078–1
ANOTHER

DOBUNNIC
E
COMUX

1082–1    1085–1

1092–1    1095–1

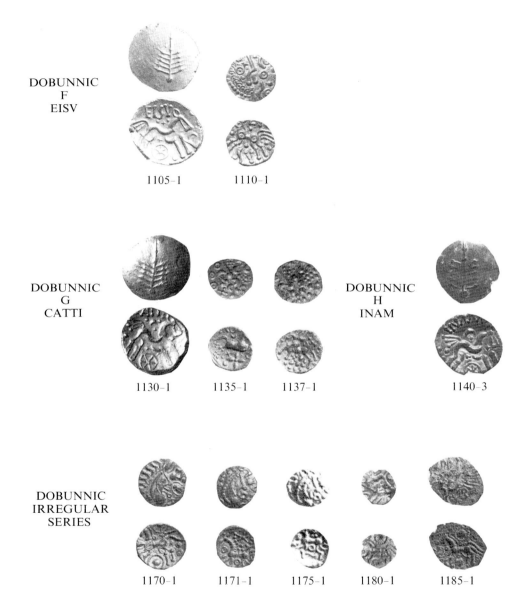

DOBUNNIC
F
EISV

1105–1          1110–1

DOBUNNIC
G
CATTI

DOBUNNIC
H
INAM

1130–1          1135–1          1137–1                    1140–3

DOBUNNIC
IRREGULAR
SERIES

1170–1          1171–1          1175–1          1180–1          1185–1

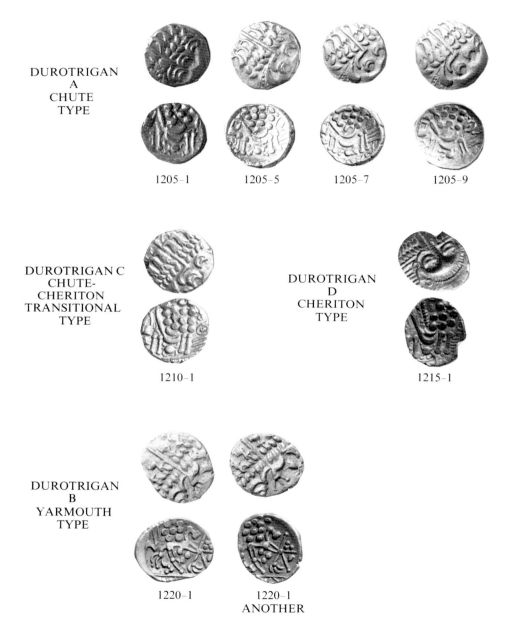

DUROTRIGAN
A
CHUTE
TYPE

1205-1        1205-5        1205-7        1205-9

DUROTRIGAN C
CHUTE-
CHERITON
TRANSITIONAL
TYPE

DUROTRIGAN
D
CHERITON
TYPE

1210-1

1215-1

DUROTRIGAN
B
YARMOUTH
TYPE

1220-1        1220-1
              ANOTHER

DUROTRIGAN
A
GEOMETRIC
TYPE

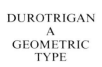    

1225–1            1227–1            1229–1            1229–1            1229–1
                                                       ANOTHER          ANOTHER

DURO-
TRIGAN
UNCERTAIN

DURO-
TRIGAN
E
ABSTRACT
TYPE

1231–1            1235–1            1235–3            1235–7            1242–1

DUROTRIGAN
F
SPREAD-TAIL
TYPE

DUROTRIGAN
G
LATER
BILLON
TYPES

1238–1            1246–1            1246–1            1249–1
                                    ANOTHER

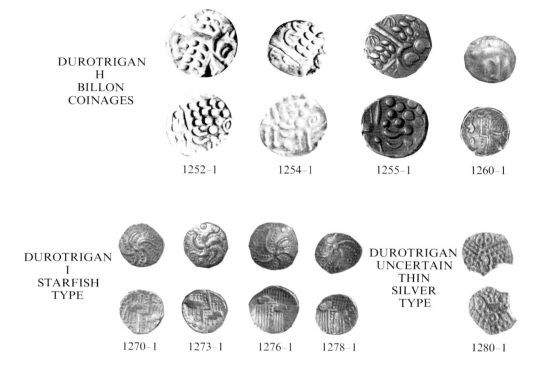

DUROTRIGAN
H
BILLON
COINAGES

1252–1          1254–1          1255–1          1260–1

DUROTRIGAN
I
STARFISH
TYPE

DUROTRIGAN
UNCERTAIN
THIN
SILVER
TYPE

1270–1     1273–1     1276–1     1278–1                    1280–1

DUROTRIGAN
UNCERTAIN
CRAB

DUROTRIGAN
J
STRUCK
BRONZE

1285–1          1286–1                    1290–1          1290–1
                                                          ANOTHER

DUROTRIGAN K   CAST BRONZES

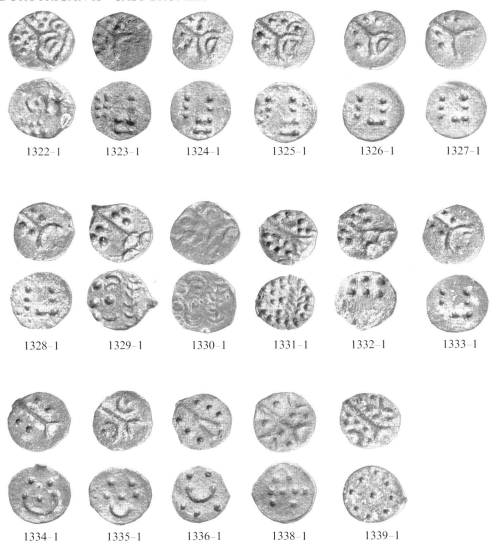

1322–1        1323–1        1324–1        1325–1        1326–1        1327–1

1328–1        1329–1        1330–1        1331–1        1332–1        1333–1

1334–1        1335–1        1336–1        1338–1        1339–1

DUROTRIGAN K    CAST BRONZES

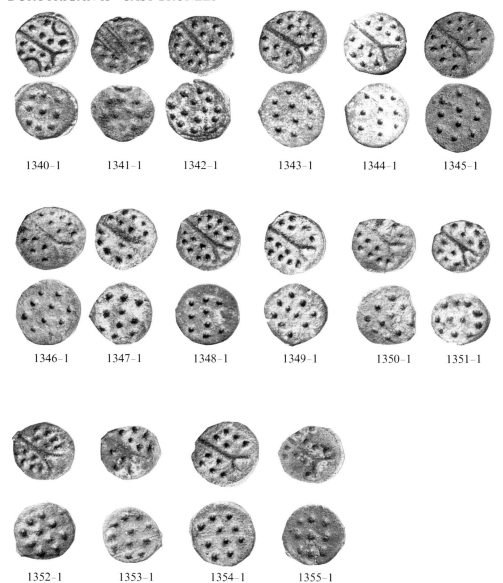

1340–1        1341–1        1342–1              1343–1        1344–1        1345–1

1346–1        1347–1        1348–1              1349–1              1350–1        1351–1

1352–1        1353–1        1354–1              1355–1

## DUROTRIGAN K    CAST BRONZES

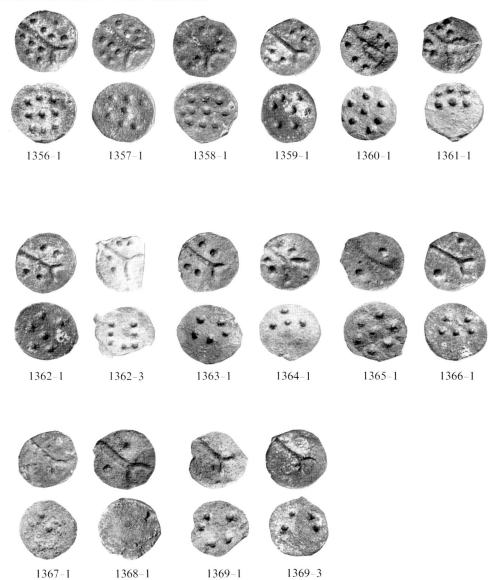

1356–1      1357–1      1358–1      1359–1      1360–1      1361–1

1362–1      1362–3      1363–1      1364–1      1365–1      1366–1

1367–1      1368–1      1369–1      1369–3

## TRINOVANTIAN A THURROCK TYPE

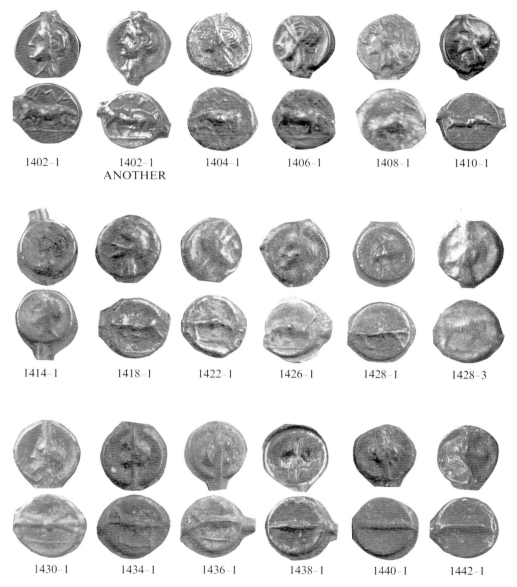

1402–1        1402–1        1404–1        1406–1        1408–1        1410–1

ANOTHER

1414–1        1418–1        1422–1        1426–1        1428–1        1428–3

1430–1        1434–1        1436–1        1438–1        1440–1        1442–1

## TRINOVANTIAN  B  CLACTON TYPE

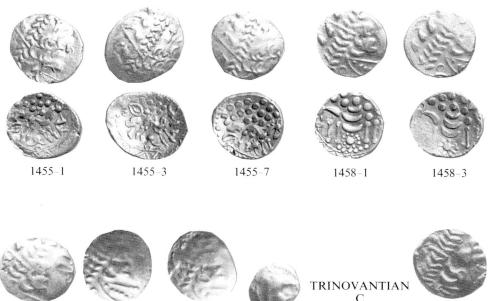

1455–1          1455–3          1455–7          1458–1          1458–3

TRINOVANTIAN
C
WALDINGFIELD
TYPE

1458–5          1458–7          1458–9          1460–1                              1462–1

TRINOVANTIAN
D
WHADDON
CHASE
TYPE

1470–1          1472–1          1474–1          1476–1          1476–1
                                                                        ANOTHER

## TRINOVANTIAN D WHADDON CHASE TYPE

| 1476–3 | 1476–3 ANOTHER | 1476–5 | 1476–5 ANOTHER | 1478–1 | 1478–3 |

TRINOVANTIAN E MIDDLE WHADDON CHASE TYPE

| 1478–5 | 1478–7 | | 1485–1 | 1487–1 | 1487–1 ANOTHER |

| 1487–3 | 1488–1 | 1491–1 | 1493–1 | 1493–1 ANOTHER | 1493–3 |

TRINOVANTIAN
F
LATE
WHADDON
CHASE TYPE

1498–1 1500–1 1502–1 1505–1 1507–1

TRINOVANTIAN
G
WONERSH
TYPE

1507–1
ANOTHER

1509–1

1520–1

1520–1
ANOTHER

1520–1
ANOTHER

TRINOVANTIAN
H
SAVERNAKE
FOREST
TYPE

1520–5 1522–1 1522–5

1526–1 1526–3

TRINOVANTIAN D, E, F   WHADDON CHASE TYPES

1540–1        1543–1        1546–1        1549–1        1552–1        1555–1        1558–1

TRINOVANTIAN I
ADDEDOMAROS
FIRST
COINAGE

1605–1        1608–1        1611–1        1613–1        1615–1

TRINOVANTIAN J
ADDEDOMAROS
SECOND
COINAGE

1620–1        1620–3        1623–1        1626–1        1629–1

TRINOVANTIAN K
ADDEDOMAROS
THIRD
COINAGE

1635–1      1638–1      1643–1      1644–1      1646–1

TRINOVANTIAN L    DUBNOVELLAUNUS-IN-ESSEX

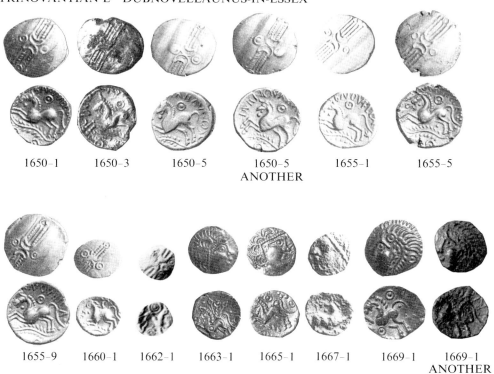

1650–1      1650–3      1650–5      1650–5      1655–1      1655–5
                                    ANOTHER

1655–9    1660–1    1662–1    1663–1    1665–1    1667–1    1669–1    1669–1
                                                                     ANOTHER

TRINOVANTIAN
M
TASCIOVANUS
FIRST
COINAGE

1680–1          1680–3          1682–1          1684–1

1688–1     1690–1     1692–1     1694–1     1698–1     1699–1     1705–1

1707–1     1707–3     1709–1     1711–1     1713–1     1715–1     1717–1

TRINOVANTIAN N
TASCIOVANUS
SECOND COINAGE

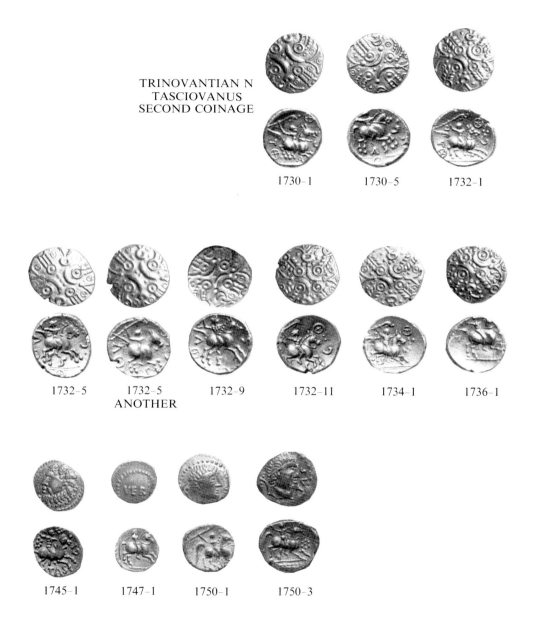

1730–1      1730–5      1732–1

1732–5    1732–5    1732–9    1732–11    1734–1    1736–1
         ANOTHER

1745–1    1747–1    1750–1    1750–3

TRINOVANTIAN O
TASCIOVANUS
THIRD COINAGE

1780–1        1780–3        1780–5        1780–9

1786–1        1786–1        1790–1    1792–1    1794–1    1796–1    1798–1
              ANOTHER

1800–1        1808–1        1810–1    1812–1    1814–1      1814–1
                                                           ANOTHER

TRINOVANTIAN O
TASCIOVANUS
THIRD COINAGE

1816-1              1818-1              1818-1
                                       ANOTHER

1820-1        1822-1        1824-1        1826-1

TRINOVANTIAN P
INTERREGNUM
SEGO

1845-1          1848-1          1851-1          1855-1

PLATE 48

TRINOVANTIAN Q
INTERREGNUM
ANDOCO

1860–1  1863–1  1868–1  1871–1  1873–1

TRINOVANTIAN R
INTERREGNUM
DIAS

1877–1  1882–1  1882–1
ANOTHER

TRINOVANTIAN S
INTERREGNUM
RUES

1890–1  1890–3  1892–1  1895–1  1903–1

TRINOVANTIAN
T
CUNOBELINE
BIGA TYPE

1910–1        1910–2        1913–1        1918–1

TRINOVANTIAN U    CUNOBELINE LINEAR TYPE

1925–1        1925–2        1925–3        1925–5        1927–1        1927–3

TRINOVANTIAN
V
CUNOBELINE
WILD TYPE

1931–1        1931–3        1931–5        1931–7

TRINOVANTIAN V
CUNOBELINE
WILD
TYPE

1931–9          1933–1          1933–3          1935–1

TRINOVANTIAN
T
CUNOBELINE
EARLY
SILVER

TRINOVANTIAN
U
CUNOBELINE
MIDDLE
SILVER

1947–1    1948–1    1949–1                          1951–1    1953–1

TRINOVANTIAN T
CUNOBELINE
EARLY
BRONZE

1963–1          1965–1          1965–1          1967–1
                                ANOTHER

TRINOVANTIAN U   CUNOBELINE MIDDLE BRONZE

1969-1        1971-1      1971-1      1973-1      1973-1      1973-3      1977-1
                          ANOTHER                 ANOTHER

1977-5        1979-1      1981-1      1983-1      1985-1      1987-1      1989-1

TRINOVANTIAN W
CUNOBELINE
PLASTIC TYPE

2010-1          2010-2        2010-3        2010-5

TRINOVANTIAN W
CUNOBELINE
PLASTIC
TYPE

2010-7     2015-1     2017-1     2020-1

## TRINOVANTIAN X    CUNOBELINE CLASSIC TYPE

2025-1     2025-3     2027-1     2029-1     2029-3     2038-1     2038-3

## TRINOVANTIAN W    CUNOBELINE LATE SILVER

2045-1     2047-1     2049-1     2051-1     2053-1     2055-1     2057-1     2059-1

**TRINOVANTIAN W CUNOBELINE LATE SILVER**

2061–1    2063–1    2063–1    2065–1    2067–1
                     ANOTHER

**TRINOVANTIAN W CUNOBELINE LATE BRONZE**

2069–1    2071–1    2073–1        2081–1    2083–1

2085–1    2087–1    2089–1    2089–1    2091–1
                               ANOTHER

TRINOVANTIAN W
CUNOBELINE
LATE
BRONZE

2093–1     2093–1     2095–1     2097–1
ANOTHER

2099–1     2101–1     2103–1     2105–1     2107–1

TRINOVANTIAN
UNCERTAIN
CUNOBELINE
BRONZE

2109–1     2109–1     2109–1        2131–1
         ANOTHER    ANOTHER